SYRACUSE UNIVERSITY
VOLUME III

The Critical Years

Syracuse University, circa 1922.

SYRACUSE UNIVERSITY

VOLUME THREE

The Critical Years

Revised and edited by
RICHARD WILSON
former University Editor, Syracuse University

From a text prepared by
W. FREEMAN GALPIN
late Professor Emeritus of History, Syracuse University

and

OSCAR T. BARCK, Jr.
Professor Emeritus of History, Syracuse University

SYRACUSE UNIVERSITY

1984

First Edition

For a listing of books published and distributed by Syracuse University Press,
visit https://press.syr.edu.

ISBN: 978-0-8156-8108-3 (hardcover)

Library of Congress Cataloging in Publication Data
(Revised for volume 3)

Galpin, William Freeman, 1890–1963
Syracuse University.

Vol. 3 rev. and edited by Richard Wilson, from a text prepared by W. Freeman Galpin and Oscar T. Barck, Jr.
Includes index.
CONTENTS: v. 1. The pioneer days.—v. 2. The growing years.—v. 3. The critical years.
1. Syracuse University—History. I. Wilson, Richard, 1920– . II. Barck, Oscar Theodore, 1902–
III. Title.
LD5233.G3 378.747 52-2118
ISBN 0-8156-8108-9 (v. 3)

To Edith S. and the late John S. Mayfield,
and to the Mayfield Library at Syracuse University,
where this book became a reality.

Contents

Foreword

WITH OTHER MEMBERS OF THE UNIVERSITY COMMUNITY I owe a debt to two of my former colleagues in the Maxwell School for their roles in this continuing chronicle of Syracuse University. W. Freeman Galpin, author of the first two volumes published in 1952 and 1960 by Syracuse University Press, died before he could finish the third. Oscar Theodore Barck, Jr., his fellow professor of history, then completed the chapters left in draft form and wrote others from Dr. Galpin's notes and from his own research. Dr. Barck worked valiantly against difficulties imposed by his teaching duties at Maxwell and by the deadline of his approaching retirement.

Unfortunately, the manuscript failed to reach the Press in time for publication during the University's observance, in 1969–70, of its centennial year. The late sixties and early seventies had seen American campuses embroiled in bitter and sometimes violent dissent. One result was that many projects were delayed or postponed, including the volume dealing with the administrations of Chancellors Charles W. Flint and William Pratt Graham.

When the project was reactivated, the director of our News Bureau, Richard Wilson, volunteered to see the book through the press. His task involved revising the manuscript to meet the editorial requirements of the 1980s. Mr. Wilson brought to the assignment a background as reporter and editor for newspapers and wire services and a free-lance writing career that has seen publication of five of his books and more than a hundred short stories.

Perhaps it is always the best of times and in some ways the worst of times for universities. It is the case that times at Syracuse were not easy during the administrations of Chancellors Flint and Graham. Chancellor Flint had to liquidate debt and cope with economic depression, and

Chancellor Graham was faced with the cataclysmic effect on universities of the first years of World War II. Both chancellors labored for the well-being of the University with wisdom, fidelity, and success.

If there were but a single outstanding impression to be gleaned from the Flint and Graham years, it is that Syracuse University was blessed by a remarkably dedicated and talented teaching faculty.

MELVIN A. EGGERS
Chancellor and President
Syracuse University

Syracuse, New York
Spring 1984

Introduction

I do not bring along with me
a clientele of wealthy supporters.
—Charles W. Flint

James Roscoe Day, the legendary fourth Chancellor of Syracuse University, was seventy-five years old and had served the University for more than a quarter century when he opened his report to the board of trustees on June 10, 1921, in valedictory fashion.

At least twice earlier he had considered resigning. He discussed the matter in 1914 with John Dustin Archbold, his close friend, adviser, board chairman of Standard Oil, and benefactor of the University, but Archbold persuaded him to remain. Then in 1919 Day told the trustees at their spring meeting: "When you feel that somebody should come with more youth and energy, you will be kind enough to intimate such to me, and I hope I will not be too old or mentally decrepit to resent it." But the trustees declined to act on this oblique offer.

Day was more forthright in 1921. He said: "With a devout appreciation of Syracuse University, which only God who sees into the secrets of the human heart can know, and with gratitude to you for your loyal friendship, which I cannot put into human language, I submit respectfully, and affectionately, my resignation as your chancellor to take effect at such time as you may choose my successor."

This time the trustees accepted Day's resignation. They conferred on him, effective with the election of a successor, the title of Chancellor Emeritus and full salary, $7,500 a year, for life. Next the board appointed a committee, headed by William H. Peck—a trustee and Scranton, Pennsylvania, bank president—to recommend a new chancellor.

Thus we come to the period of the history of Syracuse University covered by this book, 1922 to 1942. Those years between world wars encompassed the boom time of the 1920s, Prohibition, "The Era of Wonderful Nonsense," the heyday of flappers and flivvers and flagpole sitters, the Wall Street crash, the Depression, the years of Franklin D. Roosevelt and the New Deal, Repeal, and Pearl Harbor.

In those two decades the nation reeled under a series of stunning events. There were drastic changes in the world, and Syracuse University would never be the same as it had been in Chancellor Day's time and earlier.

The years up to 1922 were chronicled in the first two volumes of this history, written by W. Freeman Galpin and subtitled *The Pioneer Days* and *The Growing Years*. Let us summarize them, before going on, by returning to the year 1870, when Syracuse University received its charter.

The charter granted by the state of New York in March 1870 described the new University as an educational center at which "Christian Learning, Literature and Science, in their various departments, and the knowledge of the learned professions shall be taught." Admission to the University was not to be denied on the basis of sex, race, or religion. Although sponsored by a church, religious toleration was widely observed, and today Syracuse University is a nonsectarian, private university.

On the morning of September 4, 1871, forty-one students, including seven women, gathered in a college chapel for devotions before attending the first classes at Syracuse University, a new educational center founded by the Methodist Episcopal Church with financial assistance from the city of Syracuse.

A few days before that historic September morning, those same forty-one students may have been among the more than five thousand persons who had witnessed the laying of the cornerstone for the new University's first building, the Hall of Languages. This building was to be on the new hilltop campus on the southeastern edge of the city and would replace the temporary classroom, library, office, and chapel facilities in the Myers block in downtown Syracuse.

The laying of that cornerstone, however, marked more than the location of a new building. It marked a commitment to a philosophy of education which placed the liberal arts at the center of Syracuse University.

Throughout the years the Hall of Languages, familiarly called HL, has been the home of the liberal arts at Syracuse University and an ever-present reminder of that commitment. It was dedicated in May 1872. About a century later Philip Booth, poet and professor of English, was to say that the Hall of Languages was named by a "one-poem poet." No one knows the name of that early poet.

The University's first students were well aware of the importance of the liberal arts. Students were admitted to study for the bachelor's degree in either the classical or the scientific course.

A cautious vitality marked the growth of the University in those early years. After HL, the Holden Observatory was built in 1887, and the new Crouse College became the home of the College of Fine Arts in 1889. Founded in 1873, the College of Fine Arts offered courses in art, architecture, and music and was the first institution in the United States to grant the bachelor of fine arts degree.

Student population, too, showed a steady growth in those early years. By 1884 there were 955 students matriculated at the young University, and 551 had earned the bachelor's degree.

The University's growth during those early years soon meant that consideration had to be given to a library. From temporary quarters in the Myers building the library had been moved to a central room in HL, but within a few years pleas for more room became a continuous cry. In 1887 the University surprised the academic world by purchasing the entire library of the noted German scholar and historian, Leopold von Ranke. A condition of the sale was that the materials would be housed in a fireproof building. That condition was fulfilled with the dedication of the von Ranke Library in June 1889.

In 1894 Dr. James Roscoe Day became the fourth Chancellor of the University, with its three colleges. By the time of his retirement in 1922, there were eight more colleges. The eleven were (in chronological order, with present names in parentheses) Liberal Arts (College of Arts and Sciences), 1871; Medicine (State University of New York College of Medicine at Syracuse), 1872; Fine Arts (School of Architecture and College of Visual and Performing Arts), 1873; College of Law, 1895; Applied Science (L.C. Smith College of Engineering), 1901; Teachers College (School of Education), 1906; Oratory and Agriculture (both now defunct), 1913; Library School (School of Information Studies), 1915; Home Economics (College for Human Development), 1918; and Business Administration (School of Management), 1919. Also during Dr. Day's tenure four schools were added to the SU family: Summer Sessions in 1910; a cooperative arrangement with the State of New York which established a forestry school (State University of New York College of Environmental Science and Forestry), 1911; the Graduate School, 1912; and the evening division (forerunner of University College), 1918.

The increase in the course offerings in the various schools and colleges brought about a corresponding increase in the student and faculty population. When Dr. Day came to Syracuse, he found a student body of 751, a faculty of 60, and 5 buildings. At the time of his retirement, the student population had grown to 5,600 and the faculty to 350, and 24 buildings dotted the campus.

The first administrative head of the University was the Reverend Daniel Steele. Dr. Galpin explained in *The Pioneer Days:* "The decision to open classes in September 1871 probably explains why the offices of Chancellor and President of the College [the College of the University] were not filled. Although there is not evidence to warrant any definitive conclusion, it does seem reasonable to assume that the trustees realized the importance of obtaining the very best man possible and, since this end could not be attained at once, had made no appointments for the time being. However, by July of the year, a faculty had been engaged, of whom the Rev. Daniel Steele was appointed professor of mental and moral philosophy, and vice-president of the college. Dr. Steele, therefore, became the first administrative head of Syracuse University."

The first chancellor was not appointed until the following year. For the record, these have been the Chancellors of Syracuse University:

1872–1874	Alexander Winchell
1874–1881	Erastus O. Haven
1881–1894	Charles N. Sims
1894–1922	James Roscoe Day
1922–1936	Charles Wesley Flint
1936–1942	William Pratt Graham
1942–1969	William Pearson Tolley
1969–1971	John E. Corbally, Jr.
1971–	Melvin A. Eggers

In July 1921, when Chancellor Day was away on vacation, there was a preliminary meeting of the committee named to find his successor. At the suggestion of Henry A. Peck, dean of the College of Liberal Arts, the group met in the Chancellor's office. The dean later wrote to Dr. Day: "I suggested they use your office. I thought perhaps on looking at your empty chair they might be moved to think of a good sized man to fill it."

Dossiers were compiled on suggested candidates. One after another was eliminated until there was general agreement in favor of Charles Wesley Flint, president of Cornell College in Mount Vernon, Iowa.

Flint was forty-two, having been born November 14, 1878, at Stouffville, Ontario. He taught school in Canada and was a public school principal before he graduated from Victoria College, now the University of Toronto, in 1900. For the next four years he was the Methodist minister in Pocahontas and Marathon, Iowa. From 1904 to 1906 he had a congregation at Bayville, Long Island, at the same time attending Drew Theological Seminary, from which he received a bachelor of divinity degree in 1906.

During the next nine years he was pastor at the St. James Methodist Church in Brooklyn, New York, the First Methodist Church of Middletown, Connecticut, and the New York Avenue Methodist Church of Brooklyn. He earned a master of arts degree at Columbia University in 1908. Wesleyan University honored him with a doctor of divinity degree in 1912. Three years later he was elected president of Cornell College, where his administrative record and academic attitudes soon earned him a reputation throughout the Methodist Church and in the collegiate world. He had married Miss Clara J. Yetter in 1901 and subsequently became the father of Lois H. and George Y. Flint.

Satisfied with their findings, the trustees made formal overtures to Dr. Flint that led to personal interviews. In a letter dated December 22, 1921, to committee chairman William Peck, Dr. Flint carefully balanced his existing prospects at Cornell College against his possible future at Syracuse. He said frankly that he had heard from several persons "qualified to speak" that Syracuse University was "the most difficult educational situation in the United States." Such a situation did not dismay him, he said; it was a challenge he was not afraid to face.

But Dr. Flint sought certain assurances before he made a commitment. First, he said, there should be a clear understanding of the "sphere and program" of the University. He expressed alarm over past and current deficits: "I am convinced that I but echo your conviction when I say that all present indebtedness should be provided for, both bank indebtedness and all other obligations, before any man should be brought in." But he did not raise that objection again. Although he deplored the lack of endowment, he expressed admiration for the physical plant and the spirit of the student body.

He expressed personal affection and esteem for Dr. Day, whose counsel he said he would seek. But he said all discussions of policy and administration between the two must "be private and ... no public criticism or statement should ever raise the question or suspicion of a lack of harmony" between them. "We all recognize the difficulty of any great man in separating himself from an institution into which he has put his life and which is largely his creation," he said.

Then Dr. Flint asked the trustees what they expected from a new Chancellor. If there were differences of opinion, they should be faced now, not later. Moreover, he made it clear that "I possess no magic for extracting financial resources, that I do not bring along with me a clientele of wealthy supporters." He was equally emphatic about any desire for advancement in the Methodist Church: "I have freely said that I regard the chancellorship of Syracuse University as one of the greatest tasks of the Church and recognize that it demands an extended period of devoted service for an accomplishment worth while. It would be as much beneath the dignity of my Christian manhood as it would be offensive to my conception of the dignity, honor, and opportunity of the Chancellorship, to consider using such position as a stepping stone to ecclesiastical preferment."

He concluded his letter with a request that any call to him should be "reasonably unanimous" and that, if he accepted, he would have the support of trustees, faculty, alumni, and Methodist conferences without "serious mental reservations [and] through all vicissitudes." Furthermore, in justice to Cornell College, all issues should be settled and a decision reached by early January of 1922.

Impressed by Dr. Flint's sincerity, the committee deliberated only briefly before inviting him to visit Syracuse. He received a warm welcome on his arrival. The committee said it was particularly delighted with his willingness to accept the responsibilities of guiding the fortunes of the University. Dr. Flint replied: "I appreciate very highly the unanimous action of your nominating committee and informal approval of the considerations of my letter of December 22nd. If the Board of Trustees act with the same unanimity and approve also the considerations in my letter ... I will accept the offer of chancellorship on their election."

The trustees did give their unanimous approval at a special board meeting January 25, 1922. They immediately informed Dr. Flint of their action. Before the month was over he replied: "I accept the position and will give myself to the task to the fullest of my ability." The remuneration was $10,000 a year and use of the Chancellor's Residence.

Dr. Flint visited the campus in mid-June for a brief meeting with the executive committee and a chat with Vice Chancellor William Pratt Graham, who was to be a loyal and faithful aide throughout the Flint administration. Then the Chancellor-elect went to his camp in Maine for the rest of the summer. Letters from Graham kept him informed of the latest developments at the University. In mid-September he was at his desk in the Administration Building.

For the next few weeks, as Chancellor Flint became familiar with the campus, Vice Chancellor Graham was busy planning the inauguration of the new executive. The two-day celebration, November 16–17, 1922, opened with a formal banquet at the Onondaga Hotel. Many colleges and universities, learned societies, religious groups, educational associations, and the city of Syracuse were represented among the 200 guests. Chancellor Emeritus Day was the chief speaker. Others included Drs. Charles F. Thwing of Western Reserve and Livingston Farrand of Cornell University, and Justice William Riddell of the Supreme Court of Canada.

Several thousand people gathered the following morning for the inaugural ceremonies. It was a cool, bright day. From different parts of the campus lines formed to converge on Archbold Gymnasium. Led by Dr. Perley O. Place, the University Marshal, and followed by Chancellor Flint and Vice Chancellor Graham, the ceremonial procession entered the building to the tune of "Pomp and Circumstance," played by the Syracuse Symphony Orchestra under the direction of William Berwald of the College of Fine Arts. Although reservations had been made for five thousand guests, hundreds more crowded the running track or stood along the walls. President Richard Bowles of Victoria College, the new Chancellor's alma mater, prayed for the University and Dr. Flint. Hurlbut W. Smith, president of the board of trustees, formally invested Charles Wesley Flint with the regalia of office.

Chancellor Flint's inaugural address was hailed by the city press as a brilliant delineation, a critical survey of past and future educational trends, and a penetrating insight into his own educational philosophy. He began by reviewing the objectives of higher education in the United States. Those ends, he said, provided the basis on which students fashioned a way of life and stained the alumni once and forever. In former decades universities were wont to emphasize an educational system centering on individuals, whereas in 1922 the stress was on "social responsibility." The individual, he said, remained the heart of the matter, although a university's prestige rested upon what "graduates do for the community, state, and society."

Teacher-student relations, Dr. Flint said, should be improved wherever possible. Less formal lecturing, more recitation, class assignments stripped of rigidity and selectiveness, greater freedom of approach to faculty, increased facilities for individual study—these were the avenues to the University he contemplated.

In his closing remarks he said: "If I understand the church which founded and fostered Syracuse University, being born not out of schism in dogma but out of a passion for vitality and reality, it has always stood primarily for the vital and real in religious life and experience." Within the framework of complete religious toleration, he continued, all within the University family, regardless of individual creed, would become "better servants of the Kingdom of God." Without achieving such a goal, Syracuse University, as well as other institutions, would totter and fall. He concluded: "I pledge the fullest investment of my time, talent, and strength to make our institution, working harmoniously with all other institutions, fill the largest possible place and render the highest possible service." An ovation lasted several minutes as the Chancellor resumed his seat.

The inauguration was timed to coincide with the alumni frolic and "fallspree" held annually on the eve of the traditional football game with Colgate. The sun must have set the traditional orange: the next day Syracuse defeated its arch rival 14 to 7.

Dr. Flint, over the fourteen years of his chancellorship, carried Syracuse University through wild swings of the economic cycle. During the mid-1920s the country enjoyed a few years of giddy prosperity but then plunged into the worst depression in history. During those years he succeeded in wiping out the deficit left by his predecessor, and he raised academic standards throughout the University. It was during his administration that the School of Journalism and the Maxwell School of Citizenship were founded and the School of Education was expanded significantly. Chancellor Flint headed the largest Methodist-affiliated university in the United States, with more than three thousand students. It was during his administration that the interdenominational Hendricks Chapel was built.

He encouraged self-government by students but was quick to react to bigotry, as he did in 1923 when the Senior Council appealed unofficially for a limit on the admission of Jewish students. The Chancellor, without waiting for a formal petition, branded the suggestion "childish" and "asinine" and said he had no intention of limiting admissions in any way, provided the applicants met entrance standards. Over the years he worked for stricter entrance requirements, but he explained that these were for "proper inclusion, not capricious exclusion."

Dr. Flint fought to raise retirement benefits to a level where faculty members could live in dignity befitting their emeritus status. He led Syracuse University into a national nonprofit system of retirement insurance that vested the University's as well as the employees' contributions to the plan in the employees themselves.

Charles Wesley Flint, known as "Chesty" to some students, was named for Charles Wesley, brother of John Wesley, the founder of Methodism. Dr. Flint was later to write a full-length biography of his namesake, the preacher and hymn writer.

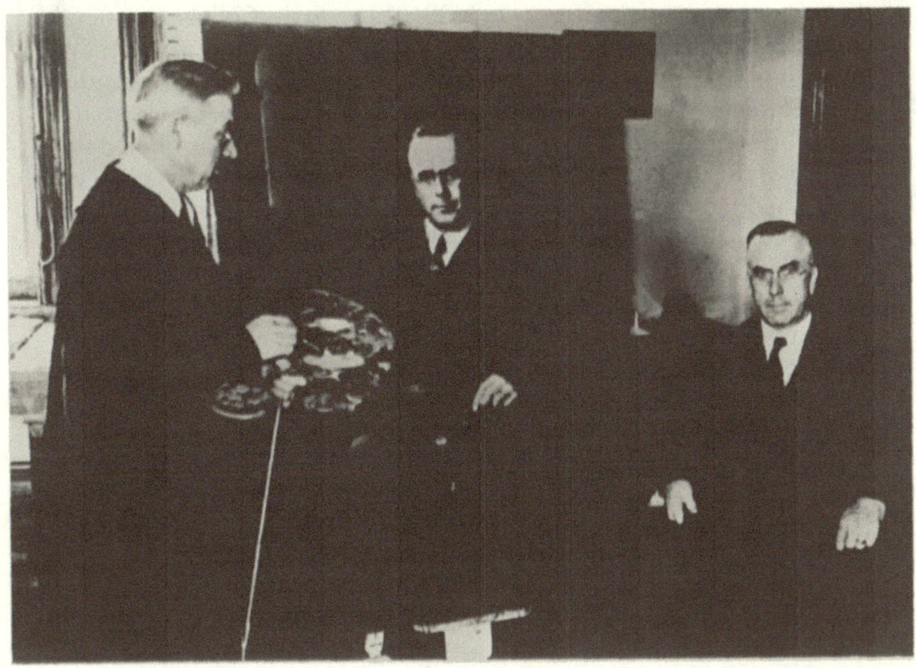

Chancellor Flint sits for artist Lee Trimm, 1936.

Dr. Flint was a man of imposing presence. An alumnus who knew him, Newell W. Rossman '39, described the Chancellor as "sound, dignified, big but not fearsome, friendly; he looked like the bishop he eventually became." He also became known, in the pages of the *Daily Orange*, as "The Phantom Chancellor," Rossman recalled, because he was often away from the campus raising money. He was seldom on campus for a whole week at a time.

"Dr. Graham, as Vice Chancellor of the University, was running it," Rossman said. "It wasn't much to run in those days. The endowment was $4 million, and the budget wasn't much more than $1 million. Everybody knew everybody else regardless of which college they were in."

William Pratt Graham was a veteran Syracusan and seasoned administrator. Born in Oswego, New York, on November 24, 1871, he was three when his parents, Jerome and Sylvia Upson Graham, brought him to Syracuse to live in a big house on the corner of Renwick Avenue and Adams Street. Graham attended Madison School and Syracuse High School, then worked at the Straight Line Engine Company before he entered Syracuse University in 1889. There, in the College of Liberal Arts, he studied mathematics, physics, and chemistry. His elective interest was Latin, and Graham took all his courses in that subject under Frank Smalley, Vice Chancellor Emeritus and head of the Latin department. After graduate work at Syracuse and abroad, Graham joined the faculty of his alma mater in 1898 as an instructor in electrical engineering. The following year he married Cora M. Dodson, an SU alumna. Later, as a full professor, he helped found the College of Applied Science and became chairman of its electrical engineering department. In 1911 he became acting dean of the college and dean the following year, a position he held until February 1922, when he was named vice chancellor.

One year after he took office Chancellor Flint told the board of trustees: "We are hampered, handicapped, cramped by debt."

This pessimistic appraisal of Syracuse University's finances was not news to the trustees. A report made available to them before Dr. Flint was sworn in on November 17, 1922, showed that since 1917 the fiscal situation had been going from bad to worse.

The report was the summary of a financial survey of the University made by the General Education Board of the Rockefeller Foundation, whose counsel had been sought by Dr. Day late in his administration. The full report of fifty-four typewritten pages, although dated November 1921, was not released until the middle of the following year. It was confined to fiscal matters, the Rockefeller group having postponed a study of academic affairs pending selection of a new chancellor.

The report criticized what it described as a policy of continued investment in unproductive real estate. It said there was an immediate need for $2 million to lift the debt and restore endowment funds. It added: "A minimum of $5 million of general endowments should be secured if the University is to continue operations on the existing basis without annual deficits."

That was the bleak picture that faced Dr. Flint as he returned from Maine late in the summer of 1922. The new chief executive discussed the matter with trustees, faculty members, and bankers, studied treasurer's reports, and reviewed annals of the Day administration—at the same time preparing for the opening of the University and his own inauguration. Then he was able to concentrate on the coming meeting of the board of trustees, where it was reported that some University investments had been sold, with the proceeds converted into more remunerative securities. At that meeting of December 22, 1922, Dr. Flint also saw the adoption of bylaw changes that more adequately defined the duties of the treasurer, created committees on finance and investment, audit, the budget, and buildings and grounds, as suggested by the Rockefeller report, and made the Chancellor an ex-officio member of all of them except the committee on audit.

It was clear that the changes, effective in June 1923, pleased the new Chancellor; they were aimed at promoting greater efficiency and at avoiding some of his predecessor's pitfalls.

But Dr. Flint had some pointed remarks to make about the University's debts. He asked the board to give the financial problem its most careful consideration. Its members responded by expressing sympathy and understanding but quickly slipped back into a well-established pattern and referred the matter to a special committee which was to report at a later date. The Chancellor agreed to this but he added: "Not later than June."

Little progress was made, however, and by June the situation was not bright. Nevertheless, discussion of finances was put off again, until November.

At the board meeting of November 16, 1923, Dr. Flint bluntly reminded the trustees that an emergency fund drive aimed at wiping out the deficit had begun while negotiations to bring him to Syracuse were still under way. It had been clearly understood that the matter of raising $1.5 million was to be settled before he took office, he remarked pointedly. He suggested several ways to erase the indebtedness.

It was then that he said: "We are hampered, handicapped, cramped by debt." The Chancellor added: "We are a live and going concern, but with growth and development denied by our financial status. Of course I cannot initiate any new policies, develop any plans, or even function normally as a chancellor until this accumulated deficit is lifted. So far as real administration, or real educational development is concerned, my chancellorship will not begin until we clear this up, recover from the effort, and are able to start over. Until then we can but mark time."

After some deliberation the trustees accepted the challenge and set July 1927 as the closing date for an all-out fund drive. Delays for various reasons slowed the drive in 1924 and 1925, but the Chancellor was able to report in November 1927 that it had been successful and that the indebtedness would disappear entirely as unpaid pledges were honored.

The board of trustees gave Dr. Flint a unanimous vote of thanks, declaring that within five years he had liquidated "the indebtedness existing when he took office."

Still much on Dr. Flint's mind was the need for faculty salary increases and retirement benefits. It was a matter he had often raised publicly. His administration was barely seven months old when he told the trustees in June 1923: "Another problem that we must face at an early date is the matter of retiring allowances for professors. We have been and now are acting on individual cases without a general policy and wise program for financing." Two years later, discussing the University's financial outlook, he noted three pressing considerations: salaries, teaching loads, and retirement funds. In 1926, speaking of the probability of added income from tuition increases, he proposed putting any surplus into a retirement fund.

He also prepared the groundwork for action. A survey of the problem had convinced him that for the time being the University alone could not handle a program of any great value to the faculty. Accordingly he investigated national organizations equipped to finance such an undertaking. He was particularly interested in the Teachers Insurance and Annuity Association (TIAA), established in 1918 by the Carnegie Foundation for the Advancement of Teaching, which he had joined at Cornell College. Although he questioned whether Syracuse would meet the association's requirements, he asked a faculty committee to examine the situation. After study, the committee recommended to Dr. Flint that the University adopt the TIAA plan for all full-time professors, instructors, and administrative staff, as well as library employees. Each qualified employee was to have the option of joining or not, but new personnel were required to become members. All who joined would contribute 5 percent of their pay each month and the University would forward an equal sum to TIAA, which would hold the accumulating total in trust for each member individually. Finally, the committee recommended that if the annual equity on retirement did not equal $1,200, the University should make up the difference. This feature was immensely attractive to older faculty members.

The Chancellor presented the plan to the trustees in June 1927. He acknowledged its shortcoming but said that potentially the TIAA program would be of untold value. He estimated that the initial cost to the University would be about $40,000. After considerable discussion the trustees endorsed the plan and, on February 1, 1928, it went into effect.

By June 1930 there were 206 faculty and administrative members of TIAA, and the cost to the University was about $68,000. Fifty years later, in June 1980, more than 1,050 faculty members and administrators were participants in TIAA and its sister organization, the College Retirement Equities Fund (CREF), and the annual cost to the University was $3.5 million.

While the retirement program was in the planning stage, Chancellor Flint had hoped to finance it and other University needs by tapping the nation's unparalleled prosperity and what seemed to be an inexhaustible reservoir of funds available to higher education. Other institutions had had marked success, and there seemed to be no reason why Syracuse should not share in the golden harvest. He told the trustees in June 1928 that the time for action had arrived. They agreed, and Dr. Flint began looking for a suitable fund-raising organization. He found one in New York City, and in August 1929 a representative of the firm visited Syracuse to begin preliminary planning for the drive. In October the trustees approved the start of the campaign. The Chancellor was enthusiastic. In a note to a trustee, Mrs. Clara Burdette, he said: "It is a long hard road, but we must travel it and we must not postpone it." Ten days later the stock market collapsed.

The financial campaign went ahead nevertheless, amid conflicting opinions about whether the Depression was a temporary phenomenon or one that might go on for twelve to eighteen months.

There was a special brochure, "Syracuse Looks Forward." The University's needs were divided into two categories. Immediate needs were to be met during the years 1930–35. Those that could be deferred would be funded by contributions received through 1945, the University's 75th anniversary year.

Dr. Flint gave priority to faculty salaries, which he wanted raised 40 percent to bring them to the level at other eastern institutions. He sought an increase in the size of the faculty and in funds for equipment and research. A scholarship fund in the amount of one or two million dollars was another goal, as was a survey of the academic life of the University. New buildings were in the plan—including a women's building, a student union, a hospital, and a campus building for the College of Law. In all, the trustees heard in June 1930, the total sought was $12 million.

The Depression continued. By the spring of 1931 it had worsened, and the role of the New York fund-raising organization had been reduced to that of an adviser. In November of that year its efforts were suspended and the fund drive ended. At the end of 1932, reviewing the decade since he became Chancellor, Dr. Flint reported: "We invested about $85,000 in ... the Endowment Campaign, but had to abandon the program on account of financial conditions."

He turned to other ways of dealing with the long-standing financial problem. All unnecessary expenses were eliminated. Faculty members took voluntary pay cuts. Contributions came from the Methodist Church. Alumni helped through an annual giving program.

The austerity program paid off. When Dr. Flint left office in 1936, the University was in sounder financial condition than it had been at any time since it was established. And Chancellor Graham carried on the conservative financial policies of his predecessor.

An expert at fund-raising recently looked back with sympathy at Dr. Flint's financial problems. Newell W. Rossman, who as Vice President for development and later Vice Chancellor for university relations successfully completed a $15 million plus campaign in the 1950s and a $76 million drive in the 1960s, said: "Dr. Flint was a very religious man who saw it as his responsibility to wipe out the debt from World War I of a million dollars—a tremendous sum in those days. He finally did wipe out the deficit, and he did it without firing anybody."

SYRACUSE UNIVERSITY
VOLUME III

The Critical Years

1

The Admissions Program

War came to Europe in 1939, and the following March the Chancellor was told more than 700 male SU students would soon be inducted into the armed forces. The future was not bright.

THE BEGINNING OF THE FLINT ADMINISTRATION in 1922 coincided with a flood of applicants to the University. The movement was not peculiar to Syracuse. Increased enrollment at the secondary level, the return of World War I veterans to the nation's campuses, and a growing realization of the importance of higher education taxed the capacity of many colleges and universities. Limited campus housing, inadequate classrooms, laboratories, and libraries, as well as understaffed administrations and faculties caused academic problems throughout the nation.

Heretofore, revenue-conscious college administrators had hesitated to reject too many applicants. Often acceptance was predicated not on how good an applicant's academic standing was, but on how poor his or her scholastic record had to be to deny admission. By 1920, however, this policy was giving way to a trend that caused drastic changes in both admission requirements and curriculum. Burgeoning enrollments, resulting from a growing population and a booming economy, created new problems for college presidents during most of the 1920s.

Syracuse University's population grew along with enrollments on other campuses: it almost doubled in just five years, rising from 3,548 in 1918 to 6,422 in 1922. Much of the growth stemmed from expansion of the Summer and Extension schools, but there were gains in all of the campus schools. Chancellor Flint was unable to give immediate attention to the resulting academic problems because of the University's shaky financial situation. Besides, judgment cautioned against tampering with an admission program that had been revised only the previous year. The new requirements were a far cry from an earlier emphasis on the classics. Between 1902 and 1911 candidates for an arts degree were required to take three years of Greek and four of Latin. Those requirements eased gradually until in 1921 candidates were "required to take in high school and college a minimum of seven years of a foreign language"—and it was merely suggested that one of these be Latin.

Obviously, the University thought well of its admissions program in 1922, and so, except for some changes within the colleges and some administrative rulings, no material revision was made until 1929. Nevertheless, undercurrents of discontent were heard at committee and faculty meetings. One of the complaints was from Vice Chancellor Graham, who deplored the devaluation of the bachelor of arts program in Liberal Arts, caused by the admission of students deficient in English grammar and composition. Responding to this and other criticisms, Chancellor Flint announced in June 1927 that surveys would be made throughout the University to help draft a new admissions program.

While the surveys were in progress, the Chancellor, the trustees, and the director of admissions, Eugene Bradford, reviewed the situation as it was depicted in a report by Bradford covering admissions since 1923. During those years there had been a steady increase both in the number of those seeking admission and those accepted. In the fall of 1923, 1,653 students had applied, of whom 1,326 were admitted; in 1927 the figures were 2,142 and 1,609. There had been a steady increase in the number admitted without conditions, and a steady decline in the number admitted conditionally.

The decline, particularly for the years 1926 and 1927, reflected an increase in the number rejected. Bradford approved of the trend, saying, "The University can and should continue to apply increasingly strict administration of the requirements for admission. It may well be that higher standards, instead of discouraging applicants for admission, stimulated the ambition of a greater number of students of a more desirable sort to enter the University."

One of the troublesome features of the admissions program in the years reported on, as well as earlier, had been what Bradford called the "flunkers and floaters" who drifted from one college to another. There had been a decline in the transfers of such people to Syracuse because the Admissions Office admitted them only under conditions that would have readmitted them to their own institutions. Moreover, since 1926, each transfer student was required to have a "C" average. Bradford suggested that Chancellor Flint consider limiting enrollment by decreasing the number admitted from among the lowest quarter of high school graduating classes.

By spring of 1929 the colleges and schools of the University had completed their surveys, and in June of that year the trustees approved a new admissions program aimed at restricting enrollment and raising academic standards. This limited enrollment as of the fall of 1929. The explanation was that Syracuse had no desire to increase the size of its student body simply for the sake of numbers; rather, it wanted students of character, ability, and promise. Nor would it admit all who sought to enter: such programs elsewhere led to a dropout rate that ranged from one-fourth to one-half of the freshman class.

Under the new program, admission to the Colleges of Liberal Arts, Business Administration, Medicine, Forestry, and certain divisions of Fine Arts and Applied Science was to be restricted to a number based on the average number enrolled during the previous three years. The Colleges of Law, Home Economics, Agriculture, Library Science, Education, and Speech, however, might equal or exceed the number of students accepted in the fall of 1928. Presumably these colleges, with relatively low enrollments, had few poorly prepared candidates.

The new program favored applicants with the intelligence, character, and physical fitness generally found among candidates in the upper half of their high school graduating classes. Those from the lower half or with conditions were to be carefully screened before being allowed to matriculate. All from the lowest quarter were required to take special examinations. In some instances, enrollment might be allowed on a conditional basis; if such students' scholastic ratings were unsatisfactory at the end of the freshman year they would be dropped. The University reserved the right to reject any applicant the director of admissions believed did not meet Syracuse standards.

Results of the new admissions program were reflected in reports prepared by Professor Frank Bryant, who became director of admissions in 1928. In the fall of 1929, 1,381 students were admitted, of 1,649 applicants. Of those accepted, 77 percent were from the upper half of their high school graduating classes. During the years 1927–29, 27.6 percent came from the lower half, compared with 34.6 percent during the three preceding years. In 1923 the University knew in 75 percent of the cases which quarter of the graduating class its applicants came from; 6 years later, the figure had risen to 80 percent, and by 1936 it was 99.6 percent.

The new program went into effect just before the start of the Depression in 1929. To the surprise of Chancellor Flint, however, enrollment in the fall of 1930, when the first effects of the Wall Street crash were being felt in academic circles, declined only 3.5 percent from the previous year. There might even have been an increase, he wrote in the *Alumni News,* had the University been willing to lower the standards it had so recently raised.

The downtrend halted in 1931, and in November of that year the Chancellor was able to report to the board of trustees that enrollment was higher by about 100 than 12 months earlier and, at 5,423, was only a hair short of the 5,430 registered in the pre-Depression year 1928–29.

Dr. Flint added: "The depression has two effects on college enrollment, one tending to drive to college because no other employment can be found, the other tending to keep from college through lack of resources. Apparently the tendencies about neutralized one another." Quoting his registrar, the Chancellor noted that nationally enrollment "generally has increased in graduate schools and tax-supported, tuition-exempt colleges, with fluctuations up and down in other institutions."

The administration was aware that if the Depression continued, the drop in enrollment, and therefore revenue, could be much greater. Alumni, faculty, and friends of the University joined the administration in a drive for students. When University recruiters visited high schools in Rochester, Buffalo, Utica, and Schenectady they discovered officials from Brown, Harvard, Northwestern, Dartmouth, and Amherst there on the same mission.

Competition was keen. A stream of letters from the deans of men and women went to prospects whose names had been furnished by alumni. Freshmen on campus were asked about outstanding students in their own communities. Establishing the cooperative houses—Nottingham, Geneva, Genesee, and Peck Cottages—enabled sixty-six women to enter who could not have done so otherwise; in terms of revenue, these women brought in more than $28,000. Also effective were a publicity drive by Burges Johnson, director of public relations, and the use of the extension centers as recruiting agencies.

When Dr. William P. Graham assumed the chancellorship in the fall of 1936, Syracuse admitted the largest number of students thus far in its history. Never before, Frank Bryant wrote in the *Alumni News,* had so ambitious a program of student recruiting been undertaken. Between June and October of that year, more than three thousand people—applicants, parents, and friends—had visited his office. As a result, of 2,243 who applied for admission, 1,940 were accepted. Of these,

Chancellor Graham portrait by Albert K. Murray from Syracuse University Collection, circa 1938.

94.9 percent entered without conditions. Chancellor Graham said it was gratifying that 49 percent came from the top quarter of their graduating classes. At the same time, however, he showed concern about a possible increase the following year, and the trustees, at his suggestion, decided to limit the number of women who might be admitted in 1937. The reason: lack of adequately supervised housing for them. No more than 500 women—except for those who lived within commuting distance of the campus—were to be enrolled.

In May 1937 Dr. Graham said in his annual report to the trustees: "We can see very clearly the time when we will have a limited enrollment." The College of Forestry, he said, admitted about one-fifth of its applicants, the College of Medicine could admit no more, and Home Economics had reached a point where it too would have to impose limits. Unless the University built new dormitories and classrooms, every college on campus would have to take similar action.

The University opened in the fall of 1937 with a record number of new students. Of 2,555 whose applications had been accepted, 2,153 actually arrived. Of these, 1,590 were freshmen and the rest transfers from other institutions. Syracuse had tried, for many reasons, to limit the number of transfers, only to find some of its best students in that category. Another phenomenon was that the large majority of entering students in the upper half of their graduation classes were women, for whom it was difficult to find suitable housing. The Chancellor was forced to announce that no new students would be admitted until the fall of 1938, when a larger entering class might be accommodated. Actually, freshman admissions declined, but transfers increased, so that the total enrollment rose from 6,448 to 6,601.

Although the number admitted in the fall of 1939 rose by eleven, it did not equal the record of 1937. In 1940, admissions fell to 1,930, and in 1941 to 1,897, mainly as a result of reductions in scholarships, the quota for women because of inadequate housing, and increased enrollments in junior colleges in New England and the Middle Atlantic states.

Further losses were on the horizon. War came to Europe in 1939, and the Roosevelt administration began to draft young men for military service in the fall of 1940. Bryant told the Chancellor the following March that more than 700 male SU students would soon be inducted into the armed forces. The future was not bright. In the fall of 1941, the beginning of Dr. Graham's last year as Chancellor, only 2,458 candidates applied for admission, a drop of about 600 from the previous year, and only 1,897 were admitted.

In the twenty years of the Flint-Graham administrations, men students outnumbered women except in 1931–32 and 1932–33. In Summer Sessions, however, women students generally outnumbered men; this was also true in the Extension School (later University College), the College of Fine Arts, and the School of Education. Those in the School of Library Science were almost entirely women then, and there was only one male student in the College of Home Economics. The College of Liberal Arts had the largest total enrollment during the period, as well as the largest number of women students, but there the men outnumbered women.

2

Liberal Arts

Syracuse University refuses to confer its degrees upon a student until he has shown ability to use the English language correctly and easily.

—*Bulletin*, 1931

CONCEIVED IN 1870 AS THE COLLEGE OF THE UNIVERSITY, the College of Liberal Arts (which in 1971 became the College of Arts and Sciences) was dedicated to the general education of young men and women, but it also prepared those seeking careers in medicine and law.

At times the college was torn between traditionalists bent on preserving the older values and progressives eager to accommodate to changing educational concepts with frequent revisions of admissions standards and curricula. This was especially true during the Flint and Graham administrations, when many revisions were pushed by deans and faculty members who did not always agree on what should change but earnestly strove to keep the college abreast of the times.

Most of the opposition to change was voiced by the classicists, who honestly believed Syracuse was weakening academic standards. They had regarded the University as an intellectual institution pledged to train a student's mind. Changes that had been made, especially from 1917 to 1921, struck the classicists as likely to transform the College of Liberal Arts into a social, commercial, and athletic center, sacrificing the intellect.

When Dr. Flint became Chancellor in the fall of 1922 the college,

Karl Clayton Leebrick, dean, College of Liberal Arts, 1929–1938. Photograph © Bachrach.

the oldest and largest subdivision of the University, had as dean William Henry Metzler, who left within the year for a similar post at the State Teachers College at Albany. For the next two years there were two acting deans, William L. Bray, who was also dean of the Graduate School, and then William Pratt Graham, an alumnus who served his alma mater in many capacities and who eventually became Vice Chancellor and then Chancellor.

In 1929 Karl Clayton Leebrick, who earned his Ph.D. at the University of California and joined Syracuse in 1928 as professor of international relations, was appointed dean. He held the post until 1938, when he became president of Kent State University in Ohio. Succeeding him was Finla Goff Crawford, a graduate of Alfred University with a doctorate from the University of Wisconsin. He began his teaching career at Syracuse in 1919 as a political scientist and was one of the original faculty members of the Maxwell School. Professor Crawford became Vice Chancellor in 1943.

Department chairmen when Chancellor Flint took office were Edward D. Roe, John R. French Professor of Mathematics; Ismar J. Peritz, Willard Ives Professor of Biblical Languages; William L. Bray, dean of the Graduate School and professor of botany; Horace A. Eaton, Jesse T. Peck Professor of English Literature; Alexander C. Flick, William Griffin Professor of History and Political Science; Frank Smalley, Vice Chancellor Emeritus and Gardner Baker Professor of Latin; George A. Wilson, William Penn Abbott Professor of Philosophy; Royal A. Porter, professor of physics; Hugh H. Tilroe, professor of rhetoric and public speaking; and William M. Smallwood, professor of comparative anatomy.

High school students seeking a liberal arts education were subject to the general admission regulations of the University, but the college had its own requirements for the two degrees it offered, bachelor of arts and bachelor of science in chemistry. These varied considerably.

Basically, candidates for the B.A. degree carried 30 hours of required study in each of the first two years. Foreign languages had a prominent place in the program, and all language and English majors were advised to study Latin or Greek for a year. In addition to the fixed requirements, the student took enough electives for a total of 124 hours for graduation. Of these, four had to be in hygiene or gymnasium, and unless the student was in a combination program, which permitted him or her to earn both a bachelor's and a professional degree, he or she could not take more than 12 hours outside of Liberal Arts.

Candidates for a science degree took specialized courses, plus French or German. Other nonscience courses included history and economics. Finally the student had to write a thesis that counted for 6 credit hours.

The passing grade in both sequences, arts and chemistry, was 65, but an overall average of 70 was needed for graduation.

Dean Bray presumably voiced the general opinion of the faculty when he applauded the curriculum in December 1923. He said it was efficiently linked to high school programs and gave the college student a wide and stimulating acquaintance with the main fields of knowledge. It afforded reasonable opportunities for specialization, including study in other colleges on the campus.

But before long it was time for intensive scrutiny of graduation requirements—a formidable task because the curriculum, an intricate pattern that had developed from an accepted philosophy of education, also reflected the desires of a competitive faculty. The study was carried out by the college's curriculum committee under the supervision of Professor Smallwood. The minutes of meetings of the committee and of the Liberal Arts faculty are aglow with sparks that flew when rival groups clashed.

The committee's survey resulted from a 1927 directive by Chancellor Flint that was part of his promotional plan for a greater University. Not only was Syracuse to become financially sound, but it was to have an academic pattern of merit and achievement for faculty and students.

Dr. Flint's interest in the curriculum of the College of Liberal Arts paralleled his interest in religious instruction and training. In 1926 he had brought Professor Clyde Wildman to the campus from Cornell College, Iowa, to strengthen the Bible department. The next year the Chancellor identified himself with the efforts of the Educational Association of the Methodist Episcopal Church, which was planning a national survey of colleges and universities affiliated with the church. The aim of the survey was to "determine the nature and quality of the services rendered the cause of Christian Education by our Educational Institutions, to appraise their work and suggest improvements of it, to cooperate in formulating a constructive policy for them, to reform the Church so that it may be inspired to increased confidence and more generous support."

The Chancellor was pleased with the project and asked that Syracuse be one of the first institutions surveyed. Although a committee did not visit Syracuse until the spring of 1930, its objectives influenced the curriculum committee in proposing a one-year course in the Bible as an alternative to English literature and composition. Bible 40, as it was known, sought to familiarize sophomores with the content of the Bible and to study it as an example of English literature.

Another curriculum committee recommendation that was adopted reflected long-felt dissatisfaction with the quality of the English written and spoken by some students. For example, late in November 1927 Dr. Graham, then a Vice Chancellor, commented on the problem in his annual report to the Chancellor. He said that if the bachelor of arts degree meant proficiency in any discipline, that field was English; yet the University had not only admitted students, but graduated some, who lacked this essential qualification. He noted that remedial steps had been taken in 1922 through the Minimum Essentials Test. Those who cleared this hurdle were excused from a part of the normal English requirement. Those who failed had to carry an additional course. In 1927 this was extended to sophomores and students in the upper classes.

The administration then applied the principles involved in the Liberal Arts program to other colleges on the campus, and in 1927 the *Bulletin* contained this:

"All undergraduates in Syracuse University, except those registered in the Colleges of Law and Medicine, are required both in their sophomore and junior year to take an examination in English usage. Candidates for degrees who reach the last semester of their senior year without passing this test will be required to take special work in English under the direction of the English adviser."

Four years later the rule was reworded to read: "Syracuse University refuses to confer its degrees upon a student until he has shown ability to use the English language correctly and easily." The requirement was continued through the Graham administration. A policy was established in Liberal Arts that no student could graduate without a certificate of proficiency in oral English. Those who failed an oral test had to take a special course.

Meanwhile the Liberal Arts faculty approved several rules, effective in September 1930, designed to "raise the standards at entrance and again at the beginning of the junior year." There were two significant provisions: (1) students who failed to maintain a "C" average in their first two years were subject to dismissal by the dean during the last two years unless definite improvement were shown; (2) the second minor was abolished, and the number of hours required for a major might vary from 18 to 36. Dean Leebrick said of the change: "This is a result of a very careful study by the curriculum committee of the College of Liberal Arts under the leadership of Dr. Smallwood. This action completes what was started a number of years ago and attempts to divide Liberal Arts into an upper and lower division. We are insisting that when students become juniors and seniors, they shall have cleared their records and be in good standing in the University. In the upper division they will be given greater freedom."

The dean's compliment to Dr. Smallwood recognized him as the expediter whose enthusiasm and understanding of curriculum trends carried the program through a series of faculty meetings. Few of his colleagues questioned the need for a new approach to education. They knew of the tremendous political, social, and economic changes that had swept the United States since the turn of the century—a trend that had impelled revisions at Syracuse. Nor were they blind to the shifts in emphasis and depth that had appeared in the curriculum of practically every American institution of higher learning.

Support for curtailing foreign language requirements appeared in the Methodist Church's Reeves Survey of 1930. Dr. Reeves and his team noted that the College of Liberal Arts required four years of foreign languages for admission and a student, if deficient, had to take two languages in college. "In comparison with the language requirements that generally obtain this is heavy," the survey said. "The faculty undoubtedly had some reasons which it felt justified it in making the requirement so heavy but it should recognize the fact that it is moving in opposition to the present trend in this matter. The survey staff seriously questions the wisdom of the present language requirements."

This section of the report must have reminded some of the faculty of a prophetic statement made by Chancellor Day in October 1911. Speaking on the campus to a meeting of state school superintendents, Dr. Day said: "It will be a calamity if the time comes in two decades when we will not have teachers in public schools to teach Greek.... [The] present trend away from the classics is lamentable.... I wish [Greek, Latin, and mathematics] requirements in all colleges."

The Reeves report endorsed the idea of upper and lower divisions and hoped they would be started as soon as possible: it urged appointment of a dean to promote counseling at the lower level. The report favored greater freedom of election in other campus colleges and suggested an all-university committee to investigate course encroachments on Liberal Arts by other schools and colleges on the campus. According to Dr. Reeves, the College of Liberal Arts had three main objectives: education for a purposeful life; education for vocational or professional service; and education for cultural ends. His survey group envisaged Liberal Arts as the college of the University that prepared students for professional and specialized study.

The various proposals to liberalize the curriculum, including the idea of a lower division under a separate dean for the freshmen and sophomores, were generally acceptable to the faculty members, but some believed attempts to put them into effect would provoke countless hours of debate and perhaps end in stalemate. Among those who took a major role in the discussions was Ernest S. Griffith, who had joined Syracuse in 1930 as associate professor of political science. Griffith, a graduate of Hamilton College, continued his studies in England and received his Ph.D. from Oxford University. He came to Syracuse with boundless energy and made a deep impression on many phases of the academic life on the Hill. He then spent a year at Harvard University studying the tutorial system.

Chancellor Flint watched his progress with interest and in January 1932 informed Dean Leebrick that Griffith would return to Syracuse not only as dean of the lower division but as associate dean of Liberal Arts as well. Softening the impact of his announcement was a comment by the Chancellor that the plan did not imply a separate lower division and did not threaten the traditional four-year program, but would benefit the freshmen and sophomores by giving them their own dean.

Dr. Flint told Dean Leebrick he saw this as a cooperative arrangement whose success depended on a "common mind" between the two deans. Any misunderstanding was to be cleared between them before being referred to anyone else, the Chancellor said.

Professor Griffith became dean of the lower division in June 1932 and initiated some changes before he left the University in 1935. (Dean Leebrick left in 1938.) One Griffith innovation was a freshman survey course, approved by the faculty and trustees, consisting of a tutorial program for twenty-five selected students, who were excused from many of the normal requirements. The course, offered for the first time in the fall of 1931, continued to be taught until 1935. Presumably Depression-connected cutbacks contributed to its demise, but it is known that the course was not popular with many faculty members, who saw it as a departure from traditional ways.

At about the time the tutorial program was introduced, the Liberal Arts faculty began to discuss the wisdom of the University's adjusting its curriculum to national trends. In November 1931 Professor Smallwood, addressing the faculty on the subject, stressed the fact that increasing numbers of Liberal Arts students were seeking degrees in professional colleges. To meet their needs, he said, Liberal Arts had been forced to devise many interlocking courses that became so entrenched they could not be disturbed without causing chaos. The result, he declared, was that the college was being slowly transformed into a service institution. Of sixteen hundred students enrolled that year in Liberal Arts, a thousand were in the combination programs in medicine, law, and education. Similar concerns, that Syracuse might become a service institution, were to be voiced fifty years later.

Chancellor Flint met with the faculty on many occasions to outline his views for the future. He called for a constant review by the divisions and departments of their aims and courses, invited an appraisal of the tutorial system and the upper division, and suggested that comprehensive examinations be introduced.

Professor Smallwood, at a faculty meeting in December 1934, commented on the many proposals the curriculum committee had received. He said the college provided all students with a rounded education suitable for their future and with a sound foundation for their individual needs, but he added that the committee was ready to examine any constructive plan and to experiment with worthwhile projects.

A project the Chancellor favored was an introductory course in the social sciences. He corresponded with Leon C. Marshall, executive secretary of the National Industrial Recovery Board and a former University of Chicago faculty member, ultimately inviting Marshall to survey the situation at Syracuse and accept a teaching assignment. Marshall declined to join the faculty, but he submitted a comprehensive report outlining a new social science course.

Marshall's failure to join the faculty postponed positive action on the course, much to the apparent delight of Dean Mosher of the School of Citizenship and most of his staff, who had seen the proposal as a rival to their own course in responsible citizenship. The School of Citizenship faculty countered with a new course idea of its own, which the Liberal Arts faculty authorized to be given in the Extension School on an experimental basis. Because it was never offered, it may be assumed that Dean Mosher and his staff had introduced it only as a means of defeating the Chancellor's proposal.

Later, in December 1937 when Dr. Graham had become Chancellor, the science faculty of the college proposed a radical curriculum revision to abolish the mathematics and philosophy requirements and thoroughly revise others. But after debate the faculty accepted a recommendation of the curriculum committee and tabled the proposals.

A year later a special faculty committee, after an exhaustive study of nationwide curriculum trends, submitted a statement of findings and recommendations that concentrated on the entering freshmen, the lower division, and the upper division.

The problem of the freshmen concerned the unevenness of their preparation for college. The special committee thought that placement tests in English, the social sciences, foreign languages, mathematics, and science would improve the college's program and allow superior students to enroll in advanced courses without taking beginning ones. Those who did poorly in the tests would have to carry courses without credit or increase the number of hours needed for graduation. But the committee was not ready to adopt placement tests without further study.

The committee approved in general of the lower division's objectives but raised many questions about the upper division: Should an examination be required for admission? What should be the minimum requirements in science, languages, English, and the social sciences? Should a speech test be continued? And because the departmental major was "rapidly passing in the American college," should a major concentration take its place? Should honors courses be established? Should there be comprehensive examinations at the end of the senior year?

There were so many pertinent questions that the college undertook a survey of its resources. It was another of the many such appraisals, reviews, studies, and surveys that took place as the college weighed its responsibilities to students against the concerns of its faculty. The study centered on the faculty's working conditions and the substance of the curriculum. The issues were closely related; if teaching loads were too heavy, any change in curriculum would be of little value. In general, the faculty wished a maximum load of twelve hours a week, with adjustments for supervision of upperclass and graduate students, as well as for administrative work and research. Other faculty complaints were that classes were too large and there was need for more secretarial help and improved library resources and laboratory equipment.

The college committee that made the self-investigation, reporting in May 1939, said the curriculum rested on courses that should not be increased without larger budgets. Generally, there was little demand for more survey or integration courses. The greatest pressure for change, the committee discovered, was in the lower division, where the faculty wanted students in their first two years to have English language and literature, a foreign language, science and laboratory training, and a knowledge of the social fields and human nature. The committee members emphasized the need of students to learn how to study systematically and to think reflectively.

In the upper division, the committee believed, the chief defect was the requirement that students wishing to teach must take eighteen hours of work in the Teachers College; it did not fit into the objectives of the College of Liberal Arts. It said this might be remedied by adding a fifth year that would concentrate on teacher training.

For better or worse, little was done to implement the committee's findings and recommendations. This may have been because the faculty had wearied of debates on curriculum matters and did not really want to change requirements. Another possible factor was a growing conservatism that spread through the University in the years just before the United States entered World War II. Thus the Graham administration ended in June 1942 with no marked changes in curriculum.

Indicative of services the College of Liberal Arts provided for the professional colleges were the combination courses allowing a student to earn both a bachelor's and a professional degree.

The oldest of these arrangements was with the medical college. Admission requirements generally followed those of Liberal Arts, and during the first three years in that college a course of study weighted in favor of science was required. The fourth year was taken in the College of Medicine; on successfully completing it, the student received an A.B. degree from the College of Liberal Arts. The student then finished the medical course in another three years and received an M.D.

Somewhat similar was a six-year combination program in Liberal Arts and Law. In 1922 those in the sequence had to complete 104 hours in Liberal Arts before entering the College of Law. Of these, 48 consisted of courses in English, public speaking, mathematics, psychology, history, political science, and foreign languages, with Latin preferred. The A.B. degree was awarded at the end of the first year in law school and the law degree the following year. In 1929 the program was altered; only 96 hours were needed in Liberal Arts. There was another slight revision in 1942.

Syracuse did not offer a degree in dentistry but had a predental program coordinated with the Regents' admissions requirements to state dental schools. There was a six-year combination course with the College of Applied Science, a four-year sequence with the School of Journalism, and several others with the School of Education.

Despite the assaults on foreign languages, their importance was stressed repeatedly—although it had to be admitted that students trained to read and write another language could not always be understood in its home country. Worse, it was often true that graduates could not speak or write good English even after the proficiency tests were introduced. Broadly speaking, the College of Liberal Arts, 1922–42, was not afraid to experiment. Its faculty hoped to educate its students to play vital roles, more meaningful than in the previous century, in the new America that was in the making.

3

The Fine Arts

In my travels practically all over the East, Middle West, and parts of the South during the past fifteen years, I know it to be a fact that the College of Fine Arts is better known over the country than any other college of the University and its reputation is as fine as that of any other college.

—Dean Harold L. Butler, 1930

THE ARTS AT SYRACUSE UNIVERSITY are in perpetual motion, changeable as the seasons. They have moved from basement to belfry, from factory building to warehouse to studio, from opera house to movie house to theater, from classroom to concert hall. The arts have adapted to reorganization and shifts in public taste, evolving from program to sequence to department to school, hurtling apart or merging into new combinations.

A roll call of artists, architects, musicians, critics, and historians of the arts who have been associated with Syracuse during the century and more of the University's existence would be impressive and lengthy. Their names can be found in department records and in the University archives. But many of the names are perpetuated more warmly on the tongues of their colleagues and artistic descendants, two of whom have been interviewed for this chapter.

A portion of one interview answers the question *What is (or are) fine arts?* The explanation is from David F. Tatham, M.A. '60, Ph.D. '70, professor and chairman of the department of fine arts.

The second interview was with D. Kenneth Sargent, professor emeritus and former dean of the School of Architecture, who was a student when architecture was part of the College of Fine Arts.

First, the definition of fine arts:

Q: For the record, would you distinguish between art and fine art? How would you define fine arts, and what relationship does it have to the college?

DFT: There are local shadings of meaning for those words. At Syracuse "fine arts" was an umbrella term that originally meant professional training in the various visual arts—painting, sculpture, printmaking, as well as music and architecture. Beginning in the 1960s the term *fine arts* seemed to some to have too much of an elitist flavor to it. Certain programs didn't fit the image very neatly—such programs as industrial design (which is now simply called design) and fabric design, that once were called applied arts rather than fine arts—and in 1970 it seemed to make sense to adopt a more inclusive name. When the college was reorganized to include the drama department, the name Visual and Performing Arts came into being. In this new entity the School of Music remained pretty much intact, as did the School of Art. The School of Architecture had become a wholly independent unit back in the 1940s.

In 1945–46, at the end of World War II, the department of fine arts had been established in the College of Liberal Arts by Professor William Fleming. It had quite a different mission than did the old College of Fine Arts. Since 1873 that college had taught the history of the arts (history of art, history of music, history of architecture) as part of the professional training for those fields. But over the years, especially in the 1930s, there was a steadily growing interest on the part of students elsewhere in the University in learning, at least in an introductory way, something of the history of art and the history of music. Many students enrolled in other colleges had a genuine interest in the arts as an avocation. Others simply sought cultural enrichment, wanting to understand the classical music they heard, and to have some intellectual and historical background from which they could view works of art in museums and elsewhere. A few intended careers of scholarship in art history or music history.

Anticipating the influx of veterans after the war, Vice Chancellor Finla Crawford decided to set up a department of fine arts in the College of Liberal Arts with the purpose of teaching while also emphasizing research and publication in these historical descriptions. That same division exists at many other major universities. The College of Visual and Performing Arts continues to teach the history of art and music to students preparing to be professional artists, musicians, and people of the theater. The School of Architecture has its own faculty of professional architectural historians.

August L. Freundlich, dean of the college when it was reborn in 1971 as the College of Visual and Performing Arts, paid tribute to two long-lived faculty members who happened to be musicians. He wrote:

"One of the longest tenures of any faculty and certainly the record for this one is that of George Albert Parker, who was born in Colona, Illinois, in 1856 and died in Syracuse in 1939. He joined the faculty in 1882, married Chancellor Sims' daughter, became dean and stayed on until his death, teaching organ, his favorite instrument." Parker resigned as dean in 1923 after seventeen years but was named dean emeritus.

"A second record for longevity probably belongs to William H. Berwald, born in Germany in 1864, who joined the music faculty in 1892 and taught piano and composing," Freundlich said. "While his status changed to emeritus in 1944 or 1945, he continued to teach at least until 1948. In 1935 the community honored him with a concert of his works, which numbered well into the hundreds."

In Germany Berwald had been director of the court operatic orchestra at Mecklenburg-Schwerin, and he gave new verve to the musical life of his adopted city. He was co-founder in 1921 and conductor of the Syracuse Symphony Orchestra from 1921 to 1924, earning this tribute in a *Post-Standard* editorial: "... Through the educational value of the symphony concerts [he] has raised the tone of cultural life in the city." An ancestor of the present Syracuse Symphony, it was a much more modest venture, having none of the government, corporate, or foundation support that has been available to orchestras in the past quarter of a century. It was sustained more by love than money, and at its best it was an admirable group.

A nationally published composer of anthems, cantatas, fugues, overtures, songs and sonatas, Berwald was head of the composition department of the College of Fine Arts. At a fiftieth anniversary dinner in his honor in 1942 Professor Berwald said: "Syracuse University has meant much to me aside from professional implications. It was here that I found my wife, educated my children, and found a husband for my daughter and a wife for my son."

Others who were on the music faculty during the Flint and Graham years, in a list certainly far from complete, were recalled by their colleagues, pupils, successors, or admirers.

George Richard Bunn, who returned to his alma mater in 1937 as star of the Kum Bak Show, part of the entertainment at the annual Kum Bak reunion dinner, enrolled in the College of Applied Science, but after a year he switched to the College of Fine Arts at the urging of Dean Harold Butler, who had heard him sing. Bunn, a native of Port Byron,

William H. Berwald. Photograph © Bachrach Brothers.

New York, graduated in 1912 and went on to world fame as Richard Bonelli, Metropolitan Opera baritone.

Hallie Stiles, another Syracuse graduate, made her debut with the Chicago Civic Opera Company, as did Bonelli, and later joined the Opera Comique of Paris. She spoke with affection of "my first teacher, Miss Belle Brewster."

Belle Louise Brewster taught voice at Syracuse from 1908 until her death in 1933 and for a time was director of the Women's Glee Club. She had gone to Europe as a young woman and, while a student in London and Paris, earned her way as a member of a quartet that sang American plantation melodies. At the same time she was a serious pupil of Alberto Randegger, an authority on oratorio and Italian opera, and Sir George Henschel, who instructed her in classic song. Born at Batavia, New York, Miss Brewster was a descendant of the Mayflower's Elder William Brewster. Syracuse University awarded her an honorary master of music degree in 1921.

Donald Grout '23, who earned his Ph.D. at Harvard in 1936 and taught at Cornell University, is the author of *A History of Western Music* (W. W. Norton) and a past president of the American Musicological Society. "His books on the history of opera and on the history of music are *the* standard items," said Syracuse University Professor Emeritus William C. Fleming. "Dr. Grout has an enormous reputation as a scholar and is very much of the establishment."

Hazel Jean Kirk was given a violin at the age of three and began her concert career under a Chautauqua tent in her native Ohio. She studied at the Cincinnati College of Music, graduated from Miami University of Ohio, and later was a pupil of Eugene Ysaye, the Belgian concert violinist. She taught in Missouri for five years and, amid more study, gave concerts in New York before joining Syracuse University in 1928.

Kirk Ridge, who also joined the Syracuse faculty in 1928, as professor of piano, was noted as an organist and concert pianist. He studied for two years in New York with Sigismond Stojowski, a protégé of Paderewski, and later in Vienna; he then taught at his alma mater, Oberlin College, before making a concert tour of Europe. After he joined Syracuse University he continued his concert appearances with the Syracuse Symphony at home and on tour.

Ridge taught at Syracuse University for thirty-six years and retired in 1964. During that time he auditioned many prospective students in travels across the United States. In a December 1981 interview Ridge reminisced about some of his former pupils. "I think the Syracuse University music school was at its height in 1936, '37, '38, and '39 when Richie Gale was there," he said. Richmond Gale, the organist and concert pianist, earned his bachelor of music degree at Syracuse in 1937 and his master's two years later. "He was pianist and music director for Helen Traubel for nine years. Before that John Charles Thomas chose him from twenty-one pianists to accompany him." Another of Ridge's students was Warren Angell '29 (master's '44), composer and conductor, who became an arranger for Fred Waring and later dean of music at Oklahoma Baptist University.

Jacob Kwalwasser, who joined Syracuse in the mid-1920s, was a pupil of Carl Seashore of Iowa, the music psychologist famous for his tests of musical ability. Kwalwasser teamed with Professor Peter William Dykema of Columbia University to devise a new series of talent tests. These fitted directly into Kwalwasser's work at Syracuse, where he was professor of public school music. He described the tests as "diagnostic and prognostic," revealing children's musical talent—or proving that they had none, if that were true. The latter could prevent waste and even tragedy by showing what a pupil could not do. He said of the Kwalwasser-Dykema tests, which measure sense of pitch, time, intensity, consonance, rhythm, and tonal memory: "They make it possible for us to discover the exact musical nature of the child; they reveal the magnitude of individual differences of endowment; and they make it possible for the teacher to conserve musical ability."

Another of Professor Kwalwasser's interests was Jewish folk songs, of which he said in a pamphlet on the subject: "They are not vivacious or animated; neither are they sprightly or pert. They show the same vividness and intensity that characterizes the Jew's religion. They move along with anxious tread, manifesting the supersensitiveness of the Jew neurologically. The firm, steady, and unswerving tread of the Anglo-Saxon is absent in the Jewish folk song. We can understand the extent of his suffering from these unconscious revelations."

Professor Fleming, whose book *Arts and Ideas* is in its sixth edition and has long been a standard work, mentioned that the editor of his new book, *Art and Civilization,* was James Kwalwasser, grandson of the music psychologist. James's father Edgar, an architect, built a house in Syracuse for his parents, Professor and Mrs. Jacob Kwalwasser. Professor Fleming now lives there. "I was able to acquire it," he said. "So the Kwalwassers are a very vivid memory." And a personal example of the interrelationship of the arts.

For anyone who was a radio fan in the 1930s and '40s, the name Billy Mills was synonymous with music. He was music director of the western division of the Columbia Broadcasting System, conducting the music for as many as twenty-five programs a week; in 1941 he aired his ten thousandth radio show, earning a place in Ripley's "Believe It or

Not." Among the big time shows were "Fibber McGee and Molly" and "The Great Gildersleeve." William R. (Billy) Mills '18 had been conducting since his high school days in Flint, Michigan, and at Syracuse in 1916 was music director for the Tambourine and Bones production of the operetta "The Girl Ione."

"Cosmopolitan" is the word for André Polah, born in The Hague, Netherlands, of Portuguese-Spanish parents, a prodigy who took up the violin at the age of six and won the gold medal of the Royal Conservatory of The Hague at twelve. At fifteen, in competition with more than 200 violinists, he won an Amati violin and a fellowship in Belgium. He studied with Jules Massenet, the composer, and Eugene Ysaye, the violinist. He began concertizing when he was sixteen and toured Europe with such composer-artists as Maurice Ravel and Cyril Scott. With Ysaye, he reached the United States in 1917, and they were for a time guests of Isadora Duncan, the dancer. Later Polah met Rose O'Neill, creator of the Kewpies, who commissioned him to write a light opera. Then he joined the Irish tenor John McCormack on a bond-selling tour. All this took place before he joined the Syracuse faculty in 1929 as professor of violin. He was named conductor of the Syracuse Symphony in 1934. He also conducted the University orchestra and was a frequent guest conductor of symphonies around the United States. As a composer, he was noted for his transcription of the Prelude and Fugue from Bach's Sonata in G Minor and for his opera based on Jules Verne's *Michael Strogoff*, produced at Théâtre de Chatelet, Paris. Polah's wife was the Norwegian-born Sophie Hansen. They had twin daughters.

Composer Halsey Stevens '31 majored in composition and returned to Syracuse in 1935 to study for his master's and teach music theory. He was music editor of the *Daily Orange* in 1935–36. Stevens also taught at Dakota Wesleyan, Bradley, and Redlands before settling in Los Angeles at the University of Southern California, from which he was summoned in 1966 to receive a doctor of literature degree from his alma mater. The literary honor reflects his book *The Life and Music of Béla Bartók* and his contributions to many periodicals, as well as to the *World Book*, the *New Catholic Encyclopedia*, and the *Encyclopaedia Britannica*. Stevens has composed symphonies, concertos, and other orchestral, chamber, piano, and choral music and has been the guest conductor of major orchestras. Among his compositions at Syracuse is "A Quartet for Mixed Voices," which he inscribed to Fine Arts Dean Harold L. Butler in 1939 "in appreciation of his interest and encouragement." The quartet consists of Stevens's music for poems or songs by A. E. Housman, Richard LeGallienne, Christina Rossetti, and Bernard de Ventadorn (A.D. 1145–95).

Professor Fleming paid tribute to George Mulfinger, who joined the faculty in 1928, as "a tremendous pianist... a specialist in German romantic music, especially the work of Schumann." The Crouse Concert of November 12, 1967, was a remarkable one. It was the farewell composition recital of Professor Mulfinger, M.M.U. '37. Seventeen of his works—for clarinet, cello, piano, voice and piano duo—were on the program. He and his wife, Elizabeth Bartenslager Mulfinger, B.M.U. '31, and their son David were featured on pianos, and their son George, Jr., A.B. '53, M.S. '62, was on cello. Thus four of the six musicians on the program were Mulfingers. Professor and Mrs. Mulfinger had three sons, all of whom play instruments; David followed in his parents' footsteps and became a concert pianist. As duo pianists Professor and Mrs. Mulfinger gave hundreds of concerts in Syracuse and the eastern United States for nearly half a century before they retired to a warmer climate.

Mihail Stolarevsky, born in Kiev, fled his homeland during the Russian Revolution. A violinist, he continued his concert career in Berlin, then came to the United States and joined the Syracuse faculty as an instructor. He left for a symphonic career with Fritz Reiner in Cincinnati and later the Pittsburgh Symphony.

In his interview on October 1, 1981, Professor Tatham looked back at his department and its parent college.

> Q: The College of Fine Arts was a nationally distinguished school when Dr. Flint arrived in 1922, wasn't it?
>
> DFT: Indeed it was. Some faculty members from that era were truly distinguished, having more than local reputations, and some of them have important places in the history of the arts in America. Others were colorful and memorable people of the era. In the art group for example, is Adelaide Alsop Robineau, whose reputation as ceramist and porcelain-maker has always been high. An older contemporary of hers was Irene Sargent, a distinguished author and teacher of the history of art and esthetics, as well as a teacher of foreign languages to singers and others. She was editor of the influential *Craftsman* magazine early in the century, and had much to do with the popularization of the famous Stickley furniture, the Mission style, and the Craftsman House when Syracuse was a center of the Arts and Crafts Movement.
>
> Jeanette Scott was a professor of painting, specializing in portraits of children. A good deal of her work remains in Syracuse.
>
> Montague Charman was another outstanding teacher of the 1920s and for many years thereafter. The whole School of Art was one of the best in the country not only in the quality of its faculty but also in its students, some of whom had distinguished careers.

Bradley Walker Tomlin graduated in the class of 1921 but continued on as a Hiram Gee Fellow. The fellowship required that he visit Europe to copy a painting approved by the painting faculty. One of the conditions of the fellowship was that the painting be brought back to Crouse College. In this way, the building gradually became decorated with high quality copies of masterworks from European collections. Many of these may still be seen there, though Tomlin's copy of Monet's *Balcony* is kept in the University art collection at Sims Hall. He also did some paintings for Memorial Hospital. In the early 1940s he was a leading member of the abstract expressionist group in New York, a close associate of Jackson Pollock. A major retrospective exhibition of his work toured the country in the late 1970s.

In the 1920s another alumnus of a much earlier generation came to fame in America, and this was Bolton Brown, who had been a student back in the 1880s, earning both an undergraduate and a master's degree in painting. After limited success as a painter, he went to England to study the art and craft of lithography in 1914. He was then fifty years old. When he returned to America in 1916, he almost single-handedly gained for lithography the kind of acceptance as a fine art medium that etching and wood engraving had long had. Syracuse awarded him an honorary doctorate in 1921. His two books on lithography, published in 1923 and 1930, remain classics in their field. He was also a founder of the Woodstock art colony, as well as an early member of the Sierra Club and a noted mountaineer.

But back to the faculty of the era. When illness caused Mrs. Robineau to leave the faculty, her successor was one of her best students, Ruth Hunie Randall. Ruth Randall taught ceramics until her own retirement in the early 1960s, after which she remained very active as a ceramic artist. The Everson Museum mounted a retrospective exhibition of her work in the spring of 1981. Where Mrs. Robineau specialized in vessels, Ruth Randall was essentially a sculptor. Among her recent works is a relief portrait of Winslow Homer executed for me in 1981.

When the College of Fine Arts was established in 1873, from the first year it had a professor of photography, probably the earliest professorship of that subject at a degree-granting university in America. Ward V. Ranger held the post. He was a well-known photographer in his own right and did some work for the Smithsonian Institution. His son, Henry Ward Ranger, who had been a student in painting at the University in the 1870s, had a distinguished career as an artist.

Q: Could you talk about the University art collection? Of course it expanded tremendously under Dr. Tolley, but it did exist, did it not, in earlier years?

DFT: Yes, in an unorganized way. It was essentially the College of Fine Art's collection used primarily for teaching. The School of Art was disadvantaged in not having a major museum nearby. Art schools in New York or Boston or Philadelphia have Rembrandts and Titians a few blocks away, but the old Syracuse Museum of Fine Arts, which became the Everson Museum in the 1960s, had always collected American art above all else and had a small collection. The University's collection was meant to complement that, but it grew very slowly in the 1920s and 1930s, never acquiring any major painting or works of sculpture. Real growth began in the Tolley years. There was, however, an important print collection, though it was little used until the 1950s. Because the painting collections of Syracuse were so modest, the Hiram Gee Fellowships assumed great importance, for they placed the best graduating seniors in the major collections of Europe.

Without question the most important single acquisition in the first seventy-five years of the University's existence was the big painting by Samuel F. B. Morse, *Exhibition Gallery of the Louvre.* This important and now famous painting by the man who invented the telegraph in the latter part of his career is a view of part of the Louvre Museum, about six by nine feet. Morse painted it in France, brought it to America in 1833, added some figures to the foreground, put it on public exhibition in the fall of 1833, and was deeply disappointed when no one came to see it.

He sold it to a friend of James Fenimore Cooper near Cooperstown and within a few years the painting was in private hands in Syracuse. It came to the University in the 1880s, where it hung in the Hall of Languages and then in Crouse College. In the 1920s the picture was little more than a historical curiosity, but in the early 1930s when the Metropolitan Museum of Art in New York planned a major retrospective exhibition of Morse's work—the first since his death—the *Louvre* was included and that marked its first public showing outside the University in almost a hundred years. Since then it has become an ever more famous painting, and worth a great sum. But in the 1920s it had been so little appreciated that it was for a while kept in a closet in the Crouse College tower. [In 1982 Syracuse University sold the painting for $3.5 million to go on public display at the Terra Museum of American Art in Evanston, Illinois.]

Two of the faculty members mentioned by Professor Tatham who achieved national reputations, Adelaide Alsop Robineau and Irene Sargent, have been written about by two scholars of a later generation with ties to the University.

The Syracuse University Press book *Adelaide Alsop Robineau: Glory in Porcelain,* published in 1981, was edited by Peg Weiss, adjunct professor of fine arts at Syracuse University and visiting associate professor at Cornell University.

Adelaide Robineau, born Adelaide Beers Alsop in Middletown, Connecticut, on April 9, 1865, was world renowned for her craft as a

Adelaide Alsop Robineau.

ceramist and porcelain-maker. She was awarded international prizes and had exhibitions in Italy, France, and the United States. Her work is in the permanent collections of the Metropolitan Museum of Art in New York City and in the Everson Museum of Art in Syracuse. She and her husband built their pottery and later their home, Four Winds, on a hill overlooking Syracuse. Mrs. Robineau designed the house with her architect friend, Catharine Budd, in a style typical of the Arts and Crafts Movement in which the ceramist figured so prominently. Among her most famous pieces are the *Viking Ship Vase* (1905), *Scarab Vase* (1910), *Snake Bowl* (1919), and *Urn of Dreams* (1920).

At her death in 1929, the Metropolitan mounted a memorial exhibition in which seventy-one of her pieces were shown. The museum's curator, Joseph Breck, wrote that it was a tribute "to the memory of one who may with every reason be called a master craftsman."

At Syracuse University Adelaide Alsop Robineau was assistant professor of design in 1920–21 and assistant professor of ceramics from 1921 until her death. In 1917 the University awarded her an honorary doctor of science degree in ceramic art. Dean Harold Butler mourned her passing as "a great loss to the College of Fine Arts because of the high artistic ideals which she implanted in her students.... Honesty and sincerity were the outstanding features of her character.

The best word picture of Professor Irene Sargent, by Cleota Reed '75, M.A. '76, a researcher and art historian, is in the summer 1979 issue of *The Courier,* published by the Syracuse University Library Associates. The copyrighted article was based on interviews and research in the University archives, the Library of Congress, and the Boston and New York public libraries. Here are excerpts:

> Professor Irene Sargent was a distinguished teacher of the history of fine arts at Syracuse University for 37 years, from 1895 to 1932.... We can begin to form an image of her as an awesome pillar of knowledge and a great lady with a colorful personality through the vivid memories of her former students. Interviews with some of her students brought forth the following recollections:
>
> > "She insisted on being called Doctor or Madame, *never* Miss. We freshmen were terribly in awe of her."
> >
> > "She always looked the same—dark blue suit, dark blue shirt waist, and dark blue hat with a broad brim."
> >
> > "One principle she dwelt on was that to be great, a work of art, no matter how exciting its subject matter, must leave one with a feeling of peace."
> >
> > "She believed that architecture is the greatest of the arts. The architecture students were her pets. She told them, 'Never work for money. Work for the love of your art.'"
>
> Jesse Irene Sargent, to give her full name, was born in Auburn, New York, on February 20, 1852, the fourth daughter of Rufus and Phebe [sic] Sargent....
>
> At age 43 she was appointed to the faculty at Syracuse University to teach French for the school year 1895–96. She was reappointed in 1901 to teach Italian in the College of Fine Arts to music students, so that they might better understand and pronounce the words they were singing. In succeeding years she also taught esthetics; the history of art which included architecture, painting, and sculpture; and the history of orna-

Irene Sargent, circa 1916.

ment, a course vital to careers in architecture, illustration, and design, in which it was important to have a historical vocabulary. . . .

Perhaps even more significant than her two honorary degrees from Syracuse University, in 1911 and 1922, was the honorary membership awarded her by the American Institute of Architects, in 1926, for a lifetime of outstanding contributions to architecture and its allied arts. She was the second woman in the history of that distinguished organization to receive such an honor.

Dr. Sargent taught until the end of the spring term in 1932. By then she was 80 years old. . . . She fell in her room at the Yates Hotel on July 5 and was hospitalized until her death on September 14. She is buried in the Syracuse University plot at Oakwood Cemetery.

Architecture students were her favorites and Miss Reed, who is married to Professor Tatham, has a touching account of Professor Sargent's final years of teaching:

> Most people now alive who remember Irene Sargent recall her in her last years, when she was in her middle-to-late seventies, the years in which on snowy midwinter days the architecture students formed a human chain to assist her, in the most proper manner, from the door of her taxi to the door of Crouse College.... Only an echo of her magnificent abilities as a teacher remained; but this was enough to convince her last students that she was... a force that opened minds to the intellectual and spritual power of the fine arts.

D. Kenneth Sargent, a 1927 graduate, taught in the department of architecture in the College of Fine Arts starting in 1930. He was the second dean (1958 to 1969) of the School of Architecture, which came into being when the college was reorganized in 1945. Dean Sargent was interviewed at his home in Liverpool, New York, on November 11, 1981.

> DKS: I feel and always did feel it was important that architects have a better background, wider background.
>
> It was then a College of Fine Arts and that's where I attended. The teachers of architecture—really a part-time faculty—were local architects. They were practicing architects coming up to instruct others when they could and in subjects that they were deemed expert in. We never had too much money for faculty, but we could always pick up some good men in the city.... I'll mention a few names: Paul Huber was an expert in the field of domestic architecture, and he did a lot of church work. He did fine design. An alumnus of the school, Lester Maxon, was a very sensitive designer; he has fine houses all over Syracuse. He taught several courses. Descriptive Geometry is the one I think of right offhand, but he taught more than that. Edwin Bonta did several buildings that are mentioned in the history of Syracuse. He did the old YWCA, the University Club, and the parish house of St. Paul's Church. He taught. I remember I studied First Year Construction under Edwin Bonta, and he did some very significant, outstanding work. When there was a new building on campus, rather than pay fees it was the staff of the school of architecture who designed it. Professor Frederic William Revels and Professor Earl Hallenbeck worked together on the design of Slocum and Lyman halls, among numerous other buildings on campus, including Carnegie Library and the chemistry building, Bowne Hall. They were practitioners; they knew something about the realities of practice, so the school did have that kind of staff.

Professor Fred Roy Lear did some practice outside. I think that's the most important aspect of the school and its early success. It did graduate men who went out and made names in the field. Louis Gill of San Diego, California, is one of us. Of course they always mention Lorimer Rich and the Tomb of the Unknown Soldier. Dwight James Baum did work on campus, excellent work; he did Memorial Hospital. I probably could name a lot more. Edwin Gaggin, who at one time directed the school, did the First Trust and Deposit, the original bank. I started to say something about Fred Lear—he practiced, as I said, but he also had a background in design. He studied at the Beaux Arts School in Paris, so he had a good background. Professor Hallenbeck got his M.A. at the University of Pennsylvania under Paul Cree, a French architect who came to this country and was one of the greats. So the faculty were exposed to a great many minds in the field of architecture. They had a perspective of the profession and what it should be doing. Professor Revels was director of the school when I entered and when I left. I suspect he's the one who called me back at the death of Professor Hallenbeck. That's how I got started up there teaching, and I was practicing. I've always practiced. There've been times when I've had some good major partners to help, but I've always practiced.... Justus Scrafford was there when I entered, and he also was a Beaux Arts graduate, an excellent designer, but he was then ill and he would come only once in a great while up to the drafting room. Arthur Moore—he was always the academician. He taught drawing courses, but he never really practiced.

Noreda A. Rotunno was a practicing landscaper. He had a feeling for plant materials and was a good designer. He knew plant materials better than anyone I've ever known. His father was a gardener and he was brought up in it. In fact, he designed the first stage of my own flower garden out in back.

Q: Could you relate him to Frederick Law Olmsted? Didn't he rework some of Olmsted's plans?

DKS: Yes, he reworked them and made changes because he was designated landscape architect of the University at one time. He was a member of the design board.

Q: Is the Olmsted we're talking about the one who designed Central Park?

DKS: Yes, he did a tremendous amount of work.

Q: And he did a lot of work for the University?

DKS: He did the original landscape plan.

Q: Didn't he also have some ideas about where buildings should be?

DKS: That's really landscape. It isn't a hundred percent because you get into the teamwork aspect of location.

In those days we worked in the College of Fine Arts because architecture was very definitely a part of fine arts. We had to take two years of cast drawing, and Professor George Hess, well known in the field, was professor of drawing in the art college. Those were beneficial years. You picked up a great deal of his techniques and ways of seeing things and so on, learning the ability to observe, just from that.

And in those days we had to take language. I know; I suffered through two years of French in the College of Fine Arts. So it was a school that did depend on other schools, and very good that it did. We didn't have to take economics and I'm sorry, and we didn't have to take sociology, although I pursued sociology after I graduated because I felt it was essential to know something about it. I did some graduate work at the tail end of the Great Depression because there wasn't anything else to do. But then I got a job and that ended the graduate work. I got a big school job, all by myself.

Q: What was the job?

DKS: It was a big job in those days but it wouldn't be big today. It was a large addition for Belleville Academy up in Belleville, New York. That really started my practice.

The school gave a good background, a wonderful background. I value it. There were two courses that were cancelled under Dean Dillenback, but I still value them because I remember them and I use them so much today. Professor Lear taught a course in stereotomy, which is the theory of cutting stone and making patterns for the cutting of stones. We had to make models of stones, complicated stones. I learned to visualize three dimensions in that course—even though I was drawing two—more than in any other course except perhaps in descriptive geometry. Descriptive geometry was also a course in abstract projections, which really was more than just learning to project—you learned to visualize. Architects normally work in two dimensions but we better well think in three. We draw in two, but we must think in terms of three, and intersections, how parts come together, and that's where you learn those things, and it isn't just stereotomy or descriptive geometry, it's the total idea.

Q: Is this something that a computer can do for you today?

DKS: I think it probably could, but I'm not sure it's worth it because you have to think when you're designing. I think it would be like a fifth wheel on a steamroller, to ask a computer how these intersections would be. You have to really sense them and think about what this plane is going to do when it meets that plane or that object.

Q: It's creative process, not a mechanical one?

DKS: It's a creative process but it is mechanical; it's scientific. But you really learn to think, and that's the importance of those courses and I regret that they're cancelled. Of course, we have so much to learn. I don't think we really learn enough, and I think it's time that architecture becomes a six-year course with two degrees, the way I had to start, the liberal arts integrated with the architecture, so that you're motivated to what you think is architecture and forced to learn the things that you will be thankful for later—the breadth of understanding, including learning to read and write.

The arts at Syracuse University have been a kaleidoscope of culture and creativity. Professor Freundlich, who was dean of the College of Visual and Performing Arts from 1971 to 1982, has looked back at the way it evolved since George Fisk Comfort, the original dean, opened it in 1873. Comfort came to Syracuse as professor of modern languages and esthetics—also his title at Allegheny College, from which he had been recruited. He was instrumental in establishing the Metropolitan Museum of Art in New York City and the Syracuse Museum of Fine Arts, now the Everson.

Professor Freundlich noted that at Syracuse, Dean Comfort founded the first degree-granting fine arts college in the United States and said: "It remains today a strong, viable, and professional college in a University setting. In over a century his child has schooled thousands of artists, musicians, architects, and theater people, but in various amalgamations and formats it has continued and will continue."

4

The Library and Library School

The situation brightened and, during 1934–35, the library budget actually rose by $200—the first sign of better days.

WHARTON MILLER WAS NOT PREPARED for what he found when he arrived from Schenectady late in June 1927 to take up twin positions as librarian of the Syracuse University Library and director of the Library School.

Miller had toured the Carnegie Library building, which housed both, but not until he had actually lived with it was he fully aware of the contrast between Carnegie's attractive exterior and its dismal and inadequate interior.

He felt cramped in his office at the southeast corner of the main floor, which he shared with the order department. He did not relish the fact that the room opposite, designed as the librarian's office, was then occupied by the YWCA, which—literally maintaining an open-door policy—spread din and confusion through the lobby and into the reading room. The reading room, in turn, had space for 300 students—on a campus with an enrollment of 3,000! The rest of the main floor was used by the periodicals department, the Library School, the cataloging department, and the English seminar room. Large card files and a delivery desk south of the reading room formed a metal curtain separating the students from the stacks, which extended from the basement to the second floor.

Carnegie Library, circa 1928.

On the second floor reposed the von Ranke Library, kept under lock and key and accumulating dust. The working library of a great German historian, this collection was acquired in the latter part of the nineteenth century as the nucleus of Syracuse University's research library. Many of the rare volumes were in need of repair but restoration was expensive. In fact that process was still incomplete as this book was being written. Elsewhere on the floor were seminar rooms, not generally used, and the office of former dean Frank Smalley, then doing historical work for the University. On the third floor, just above the von Ranke Library, was a large room with the provocative title "Treasure Room." But the "treasure" consisted chiefly of the janitor's flock of prize doves. In the basement, in addition to the stacks, were the janitor's living quarters, the binding and receiving room, and a large storage space shared by newspaper collections and the University painters. There was also a big central area popularly referred to as "the dungeon," an appropriate name for a poorly lighted space containing two tiers of stacks and a conglomeration of odds and ends.

It was obvious a thorough reorganization of the building, which had opened in 1907, was needed.

The Library School itself was an embarrassment. It lacked accreditation by the American Library Association, which was only one of the authorities from which Chancellor Flint was receiving clear signals to the effect that the school either should reorganize or close.

Things were no better than they had been in 1922, when Chancellor Flint first arrived. Even then the school had cried out for emergency treatment if it was to survive.

The school sprang originally from librarian Henry O. Sibley's way of recruiting assistants for an understaffed library. The experiment was successful, and in June 1908 the trustees approved establishing the Library School. Before that courses in library economy were given through the College of Liberal Arts.

In 1908 admission to the Library School required completion of 15 units of high school work. After two years at Syracuse or another institution, students finished their schooling with specialized instruction at the junior and senior levels and earned the degree of bachelor of library economy. Those who simply wished a certificate took technical courses for two or three years.

During most of its early years the Library School probably did not suffer from comparison with similar institutions, but by 1915, and especially after 1920, it was rapidly falling behind the growth and prestige of Pratt Institute, the New York State Library School at Albany, and the University of Illinois.

When Dr. Flint became Chancellor in the fall of 1922 a committee of concerned women wanted him to be aware of the problems facing the school. They were alumnae of the school who had discussed the matter at length the previous July at a meeting in Detroit of the American Library Association (ALA). They made an appointment with Dr. Flint, and to prepare for it they interviewed Elisabeth G. Thorne.

Miss Thorne, a Vassar graduate, served in the Utica, Port Jervis, and Kingston public libraries before joining Syracuse in 1910. For the next ten years she was instructor in classification and reference in the Library School. She was named assistant librarian in 1921 and librarian the following year. Since 1920 she had been acting director of the Library School, following the retirement of director Earl E. Sperry.

After seeing the Chancellor the alumnae submitted to him and the trustees a number of recommendations designed to raise scholastic standards and bring about greater cooperation between the alumnae and the director.

In the spring of 1923 the ALA set up a temporary committee to survey library training throughout the country and to suggest new standards. Meanwhile the association urged each library school to review its own organization and curriculum. In June 1924 the council of the ALA, on the recommendation of the temporary committee, established the Board of Education for Librarianship, which, among other things, was to publish a list of accredited library schools. The board visited Syracuse University in October that year and made a report to its parent association. The officers of the association also heard from Florence Wagner '18, then on the staff of the *Wall Street Journal,* who sent them a lengthy and critical report on the administration of the Library School, the quality of its instruction, and the courses offered. She forwarded a copy to Chancellor Flint, commenting that she doubted whether Syracuse could measure up to the new accrediting standards the association had in mind.

The confidential report of the ALA Board of Education for Librarianship reached the campus early in June 1925. Dr. Flint gave it meticulous attention, marking in red ink the points he considered significant. For example, the report said past and present administrations had suffered because the director of the school was also librarian of the University. Each area should have separate leadership, it said. Equally critical were comments about the faculty, the immaturity of the students, the inadequate equipment, the "troubled, apologetic attitude" that permeated the school, an atmosphere of "restlessness and uneasiness," and the absence of administrative records and financial reports. Finally, the report contained this pointed remark: "The school should be thoroughly reorganized or discontinued. Full information on many matters [about] which the board should be informed has been very difficult to obtain." This was a fair indictment, the Chancellor realized, although there was little he could do about the omissions of a previous administration. Nor would it be fair to suggest that he should have tapped his limited resources for a school whose future was uncertain.

Elisabeth Thorne, in letters to the Chancellor of June 4 and 5, acknowledged the validity of most of the ALA findings. She requested reasonable monetary appropriations and stated: "The Library School is at the crossroads. If it is to continue, someone with a vigorous constructive program must carry it on." She offered to take a year's leave at a reduced salary to study other library schools and their methods. During her absence, she suggested, an associate director with full and independent authority should be named to administer the school, while one of the staff should act as the University librarian. Finally, she declared: "If you feel the University is doing its utmost for the Library School with no definite hope of strengthening it, I should personally rather discontinue it now or at the end of the next year than incur the inevitable stigma of loss of professional prestige from the constituted authorities of the American Library Association, with the resultant loss of students, confidence, and prestige."

She also mentioned some favorable aspects of the school: it had provided workers in a field that badly needed trained personnel, it had acted as a feeder to the library staff, and it meant that "we have a plant already established and are merely strengthening it."

The Chancellor continued to receive complaints about the school from alumni who suggested he appoint a new director. In handling this delicate phase of the problem Dr. Flint was loath to take immediate action, a decision some interpreted as indifference or ignorance. But, in a letter to an alumna, J. Winifred Hughes '14, he said he had pledged himself not to "manifest openly an enthusiastic endorsement of their complaints." He said it would be unwise "to express sympathy with complaints about one of my associates, knowing that such expression of sympathy is always taken for even more than its face value." Nor would he hurry his decision, he said, for he was in no position to finance any great change or improvement in the school.

Dr. Flint discussed the situation thoroughly with Miss Thorne, particularly enrollment and financial reports since the fall of 1921. For the 1921–22 academic year, forty-six students had registered in the school, of whom twenty-nine were candidates for the degree of bachelor of library economy; the rest were seeking certificates. For the same period the educational and administrative expenditures amounted to slightly more than $5,200, of which $4,991 was for salaries, a sum about $300 below income. The following year, with no appreciable change in enrollment but with an increase in tuition, there was a net profit of nearly $1,900. During the next three years the picture brightened somewhat, and as a result Elisabeth Thorne suggested both salary increases and additional personnel.

But in the spring of 1926 the American Library Association privately informed the Chancellor that it could not accredit the Library School "until such time as it can conform to current standards." The ALA stood ready, however, to advise and encourage the University in meeting the requirements. It said: "Forget the past and see if you can rebuild." Clearly, in view of the small number of library schools in the country, the association did not intend to force Syracuse's to close. Accordingly, after announcing in its May 1926 *Bulletin* its list of accredited institutions, the ALA softened the omission of Syracuse by stating that the Syracuse Library School was "in the process of reorganization."

All this distressed and embarrassed Dr. Flint. He was distressed because the University had not been given enough time to set its house in order. He was embarrassed because he did not know how the failure to accredit might affect the University's prestige. Nor did he welcome the view in some quarters that, despite recent improvements in curriculum and requirements, the school would continue at a junior undergraduate level for years to come. He made these and other sentiments known to the ALA. "We have discontinued certificates... [and] we want only those who are studying for degrees," he declared, implying that there should have been greater recognition of growth and development at Syracuse. He closed his letter with the suggestion that if Syracuse were not given a senior undergraduate rating in the near future, the school might have to close.

Pending further developments, Chancellor Flint again asked the alumni for remedial suggestions. Most replies favored immediate reorganization of the school to win ALA recognition. Others stressed the need for increased publicity and a new library administration. The ALA suggested meanwhile that the University increase the budget for the School to $20,000 or $25,000, with a $5,000 salary for the director. It also favored four full-time instructors for fifty students.

Miss Thorne realized that the University could not meet these proposals, but she pressed the Chancellor for increased appropriations, specifically asking for the appointment of a professor of cataloging, without whom it would be difficult to operate the following year.

Assailed by doubts as to the wisdom of continuing the school but hoping to avoid the drastic step of closing it, Dr. Flint asked the ALA how Syracuse, with its limited resources, might qualify for an undergraduate rating. The association replied with a series of suggestions that encouraged the Chancellor to move ahead with reorganization. Early in October 1926, he addressed the school's alumnae at the ALA annual meeting. Touched by his concern for the future of the school, they approved a series of resolutions favoring prompt reorganization. Dr. Flint also sought the counsel of his deans and directors, some of whom had a dim view of the school, and frequently consulted Paul Paine, head of the Syracuse Public Library. Then, in November, he obtained the consent of the trustees to a reorganization.

Rough notes in his official files show what the Chancellor had in mind. He was ready to increase the budget and the number of faculty. From time to time he noted the need for a new director. Several names had been proposed, but his choice was Wharton Miller, librarian at Union College, Schenectady, New York. Miller had degrees from Columbia University and the state library school. He had been on the staff of the Free Public Library in Newark, New Jersey, and for four years before he went to Union in 1920 had been assistant librarian at the Syracuse Public Library. After several conferences with the Chancellor, Miller accepted the offer to become librarian of the University library and director of the Library School and assumed the posts late in June 1927.

Miller quickly began reorganizing the school, renamed the School of Library Science, to meet the ALA guidelines. The first important step was to concentrate the work in the senior year and to limit the number of students to fifty. At the same time it was decided no one should be admitted to senior standing without a "C" average for the first three years. Nor should anyone graduate who did not maintain a similar average as a senior.

More important in the history of the school was the decision early in 1931 to change its status from that of a senior undergraduate institution to a graduate one beginning in the fall of 1935, when the so-called five-year plan went into effect. The first four years were to be devoted to the study of liberal arts subjects leading to an A.B. degree—a prerequisite for admission to the library school. Candidates also needed a thorough reading knowledge of French or German and had to know how to type.

The new curriculum concentrated in the first semester on general training in the whole field of library science. All students were required to take 16 hours of course work that included Book Selection Principles, Children's Literature, National Bibliography, General Reference, Classification, Cataloging, Organization, and Management, together with field work that entailed visiting library supply houses, binderies, a three-day visit to New York City, and two weeks at representative libraries of the area.

Wharton Miller, director, Library School, 1927–1955. Photograph © Bachrach.

The second semester was devoted to training those with special interests. For those who planned to work with adults in public or college libraries, the sequence consisted of 16 hours in Book Selection, Book Appreciation, Government Publications, History of Books and Libraries, Methods, Subject Bibliography, Special Reference Material, Cataloging, Public Library Administration, and College Library Administration, together with additional field work. The other specialty was for those who expected to work with young people in school libraries or in children's rooms of public libraries. On successful completion of either program, the candidate received the degree of bachelor of library science.

By the end of the Graham administration in 1942, the library school had overcome its earlier problems and was recognized as one of the outstanding institutions of its kind in the United States.

Because the director of the school was also the University librarian and the faculty of the school generally served on the library staff during the Flint-Graham administrations, it is impossible to separate the story of the school from the problems of the library itself. Probably no one looked forward to the arrival of Chancellor Flint in 1922 more than Elisabeth Thorne. Thoroughly familiar with the library and its building, she informed the new Chancellor about existing conditions and sought increased appropriations for staff, books, equipment, and maintenance. Dr. Flint was sympathetic to her requests, but he knew the University was in no position to honor them. Indeed, during his first year on campus, the actual expenditures for library salaries and services were less than in the previous year—for the year ended June 1922, $15,721; in June 1923, $15,109.

Although conditions improved during the next four years, the situation was still far from satisfactory. Total expenditures for the year ended June 1927, when Miss Thorne left Syracuse, were $34,565, including $27,270 for salaries and services. Repeatedly she had told the Chancellor of the impoverished conditions. In a letter in March 1925 she said she hoped he would realize she was "only asking for the number on the staff we had in the pre-war period of 1913–1914." She added that if the library were compared with others of similar size, Syracuse would be found wanting in the amount of salaries and in the number of volumes. A year later she quoted a report of the American Library Association to show that salaries at Syracuse were comparable only to colleges whose enrollments were much smaller. In 1926, speaking of a projected ALA study, she said: "I do not know why we are chosen for [a survey] except as an example of the insufficient budget, providing wholly insufficient material both in book content and in the rendering of the largest potential availability of book knowledge through services."

There was criticism also in a report by Professor George Works of Cornell University, who surveyed the library late in 1926. He compared the Syracuse library with those of Vassar, Yale, Tulane, and other institutions, concluding that "there was only one ... in which I considered library conditions at a lower ebb than in Syracuse."

Wharton Miller moved quickly following his appointment in 1927 to stem the cannonade of criticism that for so long had assailed his new domain, the Library School and the twenty-year-old Carnegie Library building.

He urged the YWCA to find space elsewhere. The room it had occupied and an adjoining one were combined into a reading room. He moved his office to bigger quarters which he gradually enlarged and partitioned to accommodate rare books and selected exhibits from the University's collections.

By 1928 the Library School, now called the School of Library Science, had moved from the first floor to the basement, allowing the periodicals department to take over the vacated space. Other rooms on the first floor were converted into a bigger reference room that included an art book collection. Soon after that the von Ranke Library was moved to the top floor, with the history seminar room taking its place on the second floor. A few years later some of the rooms on the main floor became a recreational reading and open shelf room. Meanwhile the stacks at the rear of the building were completed to the top floors.

Miller sought to attract male students to an area that was predominantly female. A 1928 information sheet emphasized that the school "accepted men as well as women." Great need for men in library work," it said. "Step into administrative positions. Course well-fitted to man who has bookish or scholarly interests but who doesn't want to teach."

For whatever reason, the number of male library science students went from zero in 1928 to one in 1929, then to two in 1930 and 1931. The number of women in the school in those years ranged from 87 to 139. The high points of male attendance in the Flint-Graham years came in 1937 and 1938, when seven men were enrolled, and the number of women had dropped to twenty-nine and forty-two respectively.

Not only was the school within the library, but there came to be a library inside the school. This was another of Miller's early innovations. Called the Project Library, it was administered by students in the School of Library Science. Occupying a small room near an entrance to the Carnegie, it functioned as a model free public library, offering a selection ranging from the classics to recently published fiction and biographies, as well as history, science, and travel books. Miller explained the name of the miniature library by saying: "Supervision will be given no more than help is given in project teaching. The faculty of the school will function as the board of trustees."

The Project Library fitted a theme Miller was to return to again and again—encouraging the love of books and the reading of more of them. The student-run library served faculty, spouses, and children as well as other students. Library school students drew lots to see who would be librarians and assistants in the order, catalog, loan, and children's departments, and then rotated in those offices. Miller said the students ran the Project Library "almost as a frolic." But, he added, if it gave them practice and experience, and gave a love of reading to other students, "will it not be a contribution to education?"

Years later the novel ways the library found to encourage learning caught the fancy of the *New York Times.* The newspaper in its issue of December 13, 1936 described as a "new conception of university library science" services to students and faculty members that included attention to music and art as well as contemporary books. "The modern library must function as something more than a tool for digging out scholastic facts and theories," the librarian in charge, Ida O. Benderson, said. A thing that tickled the *Times* was "brilliant-jacketed" detective novels such as Sax Rohmer's *President Fu Manchu* and Agatha Christie's *The A.B.C. Murders* sharing shelf space with more serious works such as Thomas Mann's *Stories of Three Decades* and James Truslow Adams' *The Living Jefferson.* In the music listening room twentieth-century compositions as well as classics were among 125 new phonograph records. Mrs. Benderson told the *Times:* "We are not trying solely to educate students. Rather, we are attempting to interest them in reading as one form of recreation." She mentioned an art loan program in which reproductions of famous paintings were rented to students for fifty cents a semester, with the proceeds going toward purchase of more pictures.

Library holdings had grown slowly in Dr. Flint's first years at Syracuse. In May 1922 there were 113,998 volumes. Five years later, when Miller took charge at the library, there were 135,874. Thereafter, except during the Depression, purchases mounted constantly so that in 1942 there were 287,000 volumes. Some of the increase resulted from the birth of the School of Citizenship and grants by donors for departmental and branch libraries, which Miller enthusiastically supported. (Nearly forty years later, in 1981, the Ernest S. Bird Library of Syracuse University counted 1,952,594 volumes plus 1,970,000 pieces of microform, which is the generic term for microfilm, microfiche, and microcards. Gregory N. Bullard, assistant director of administration, described the microform holdings as "equivalent in bibliographic resource to the existing library of 1.9 million volumes all over again, but taking up only a fraction of the space.")

But during most of the Flint administration the library existed in a chronic state of poverty. During Miller's first three years his hopes rose as library income went from $44,736 to $69,250, but it declined again by 1930. In staff salaries, Syracuse then stood eighteenth among twenty-seven institutions surveyed by the ALA. There was alarm when Dr. Flint urged immediate retrenchment in book purchases, apologizing: "I am ashamed to suggest this, and only desperate circumstances lead me to raise the question." Miller consented reluctantly, knowing how severely the University had been hit by the Depression. Until July 1935 library appropriations declined steadily.

Then the situation brightened and, during 1934–35, the library budget actually rose by $200—the first sign of better days. Each year thereafter the administration increased its appropriations, the sum for 1941–42 being $91,400, slightly more than double the figure when Miller took over in 1927. When he retired in 1955 he was able to report that the number of books in the library had increased fourfold in his twenty-eight years as director. The library and the Library School were budgeted separately later. For example, in the treasurer's report of 1937 Library costs came under the heading of general expenses ($48,216), and those of the Library School under instructional expenses ($10,248).

Gifts of books, manuscripts, and magazines from student organizations and friends of the University helped the growth of the library and its branches. In 1937 F. W. Christmas of Herkimer, New York, donated more than five thousand books and periodicals. In 1939 Edwin R. Whiffen established a poetry fund. Owen D. Young made a donation to purchase books about radio. A memorial fund honored Earl Sperry of the history department, the former librarian. One of the most significant gifts was that of more than fifty thousand pieces of manuscript material relating to Peter Smith, long a partner of John Jacob Astor, and his son Gerrit Smith, the noted reformer and abolitionist. The papers, including journals, letter books, maps, and accounts of the Smith family and its estate at Peterboro, Madison County, New York, from 1780 to 1880, were given to the University in 1928 by Gerrit Smith Miller, grandson of Gerrit Smith.

The special collections begun under Wharton Miller included a section of books and other writings by alumni and faculty members. Among them are *My Friend the Working Man* by James Roscoe Day, *The New Russia* by Dorothy Thompson, *Old Testament History* by Ismar J. Peritz, and *The Idea of God in the Philosophy of St. Augustine* by William Pearson Tolley. Others are *Method in History* by William H. Mace, *Second Year Latin* by Perley O. Place, *Campus Versus Classroom* by Burges Johnson, Chancellor Flint's public relations director, and many of the works of Stephen Crane, who as a student spent one semester of his short life (1871–1900) at Syracuse University, much of it in the Delta Upsilon house writing his first novel, *Maggie: A Girl of the Streets.*

Formal beginnings of the Syracuse University Archives also may be credited to Miller. Two years after he arrived on the campus, in 1929, he started to gather what he called Syracuse memorabilia, or Syracuseana. He appealed for documents, printed matter, and other material needed to compile a complete history of the institution. With the help of librarian Marjorie Thorpe he assembled such records as reports and speeches by the chancellors and other officials, minutes of meetings of the board of trustees, theses, dissertations, bulletins, catalogs, commencement programs, photographs, and files of campus newspapers and magazines. This Syracuse Collection, as it was also known, became the Syracuse University Archives and is today a key component of the George Arents Research Library.

As Chancellor Graham's administration neared an end in 1942, Wharton Miller felt encouraged with the progress the library had made in his fifteen years as director of libraries. Reporting in *Alumni News,* he noted that the number of librarians on the permanent staff had increased from fifteen to forty-four. Library expenditures had gone from $34,800 to $100,000. There were eleven branch libraries, professionally staffed. The University was adding ten thousand volumes a year, and it subscribed to fifteen hundred periodicals. He seemed proudest of the increasing use that was being made of the library, noting that while the number of students at the University was 18 percent higher than fifteen years ago, the number of library books the students borrowed in that time had risen 198 percent.

"Perhaps the library is not yet a competitor of the gymnasium or the movies," Miller said, "but it seems obvious that students do read or, at least, that they withdraw books from the library for that purpose." He added that, for the future, "all plans are directed to the development of the book collections because . . . good teaching and good preparation for the student's endeavors after he leaves the University are more and more dependent on his reading and his access to books."

5

The College of Forestry

Had the College of Forestry at Syracuse been discontinued and forestry education left entirely to Cornell, it would have grown under the shadow of the College of Agriculture, as forestry has developed in all land-grant colleges.

—Hardy L. Shirley

EVENTS LEADING TO THE FOUNDING of the New York State College of Forestry at Syracuse University in 1911, including Chancellor Day's stormy and sometimes intemperate attacks on Cornell University, are detailed in W. Freeman Galpin's *The Growing Years,* the second volume of the history of Syracuse University (1960, Syracuse University Press).

In brief, Dr. Day, Louis Marshall, and two state senators, Hendrick S. Holden and J. Henry Walters, are among those credited with creating the forestry college at Syracuse. A state college of forestry had been established at Cornell in 1898, but it closed in 1903 when appropriations ended. A bill to set up such an institution at Syracuse passed the legislature in 1910 but was vetoed by Governor Charles Evans Hughes on the grounds of economy.

Reintroduced in 1911, the bill passed both houses of the legislature, then lay on the desk of Hughes's successor as governor, John A. Dix. Marshall, a constitutional lawyer, lover of the outdoors, conservationist, philanthropist, and trustee of the university, wrote an impassioned letter to the governor. He said, in part: "Our virgin forests are disappearing, and dismal wastes have succeeded to mark the tragedy of their extinction.... An era of creation must follow that of devastation.... What the state requires is trained foresters, more trained foresters, and again trained foresters."

Governor Dix signed the bill.

Marshall used a different tactic on a third governor, William Sulzer, in 1913. A bill authorizing $250,000 for a forestry building on the Syracuse campus had won legislative approval, but Sulzer, aware that Cornellians hoped to revive a forestry program at Ithaca, scheduled a public hearing to help him decide whether to sign the bill. More than 100 people at the hearing in the Capitol Building opposed the measure, outnumbering its supporters three to one. Each side made forceful arguments, and the discussions became heated. Eleven days after the hearing the governor still had not signed the bill; Chancellor Day and Marshall took the train to Albany to see him. An emergency sent the Chancellor back to Syracuse, and trustee Marshall saw the governor alone. Marshall recounted later that immediately after shaking hands with Governor Sulzer, he asked if he had signed the bill. When the governor said he was still studying it, Marshall put a pen in his hand and asked him to sign it at once. Governor Sulzer did—and the appropriation for the college's first building was assured. The fateful pen, framed, hung for many years in the dean's office.

Louis Marshall was president of Forestry's board of trustees from its birth until his death in 1929. His continuing affection for and influence on the college was enormous. Dean Baker summed up the first board president's contribution to the college at a ceremony laying the cornerstone of the Marshall Memorial building in 1931. He said: "If there is any one man to whom we owe not only our present buildings but the spirit and the vision which have been followed in the development of the college it is Mr. Marshall."

In the early years of the New York State College of Forestry at Syracuse University (now the State University of New York College of Environmental Science and Forestry), almost from its founding in 1911, there had been differences of opinion between two dominant figures over what constituted a sound curriculum. They were Hugh P. Baker, with experience in both forestry practice and forestry education, and Franklin F. Moon, a man of broad cultural background with degrees in the sciences and the arts.

Baker had three separate terms as dean for a total of eight years and two months. Moon in his four administrations was twice acting dean and twice dean, for just under eleven years, the longest tenure for a chief executive of the college in its first quarter century.

Baker and Moon virtually alternated in office for twenty-one years after William L. Bray (Syracuse University professor of botany, who served as first head of the college, with the title acting dean for six months starting August 1911) returned to the neighboring campus. The roster from February 1912 to February 1933 looks like this: Baker, Moon, Baker, Moon, Moon, Brown, Moon, Brown, Baker.

Nelson G. Brown was acting dean twice, in 1927–28 and 1929–30.

Hugh Baker, who became dean in February 1912 after field work with the federal Forest Service and as head of the department of forestry at Pennsylvania State College, wanted forestry tied to everything the college did. He stressed general forestry, city forestry, and forest utilization broadly interpreted to include the lumber industry, the pulp and paper industry, and the wood chemical field.

Franklin Moon had a broader conception of the college's responsibilities. He too stressed professional education, but he knew that many students could not afford the tuition at private colleges. He also recognized that forestry involved a broad general training that would fit students for good citizenship and for many types of work. Therefore he sought to expand the liberal arts aspects of the curriculum, somewhat at the expense of professional courses—which he said "might be referred to today as vocational courses."

Moon's position was supported by others in forestry education who valued a broad foundation in the biological, physical, and social sciences.

There were sharp differences of opinion between the men and when Baker left for World War I service, Moon immediately revised the curriculum. On Baker's return the older approach was again stressed. But when Baker left in 1920 for a business career (he was to return a decade later), Moon as dean broadened the curriculum and kept it that way for the rest of his tenure.

As a subsequent dean, Hardy L. Shirley (1952–66), wrote to W. Freeman Galpin in 1962: "These curriculum switches were not sufficient to disrupt seriously the work of the students, but they did represent a fundamental difference in philosophy between the two men and one that persists to this day among forestry educators."

Moon, who was dean when Dr. Flint became Chancellor, was a graduate of Amherst College and received a master of forestry degree from Yale University in 1909. For two years he was a forester with the New York State Conservation Department then was on the faculty of Massachusetts State College. He joined the New York State College of Forestry in 1912 as professor of forestry engineering. Eight years later he was named professor of silviculture. He first became acting dean in

Chancellor Flint, center on log, and Professor Nelson C. Brown, in knickers at end of saw on right, in 1926 at the annual College of Forestry barbecue.

1917, and then again in 1920 before he was appointed dean later that year. He remained dean, except for a year's leave of absence, until his death in September 1929.

Dean Moon's career is detailed in *Forestry College,* a book published on the fiftieth anniversary of the institution by its alumni association. In the book, Moon's colleagues recall his revision of the curriculum, expansion of extension teaching and public service, acquisition of Adirondack forest lands, and his 1926 "grand tour" of Europe that brought him and the college international recognition. Moon is described as a "top administrator," a scholar, educator, and friend to all students and faculty members. The college library bears his name.

Interim appointments in 1927–28 and 1929–30 made Professor Nelson C. Brown acting dean before and after Moon's leave of absence. Brown received his baccalaureate and master of forestry degrees from

Yale, then spent four years as a forester in the United States Department of Agriculture and as assistant professor of forest utilization. He went to Syracuse in 1912 at the same rank and with the same specialty. Two years later he was named professor of forest utilization and subsequently became chairman of that department. During World War I he was a civilian engineer in France and Spain and an adviser to the Czechoslovakian government in 1919–20. As acting dean he won the applause of his faculty by obtaining salary increases and a state grant of $10,000 for forest investigation, the first state appropriation to the college for research. He had good personal relations with Governor Franklin D. Roosevelt and thanks to Brown's efforts, the governor announced in January 1930 that his proposed budget would include $600,000 for a building in honor of Louis Marshall, president of the college's board of trustees, who had died the previous September.

At about this time Roosevelt named a committee headed by Chancellor Flint to look over the candidates for a permanent dean. By July 1930 the committee members had made their choice, and Hugh Baker was again dean.

During his second deanship, 1930–33, Baker carried through the construction of Marshall Hall. There had been an imperative need for the building for some time. In 1926, for example, Moon had sought state aid for a science hall, as well as a greenhouse, pulp and paper laboratory, a sawmill, and a woodworking laboratory. His efforts were blocked, however, by the commissioner of education and the state finance committee. Thus it was not until October 1929 that Brown, as acting dean, submitted plans for the building to the state commissioner of architecture. Early the next month Alfred E. Smith, former governor of New York and 1928 Democratic presidential candidate, was named president of the board of trustees of the college. Chancellor Flint hailed the appointment and sent Smith an enthusiastic letter in November 1929. He also said in the letter:

> The need for the new building at Syracuse is so clear and so taken for granted by everyone that it is unnecessary to discuss this phase of it. Governor Roosevelt has raised the question if it might not well be called the Louis Marshall Hall. I think this an admirable idea and hope that the whole amount of $600,000 may be included in this year's budget. . . . We should not be "skimpy" about this building, especially if it is to carry Louis Marshall's name. As you know he has been the only president of the board of trustees from the beginning of the college until your election today. When we realize that we have only one building for all the work of the College of Forestry with nearly 400 students enough has been said.

"It was Alfred E. Smith, former Governor of New York and President of the College's Board of Trustees from 1929 to 1944, who laid the cornerstone of Marshall Hall" (*Forestry College*, 1961).

Meanwhile Brown advanced the cause through conversations with Roosevelt, of which Dr. Flint was kept informed. In January 1930 the governor publicly announced his support, and the legislature approved the necessary appropriations two months later.

Construction began the following February, and in late February 1933 Marshall Hall, which ultimately included the Franklin Moon Library, was dedicated. At the ceremonies Dr. Flint said Marshall might have many memorials, "but New York . . . memorializes her great citizen in the sphere of his interest which made him a forester by avocation, and most appropriate also, in this college, for whose origin he had so large a share of the responsibility."

Marshall Hall was the second building on the Forestry campus. The first had been known simply as "the forestry building." With Marshall Hall completed, the other was named Bray Hall in honor of William L. Bray, first head of the college. Bray had taught a course in forestry at the University as early as 1908 and was often called the father of the college. For many years he was known affectionately to students as "Daddy" Bray. Although he served as acting dean only half a year, his contribution to the college has been described by its historians as extremely important in the formation of its spirit and development of its ideals.

Under Dean Baker the College of Forestry continued its advance. In the summer of 1932, the Pulp and Paper Laboratory was built. The faculty was also strengthened. Dean Baker brought back Professor Edward McCarthy as chairman of a reorganized department of silviculture. From Pennsylvania he drafted Joseph Illick, former Pennsylvania state forester, whose skills were needed to promote the department of forest management. At about the same time Baker engaged Samuel N. Spring, widely known for his work in silviculture at Cornell University. Spring's administrative abilities soon led to his appointment as assistant dean. Baker also helped in the early development of the Huntington Wild Life Forest.

Dean Baker's abilities as a promoter and administrator were recognized by other institutions. In June 1932 Massachusetts State College intimated it wanted him as its president. Chancellor Flint tried to persuade him to remain, and it seemed for a time he had succeeded. One factor influencing Baker's thinking was the possibility that his title would be changed to president. When he mentioned this to the Chancellor, however, Dr. Flint said such a change might result in a new relationship between the University and the college. He therefore conducted a lengthy correspondence with state commissioner Frank Graves, who was also a trustee of the college. In a letter to Dr. Flint on June 21, 1932, Graves wrote: "I cannot think of any greater calamity than to lose Dean Baker, except the misfortune of creating an unsound administrative situation." About a month later, after the commissioner had a conference with the dean, he wrote Dr. Flint again:

> We ought not, because of our high regard of Dean Baker and our great desire to recognize him, to build up a new university policy out of a temporary situation. Dr. Baker may tomorrow be offered a university presidency of such a caliber that he could not properly decline it, or he (or any or all the rest of us) might die tomorrow, and the University would

> find itself saddled with a position for which it had no fitting incumbent. Moreover, I think you would be inviting discussion from other colleges of the University. The law school and the medical school are even more distinct from the College of Liberal Arts and the other schools on the Hill than the College of Forestry. What would you say if their deans requested the right to be presidents?

This advice from Commissioner Graves and the Massachusetts offer persuaded the Chancellor not to stand in Baker's way, and in February 1933 the dean left to head Massachusetts State College. The title of the chief executive of the College of Forestry was changed to president much later, in 1970.

Samuel Spring, Baker's successor, earned his bachelor's and master's degrees from Yale, then had a successful career as a practical forester in the federal and Connecticut forest services and taught at the University of Maine, the Yale School of Forestry, the University of Missouri, and Cornell. As dean of the College of Forestry, despite the handicap of a national Depression, Spring constantly sought to improve the curriculum, to prevent salary cuts, and to furnish the Pulp and Paper Laboratory with modern equipment. He persuaded Albany to erect a greenhouse and insectary south of Bray Hall and saw the Roosevelt Experimental Station reorganized. After World War II broke out in Europe, Spring had to simplify the curriculum and otherwise retrench. Adding to his worries were the departure of some of his faculty and a drop in enrollment.

Between its founding and 1922, the College of Forestry generally followed the entrance requirements of the College of Liberal Arts. No one was admitted to a professional course if deficient in more than one entrance unit, nor could anyone register except at the opening of the fall term. Students could transfer from accredited colleges and universities. In those years there was spirited debate over the requirements. One view was that transfer students should not normally be expected to make up entrance requirements. At another time Dean Moon sought the University's advice about accepting students deficient in academic standing but strong in practical farm and forestry experience. Moon said those rejected at Syracuse entered the agriculture college at Ithaca, which tolerantly waived language requirements. The dean did not wish to stir up the state department of education, but he hoped the college might accept candidates who otherwise were qualified for forestry study.

A more elastic admissions program was also urged by Louis Marshall for applicants with rural backgrounds who, he held, had qualifications most city candidates did not possess. Moreover, he believed all applicants should pass a physical examination before registration.

Some minor changes were made, but the admissions program of 1941–42 was much like that of 1922–23 except that 16 entrance units were necessary. In addition, each candidate had to submit a certificate showing a grade of at least 70 on the Regents examinations. Others whose preparatory work averaged 75 might be admitted on certification from a high school principal. Applicants were also told that admission to the college was restricted by its limited physical facilities. Undergraduates were offered several courses of study. One was a program of General Forestry, with Forestry as its major subject. A second was Landscape and City Forestry, and a third was Pulp and Paper Manufacture. A total of 132 hours led to the degree of bachelor of science. In 1924 a new curriculum provided for a broader program, which remained unchanged until 1933. All work in forestry was then divided into two major divisions: General Forestry and Forest Production. Under this arrangement, which was frequently amended, greater specialization was allowed in the upperclass years.

The relationship between the college and the University was spelled out in *The New York State College of Forestry at Syracuse University: A History of its First Twenty-five Years 1911–1936*, a book edited by faculty members Raymond J. Hoyle and Laurie D. Cox and published by the college in 1936. They wrote:

> Although an integral part of Syracuse University, the New York State College of Forestry, almost from its inception, was a definite legal entity and governed by a separate board of trustees directly responsible to the State of New York. The only legal liaison between the College and the University is an ex-officio member of the board of trustees.

The work and influence of the College of Forestry, extending far beyond its Syracuse campus, includes the Ranger School and two wildlife stations.

The Theodore Roosevelt Wild Life Experiment Station, established in 1919, is a specialized unit of the department of forest zoology named for the late president. The experiments were for the protection and propagation of animal life in the forest and its waters. In years to come it was to serve as a zoological research center for the nation as well as the state. Its first director, Charles C. Adams, was succeeded in 1926 by Charles E. Johnson. With Professors Wilford A. Dence and Justus F. Mueller, they initiated a series of research projects that included an ornithological study of the Finger Lakes and the Catskill Mountains.

Zoological research was also fostered with the gift to the University in 1932 of thirteen thousand acres of forest in Essex County from Mr. and Mrs. Archer M. Huntington. The land was given in trust for the college to use "for investigation, experiment and research in relation to the habits, life history, methods of propagation, and management of fish, birds, game food and fur-bearing animals and as a forest of wildlife." It became the Archer and Anna Huntington Wildlife Forest. In 1938 the Huntingtons deeded more than eighteen hundred acres adjoining the original tract and later provided funds to maintain the forest.

The New York State Ranger School, established in 1912, is on Cranberry Lake, two miles from the village of Wanakena in St. Lawrence County. Its director when Chancellor Flint took office was James F. Dubuar, who held the post from 1921 until his retirement in 1957. The admissions procedure in 1922 was simple. Any applicant between the ages of eighteen and thirty-five who had a grammar school education and was physically fit was accepted. The purpose was to train young men "to fill the gap which exists between the woodsman and the professional forester." In other words it was a school for secondary education in forestry. The ranger course lasted forty weeks and actual instruction, according to the curriculum, was largely vocational in nature and method. The so-called rangers chiefly studied forest production and harvest, surveying and engineering, management and business, wood technology, grazing, and rudiments of the history of forestry. In each week there were forty-four working hours. Of the thirty-five students registered during the 1921–22 school year, twenty-two received certificates.

The forest, over which the Ranger School and College of Forestry had direction, had been given to Syracuse University by the Rich Lumber Company and consisted of 1,814 acres. The deed provided that the University was to hold the land for the use of the forestry college. For a time this arrangement precluded the possibility of state support for the school, and during its early years and the school's needs were met by loans from the University. The situation was rectified in 1913 when the state bought twenty-two acres of the original Rich grant from the University. On that the school undertook a state-financed building program, and by 1922 there were several structures, including a new dormitory, a dining hall, a workshop, and a main building.

In the summer of that year Louis Marshall paid a surprise visit to the Ranger School. He was particularly interested in seeing the dormitory which had been built with a $5,000 state appropriation. As recounted in the book *Forestry College:*

Joseph S. Illick, professor of forest management and later dean of the College of Forestry, with a student, tramping the woods along a trail at Green Lakes State Park. Photograph by C. Wesley Brewster.

At that time, $5,000 had considerable purchasing power. It more than paid for a one-story building, without a basement, built by the Ranger School handyman, the teamster, and a laborer who was paid $17.50 per week plus board. The building, only 16 ft. wide but 90 ft. long,

> was called "the long dormitory." It contained eight 10 x 12 ft. rooms which provided ample space for 16 students. The money remaining after construction purchased some new furniture; an efficient hot water heating system ... and an electric generator, storage batteries, materials for wiring, and the labor for installing electric lighting in all the buildings. The change from kerosene lamps was welcome; after a time, the main building and the old dining hall no longer smelled of kerosene. The new lighting system served until 1926, when the utility company built a power line to the school.

Marshall became enthusiastic about the school and heartily promoted its program. Assured of Marshall's goodwill and profiting from a combination of recovery from an economic depression and a change in the college administration, Dean Moon moved ahead with his expansion plans and in 1923 obtained a state appropriation of $200,000 for a new main building. But only after five years of delays was the stone and concrete structure opened, in March 1928. It was formally dedicated the following August in ceremonies attended by distinguished educators, foresters, and conservationists. Marshall, as president of the college's board of trustees, gave the principal address.

In the same year the Ranger School had the first addition to its land: James Dubuar told the story behind the acquisition in *Forestry College:*

> An adjacent tract of 15 acres had been subdivided into lots for hunting or summer camps. The director foresaw disadvantages in this development and discussed with Dean Moon the possibility of acquiring the acreage as an addition to the school forest. The dean did not consider it advisable to try to obtain an appropriation for purchase, but he wisely mentioned the matter at the next meeting of the board of trustees, and Mr. Marshall purchased the land. ...
>
> The area had never been burned or cut over for its hardwoods and he was told that among other uses it would enlarge the school's sugar bush.
>
> In the spring of 1929 the Ranger School sent Mr. Marshall some syrup from maple trees on the land he had donated. Soon after, Marshall wrote that in a long life in which he had given much of his time, abilities, and money in philanthropic enterprises, the syrup was the first material reward he had ever received.

When Nelson Brown became acting dean in 1929, he and Hall E. Shepherd, a graduate of the Ranger School, approached the International Paper Company about five thousand acres northeast of the college forest. The land, like the Rich property, had been logged and had seen fire damage. In a letter to the company on September 27, 1929, Brown said: "In itself, the tract probably represents a relatively low value. As an addition to the educational facilities at our state Ranger School, however, it has a large scientific and demonstrational value and we hope very much that your board will look upon it in this light and help us add to our facilities for turning out men who may be of some use and help to them in the operation of your company." In 1931 the company gave the University 500 acres in trust for the college, increasing the size of the forest to 2,330 acres.

During the next ten years the physical conditions of the forest underwent considerable change. In 1933, for example, the Civilian Conservation Corps set up a camp in the forest and remained there for more than four years. Roads were built, second growth stands of timber were cut, new plantings were made, and several additional buildings were erected, chiefly as living quarters for the Ranger School's faculty and their families. But World War II caused an immediate drop in enrollment, and in 1944 there was no regular Ranger School class. After the war enrollment in the Ranger School soared—from eighteen in 1946 to sixty-one in 1947. Sixty-one was the maximum number of students the school could house and train.

From 1922 to 1942 enrollments in the Ranger School rose from twenty-eight to forty-seven. The peak year was 1928–29, with sixty-three students; the number of certificates issued was forty-four, and forty-five were awarded in 1935–36. Surveying, forest inventory, and engineering had become the backbone of the Ranger School's curriculum.

Allied in many ways to the school's work was a summer training camp opened in 1913 near Tannersville in the Catskill Mountains. Starting in 1915 the sessions were held at Cranberry Lake. Because most of the summer students were second year men in forestry, the school was often called the Sophomore Camp.

Another phase of Forestry's many activities grew out of the friendship of Charles Lathrop Pack, a wealthy, retired lumberman who was past president of the American Forestry Association and American Tree Association and founder of the Charles Lathrop Pack Forestry Foundation. Forestry students were eligible for an annual prize offered by the Pack Foundation for an article or talk promoting forestry and forest education. Dean Moon cultivated Pack's friendship and, when the Barber Tract of 964 acres was put up for sale, Pack purchased it in November 1923 and deeded it to the University for the exclusive use of the College of Forestry.

The tract, lying between the Ranger School and a large state forest, became known as the Pack Demonstration Forest. It was immediately put to use as a laboratory for students, especially those who spent ten weeks each summer in field training. But Pack in his enthusiasm envisaged something more than a summer camp. What he had in mind coincided with Dean Moon's aim of providing improved field training, and Pack bought and deeded to the University for the college 2,250 acres of forest land a few miles north of Warrensburg in the fall of 1926.

A few months later Louis Marshall, in a letter to his son Robert, spoke of the tremendous impact the gift would have on silviculture and forest management. He also said the state legislature had recently appropriated $3,500 for someone to take charge of the forest. The following year Clifford H. Foster, a graduate of the college, was named director of the Pack Demonstration Forest and was its only director for the next thirty years. Foster spent two years preparing the forest for improvement and planting. Then farm buildings were repaired, a sawmill was built, and other facilities were added. "By the early 1930s," Raymond Hoyle wrote in *Forestry College,* "the Pack Forest was adding significantly to the college's instructional program."

Pack, who received an honorary doctor of business administration degree from Syracuse University in 1927, continued to interest himself in the college, its personnel, and its curriculum. During 1929–30 he contributed more than $10,000 toward the work of the forest. Then his health failed, and in 1936 he asked the University to set aside a place in the Demonstration Forest for his burial plot. With the blessing of the college his request was granted. At his death he was buried in the forest he had established. A bronze plaque on a boulder at the site reads "Charles Lathrop Pack, 1857–1937, Pioneer in Forest Education. Here He Lies Where He Longed To Be."

Arthur Pack, son of the benefactor, bought the seventy-eight-acre Raymond farm, the last privately owned land within the forest, in 1939. Ten years later he deeded it to the University in trust for the college. Shortly thereafter, in a letter to the University board of trustees, he expressed the hope that the College of Forestry would guide the people of New York State to a broader understanding of the sociological aspects of forestry as well as the economic importance of a better use of state forest reserves. The college consistently followed that policy.

The fortunes of the college and the University were shaken by the Wall Street Crash of 1929. Both institutions realized that if the Depression continued, there would be a decrease in enrollment and a forced curtailment of expenses. Actually, the result was not as serious as expected, although the college's proposed budgets were sliced by the state.

At the college, however, the problem was accentuated because the state was supporting forestry instruction at both Cornell and Syracuse, and state authorities soon questioned maintaining parallel work at two institutions. The state, like the college and University, saw a need to retrench. Anticipating the problem, Brown, the acting dean, and Chancellor Flint took steps to strengthen the college.

Dr. Flint, who was a member of the college's board of trustees, strongly urged Brown to investigate the possibility of a grant from the State Reforestation Commission for initial studies in that field. The Chancellor also wanted him to persuade the commission to endorse the college's building program; he said Brown could bolster his request with a formidable array of facts about the national reputation of the college, its ability to educate men for forestry, and a faculty capable of carrying out any assignment. The Chancellor admitted that Cornell had its just claims but insisted that the college had equally well-established rights.

The acting dean replied to Dr. Flint with a nine-page memorandum "showing reasons for increased support of the New York State College of Forestry at Syracuse University." These included data about the college's enrollment, achievements of its graduates in forestry work, and its many public services. But he said its future depended on increased state appropriations for buildings, more equipment, a broader curriculum, and better salaries. He compared state aid to the College of Agriculture at Cornell with state aid to the College of Forestry at Syracuse. In the year 1924–25 the college at Cornell received $1,429,160 and the college at Syracuse $215,950. By 1928–29 the figures had risen to $1,636,880 for Cornell and $265,220 for Syracuse. In the latter year Cornell's school had 713 students compared to 441 at Syracuse, and the state's appropriation per student was $2,295 and $601 respectively. The teaching staff of 272 at Cornell averaged 2.6 students per instructor, while at Syracuse 34 faculty members taught an average of 12.9 students each. Finally Brown said: "Is it good business, is it sound policy, to have two institutions supported by the state training men for the same profession?"

The Chancellor, saying he had "overheard in the Regents committee meeting that the College of Agriculture will take the stand that all land classified as 'agricultural' is their field for forestry," wrote to Brown: "Our attitude will be that abandoned farms or farms that ought to be abandoned or farms which no longer can be operated profitably as an agricultural proposition become thereby a forestry project, and, indeed, anything more than a minor woodlot on a farm would become a College of Forestry proposition."

The question of whether more than one institution should teach forestry at public expense was also being discussed in Albany, and the state education department asked Harlan H. Horner, assistant commissioner for higher and professional education, to study the situation. He submitted his findings in April 1932.

After tracing the history of agricultural and forestry instruction at Ithaca and Syracuse, he recommended that at the end of the academic year 1933–34 the state should stop supporting professional forestry courses at Cornell. No further forestry students should be admitted to Cornell. Those still registered and wishing to continue their studies should transfer to Syracuse. Cornell could offer elementary and informational forestry courses needed for its agriculture students, and should limit extension work to forestry problems of the farm and to cooperation with farm agencies and rural schools.

As a result of the Horner study and subsequent conferences, Cornell agreed to discontinue undergraduate courses and admit no new students. Extension work in forestry as related to farm and woodlot, and elementary education in forestry would continue at Cornell as an inherent part of the general course in agriculture and graduate instruction and research.

Within three years, however, a *Bulletin* of the Cornell Agriculture College, issued in July 1935, announced courses in wildlife conservation and management. Worried that Cornell might ask for appropriations to finance those objectives, which would amount to a duplication of the work at Syracuse, the Regents again sought Horner's advice.

The outcome was an agreement by the colleges in November 1936. Graduate work was to cease at Cornell, and nonprofessional courses were to be ancillary to those in agriculture and wildlife conservation and management. Instruction and research in wildlife conservation and at Cornell were to be recognized, endorsed, and supported. All undergraduate and graduate instruction and research in professional forestry, however, were to be concentrated in the College of Forestry, but nonprofessional courses in wildlife conservation and management were to be ancillary to the needs of a forestry program. The Roosevelt Wild Life Station was to be continued, its work confined to a study of wildlife problems and experimentation within the field of forest management.

The rivalries between Cornell and Syracuse led Dean Hardy L. Shirley to state in 1962:

> No fully objective appraisal has been made of the results to forestry education and research of having the forestry college in New York separated from the College of Agriculture and the Agricultural Experiment Station. Certainly the College of Forestry has paid a price for its location at

Syracuse University. Cornell University had, and increasingly has developed, strong departments and programs in such fields as entomology, pathology, plant and animal physiology, botany, zoology both as related to veterinary science and animal ecology, agronomy, soils, genetics, agricultural engineering, and agricultural economics. Syracuse University has properly left most of these fields to Cornell. Also the College of Forestry, if located at Cornell, would have been eligible to receive funds available to land grant colleges and agricultural experiment stations under various federal grants. All of these furnished material for arguments that Cornell could and did use for centering all forestry education and research with agriculture. Moreover, Cornell historically had the first College of Forestry.

But there is another aspect to the picture. Had the College of Forestry at Syracuse been discontinued and forestry education left entirely to Cornell, it would have grown up under the shadow of the College of Agriculture, as forestry has developed in all land grant colleges. Hence, it would not have had its own departments of botany, entomology, and zoology with their strong emphasis on the ecological approach. It is likely that its work in the forest products field would have been rather closely related to agricultural engineering. It seems unlikely that the college would have developed the strong ties with industry and its strong programs in pulp and paper technology, wood products engineering, and forest chemistry that have been developed at Syracuse. It seems almost certain also that it would not have had the special programs in landscape architecture, though this field might have been continued at a relatively high level at Cornell had the College of Forestry not developed at Syracuse. And, finally, it would not have had the influence of the strong Maxwell School of Citizenship and Public Affairs with its orientation, first toward county government, later toward state and national, and more recently toward world affairs. Many foresters have gotten a start in public administration here that has served them well since graduation.

6

A School of Country Life?

Chancellor Flint asked his friend the president of Massachusetts Agricultural College to survey local conditions with the idea of establishing a School of Country Life.

THE SYRACUSE UNIVERSITY *Bulletin* of 1910 carried this statement:

> The trustees and administration of the University have decided to establish definite courses in Agriculture and Forestry as a preliminary step and with the purpose in view of organizing soon a College of Agriculture. Provision is made for utilizing the present facilities of the University in offering students—beginning in September 1910—the opportunity of electing courses leading to specialization in Agriculture and Forestry.
>
> Syracuse University believes that there is a demand for such instruction from the common school in elementary forms through all the grades to the laboratories of the College, and that the time has come when every college should be encouraged to take up this work. Nineteen colleges in the State of New York teach the other sciences. They would doubtless teach the sciences of Agriculture and Forestry if the State were to call upon them for this instruction which to reach the popular demand must be extended to every part of the State.

W. Freeman Galpin, writing in the second volume of the history of Syracuse University, said: "This pointed statement, penned by the Chancellor [Day] himself . . . must be interpreted in its proper setting."

Galpin said Dr. Day, irked by Albany's "continued favoritism for Cornell University," became a crusader for state support for all educational institutions including Syracuse. Albany's educational program was unjust, the Chancellor believed.

Dr. Day was in the fight as early as 1904, when a bill was introduced at Albany to appropriate $250,000 for the College of Agriculture at Cornell. He and other college presidents—of Colgate, Hamilton, Rochester, St. Lawrence, New York, and Union—opposed the measure. Dr. Day's arguments appeared in two pamphlets, "A Protest and some Proposals concerning Agricultural Education" and "More Reasons Why State Money Should Not Be Appropriated This Year for an Agricultural Building at Cornell." In both pamphlets, wrote Galpin, "his case was weakened by ill-advised words and phrases and a faulty presentation of the facts involved."

The *Bulletin* of 1910 that spoke of "organizing soon a College of Agriculture" was premature, but those who registered for the courses promised for September 1910 presumably were accommodated in the College of Liberal Arts, where such instruction was given. In June 1911, a bachelor of science degree in agriculture was conferred on George Delcasse, but the college had not yet been born.

In the spring of 1912, Frank W. Howe came to Syracuse from the state education department, where he had been a specialist in agriculture. In May of that year a division of agriculture was established, and Howe was named director. The College of Agriculture opened in the fall of 1912, and the *Bulletin* of March 1913 listed thirty-five agriculture students.

A benefactor of the University, Margaret (Mrs. Russell) Sage of New York City, who earlier had set up endowments for the Margaret Olivia Slocum Teachers College (giving it her maiden name), presented Syracuse University with $83,000 in 1912 as a memorial to her father, Joseph Slocum—$50,000 for a professorship in agriculture, $20,000 for scholarships, and $13,000 to pay off a mortgage on the University Farm. The agriculture division and later the college were named for him. Not long afterward she gave $30,000 more for equipment and buildings at the farm.

The Joseph Slocum College of Agriculture had a faculty of twelve headed by Dean Reuben L. Nye when Dr. Flint became Chancellor in 1922. Under their direction, the college gave courses leading to the degrees of bachelor of science and bachelor of science in agriculture. A student seeking admission to either sequence needed 15 units of high school work, consisting of English (3 units), mathematics (2), algebra (1), geometry (1), science (2), history (1), and electives (5). Starting with the fall of 1927, a student could be admitted after passing a Syracuse University, College Board, or state regents examination, or on presentation of a certificate from an approved secondary school. About the only change during the remaining life of the college was the dropping of the requirement of two entrance units in mathematics.

Anyone seeking a B.S. in agriculture (the B.S. degree was dropped in 1925) was required to have had one year of practical farm experience and to complete 140 class hours of formal course work. This program was primarily designed for those who planned to engage in some form of vocational agriculture or to teach agriculture. During the freshman year all degree candidates had to take courses in botany, English, chemistry, and zoology—all taught in the College of Liberal Arts—and to begin specialized study in the College of Agriculture: animal husbandry, dairy husbandry, cereal crops, and plant propagation. There were some modifications after 1922, with the trend favoring more intensive work in agriculture. English, botany, and chemistry were still required, but such new courses as agricultural survey, landscape gardening, drawing and design, and special work in algebra and trigonometry were made available.

In the first semester of the sophomore year each student selected a major in a particularized field of study, to be pursued during the rest of his or her college years. The sophomore program might include courses in geology, entomology, drawing, forage crops, horticulture, poultry, soils and fertilizer, botany, mathematics, wood shop, and general pomology. During the last two years each student registered in one of these groups: agronomy, animal husbandry, dairy husbandry, horticulture, general agriculture, agricultural teaching, and poultry husbandry. Subsequently, landscaping gardening, science, and agricultural administration were added to the list of majors.

A major problem facing Chancellor Flint on coming to Syracuse was that of finances, and the situation in the College of Agriculture did nothing to help him. Against a total operating cost of $34,904 for the college year 1922–23, most of it for salaries, there were earnings of $12,059, mostly from tuition. To this deficit of nearly $23,000 had to be added $9,000 more for overhead. Offsetting this in part was the income from endowment, making the net loss slightly more than $21,000. The total valuation of educational equipment was listed as $23,039, and the University Farm and its buildings were valued at $139,615.

Had the University been more prosperous, Chancellor Flint might have been able to overlook the college's financial troubles, but with a large inherited debt he realized that remedial measures were sorely needed. Consequently, during the summer and early fall of 1923, he explored the problem at length and reported his findings to the trustees. The enrollment in agriculture, never large, had declined again, he said, partly because of increased tuition and partly because of general trends affecting all agricultural institutions in the state. He added: "The question of some form of specialization or differentiation should be considered within the next two years; meanwhile the field is being studied and various lines of development investigated." But the college and the farm continued to show annual deficits.

The Chancellor wrote to his friend Kenyon Butterfield, president of the Massachusetts Agricultural College, frankly admitting his pessimism over the future of agriculture at Syracuse, but inviting Butterfield to survey local conditions with the idea of establishing a "School of Country Life." Butterfield accepted the invitation, studied the situation, and outlined a plan. In general he proposed a continuation of the college with agriculture as its nucleus, but subject to a reorganization that would transform its curriculum and objectives into a service institution for rural life. The bachelor's degree would be dropped because agriculture was being adequately handled by existing land-grant colleges. In its place would be a battery of new courses, at the undergraduate and graduate levels, designed to acquaint students with the farmer's problems and to train them to become social workers, preachers, doctors, school administrators, nurses, government agents, and journalists in rural areas.

Chancellor Flint was pleased with the plan, and his enthusiasm rose as he realized how various university departments could help promote the new school. Architecture, for example, could train students to design and build rural schools; journalism could prepare others to become owners or editors of rural newspapers, and the prospective School of Citizenship could fashion a course in local government. The Chancellor believed an experiment in rural sociology might enhance the reputation of the University. Moreover, it would mean retaining the college, which he believed the University was morally bound to continue. Therefore he urged Butterfield to prepare a final draft of the proposal, because he had his eyes on an "angel" who had shown an interest in the school.

Unfortunately Butterfield's original enthusiasm waned in late 1924, chiefly because of his decision to become president of Michigan Agricultural College. Nevertheless, Chancellor Flint continued to seek his help and advice, and from time to time he received letters from his friend containing more recommendations. Should Dr. Flint raise an endowment of $2 or $3 million, Butterfield wrote once, Charles J. Galpin of the United States Department of Agriculture might be persuaded to head the proposed school. On the other hand, if the endowment were as large as $10 million, he himself might consider the position. Optimistic as the Chancellor was, both figures were much too high. Thus plans for a School of Country Life came to an end. Only the elimination of the bachelor of science degree and some major changes in curriculum remained to remind him of his efforts to solve the problems of the college along more conventional lines.

Still Dr. Flint was not ready to surrender. Repeatedly his thoughts returned to the idea of the college becoming a service institution, and the introduction of new courses in agricultural administration and journalism, both suggested by Butterfield, may be credited to the Chancellor. But these innovations did little to check a downward trend in enrollment and in income. By 1928, for instance, only sixty students were registered. The following year Dr. Flint continued his search for an "angel," but pessimistic forecasts about the college obviously discouraged potential benefactors. Anxious as he was that the college should "function in a significant way" and be distinguished from the state agricultural schools, Dr. Flint said, as things then stood he had "no pride in its continuance and if there were no real job for it I would just as soon discontinue it."

Still unable, however, to accept what seemed to be inevitable, the chancellor authorized a publicity campaign to increase enrollment. Some favorable reaction followed, and in the fall of 1928 the registration climbed to seventy-two, although part of the gain stemmed from the temporary placement of some university students in agriculture. This helps to explain Vice Chancellor Graham's remark at the time: "It is difficult to offer any constructive suggestions for an advertising program in connection with the College of Agriculture, for it is impossible to give any satisfactory answer to the question as to why a young man should come to Syracuse for a four-year course in agriculture."

In 1930, when a committee of the Board of Education of the Methodist Church surveyed the University, it said very little about the College of Agriculture. Earlier, Floyd W. Reeves, the committee chairman from the University of Chicago, had intimated to the chancellor that the Margaret Sage endowments placed a moral obligation on the University to continue the college. Dr. Flint replied: "This moral obligation would make necessary the effort to function successfully as a School of Agriculture, but if it were found impossible to function successfully, we would then feel free to concentrate her gifts upon the other phases of her interest in Syracuse University."

The 1930 Reeves Survey made it clear that Syracuse was the only agricultural college in the country not receiving state or federal funds,

University Farm scene.

and that consequently it was not under any immediate government inspection or control. It also stressed the need to maintain enrollment in the college within a number that could be adequately handled by the staff—between 100 and 125. Finally, the survey brusquely recommended "that the College of Agriculture be discontinued."

The Reeves Survey provided this contemporary description of the University Farm, which had grown from a one hundred-acre tract Chancellor Day had bought at the end of Lancaster Avenue on Colvin Street in 1910 and sold to the University at cost:

> The University Farm consists of 196 acres within the city limits and is easy of access to campus. There are on the farm three houses and more than a half dozen barns. The barns are in a very bad state of repair. There is no dairy herd, only a sire and three or four cows. There is a limited number of hogs. These are kept largely as a commercial proposition for the consumption of University garbage. ... There are no horses except those used for farm service. There are no sheep, their absence being

> explained because, when effort was made to keep them they were killed by dogs. Poultry is the only project carried on respectably for instructional purposes. There is an old apple orchard but no care is taken of it.

At about the same time Dr. Graham submitted his findings about the University Farm, whose management, except for poultry operations, had not been under control of the University. Among other things, he objected to Dean Nye's proposal to make the farm a laboratory for the college because of added expense; the deficit for 1929–30 was close to $3,000. He believed that mounting labor costs were largely responsible for this deficit and felt that to employ a farm manager would be extravagance. But, he added, "of course we can not get on without one. We are the victims of a situation. I do not see how these costs can be reduced." Later, in May 1931, Dr. Graham told the Chancellor it would be unwise to abandon the college.

Matters drifted along for a year, but in the spring of 1932 the Chancellor directed Dean Nye to assume management of the farm with the understanding that he must make ends meet. This foreshadowed the demise of both farm and college, and few were surprised when, at the board of trustees meeting in June 1932, Dr. Flint recommended that the executive committee be instructed to decide what should be done. Instead, however, the trustees voted that the committee discontinue the college at such time and under such circumstances as were deemed best. The following spring the committee agreed to abandon it after all the current students had been graduated or otherwise provided for. It remained for Dean Nye and the Chancellor to implement this action. Formal instruction ceased in June 1934, although graduations in agriculture are recorded as late as 1939.

Since 1928 Dean Nye and his faculty had fought a strong rear guard battle against the closing. Evidence of this exists in a "Memo Concerning Important Considerations Relating to the Future Development of the College of Agriculture," found in Dr. Flint's official correspondence. The memo, apparently written by a member of the faculty, pointed out that 25 percent of the teachers of high school agriculture in New York State were graduates of Syracuse, and that there were many other such teachers in Ohio and Pennsylvania. It added that because teacher training in agriculture was closely interwoven with the other departments of the college, any change from collegiate standing would prevent future graduates from entering a field so productive of good results.

At the time the College of Agriculture was rebutting various proposals circulating on the campus that threatened its future. For example, the memo declared that the college had been criticized for its low enrollments in comparison with other agricultural colleges. But it said that unlike them, Syracuse did not include home economics and engineering students. Nor should the critics forget that "our very fine" combination program with the College of Business Administration had not grown because the college did not have a staff member to publicize it. Texas had done this with great success, and it was rumored that Cornell was considering such a combination. Although Cornell was a serious competitor in agriculture, there was no reason why Syracuse University could not do more for the college. Increased publicity, the opening of agricultural courses to other students on the Hill, and a helping hand to the dean and faculty would more than justify its continuance. Finally, the memo concluded, there was a definite place for a private agricultural college in the state.

Chancellor Flint weighed these and many other suggestions. He had struggled to keep the college alive, but he had tried to direct its future into more fruitful channels. Declining enrollment and mounting costs were more than the impoverished University could stand, especially in the face of increased competition from state-supported schools. The Chancellor finally did what many thought should have been done long before 1934.

The closing of the college was followed by gradual curtailment of the program on the farm, which continued to operate for some time after the Graham administration. Later, under Chancellor Tolley, the farm property was converted into more useful purposes, and the Sage endowments, as well as Slocum Hall, were diverted to the needs of other colleges on the campus.

During its life the College of Agriculture, in spite of severe competition, maintained creditable academic standards. Many of its alumni gained recognition in the state and nation. After the demise of the college, Nye served for several years as superintendent of the farm and retired in 1956.

7

The College of Applied Science

The appointment of William Pratt Graham as Chancellor was talked about as *"anticipating the wave of the future. . . . One of my mentors at Middlebury College said when I decided to go to the Maxwell School, 'You're going to a forward-looking university. I don't know whether it's due to the Methodists or to their new Chancellor.' He knew who the new Chancellor was, knew he was a technologically based person; it had filtered up to an economist in Vermont that here was a professionally trained engineer."*

—Frank P. Piskor, 1981

In 1978 Milton A. Wise '24 of Pasadena, California, wrote to the College of Engineering for information about his surviving engineering classmates. He wanted them to report on their professional and personal experiences since graduation so he could compile their replies for the fifty-fifth anniversary of the class in 1979.

From the dean's office he learned that forty-five of the seventy-four graduates were living. He circularized them "to obtain the work-life review of all of you who are still alive and able to write." He received thirty-one replies; many of them were handwritten, and these Wise painstakingly typed. Then he photocopied the lot, titled the compilation "The Tales of the Survivors," and sent each responding classmate a complete set in time for the fifty-fifth reunion. But he himself did not attend because "I get depressed in seeing all those old people!"

He was sure time had taken its toll, noting in 1978: "Our youngest man would be John Oehrle; most will be at least seventy-five."

The engineering graduates of 1924 included a clergyman, Charles L. Montgomery of the Central New York Conference of the United Methodist Church (a mechanical engineer); Francis William "Bill" McCarthy (chemical), a baker and later president of Fleischmann's Bakery, Philadelphia; Henry H. Graley (electrical), inventor of an electric oar and other "contraptions"; J. Park Bailey (civil), who helped bring water from Skaneateles to Syracuse; General LeGrande A. Diller (chemical), an aide to General Douglas MacArthur in World War II; and Forman H. Craton (mechanical), who helped adapt locomotive propulsion apparatus to oil-well drilling. Excerpts from some of their histories are at the end of this chapter.

The *Bulletin* of the College of Applied Science for the year Milton Wise and his colleagues graduated has an air of quaint modernity. For the year 1924–25 the catalog was completely rewritten. For the first time it was illustrated and printed on glossy paper. Photographs show squared-off motor cars, with running boards and high-arching fenders, parked near Lyman and Machinery halls.

A portion of the section on mechanical engineering says, "the present age has frequently been called the *Mechanical Age,"* which began with invention of the steam engine and was followed by "the building of numberless engine- and motor-driven pieces of machinery and machine tools." The description of electrical engineering refers for the first time to the new and growing field of radio engineering. Potential civil engineers are told, "The trend toward the City Manager form of municipal government opens an attractive field to the civil engineer with executive and business ability." And finally, the prospective student is told, the chemical engineer "is now found in practically every line of manufacture even where no chemical processes are concerned."

The college is formally listed as the Lyman Cornelius Smith College of Applied Science, in memory of the typewriter pioneer who was a University trustee and vice-president of the board of trustees at the time of his death in 1910.

The enrollment was small by later standards. A photograph of the class of 1925 shows fifty-six engineering students, all male, one of them black. In that year the total enrollment of the college was 195, and of the University 7,546.

Before long, courses in administrative and aeronautical engineering had been added to the catalog, which defined engineering as "the art and science of directing the great sources of power in nature for the use and convenience of mankind."

Louis Mitchell, dean, College of Applied Science, 1911–1950.

In January 1922, when Charles W. Flint was being considered as a successor to the ailing Chancellor Day, William Pratt Graham, dean of the College of Applied Science since 1911, was named acting vice-chancellor of the University. Five months later the prefix was dropped and he became Vice Chancellor. Fifteen years later he succeeded Dr. Flint as Chancellor. The choice stirred wide interest. Because of Dr. Graham's engineering background there was talk about the forward-looking nature of his appointment and speculation that it might be part of a wave of the future.

But that was to come. As Dr. Graham left the engineering deanship he was succeeded by Louis Mitchell, a graduate of Purdue University with advanced degrees from the Massachusetts Institute of Technology and Harvard University. Mitchell, who had joined Syracuse in 1910 as a member of the department of civil engineering, continued as dean and professor throughout the Flint and Graham chancellorships and until 1950. The name of the school, founded in 1901, was changed to the College of Engineering in 1952.

On the Applied Science faculty when Dr. Flint became Chancellor were seven full professors—Albert Acheson, mechanical engineering; Rich Whitney, electrical engineering; Charles Easley, chemical engineering; Ernest Keenan and William Taylor, applied mathematics; Simeon T. Hart, industrial engineering; and Leon Howe, drawing. There were also three associate professors, four assistant professors, and eight instructors.

Those seeking admission to the college in the fall of 1922 had to present 15 entrance units—3 in English; 3 in language from among Greek, Latin, French, Spanish, and German; one each in elementary algebra and plane geometry; a half unit each in intermediate algebra and solid and spherical geometry; and 6 units of electives.

Four major programs were offered. Three of these four-year programs led to the degrees of bachelor of civil engineering, bachelor of electrical engineering, and bachelor of mechanical engineering. The fourth earned the degree of bachelor of science in chemical engineering. By 1925, however, the other three areas also gave the bachelor of science degree.

Regardless of the degree sought, all freshmen were required to take the same course of study. The subjects were chemistry, advanced trigonometry, calculus, analysis, mechanical drawing, sketching, lettering, shopwork, orientation, and English. Sophomores then branched out into their specialized areas, each with another common denominator—six months of practical experience for those taking civil, electrical, or mechanical engineering, along with attendance for two weeks at a summer surveying camp.

The camp was on Panther Lake near Bernhard's Bay, a village on the north shore of Oneida Lake. Among the subjects given there were general and topographical surveying, highway location, railroad survey, and hydrographic survey. Civil engineering students had to attend the camp at the beginning of their sophomore and junior years. A student seeking a degree in electrical, mechanical, or administration engineering went only in the summer before the sophomore year. In the mid-1930s the camp was moved to Sandy Pond on Lake Ontario.

For those aiming at a degree in civil engineering, which could lead to eventual private practice or employment by municipal, county, state, or federal agencies or by industrial or public utility corporations, there was instruction in highway, structural, railroad, hydraulic, sanitary, municipal, or geodetic engineering.

The field of electrical engineering was broadening constantly with the diversity of industry. There were two main areas of concentration in the electrical engineering sequence: the transmission of power and the problems of communication. Within those areas students could specialize in one of the following: central station operation, high voltage transmission systems, design and manufacture of electrical equipment, railroad electrification, telegraph engineering, telephone engineering, radio engineering, illuminating engineering, and sales engineering.

Starting in 1925 the college introduced a fifth major area of concentration, leading to a degree of bachelor of science in administrative engineering. In this sequence students were trained in the principles of engineering and business. It was specifically designed for those with scientific ability who wished to enter the industrial, public utility, and commercial fields. The academic program for the first year was the same as in the other four areas. But in the sophomore year and particularly during the two upperclass years, some of the advanced technical subjects of the other fields were omitted in favor of courses in accounting, business law, American government, money and banking, marketing, psychology, and engineering and business management.

In 1927 a report of the Guggenheim Foundation for the Promotion of Aeronautics said in part: "We must consider, too, that our graduate aeronautical engineer is primarily a mechanical engineer so that his training can be put to good use in other fields if we shall have misjudged our own future market in aviation."

Despite the foundation's caution, the college in 1927 began a program in aeronautical engineering. Students entering the field were advised to complete first one of the regular courses in mechanical or electrical engineering to obtain the necessary basic training in engineering theory and design, and perhaps also take allied subjects in other colleges of the University. Then the candidates would concentrate on a program consisting of meteorology, climatology, aerial photographic surveying and mapping, aerial navigation, and elementary aeronautical engineering.

The College of Applied Science cooperated with Teachers College

Between classes at Smith Hall, 1927.

in a dual program that provided teacher preparation for future engineering instructors. Another example of the broadening scope of engineering interests was a dual program in engineering and law. In addition to a basic foundation in engineering, students wishing to continue their education in the College of Law were advised to take as many courses as possible in the liberal arts—English, political science, history, and economics.

Throughout the two decades after 1922 the college was handicapped by its cramped quarters in the L. C. Smith Hall of Engineering (which it shared part of the time with the mathematics department), and nearby Machinery Hall. A constant problem also was the scarcity of up-to-date machinery and other equipment, a byproduct of the University's stringent budget. As did other areas of the University, the Applied Science faculty worked loyally under adverse conditions. By the end of the Flint-Graham era, there were eight full professors, four associate professors, eight assistant professors, and six instructors. Throughout the period, faculty from the Colleges of Liberal Arts and Business Administration, as well as many outside lecturers, helped to liberalize the engineering programs in line with the example set by the earlier deans, notably Dr. Graham, who insisted that Applied Science should be broad in scope.

With several other colleges on the campus, Applied Science enjoyed a post–World War I boom in enrollment that lasted through the academic year 1922–23, when 343 students were registered for engineering degrees. Thereafter a steady decline set in—by 1927–28, only 158 enrolled in the college. From then until 1941–42, however, there was a slow but steady increase until a peak of 486 was reached at the time of Pearl Harbor.

The war years were to bring problems. Dean Mitchell spoke of them in a June 1942 report to the trustees. In the previous year there had been an unprecedented demand for engineering graduates, especially in the field of electrical communications, he said, but the college was finding it difficult to keep both faculty members and equipment. He noted that the War Department and other agencies of the federal government had requisitioned some expensive instruments which the college finally agreed to release.

When Dr. Graham succeeded Dr. Flint in 1937, the fact that Syracuse University had, for the first time, a Chancellor with a high earned degree attracted attention in the academic world. Frank P. Piskor, who like the former engineering dean had gone from graduate student to Vice Chancellor at Syracuse—and then became president of St. Lawrence University—commented on this in an interview in Canton, New York, on the eve of his retirement from St. Lawrence, and added:

"And wasn't Dr. Graham's really the first non-liberal arts doctorate, because his was a professional degree in engineering rather than in the humanities or social sciences? At the time that was talked about among the graduate students as really a very forward-looking appointment on the part of the board [of trustees] because it was anticipating the wave of the future."

Dr. Piskor went on: "Maybe this Methodist school was ahead of its time. One of my mentors at Middlebury College, the head of the economics department, said when I decided to go to the Maxwell

School, 'Well, you're really going to a forward-looking university. I don't know whether it's due to the Methodists or to their new Chancellor.' You see, he knew who the new Chancellor was, knew he was a technologically based person; it had filtered up to an economist in Vermont that here was a professionally trained engineer."

The 1924 engineering graduates who were persuaded by Milton Wise to profile themselves manifest a diversity of skills and personalities. In some ways they form a composite of the ideal engineering student Dr. Graham often spoke of. In one such talk the Chancellor-to-be said: "The engineer is a dreamer. He must have a vivid imagination and must be able to picture to himself a machine, a bridge, a dam, ... must be able to reduce the picture to detailed drawings which can be placed in the hands of skilled workmen ... to make the dream a reality." Dr. Graham struck what was to be a recurrent theme when he also said: "It is impossible to overestimate the importance of the ability to write and speak clear and forceful English. The engineer must not only be able to plan, but he must be able to explain his plans in a convincing way to others. It is impossible to write clearly unless the thoughts which are to be expressed are clear. The engineering school must therefore aim to train its students to habits of clear thought."

Wise classified his fellow engineers as "mechanical, electrical, chemical, civil, and not sure." He listed himself as a chemical/mechanical. He said the personal histories ranged from long and detailed accounts to short statements, in a variety of styles.

Here is a selection:

Mechanical engineer Frederick G. Amey went to work in the sales department of Ingersoll Rand Company in New York after his graduation and stayed with the firm until the Depression year 1930, when he was laid off. He wrote from St. Petersburg, Florida:

> I was lucky to get a job with the George J. Atwell Foundation, which had a contract to do the excavation for the foundation for Radio City. I worked developing a rock-drilling dust control for mining and rock drilling. We had about forty to fifty rock drills going every day, and we kept this dust from entering St. Patrick's Cathedral and the Saks Fifth Avenue store.
>
> After the Second World War began I went with Brewster Aeronautical Corporation in Johnsville, Pennsylvania, which was taken over by the U.S. Navy. I applied for a position with the Navy, was accepted, and worked twenty years in aeronautical design until I retired December 30, 1966.

The thrill of railroading, an occupation he often wrote about for *Trains* magazine, was described by Forman H. Craton, "born, raised and educated in Syracuse, graduated from the University in 1924 with the degree of mechanical engineer magna cum laude."

He continued:

> On July 7, 1924, I reported in Schenectady for General Electric's new factory management course. Long fascinated by trains and discovering GE's deep involvement in rail transportation apparatus, I soon transferred to the Erie, Pennsylvania, plant where I finally headed traction motor test nights and later took a locomotive test. The latter was an impossible dream come true, involving electric locomotive riding and operation on the four-mile test track.
>
> In 1930 the Lackawanna suburban electrification out of Hoboken was inaugurated. It included two 3,000-volt trolley-battery–diesel locomotives for transfer freight service between the Jersey City and Secaucus yards. I'd done the control engineering on these locomotives and helped put them into service. This included the thrill of operating the locomotive pulling a 105-car freight train up grade out of Jersey City, through the Bergen hill tunnel, and on to Secaucus, to me an incredible experience. This assignment was my first intimate exposure to railroading.
>
> In 1931 we were fast sinking into the abyss of the Depression. By 1932 the only active job we had was apparatus for the Pennsylvania Railroad electrification; if you weren't fortunate enough to be working on that, and I wasn't, it was touch and go whether you'd be short-timed or dismissed. I got down to four days a week and $157 per month with a wife and two children to support, but I hung onto my job. That was the bottom. In 1933 things began to improve slowly.
>
> In 1940 I became manager of industrial haulage at Erie, which had responsibility for the GE mining and industrial locomotive business, about to come on strong with World War II in the immediate offing. This was my first managerial job. I spent much of 1942 in Washington as a dollar-a-year man on the War Production Board and was responsible for scheduling the manufacture of all locomotives in the United States below 100 tons; these included diesel and steam as well as the military requirements.
>
> "I retired at age sixty to relax, travel with my wife, and write. Writing is my principal hobby. I've written many technical papers and articles, but I'm most proud of my forty-volume autobiography. I've long kept a diary intermittently, and since retirement have filled in the blank periods so I now have virtually a continuous story of my life since birth. I estimate there are at least three million words in this record, which is illustrated with our photographs.

An electric oar and a mechanized two-person saw were among the gadgets Henry Graley of Syracuse developed as an electrical engineer with area-based corporations, including Semet-Solvay Company, the Bear Street plant of the Standard Oil Company, Syracuse Lighting, and its successor, Niagara Mohawk.

Graley wrote:

> I spent considerable time at my bench and desk developing contraptions which took my fancy. One was an electric oar on which was mounted a truck generator converted to a motor to rotate the shaft and propeller, control box with switches, ammeter, etc. This was operated by three 6v. batteries that I rebuilt for the purpose, along with a 30-amp. variable rectifier, converted from a 15kv current transformer. This oar was used for trolling and cruising in the local lakes and provided enjoyable recreation for many years.
>
> One fall while Niagara Mohawk was converting the distribution system in Syracuse to higher voltage, many poles, replaced for height, were dumped on our side lot by their line superintendent. Hand sawing being out of the question and the chain saw not yet in common use, I worked out a pipe rigging to handle a two-man cross-cut saw mounted on a plank with jack and motor, controlled by a system of pulleys and bomber cables, and counterweighted by a sand pail which controlled the speed of cutting by adding or removing the sand. The pile of poles diminished rapidly.

John G. Hummel (electrical) first went to work for the Western Union Telegraph Company, attending its training school at Red Bank, New Jersey, and learning "to dig postholes, climb poles, and splice 200 pair cables," then reporting to the main office at 195 Broadway, New York. But big city commuting was unsatisfactory, and

> during my second Christmas vacation after graduation I accepted a job with the Crouse-Hinds Company of Syracuse. Rich D. Whitney, one of our electrical engineering professors, had previously accepted a job there to help introduce the use of the first traffic signals. I worked in the same department, as a sales engineer and field assistant. This proved interesting and challenging as we had to pioneer many ideas which are standard today. This job put me in touch with William Lawyer Hinds, vice president of the manufacturing department, and later president and chairman of the board.

Mr. Hummel noted that William Lawyer Hinds Hall became the "first new engineering building," next to Smith Hall.

He went on in his report from retirement in DeWitt, New York:

"Mr. Hinds offered me the opportunity of being 'office boy' to the plant superintendent, which I grasped. This gave me the opportunity to know all the plant foremen, as well as the various group leaders and many of the workers."

When the superintendent retired "I took his place and later became vice president in charge of manufacturing."

Of his retirement Mr. Hummel wrote that he and his wife "have been driving to Florida, where we generally spend several months. We sincerely hope that OPEC doesn't make this impossible. Perhaps some bright young engineer will find a way to move our cars without gasoline."

Eric E. E. Johnson, a chemical engineering graduate, wrote: "Directly after graduation I went to work for the Western Gas Company in Fort Wayne, Indiana, for $125 per month as a cadet engineer. With room and board at $7 per week, this was good." (What Eric Johnson considered good pay for a month's work in 1923 was not much more than a day's pay for beginning engineers in 1982. According to a United Press International story, a survey by the Wharton School of Finance, University of Pennsylvania, concluded that 1982 recipients of either bachelor's degrees in engineering or master's degrees in business "will be able to step immediately into jobs with a pay range of $24,000 to $30,000 a year to start—and in some cases even higher than that.")

Eric Johnson, in his report to the class of 1924, said that within a year Koppers bought Western Gas, let all the employees go, and closed the plant. Johnson worked toward a master's at Northwestern University but did not finish, "partly because I became convinced that a M.S. was not too rewarded unless I went for Ph.D." He joined Pittsburgh Plate Glass Company and remained for forty-two years until he retired in 1965.

Johnson concluded, as he looked back and recalled his contacts with engineers and chemists, "it does seem that there is a great need for orientation courses to prepare engineers for the world—how to get jobs, how to bargain, how to provide for future advancement in responsibilities and salary, how to select employers and how to avoid dead ends."

Chemical engineer Norman Longbottom wrote from Silver Springs Shores, near Ocala, Florida, of his forty years with the federal government. This included work for the Bureau of Standards in Washington, D.C., and Anniston, Alabama. "There, as a member of a crew, I helped develop a method for making zylose, a rare sugar at that time [1930], from waste cotton seed hulls on a semicommercial scale." Then for four years he was with the Department of Agriculture, doing research on leather and tanning material. "In 1934 I started in the Naval Boiler & Turbine Laboratory, later named Navy Ship Engineering Center, Philadelphia Division, at the Navy base. My work was standardizing the special fuel oil used to fire the large water tube boilers installed on the ships of the fleet. The work also involved removal of boiler tube scale by chemical means. Later I developed analytical procedures using electronic equipment for this work."

In 1926 the electrical industry decided to adopt as a nationwide standard an operating frequency of 60 cycles. Until then different frequencies had been used in different systems. For example, in Los Angeles it was 50 cycles; in Glens Falls, New York, it was 40. Adopting a national standard facilitated system interconnections and the economical transfer or exchange of electric power.

A year and a half after he graduated with an electrical engineering degree, J. Kenneth Savage participated in this historic changeover. He wrote from Rochester, New York: "On January 1, 1926, I reported to the Adirondack Power and Light Company at Glens Falls as a result of the first frequency changeover in the United States, from 40 to 60 cycles. They changed everything—motors, transformers, even carbon filiment bulbs—to the new Mazda lamps."

Milton A. "Sock" Wise, the chemical and mechanical engineer who persuaded his classmates to let one another know what they had done with their lives, exceeded his own rule and wrote a lengthy account. He half-apologized for being a compulsive writer, saying his writing ability had helped him in his career. "The best engineering report of my life" led to a job in the depths of the Depression. "All engineering students should be thankful for their brief course in written English," he said.

8

The School of Education and Teacher Training

One of the most important services rendered by Syracuse University is the training of teachers and school executives for New York and surrounding states. . . . more than one-fourth of the graduates of Syracuse University are now engaged in educational service. This is the largest of any of the occupational groups of alumni.

—Reeves Report, 1930

IN HIS FIRST ANNUAL REPORT to the board of trustees in 1923, Chancellor Flint declared: "Teachers College is embarrassed by its success and is calling for more room and more teachers. This is a field in which Syracuse University has signally served the state and for such service is admirably located and equipped. The opportunities ahead are limited only by its resources."

The beginning of the Flint administration in 1922 foreshadowed an era of remarkable growth and development for Teachers College, later the School of Education. At the time, Albert S. Hurst was dean and had been a faculty member for most of the period since its inception in 1906. When Dean Mark Penney retired in 1920, Chancellor Day appointed Canadian-born Professor Hurst to that position, much against his wishes. Those who knew Hurst understood that by temperament he did not naturally take to office details. He was at his best in the classroom stimulating students, in visiting and corresponding with those

Professor Helene W. Hartley of Teachers College, oil portrait by Hilda G. Taylor.

who became teachers, and in pursuing a philosophy of education that, without causing a breach with the past at Syracuse, embraced much that was new and vital.

During his deanship Hurst saw the foundations laid for the School of Education that was to come. Assisting him was an exceptional corps of teachers, among them Arthur C. Fleshman, professor of the history and philosophy of education; Clarence H. Thurber, associate professor of educational administration; and Helene Willey, instructor in education. Miss Willey, later known as Dr. Helene Willey Hartley, joined Syracuse University in 1921 and quickly proved her worth through splendid teaching and a firm grasp of the problem of professional education. Especially outstanding were her record in teacher preparation and her many years of service as chairman of the curriculum committee. Her reputation soon spread, and in due time she was elected president of the National Council of the Teachers of English in the United States. She became one of the most brilliant women in professional education, but her greatest achievement, as recognized by her many students and friends, was her unending loyalty to Syracuse University.

William T. Melchior was brought to Syracuse from St. Lawrence University in 1926 to take charge of the assignment of teachers and to direct teacher extension work. Harry S. Ganders, who succeeded Hurst as dean in 1930, subsequently appraised Melchior as someone "who helped more people to the square mile than any other educator I have known." Melchior made friends quickly and built a large and loyal following among the teachers and administrators of New York State.

Another distinguished faculty member was Ralph F. Strebel, a 1916 graduate of the University whose teaching appointment in 1925 followed his service as a public school administrator. During his first year on the Hill, Strebel initiated an experimental, noncredit program in practice teaching at suburban centers including Solvay and North Syracuse. Soon he carried the plan into the Syracuse city schools. His success prompted Dean Hurst to use him in the field of teacher placement, and Strebel became director of the placement bureau. Much later he was dean of Utica College (1947–59), and the Strebel Center there is named for him.

After Ganders became dean of Teachers College, Hurst assumed direction of student teaching, where he probably made his greatest contribution to the University.

Harry P. Smith, a former school superintendent, was teaching at the University of Kansas when he was invited to Syracuse. He was placed in charge of educational research and school administration—activities that brought him national recognition. He cooperated with the research department of the City of Syracuse in connection with local educational problems and needs. Others on the Teachers College faculty during the Flint regime were Robert P. Carroll (1923–32), who in his later years ran for governor on the Prohibition ticket; Grover C. Morehart (1923–52), well known as a specialist in secondary school matters who had the knack of discovering students of exceptional ability and encouraging them to greater accomplishments; Orlie M. Clem (1924–34), a prolific contributor to educational journals who was noted for his emphasis upon the discussion method; and John N. Washburne (1938–41), a specialst in educational psychology who was attacked by the Hearst newspapers because of his political liberalism.

The hopes and fortunes of Teachers College rested principally on this staff. Theirs was the privilege of counseling Dean Hurst on matters of general policy and of implementing that policy in the classrooms and through visits to the public schools of New York State. Probably a good index of their labors may be seen by evaluating the curriculum as it unfolded between 1922 and 1930.

The purpose of Teachers College at the beginning of the Flint administration, as stated in the *Bulletin,* was: "The preparation of teachers for the secondary and elementary schools, the training of superintendents, supervisors, and principals, and also normal school and college teachers of education. Further provision is made for the preparation of teachers of art, music, and physical education in the public schools. The college also affords opportunity to advanced students for the study of educational problems in their proper scientific and philosophical aspects."

Broadly interpreted, the program was virtually the same as when Jacob Richard Street had been dean, from 1906 to 1917, with the emphasis primarily on teacher training at the elementary and secondary school level and the preparation of those seeking administrative positions at the same level. Graduate work was not ignored, but it lagged far behind the other areas.

The years 1922 to 1930 saw many changes, one of them involving religious education, about which the Teachers College faculty members had misgivings as early as 1924. They favored transferring the program to the Bible department in the College of Liberal Arts. Dr. Flint was not receptive to the suggestion, however, and the sequence stayed. But the courses in public school art and music were turned over to the College of Fine Arts for financial reasons. Relinquishing these programs proved advantageous to Teachers College, allowing greater concentration in more pressing fields.

For example, there was a rapid growth in extension work. In 1922 there had been two small classes; five years later about a thousand students were enrolled in such urban centers as Binghamton, Schenectady, Utica, and Watertown. Dean Hurst believed it was the duty of the University to introduce to teachers of the state elementary and secondary subject matter, both practical and theoretical. Undergraduate and graduate degrees were offered in the extension field, and the University gained an interested and loyal clientele throughout the state.

Another measure of the college's growth in the 1920s was the promotion of the Summer School. During 1928 and 1929 attractive programs were offered, and provision was made for students to obtain credit for special education work done off campus.

By the fall of 1928, an ailing Dean Hurst offered his resignation, but the Chancellor persuaded him to remain until a successor was selected. Dr. Flint moved with characteristic caution. He considered several candidates but had made no decision by June 1929, and it was Hurst who made the annual report for the college that spring. "For twenty-five years," he said, "we have been engaged in teacher training. This is very important work, but it is dependent upon a scientific study of education." He said the essentials for a new curriculum were increased graduate work, establishment of a research bureau, an improved placement office, and a practice school on campus. Only by instituting these services could the University be prevented from falling behind in the education field, he said.

Chancellor Flint meanwhile had been adding to his dossier on Harry Ganders, chairman of the department of school administration at the University of Cincinnati. Ganders, a relatively young man, was a graduate of the University of Washington, received his doctorate at Columbia in 1925, and had taught at the State College of Education at Greeley, Colorado. The Chancellor invited Ganders to Syracuse for an interview in July 1929, and then offered him the deanship of Teachers College. Ganders accepted, and he and his family moved to Syracuse in time for the Christmas holidays. His arrival coincided with a state meeting of high school principals at Syracuse, where Ganders made the most of the opportunity to get to know them. In January he familiarized himself with the general conditions at the college and University and visited Albany, where much of his future work would center. By the opening of the second semester in February 1930, he was ready to assume the deanship officially.

Ganders had no illusions about the problems he would face in his new post. Teachers College was at a crossroads. Overshadowed and influenced by the College of Liberal Arts, whose educational attitudes and philosophy sometimes conflicted with those of the School of Education, the time had come when the latter must free itself from these entanglements if it was to achieve the ends a Teachers College should attain in the state and nation. To this purpose the new dean wrote in his November 1939 report to the Chancellor: "The accomplishment of a quarter of a century of Teachers College is recognizable in the significant contributions being made by several thousand Syracuse alumni in

Harry S. Ganders, dean, Teachers College/School of Education, 1930–1952.

school systems in New York, Pennsylvania, and other neighboring states." With this reservoir of human resources behind it, he said, Syracuse could become the educational center in the state in which it was the geographical center. "It is to the realization of this objective that Teachers College should shape its policies and develop its program." The dean concluded: "At the beginning of the second quarter of its existence the college seems to stand at the threshold of unprecedented opportunities for development and the assumption of fundamental positions of leadership."

Development of the Teachers College that Ganders desired posed the kind of challenge he relished. He harbored no misconceptions about the long, difficult efforts that the fulfillment of his program entailed. There were still, for example, the financial limitations that had dogged the University since 1870. There was also the task of establishing sound administrative practices in the college and proper protocol with colleagues in other colleges on campus. In addition, there had to be faced the keen, and at times unhappy, competition from rival institutions in the state. These and other problems had been reviewed in the all-University survey undertaken by the Board of Education of the Methodist Church—the so-called Reeves Survey of 1930, in which Ganders found many helpful suggestions.

The Reeves team reported: "One of the most important services rendered by Syracuse University is the training of teachers and school executives for New York and surrounding states. ... more than one-fourth of the graduates of Syracuse University are now engaged in educational service. This is the largest of any of the occupational groups of alumni."

Bolstered by this survey and by his own findings, Ganders was ready to announce his immediate objectives and stake out claims by the winter of 1930–31. These were based on an analysis of recent trends in American education, an appreciation of economic and social changes that had surged through the nation since the turn of the century and their effect upon secondary schools, and the role Teachers College had played on the campus.

The United States, as a result of a rapid population increase and an astonishing growth in big business, wealth, and industrialization, had found itself with an educational system that was becoming outmoded. During the 1920s, for instance, most high schools offered primarily college preparatory courses. By 1930 the same schools served a larger number of prospective college students with scores of different curricula. Those aware of these trends wondered where they might lead by 1940 and asked what the colleges and universities were doing about it. As far as Teachers College was concerned, there was the fact that only 10 percent of the Syracuse University students preparing to teach were under its control. Functionally, it was the University and not the college that directed teacher training. The basic difficulty, Ganders said, was "an inappropriate organization of curriculum and administration." He asked the Chancellor in the fall of 1931: "Is it possible that in the absence of such differentiation there has developed an anomalous situation ... equivalent to having in the same University two law or two liberal arts colleges on the same campus?"

It was to correct the University's teacher training program that the dean frequently spoke his mind throughout 1930 and 1931. He favored several changes. The first required greater unity between his college and others, especially Liberal Arts. The interest of the College of Liberal Arts in teacher preparation he understood and appreciated; what he deplored was the failure of the trustees to assign any exclusive function to Teachers College when it was founded in 1906. This omission led to divisiveness and spirited competition. Whether right or wrong, Liberal Arts, as evidenced by its *Bulletin* and its faculty meetings, believed that control over academic matters was within its jurisdiction by right and by law. Another concern of Teachers College was the perennial problem of maintaining cordial relationships with the state education department and the Board of Regents. Finally, the situation argued for the promotion of objectives beneficial not only to the college itself, but also to the University, to prospective teachers, and to administrators in the state.

Ganders listed no fewer than forty-seven such objectives in his report to the Chancellor. Some had been achieved; in others, a toehold at least had been gained. For example, he said there was less prejudice against teachers colleges at Syracuse than elsewhere in the nation. Moreover, in certain methods courses heretofore entrenched in Liberal Arts, instruction had been yielded to his college. This was especially true in English, where Professor Hartley was demonstrating unusual excellence in teaching methods. Methods courses in Liberal Arts largely concerned themselves with methods relating to subject matter, not to the art of teaching.

In 1931 and 1932 these and other preliminary steps were taken—curriculum improvements, curtailment of extension services, reorganization and expansion of practice teaching, and the inception of a doctoral program in education.

Achieving these objectives, which were sanctioned by the trustees in 1932, had not been easy. A hint of discord between the College of Liberal Arts and Teachers College may be seen in enrollment in Teachers College. During the 1922–30 period, registration under a four-year program ranged from 108 to 180. But in 1931, as a result of the determined drive for students by Teachers College in the high schools of Central New York, freshman enrollment jumped. The following year a peak of 248 was reached. Liberal Arts was astonished at the large increase and naturally questioned what the future held for its own teacher training program and its academic courses. On the other hand, Teachers College was critical of the Liberal Arts policy under which it counted as its own "all education courses required by the State [21 credits in all] by designating even methods courses *Liberal Arts content,* and by accepting other education courses for the Liberal Arts degree."

This meant in practice that prospective teachers could qualify for degree *and* certification by enrollment only in Liberal Arts—a situation that was anathema to Teachers College. Dr. Hurst in a letter to Dean Ganders November 27, 1932, summarized what he understood to be his successor's aim: "As I am able to interpret your paper, your plea is for a complete cooperation between the Liberal Arts College (and likewise the other colleges giving the core subjects for teaching) and the College of Education that there should be in all cases a broad cultural background, given chiefly by L.A. coll., but also in cooperation with Education, always keeping in mind the fact that the student is training for teaching; that from the beginning, perhaps, the student should be in an atmosphere of teacher preparation, and that great care should be exercised (again cooperatively) in the selection of candidates for teacher training.

"In short, all the colleges concerned should recognize the need for teacher preparation in the light of the needs of a changing education, and all should cooperate to this end. Only in this way can efficient teacher training be accomplished and a teaching profession be developed on a par with the other professions. To all this I most heartily subscribe and hope some day it will be realized, but not until your hair and that of many others has turned gray."

But Ganders and his faculty did not intend to wait for old age. "Do it now" was an expression he used frequently in letters and reports. During 1933 and early 1934 many staff meetings resulted in drafts for a new curriculum and improved teacher placement. There were closed sessions among the dean, Chancellor Flint, Professor William M. Smallwood of Liberal Arts, and other key people. Many conferences, formal and informal, were held between the colleges concerned, and there were lengthy discussions at Liberal Arts faculty meetings. Step by step the issues were taken up in detail, climaxing when Ganders submitted a program to the Chancellor late in January 1934 with this comment: "I find that in any discussion of reorganization with other deans I am inevitably placed in the position of *advocate for* my own unit—somewhat in a position of getting *something for myself from* them. I think this inherent in my position and the situation. . . . As these deans have told me for years, I now believe that in trying to adjust the matter myself I am attempting the impossible. It is an all-University problem, they say, which only the chief administrator can decide. Realizing that organization is but a 'first step' and that a real strong program must follow after that, I am naturally anxious for a decision which will give me a setting for a more constructive effort in the real business of developing a program."

Chancellor Flint took Ganders's report and letter with him on a trip to Chicago, where he wrote encouragingly to the dean: "You're on the right track, I firmly believe. Will want you at quite an early date to go to Iowa City, Iowa, and Chicago to confer on both situations. I've just had a long visit with Jessup of Iowa... and Iowa has worked this out even more radically than proposed." The Chancellor added: "Keep your shirt on—can be done—is what should be done for next year. Believe you've got the right idea—you may want to go further and may not. One result will be a *whole campus* enthusiastically with you and Education! This is personal and unofficial."

To Ganders the many hours of hard labor were over, at least for the moment, for the Chancellor had given his unofficial approval. Then, on March 2, 1934, Dr. Flint made good his promise by notifying the heads of all departments of his decision to authorize a new School of Education and the drafting of a curriculum to take effect at the opening of college in September, 1934. On June 1, 1934, the Syracuse University board of trustees established an all-University School of Education, decreeing in part:

"WHEREAS, the problems to be solved in the training of teachers consist (1) in the recognition of the need for specific training in the duties and responsibilities of the teacher as such, and in educational theory and background; (2) in the shaping of progressive teacher-training curriculum, that is, the study of subject matter in the several fields of education with a view to (a) mastery of content, and (b) adaptability to the demands of the schools. And

"WHEREAS, the intimate way in which these objectives interlock requires that there be a unity of organization between those interested particularly in the theory of education as applied to teacher-training and those most concerned with subject matter. Marked changes of emphasis are taking place in secondary schools. With these our graduates need to be familiar and this requires a plan that is flexible and easily adjusted.

"RESOLVED, that, as voted by the executive committee on February 12, 1934, subject to confirmation by the board of trustees,

"We do hereby establish at Syracuse University an all-University School of Education, to include the Margaret Olivia Slocum Teachers College ... "

The program of the new school completely abandoned all control over its former four-year program and degree. In return, however, the school gained wide authority over the junior and senior years. Furthermore, it instituted a system of majors and minors that led to what became known as the plan of duality. Dean Ganders and his faculty were enthusiastic about the changes and eagerly accepted their new responsibilities, which basically involved devising a better system for selecting prospective teachers, adopting a curriculum to meet their needs, and establishing a more efficient teacher placement bureau.

The new Syracuse system was the subject of a 1941 book published by the American Council on Education, *A Functional Program of Teacher Education*. Publication of the 252-page book was especially significant, Ganders said, because the council chose the Syracuse program to describe from among more than "a thousand American institutions of higher education which are wholly or in part engaged in the business of teacher education."

Once accepted in the new school, a candidate was within the plan of duality. Heretofore he or she had matriculated, for example, in the College of Liberal Arts; now the student was dually enrolled in both Liberal Arts and Education, continuing in the former to pursue his or her major interests, including the subject the student wished to teach; in the latter he or she sought guidance in preparation for a future role as a teacher. Furthermore, under the duality plan, the student would have two deans and two major advisers. Having two deans was not an innovation, for this had been the case in certain combination courses within the University; but the concept of two advisers, foreshadowed perhaps by practices in the School of Citizenship and by recommendations in the Reeves Survey, was decidedly new in teacher training programs at Syracuse University and elsewhere. To simplify matters, there came into being the so-called *dual professors*, who held concurrent affiliation in two colleges; for example, Roy A. Price was appointed a faculty member of the Maxwell School and the School of Education. A dual professor had the major direction of a student's program during the upper division years. While his or her interest was chiefly in teacher education, the dual professor taught academic subjects as well, having been trained to counsel students in both areas. Innovation of the dual professorship received wide publicity and acclaim in many American academic circles. Nevertheless, as *A Functional Program of Teacher Education* showed in 1941, the plan undoubtedly placed an undue strain on the dual professor, and there were other shortcomings and defects requiring subsequent correction and change.

Michael O. Sawyer, professor and Vice Chancellor, recalled Professor Roy Price with admiration, having studied under him:

> My freshman citizenship and public affairs course, which was interdepartmental, was taught by this very distinguished man, who had been a student both at Chicago and Harvard. He was one of the first dual

> professors of the social sciences and education. In terms of drawing the disciplines together, particularly for people who are going to be teachers to have a close relationship between those who taught pedagogy and those who taught the substantive fields—it was done at Syracuse, and it was pioneering at the time. The School of Education and the other colleges were drawn together by this mechanism of dual professors.

But there were two problems with it, Dr. Sawyer said: "In one sense, I suppose, the fact that a teacher or professor couldn't know as much about each of the two disciplines as he might have known about one; and there were problems in terms of promotion and tenure—whose responsibility was it if the person was essentially half time? So it was a great idea, but there were complications. It still goes on at the University."

One of the more important contributions of the dual professor was in curriculum building, the second of the problems faced when the school was established. The assignment was turned over to a committee first under the chairmanship of Harry P. Smith (and later Helene Hartley) and including Professors Strebel and Troyer and Dean Ganders. Ultimately the members agreed that the curriculum should be founded on several basic principles: (1) the acquisition of knowledge, skill, and attitudes that harmonized both theory and practice; (2) the functional selection of subject matter in reference to objectives and problems; and (3) "the traditional modes of university instruction must be broadened to include a wide range of activities." The committee clarified the third principle by saying it aimed at relating prospective teachers to adolescents in and out of school and with social agencies interested in education.

On these principles, the School of Education worked out a sequence of courses carrying 18 hours of credit that entailed assigned readings, lectures, seminars, observation, leadership of nonschool adolescent groups, and practice teaching. Embodied in the program was the premise, never to be forgotten by the student, that education was designed for the pupil, not the teacher. Embedding this philosophy in the curriculum was considered of utmost importance, because by the end of their sophomore year most students had tended to become "subject-matter minded" and reorientation was needed to enable them to regard the pupil as the core of their professional study. Thus certain courses in the education curriculum emphasized adolescent development as understood through physiological, sociological, and psychological factors. Implementing these offerings, students had to work with a youth organization such as the Boy Scouts or the YWCA. Later the future teachers went into a classroom in one of the city schools. There they first observed, then assisted, and finally assumed responsibility for the class period. In general, this assignment entailed one class a week for a portion of the college year.

In February 1940 an experiment in extramural teaching was introduced. Under it a student lived the life of a teacher for three weeks in a rural or village community within a hundred miles of Syracuse. The value of this experience was never questioned in terms of results, but the impact of World War II, its aftermath, and the financial burdens the program imposed combined to bring about its abandonment except in certain disciplines.

Another form of practice teaching was available through the University Hill School, which had been organized in 1926 at the request of several women, chiefly faculty wives, who needed a nursery school for their children. Under the guidance of Gertrude S. Hayes it opened at 1033 Lancaster Avenue. When the costs of management eventually became too heavy for the sponsors to bear, Chancellor Flint, after consulting with Dean Annie Louise Macleod of the College of Home Economics and others, agreed in December 1928 to have the University assume a share of the expenses. New quarters were found at 119 College Place, and the staffs of Teachers College and Home Economics acquired a laboratory, so to speak, for the study of child care and behavior. The relationship between the Hill School and the University gradually came to an end, but eventually the University established its own nursery school.

Last among the major problems facing the School of Education in 1934 was that of teacher placement, about which the University had concerned itself for more than a quarter of a century. Successful as Teachers College had been, it became evident by 1929 that a bureau dedicated to mere job getting was not enough. Consequently, a reorganization was effected. Future teachers were screened and tested to ascertain, as far as possible, the positions for which they were best qualified. Helping Professor Strebel in the task were the other members of his staff, the dual professors, and professors at other colleges in whose departments candidates had majored. The school maintained more than a personnel and placement office. It developed an institutional follow-up to coordinate the School of Education with the public schools in continuing the professional attitude and growth of the teachers. In part this involved the growth and broadening of a summer session on the campus suited to the needs of teachers in service. It also involved periodic visits by the director to the schools of the state, maintaining an active file on each teacher, and other features. Probably the best proof of the success of the teacher placement program was the ever-mounting demand for teachers trained at Syracuse University.

Professor Strebel said in 1940 as head of the teachers placement bureau that "the average is better than four placements for each ten calls reported to the bureau." He added in an article in *Alumni News:* "Although the job-getting function of the bureau is of great importance, it performs other related activities which far transcend it in professional significance. ... By virtue of the broadened nature of its work, it has really become a bureau of educational service both to the University and to the public schools it serves."

At about the same time, supply-and-demand studies made by the bureau resulted in several curricular changes in the school. One example recognized a decreasing demand for teachers specializing in English and history, and increased need for those prepared in English and library science.

As the administration of Chancellor Graham drew to an end, he announced that the School of Education would exercise control over all masters' and doctoral degrees in the fields of professional education, thus becoming a graduate as well as an undergraduate unit of the University.

The Graduate School formerly controlled those degrees—doctor of education, master of arts in education and in teaching, and master of science degrees in education, teaching, home economics education, speech education, commercial education, nursing education, and physical education. Dean Ganders commented: "This latest change in organization of graduate work tends to raise the status of the profession of education on the Syracuse campus to a parity of the better established professions of engineering, law, and medicine."

9

The College of Business Administration

The dean questioned whether a zoologist was competent to head a study of a college that dealt primarily with economics and the other social sciences.

THERE WERE EXCELLENT REASONS IN 1919 to establish a school of business at Syracuse University. The metropolitan area was expanding rapidly, new industries were developing, and there was increasing demand for college-trained men and women in the business life of the community.

With the end of the first world war, many veterans sought a business education, and Central New York manufacturers, bankers, and newspaper editors were among those who applauded Chancellor Day's decision to establish the school, the last to be founded on the Hill during his administration. A pioneer automobile manufacturer, Herbert H. Franklin of the Franklin Motor Company, gave the University $80,000 for a chair in transportation.

The School of Business Administration, as it was called then, formally opened in the fall of 1919. The first faculty meeting was held in the Chancellor's office on October 31. Those present were the Chancellor, the director of the school, John Herman Wharton, and fifteen faculty members, some of whom were also connected with the College of Liberal Arts.

The school received much favorable publicity and high compliments from professional educators elsewhere in the country. In May 1920 the assistant director for commercial education of the Federal Board for Vocational Education, Washington, D.C, predicted that the school would soon become the largest in the University. At about the same time it was invited to join the Association of Collegiate Schools of Business. Professor Wharton, realizing that this meant national recognition, prevailed on Dr. Day to authorize spending twenty-five dollars, the initial cost of membership.

W. E. Bartholomew, commercial education specialist in the New York State education department, became interested in the school's courses in commercial teaching. He found them adequate in subject matter but lacking in methods courses in bookkeeping, business arithmetic, typing and shorthand, commercial geography, and economics. He expressed the hope that such instruction would soon be introduced and that, later, courses might be given in the organization and administration of commercial education. Bartholomew also said he hoped the school would admit students who had high school diplomas in commercial subjects. His suggestions were brought to the attention of the faculty members, and in October 1919 they approved resolutions providing for the introduction of methods courses and for the admission of those with diplomas in commercial subjects.

The faculty also agreed to give credit for stenography and typing taken at the school and talked about the possibility of a certificate program in the University's night school.

A communication from another state official was less welcome than Bartholomew's. In the summer of 1920 Augustus S. Downing of the state education department wrote to the Chancellor. Dr. Downing was assistant commissioner for higher education and director of professional education. His subject was registration of the school as an approved college under the University of the State of New York. Dr. Downing held that a school was not a college, and that the School of Business Administration was not listed in the Board of Regents *Handbook* of 1918.

The letter startled Chancellor Day. At least three other schools, two of them at Syracuse, *were* listed in the *Handbook.* These were the School of Oratory and the Library School at Syracuse and, in New York City, Columbia's School of Journalism. It also seemed clear to the Chancellor that the business school was not listed because it had been founded a year after the *Handbook* was published.

Dr. Day informed Henry A. Peck, dean of the College of Liberal Arts: "I have written Dr. Downing, but his opinions ... seem to be inspired by some deep-seated prejudice."

The Chancellor was also annoyed by the education department's refusal to grant scholarships to students attending an unrecognized school or college. He believed the University's charter allowed it to establish colleges and departments and said he failed to understand the state's position. Fortunately the state officials reversed themselves, and in September 1920 the Regents recognized the school and subsequently granted scholarship aid to qualified students.

In November, however, the state advised the school that recognition was temporary and that it would remain that way until the school was reorganized as a college. Thus when the faculty members met in February 1921 the school had become the College of Business Administration, and Professor Wharton was no longer director but dean.

John Herman Wharton, a 1911 graduate of Syracuse University, joined the faculty as an instructor in English and rose quickly to full professor and head of the English department in the College of Applied Science when William Pratt Graham was dean.

Professor Wharton had been dean of the College of Business Administration for two months, after heading it as director since its founding as a school, when he was shot to death in his office in Slocum Hall on April 2, 1921. He was thirty-one. His killer was Holmes Beckwith, an instructor in the college who then killed himself. Beckwith had been notified by Dean Wharton the previous week that his contract would not be renewed. In the ten years since his graduation from the University of California, Beckwith had been dismissed from eight positions, six of them at colleges or universities. "Professor Beckwith must have been insane," Chancellor Day said. Coroner S. Ellis Crane issued certificates of death by murder and suicide.

Charles Lee Raper, dean of the Graduate School of the University of North Carolina, had been appointed the first Franklin Professor of Transportation at Syracuse University in the fall of 1920. He succeeded Professor Wharton as dean.

Dr. Day's nemesis in Albany, Dr. Downing, was heard from again. The state education department official had become concerned about the curriculum of the college and the degrees it might confer. One of Dean Raper's first tasks was to untangle the situation. Dr. Downing asked the dean to formulate a program to be registered with the Regents. There were other exchanges of correspondence, and then in June 1922 Dr. Downing told Vice Chancellor William P. Graham that scholarships would not be available to business administration students unless "Dean Raper shall fulfill his promise and submit a course of study leading to a baccalaureate degree which can be approved by the Board of Regents."

Dean Raper mailed Dr. Downing a copy of the *Bulletin* of June

Charles L. Raper, dean, College of Business Administration 1921–1943, and later, acting Vice Chancellor.

1922, which contained a more precise statement of the college's curriculum. In his accompanying letter the dean said, "I hope you will see fit, after examining all the evidence, to recommend permanent registration," or at least temporary registration for one year. He continued:

"We have no desire to maintain anything but a first-rate college. We have no desire to make it unlike a first-class College of Liberal Arts, but we cannot think it best to make it completely or almost completely a Liberal Arts College." He said that was because "our degree is not a Bachelor of Arts, nor a general Bachelor of Science; it is a special Bachelor of Science in Business, or Bachelor of Science in Secretarial Science, or Bachelor of Science in Commercial Teaching, or Bachelor of Science in Journalism."

Dean Raper made what he said was "every reasonable effort" to satisfy the Regents, but the problem was to drag on well into the administration of Chancellor Charles W. Flint. In 1925, for example, Dr. Downing and Dean Raper were still in correspondence on the issue, with Albany reportedly wanting an increase in language requirements for graduation. There were other differences. It was not until May 1928 that a Syracuse-Albany understanding was reached and the college's courses and degrees were formally registered.

At the time of Dr. Flint's arrival in 1922 these were the requirements for admission:

Every graduate of an approved high school was eligible to be admitted on proper certification by the principal. With this certification there was to be a statement showing the applicant had completed 15 units, consisting of: English (3 units); a foreign language (2); one unit each of history, algebra, and plane geometry; and 7 units of electives. Applicants were advised that commercial subjects such as arithmetic, bookkeeping, economics, business English, stenography, and typing would be proper electives. A candidate from a nonapproved high school might be admitted after passing a special examination. College Entrance Board credits and Regents certificates were also accepted, and provision was made for the admission of special students and those with advance standing.

Dean Raper, reporting to Chancellor Flint on the first five years of the college through June 1924, said this was "a period of large expansion in student registration," with more than eleven hundred enrolled each year for three years. Of these, more than two hundred were in two temporary groups—World War I veterans being educated by the federal government, and others working toward two-year certificates "without any thought of four years in college." These students had almost entirely disappeared by the end of the first five-year period, the dean said. The group of veterans, "from its very nature," was a temporary one and the two-year courses were discontinued.

During the second five-year period of the college, which ended in June 1929, there were virtually no special students, and entrance requirements were "materially increased, both as to the specific requirements and as to the standing of the students in their high school work," Dean Raper reported. Consequently, he said, there was decreased enrollment, from 1,087 in the fall of 1925 to 953 in the fall of 1928. The drop was not unique to Syracuse, the dean said; "during those four years, most of the schools and colleges of business in the United States had a similar decrease in registration figures." He noted that the figure in the fall of 1929 was exactly the same as the year before, 953, and that for 1930 it was 977.

There was a harbinger of things to come in the last section of Dean Raper's report. "Much thought has been given to the reorganization of journalism teaching," he wrote. "At this time I merely wish to say that whatever readjustment in journalism teaching may take place, the University must put some more money into instruction in journalism."

In October 1935 the dean's report reflected the creation the previous year of the School of Journalism as a separate academic unit. Formerly it had been a department in his college. Despite the loss of journalism students, Dean Raper said, enrollment in the college went from 775 in the fall of 1933 to 779 a year later, and at the beginning of the 1935–36 academic year it was 800.

Significant in the 1935 report, written against the background of the Depression and measures being taken in Washington by the Franklin D. Roosevelt administration, was Dean Raper's mention of a new course, introduced the previous fall, called Trends in Government Control of Industry and Commerce. He said: "It deals with the recent changes in government control of industry and commerce, of banking and finance, of transportation, the trends of this enlarged government control and the effect which this control is having on management, employment, wages, and prices."

The one-hour course, for business administration seniors, was given by Professor Maurice Cross, head of the department of business organization and management, in cooperation with the heads of the departments of accounting, business law, commerce, finance, insurance, and transportation, the dean said. He added: "The course is entirely expository and analytical, with no propaganda features."

Dean Raper also saw fit to stress his faculty's "Interest in Current Affairs," as the concluding section of his report was headed. It spoke of "new" versus "old" economics.

> Each member of the teaching faculty is keenly interested not only in the things which are happening in his own field but also to a considerable degree in all the allied fields, in each of which a good many new aspects

> have appeared within the last few years. Many people feel that we are now faced with a completely new economics, that the old economics has been proven false or inadequate. I think that no member of the staff in any of our fields of instruction, each of which is a field in applied economics, has been convinced that the old economics has been disproved; their minds are open to new economic ideas; they do not accept an idea merely because it is new; neither do they reject an idea because it is old.

Elsewhere Dean Raper summed up the philosophy of his college, stressing the need for its graduates to be well-rounded human beings and public spirited citizens. A college publication quoted him in these words: "A graduate of the College of Business Administration is expected to be an effective worker in some field of business. He also is expected to be an active, intelligent and broadminded citizen. His training has had this in mind even above all other things, that he is to be an effective worker, an effective citizen, and a believer in the ideal that his life shall mean much more than the mere making of money."

Starting in 1922, business administration students followed one of four courses of study—General Business, Secretarial Science, Commercial Teaching, or Journalism. The journalism division was dropped in 1934 with the founding of the School of Journalism. The curriculum in each division was similar, and each allowed electives in the others as well as in the College of Liberal Arts. At the end of the sophomore year each student selected a major of not less than 16 hours at the upperclass level, one-third of which might be in another division. Such a program permitted a wide choice of courses within the college, as well as in other departments of the University—a feature that Dean Raper believed was most important.

In the general business division, for instance, a student could specialize in accounting, advertising, controllership, economics, finance, foreign trade, geography, insurance, domestic commerce, marketing, organization and management, political science, psychology, real estate, selling, or traffic and transportation. This program remained much the same through 1941–42.

In the secretarial science division the curriculum was similar to that in general business, except that four hours of typing and stenography were required. Kathryn L. Clippinger taught secretarial science. Among the subjects were accounting, economics, finance, political science, commerce, psychology, and languages. "We aim at a broad cultural knowledge," Mrs. Clippinger said in an interview in December 1933. "A secretary ought to know a great deal more than her technical subjects. A girl who has taken the full course should be able to run a business on its mechanical side." Not all of the graduates of the course over the previous dozen or so years had been women, she noted. One of the first alumni was Wallace F. Campbell, secretary to the president of the Fuller Brush Company of Hartford, Connecticut.

Commercial teaching, renamed business education in 1925, consisted of two groups: secretarial science and general business. They had much in common, including special work in education such as principles of education, methods, and teaching, taken in Teachers College. Neither group followed exactly the curricula in general business and secretarial science, but both drew heavily on them in their own sequences. In the business education division, dual enrollment in the college and the School of Education was required after 1935.

The accounting division was established in 1924 as a four-year sequence. Bachelor of science degree candidates took subjects much like those in general business during their underclass years. Upperclass students concentrated on advance accounting, supplemented by a liberal elective program.

In 1930 a combination course with the College of Law was introduced. Six years long, it led to a joint degree in both colleges. A requirement was a "B" average during the first three years, all taken in business administration.

Another combination program, in physical education and commercial education, was inaugurated in 1936. The hours needed for graduation varied between 145 and 161, including specified work in summer school. Most of the courses at the upperclass level were in physical education. Successful candidates received both a bachelor of science degree and a teaching certificate in accounting and business practice. In 1941 the program was lengthened to five years and led to the degrees of bachelor of science and master of science in teaching, together with a teaching certificate in physical education.

Summer or extension courses in finance were popular, and hundreds of employees of banks enrolled each year in special programs sponsored by the American Institute of Banking. Taught by Syracuse University faculty members, the courses were exactly the same as those taken by full-time students. In 1938 anyone who had taken an institute-sponsored course was entitled to transfer credits earned toward Syracuse University degrees.

Despite Dean Raper's general optimism about his college, Chancellor Flint was concerned about its academic standards. In 1927, for example, he studied the grades of 278 students who had classes in both business administration and in the College of Liberal Arts; the comparison was not favorable to the former. Nine percent of the "A"s awarded were in business administration courses while only one percent were in liberal arts courses. In the "B" category, 25 percent were in business administration subjects, while 16 percent were in liberal arts. Forty-two percent of the "C"s were in business courses, and 25 percent in liberal arts. Nineteen percent failed liberal arts subjects, but only 8 percent failed in business subjects.

Dean Raper and his faculty promised to remedy the situation. But a dozen years later Dr. Flint's successor, Chancellor Graham, was to express concern about the college and the way it was organized. In a letter to Dean Raper, who by now was also acting Vice Chancellor of the University, Dr. Graham wrote on March 28, 1939:

"There seems to be some question as to whether our College of Business Administration is keeping abreast of the times, and whether its present organization is that which best accords with the general University program.

> At other times Dr. Smallwood [William Martin Smallwood, professor of comparative anatomy] has done excellent work in making studies of a similar nature and I am asking him to study the programs at other institutions which are somewhat similar to ours and to make a comparison. This he has agreed to do.
>
> It is perhaps needless to say that no publicity of any kind will be given to his work.

The following day Dean Raper objected strenuously to the Chancellor's action. In defense of his college, he pointed out that it had been a member of the American Association of Collegiate Schools of Business for nineteen years, with no complaints. He had regularly attended annual meetings of business administration deans, who had frequently discussed organization, curricula, and the like and had made several studies. Syracuse conformed to all the latest findings, the dean said in his letter. Furthermore, the state education department had made a careful survey of the college ten years earlier and the Regents had given their approval.

Finally the dean questioned the need for the proposed Smallwood survey, which he said might be not only confusing but embarrassing. He asked whether Dr. Smallwood, a zoologist, was competent to head a study of a college that dealt not with the natural sciences but primarily with economics and the other social sciences.

In another letter to the Chancellor, Dean Raper pointed out the close association between the College of Business Administration and the other colleges on the campus. If 316 upperclass students from other colleges elected courses in his college, he said, the reputation of those courses could not be as bad as Dr. Graham had implied.

At about this time the College of Business Administration was the subject of an exchange of letters between two other University officials. The topic was entrance requirements, and the college's were defended by Frank N. Bryant, director of admissions. His letter of April 19, 1939, said a query from the registrar implied "that for some time there have been easier entrance requirements for Business Administration than for Liberal Arts." The contrary was true, Mr. Bryant said; the requirements were stronger.

According to Mr. Bryant—he was a professor of business management as well as director of admissions—the registrar, Keith J. Kennedy, had asked "what changes would have to be made in the requirements... if all Business Administration students met the entrance requirements now in force for Liberal Arts students." Mr. Bryant said:

> Students who take the academic course in high school are required to present exactly the same requirements for Business Administration as for Liberal Arts, with one exception: a student who has not had foreign language may offer as an alternate for the foreign language requirement two years of additional science or two years of additional science and mathematics. In my opinion, this not a weakening of the entrance requirements. If anything, it constitutes a stiffening, as it is emphasizing the idea of a sequence and less scattering of energy....
>
> A very large percentage of the students coming to us from groups with very limited cultural background, and with citizenship objectives different from those which the University desires to attract, enter the College of Liberal Arts. The College of Business Administration has never knowingly or intentionally been given any advantages over Liberal Arts or any other college in our set-up, from the standpoint of entrance requirements.

There is nothing in the records to indicate that the proposed Smallwood survey was made, so evidently Dean Raper's defense of his college—perhaps helped by Professor Bryant's—dissuaded Chancellor Graham from pursuing an inquiry.

On its own, meanwhile, the college improved entrance requirements and reorganized some programs. It encouraged students, especially in the upper classes, "to identify themselves with some local business enterprise." At the same time it required approved summer employment of all students between their sophomore and junior and junior and senior years, with written reports of their work experience submitted to the dean's office. The major requirements were also spelled out more effectively.

Such was the situation when the United States entered World War II.

There had been high enrollment in the years immediately after World War I, helped considerably by the two-year certificate and veterans programs. That had been followed by a gradual decline from an enrollment of 1,198 in 1922. In the academic year 1935–36, during the Depression, there was a low of 805 students in the college. After that came steady growth until a new peak of 1,286 was reached in 1939–40. Now another war made its impact on the campus, and in 1942 enrollment fell back to 1,085.

10

Medicine and Nursing

There must be ultimately developed a hospital-dispensary–medical-nursing center in close proximity to the University campus which will embrace a number of cooperating units.

—from a 1923 survey

WHEN DR. FLINT ASSUMED THE CHANCELLORSHIP in the fall of 1922, he realized Dr. Day had not exaggerated in reporting to the trustees the previous June that the status of the College of Medicine had become "the most serious problem of any of our colleges."

The views of the dean of the medical school, John L. Heffron, were on record in his final annual report of June 1922. At that time the school's budget was about $80,000, of which $59,000 was for instructional salaries for thirty-two professors and eighty-five associate and assistant professors, assistants, and lecturers.

The medical college became part of the University in October 1872. It was then located in rooms in the Clinton block near the city center. In 1875 it was moved to South McBride Street (then Orange Street) where it remained until a new building was provided at the same location in 1895. In 1914 a "Free Dispensary" for the city was erected nearby this also served as a teaching facility for the college. The next year the Hospital of the Good Shepherd on Marshall Street between University and South Crouse Avenues was taken over by the University, adding 278 general hospital beds to the teaching capabilities of the college.

The Hospital of the Good Shepherd was thereafter called University Hospital.

In addition to the teaching faculty, there was the clinical staff, none of whom had a University appointment or received compensation for services. The staff members were recruited from local physicians who, busy with private practice, could give only limited and not always regular time to the college. "Look at the college," the dean said, "and you will find there are more teachers than students." (In the 1922–23 academic year, there were 174 candidates for the M.D. degree, 10 of them women.)

Heffron thought well of the courses and quality of teaching in the freshman and sophomore years, but his views of the clinical and laboratory instruction, given chiefly in the junior and senior years, were less favorable. He proposed that the faculty devote more time to research. He believed it was vital for the college to have a closer relationship with the other branches of the University. At the time the medical school, on South Orange Street, was about one mile away from both the main campus and University Hospital. To the dean the hospital, whose plant and equipment required replacing, was a white elephant that should be converted to a dormitory; a new hospital should be built on the Yates Castle grounds across Irving Avenue from University Place. Yates Castle, a Norman replica, had been acquired in 1906 with a view to the expansion of the University's facilities on the fourteen acres that accompanied the building. The Castle itself, renamed Renwick Hall, was used for some of the classes offered by the college of fine arts. With a new hospital on the Castle grounds the college, built on "ground so swampy that delicate instruments of precision cannot be free from vibration," should be moved to the Yates Castle site. He believed a new building and an improved clinical staff would enable the college to hold to academic standards equal to those at Albany, Rochester, and Buffalo.

Heffron did not live to see his dreams fulfilled. That same June he resigned the deanship, which he had held since 1908, and his old friend and fellow teacher, Dr. Herman Gates Weiskotten, was named acting dean, an appointment that became permanent in 1925. Weiskotten graduated from Syracuse University in 1906 with the degree of bachelor of philosophy; three years later the College of Medicine granted his M.D. degree. In the fall of 1909 he became resident pathologist at the University Hospital and a member of the medical school faculty.

Working closely with Chancellor Flint and later with Chancellor Graham, Weiskotten attempted to resolve the administrative and financial problems facing the college and University Hospital. Dr. Flint appointed Dr. Charles H. Young, who had been superintendent of the

Yates Castle.

Presbyterian Hospital of Brooklyn, to a similar post at the University Hospital. But because Young could not take over his new duties until the spring of 1923, Nellie Hamill, R.N., agreed to stay on as superintendent, a position she had filled since 1915, until her replacement arrived.

The Chancellor also arranged to have a survey made of the college, the hospital, and the dispensary. In February 1923 Dr. Willard Rappleye of the Rockefeller Foundation and Dr. Winifred Smith of the Johns Hopkins Hospital submitted their findings, saying in part:

> The University has a great opportunity to serve the community.... To most effectually realize this opportunity the University will require a group of organizations in the nature of hospitals, dispensary, and education facilities in which the leaders in health work of the community may be engaged and in contact. It is clear that if the University is to realize its opportunity there must be ultimately developed a hospital-dispensary–medical-nursing center in close proximity to the University campus which will embrace a number of cooperating units.

The two doctors then made specific recommendations, many paralleling Heffron's. They also said the School of Nursing should be reorganized to prepare qualified young women for their life careers; ultimately this school should also be part of the medical center.

Rappleye and Smith realized the cost would be high, but they believed establishment of a medical center was so important that the University, community agencies, and the Syracuse residents should cooperate in financing it. In a separate memorandum Smith said the hospital staff had suffered in the past because "too large a percentage of the work ... was in the hands of men who are not members of the medical faculty. This means that a definite and progressive reorganization should be developed." In other words, the faculty should be appointed by the University, though subject to the dean of the medical college.

The University trustees, after a thorough study, established an administrative board consisting of the Chancellor, Weiskotten, Young, and the directors of medicine and surgery of the hospital; the respective presidents of the board of trustees and the hospital staff were ex-officio members. All medical directors were made consultants at the hospital, and the superintendent became a member of the medical faculty. All appointments to the hospital staff were to be made in accordance with the University bylaws. All recommendations for teaching assignments were to be cleared through the medical departments, the administrative board, and the Chancellor. The medical college faculty accepted the provisions, and late in November 1923 Chancellor Flint was able to tell the trustees the college met most of the standards laid down by the Association of Medical Colleges. He noted, however, that until the college was moved to the campus, the University could not comply with all of the association's requirements. Fortunately the University owned the Yates Castle property, and it was there that the new college and hospital structures should be built, he said. The board of trustees endorsed such use of the land, and the executive committee was asked to clear the way for construction.

As these developments took place, the pressing building needs of Memorial Hospital became entwined with those of the medical college and the University Hospital. Memorial Hospital, founded in 1887 and located at that time in a building on West Genesee Street, was where the College of Medicine students received their training in medicine and surgery, under the direction of the medical school faculty. Good as the facilities of the hospital had been at the end of the nineteenth century, the college and hospital authorities of 1922 knew a modern structure was needed for further growth.

Dean Weiskotten received a call in October 1922 from Mrs. James Pass, a trustee of Memorial Hospital, about the possibility of a "central school of nursing," combining the school based in University Hospital with the Memorial's school. The dean raised a larger issue during their conversation. He said it was time for the college and the hospital to cooperate in supporting Memorial's need for a new building. Mrs. Pass expressed interest and agreed that a survey should be the first step. Weiskotten, Chancellor Flint, and the hospital's board conferred on the matter and the result was the Rappleye-Smith report, which recommended construction of a new Memorial Hospital in the neighborhood of a College of Medicine building. The University deeded to Memorial's board the necessary land for a new hospital.

The board's building drive began late in 1926. Chancellor Flint endorsed it, saying the board had planned a campaign several times before, only to defer to other local drives. In the fall of 1924, for example, the board postponed its campaign so "the University might stage its ... drive for indebtedness." Now it was the University's turn to wait, the Chancellor said. This reciprocity undoubtedly benefited the Memorial drive, and by January 1927 nearly $2.5 million had been subscribed. In June 1929 the cornerstone was laid, and on September 20 of that year the new Memorial Hospital was formally dedicated. Chancellor Flint and Dean Weiskotten, speaking for the University and the College of Medicine, welcomed the hospital to the Hill and hailed it as "a truly educational" institution with definite teaching responsibilities for physicians and nurses. There were no formal agreements except on minor matters, but the college, by mutual understanding, used the hospital thereafter as a teaching center for pediatrics and obstetrics and gynecology, among other subjects.

The Syracuse press hailed the Memorial board and spoke of close cooperation and friendly affiliation among the University, the hospital, and the other medical units that were to occupy the Yates Castle grounds—the City Hospital for Communicable Diseases and the State Psychiatric Hospital. The University had contributed by donating the land for the latter buildings as well.

The idea of a new city hospital had long been discussed. Though owned and operated by the city health department, the medical and nursing staffs were supplied by the medical college. A similar arrangement provided that the state would own and operate the psychiatric hospital. There was no formal agreement between the state and the college, aside from a stipulation that the hospital would always be open for teaching purposes. Harry Steckel was named director of the psychiatric hospital and professor of psychiatry in the College of Medicine. Thus, by 1930, the medical center had become a reality, except for a new medical college building and a new University hospital and dispensary.

During these developments Chancellor Flint never lost sight of the role to which the University had committed itself. In June 1925 the trustees approved moving the medical college to the Yates Castle grounds. The following year a survey was made of the condition and needs of the college. This revealed that the McBride Street building housing the college was a fire hazard; that it was overcrowded with departments of anatomy, physiology, pharmacology, and pathology, together with classrooms, offices, and library; that a tunnel connected it with the dispensary on East Fayette Street, in which there were more classrooms and the offices of bacteriology and clinical chemistry; and that the medical students had to travel to the University for such subjects as physiological chemistry. Clearly this was a situation in which division and separation of labor bred confusion and retarded progress. Consequently all units should be under one roof, the survey said. Adequate endowments for salaries and the library were essential, and a men's dormitory was a must for the improvement of student morale. The survey estimated the necessary changes would cost about $3,685,000, with $2 million more for construction of a new medical college and University Hospital. Finances being what they were, the Chancellor realized he would have to be content with much less.

The medical center's architect was Dwight J. Baum, who was also the University architect. In 1927 he submitted a plan for a new campus that was to be south of the proposed new Memorial Hospital and the State Psychiatric Hospital, both to face Irving Avenue. The college and the University Hospital, which was to include an administrative unit and several laboratories, would also face the avenue. The City Hospital and the dispensary, west of the college and the University Hospital, would face Renwick Avenue. But because construction of the college units depended on private philanthropy, which in those Depression years was difficult to obtain, the Chancellor's plans had to be held in abeyance.

Nevertheless, thanks to the efforts of Dr. Flint, Dean Weiskotten, and Professor Herbert Shenton of the department of sociology at the University, the Josiah Macy Foundation made small interim grants to support work in the "sociological and preventive aspects of medicine." Heretofore, American medical students were trained chiefly in the treatment of disease, with less attention given to the patient as an individual. The Macy gifts allowed a program that permitted investigations into the life, history, living, and working conditions of the sick.

When the worst of the Depression was over, but before charitable foundations reopened their purses, Chancellor Flint explored the possibilities of obtaining federal assistance from the Public Works Administration (PWA). After much correspondence and many interviews, the federal agency agreed to help finance the construction and equipping of a new medical college building. The University gladly accepted the terms, and in February 1936 provision was made to issue $825,000 in mortgage bonds bearing 4 percent interest. Construction soon began, and on September 29, 1936, the cornerstone was laid by President Franklin D. Roosevelt before an audience that included Secretary of the Interior Harold Ickes, who also administered the PWA, New York Governor Herbert H. Lehman, Syracuse Mayor Rolland B. Marvin, the new chancellor, William P. Graham, Dean Weiskotten, and members of the board of trustees, faculty, and student body. Dr. Flint, by then a bishop of the Methodist Church, could not be present to witness the event for which he had done so much.

Completed in November 1937, the English Georgian style building was five stories high, including the basement, and contained six large student laboratories, as well as research laboratories for the faculty. Classrooms, lecture rooms, and departmental offices opened off the three main corridors on each floor. An auditorium and the college library were on the first floor.

As an integral part of the medical center, the new building was a

President Franklin D. Roosevelt with Vice Chancellor Graham wields a trowel at the cornerstone laying for the new School of Medicine building, September 30, 1936.

notable contribution by the University to medical education and community service. The center now consisted of the college, the Memorial Hospital with 335 beds, the City Hospital with 80 beds, and the State Psychiatric Hospital with 60 beds. Nearby were the Crouse-Irving Hospital with 227 beds and the University Hospital on Marshall Street with 200 beds—in all 902 beds immediately associated with the medical college.

Chancellor Graham soon became concerned over the University's debt on the college building, whose total cost was $900,000. At about the time of the formal opening, he reminded the board of trustees that the building owed its existence to a loan, on which the University had been making payments out of current funds for two years. He said this was satisfactory as a temporary expedient, but another method of meeting payments had to be found. Some amortization of the debt was made, but the disturbed condition of the national economy after Pearl Harbor postponed a solution of the problem.

During the years 1922–42 the College of Medicine Alumni Association, which remained apart from the University Alumni Association, aided greatly in the growth of the college, the hospital, and the medical center. After completion of the next college building, the medical alumni started a drive for endowments; in 1939 they gave the amount collected to the University for use by the college. Among the officers of the association during the Flint-Graham administrations were Doctors A. G. Swift, William G. Johnson, Francis J. Ryan, Edward S. Van Duyn, Alfred W. Armstrong, Henry W. Schoeneck, Henry B. Doust, J. G. Fred Hiss, George S. Britten, E. C. Rulison, and Edward C. Hughes.

Many of these and other alumni gave willingly of their time and energy to work at the University Hospital, which at a future date was scheduled to be abandoned in favor of a new hospital and dispensary which would be erected near the medical center. Financial difficulties frustrated this plan, so the University made improvements from time to time in the Marshall Street structure. In 1927, for instance, the operating amphitheater was remodeled, and the properties at 107 Waverly Avenue and 130 Marshall Street were purchased for future expansion. Despite the fact that some considered University Hospital outmoded, it continued to render valuable service to the community.

Closely related to the medical college and the University Hospital was the University's School of Nursing. During the early years of the Flint administration it functioned much as it had under Chancellor Day. Entrance requirements were few: virtually any woman between the ages of seventeen and thirty-five who had spent four years in high school was accepted. In 1928 applicants generally had to meet the admission standards of the College of Liberal Arts. By 1931 only graduates of approved high schools were admitted, and eight years later general aptitude tests were introduced.

In 1922 the courses taught were ethics, anatomy and physiology, chemistry, nutrition, dietetics, hygiene, bacteriology, materia medica, urinalysis, contagious and children's diseases, and nursing in medicine, surgery, obstetrics, and gynecology. Clinical training for nursing in hospitals or private homes was given in the University Hospital. Other instruction included work in the diet kitchen, the formula room, operating rooms, and in the departments of x-ray, obstetrics, and pediatrics. There was also a combination course in nursing and liberal arts, and provision was made for graduate study in x-ray and laboratory work. On completion of the undergraduate program, covering a period of two years and four months, the University issued a nursing certificate.

Nursing graduates in the 1940 commencement procession.

In 1929 the course was lengthened to three years to allow for special training for contagious diseases in the City Hospital; later, similar arrangements were made with the state psychiatric hospitals at Syracuse, Utica, and Rome.

A partial merger of the University and Memorial schools of nursing took place in 1936. The possibility of a central school of nursing had been discussed as far back as 1922. Nothing materialized at that time, but in 1931 there was a movement to bring about a formal affiliation of the two schools. Dean Weiskotten believed that if this were done, the University would take over two or three departments of the Memorial Hospital, giving the medical college control of all personnel and research. For two years the administration studied the proposal. The discussions led to changes in the curricula of both nursing schools, as well as to the concept of combining both schools into a Syracuse University School of Nursing.

In 1936 such a merger was strongly recommended. It was to be an independent, separate unit within the University. The program and curriculum would be professional, leading to a bachelor's degree and diploma in nursing. Provision was also made for financing the school, a feature that finally prevented the adoption of the plan by the University and Memorial Hospital boards. Those interested in the basic idea, however, pressed on with the proposal to centralize instruction in both nursing schools during the first six months of the freshman year. The idea was adopted and put into effect in February 1936. All classes during this period were combined, and the facilities of University and Memorial Hospitals were made available to the student nurses of both institutions. During this preclinical time, the students were instructed in the sciences basic to nursing and nursing techniques.

In April 1938 a special committee developed a plan whereby the two schools might become one. Two months later the Chancellor, Dean Weiskotten, and the chief officers of the schools and hospital boards adopted the proposal, subject to approval by the University and Memorial Hospital trustees. Little was accomplished until 1939, when the University's executive committee approved the merger because it was educationally wise, would not cost the University a large sum, and was in keeping with the idea of a medical center. There were many matters to be ironed out, however, and at several joint meetings the proposition was discussed in great detail. Finally, in February 1941, Chancellor Graham expressed his willingness to implement the plan by converting one of the buildings near the University Hospital into a nursing school at a cost not exceeding $15,000. He said he regretted that the University could not do more, adding that if his proposal did not please those urging the merger, each school had better go its own way.

In May of the same year the joint committees of Memorial Hospital and the University trustees submitted a clear-cut plan to combine the two schools. The hospital and the University would share the operating costs of the building to be converted by the University, with the hospital continuing to be responsible for the nurses' living quarters. But that May of 1941 was a trying month for Chancellor Graham and the University trustees. The pall of the European war hung over the campus, and the federal government's conscription program pointed to a sharp decrease in male enrollment. To offset the resulting tuition loss, Dr. Graham hoped to increase the enrollment of women; to do so, University housing, including that earmarked for the new nursing school, would be made over into living centers for women. He declared, however, that the University would honor its promise to convert the building rather than risk ill will from the Memorial Hospital board.

The next month the Memorial board, probably apprehensive about its own future, agreed to postpone the merger until conditions were more favorable. The hospital and the University voiced regret over the seeming demise of a plan on which so much time and thought had been spent, and both expressed continued good will toward each other.

Ultimately the question of a merger was reopened. But that was in the future, as was the transfer of the College of Medicine to the state university system in 1950.

11

The College of Law

Dean Roscoe Pound of Harvard Law School said in his 1927 survey that the College of Law was conducted *"too much as a sort of glorified law office, doing things after the manner of the old-time apprentice training in a law office. . . . Too much time is devoted to things of transient importance."*

SINCE ITS FOUNDING IN 1894, the College of Law had enjoyed a steady but not spectacular growth. Its foundations appeared secure, and the faculty and graduates were known throughout Central New York. Classes were held in the former mansion of John Crouse at the corner of Fayette and State streets. It is doubtful whether Dr. Flint knew more than these few facts about the law school when he accepted the chancellorship in 1922.

The college at its inception was basically a local institution preparing its students almost exclusively for the bar of Onondaga County. The new chancellor had his first inkling of what the law school was like in March 1922 while he was still president of Cornell College, Iowa. He received a letter from Ellis H. Gidley, Class of 1909, then a prominent Buffalo attorney. Gidley, basing his argument on recollections of his life at Syracuse and a study of the College of Law *Bulletin* of 1921, wrote that the course of study "now provided is in all essentials precisely the same as it was when . . . I took my law degree." He noted a score of deficiencies, especially in the curriculum, and said that unless these and other matters were speedily corrected, the college would suffer in public esteem.

Dr. Flint, always sensitive to public relations, promised Gidley he would investigate the matter in the near future, but his illness during the spring and summer of 1922 forced a delay. Then, on assuming his duties as Chancellor that fall, he was beset with problems deemed more pressing. But presumably he had conversations with Dean Frank R. Walker, Professors John W. Church, George W. Gray, and Louis L. Waters, and part-time instructors like Paul Shipman Andrews, George N. Cheney, and Crandall Melvin. In the *Bulletin* Chancellor Flint would have discovered that graduates of approved colleges had been admitted to the law school without examination, although beginning in September 1922 all candidates for the bachelor of law degree were required to have spent two years at a liberal arts college. Those not seeking degrees, but who had completed four years of high school work, were admitted without examination and on successful completion of a three-year course received a certificate. The certificate plan was soon dropped, however, and with the exception of special students, all were subject to the entrance requirements of the College of Liberal Arts.

In 1922 the curriculum for the freshman year included courses in contracts, torts, elementary law, personal property, bills and notes, jurisprudence, domestic relations, criminal law, agency and partnership, legal ethics, and legal expressions. For students in the second year there was work in criminal law and procedure, real property, evidence, Roman law, legal bibliography, medical jurisprudence, taxation, civil procedure, suretyship, bailments, equity, state law, moot court, and sales and liens. In the third and final year equity, trusts, corporations, New York civil laws, wills and administration, constitutional law, insurance, moot court, conflicts, international law, patents, and elocution might be taken.

It is unlikely that all these courses were given every year; probably the curriculum was padded, and it is doubtful moot court was offered at all. Moreover, the program sequence lacked proper order. For example, the course in partnership, given in the first year, should have presupposed a knowledge of equity, which was not given until the second year, while taxation normally should have come after constitutional law. In some instances there appears to have been an overlapping of courses and, since the college was an undergraduate institution, it seemed odd to find graduate work listed in the curriculum. Finally, the impression could be gained that the curriculum was drafted in part to meet the interests of the teaching staff, not the students.

Dean Walker's report of November 1923 gave additional insight

College of Law, downtown, 1904–1928. Dean Walker was not happy that some law books were at the University library more than a mile away. A new home was needed.

into the situation at the college. The faculty, he said, consisted of a dean and three professors who "devote substantially all their time to the work of the college." There were twelve instructors and five part-time lecturers, who spent from a few hours a semester to eight hours a week teaching. Of the 223 students enrolled in 1922–23, 129 were candidates for degrees, 86 sought certificates, and 8 were special students. The thirty-six entering freshmen represented a drop, presumably caused by a change in the entrance requirements. Most of the students came from New York, with a scattering from New Jersey, Pennsylvania, and Connecticut. As in the past, the second- and third-year students had their classes in the morning, the freshmen in the afternoon. Dean Walker was not happy with this schedule, but with limited classroom space no other plan was possible. The same handicap prevented expansion of the curriculum, especially electives. Nor did the dean think it wise to have part of the law library shelved at the University library more than a mile away.

In contrast with the year before, it appeared that little improvement had been made except to rearrange the curriculum and add a few instructors. And nothing had been done to check the undue emphasis on extracurricular student activities. All in all, the comments Dean Roscoe Pound of Harvard was to make in his 1927 survey were fair. He said the college "was conducted too much as a sort of glorified law office, doing things after the manner of the old-time apprentice training in a law office. Too much time and energy are devoted to things that can be learned without a teacher in a very short time out of school. Too much time is devoted to things of transient importance, likely to change with the advent of new legislation at any time."

As time went on Chancellor Flint, despite limited finances, was able to make improvements in faculty personnel, admission requirements, and curriculum. And while the *Bulletin* regularly repeated that the law school was "in a large and commodious structure facing beautiful Fayette Park," everyone knew the building was neither large nor commodious and that the park's beauty did not enhance the academic reputation of the college. A new home was needed to meet the demands of a modern law school.

Fortunately there was a bequest available for a new building. In the fall of 1914 Minnie H. Trowbridge of New York City gave the University $100,000 for that purpose. Placed in a local bank, the money appeared on the treasurer's books as a restricted and reserved fund, where it remained and drew interest. Meanwhile the University Hospital needed a new pavilion, and the trustees approved such an addition in the spring of 1917. Chancellor Day, refused a loan by city banks, solved the problem by temporarily borrowing from the College of Law Building Fund, which then amounted to $112,480.

After Chancellor Flint had reorganized the University, the Trowbridge bequest was restored to its proper place among the endowments and the way was paved for carrying out the donor's wishes.* In seeking a new site, the Chancellor and the executive committee found the Ely Apartments at 290 East Onondaga Street. Unlike the building

*A fuller account of the Trowbridge bequest is in the second volume of the history of Syracuse University, pages 108 and 436.

Court House and College of Law, 1928–1954.

on Fayette Street, the apartments were in a quiet neighborhood, and they were across the street from the Onondaga County Court House, which offered the students a convenient library for research and study, as well as an opportunity to witness trials. Just as pertinent was the profit from the sale of the Fayette Street property; originally bought for $50,000, it sold for $160,000. In June 1924 the Ely Apartments were purchased for $100,000 on condition they would not be used for commercial purposes nor disposed of as ordinary real estate. By this time the restored Trowbridge Fund amounted to nearly $150,000, which not only paid for the property but provided for the construction of offices, classrooms, and a library in the new structure. Named Hackett Hall in honor of Minnie Trowbridge's father, the building was opened as the College of Law in the fall of 1926.

While these physical changes were taking place Chancellor Flint began his reorganization. He asked Ralph E. Himstead, whom he had brought to Syracuse from Cornell College in 1924, to draw up suggestions for the improvement of the law school. Dr. Flint was to say before he left Syracuse that he discovered Himstead "teaching in a high school in Omaha and offered him his first college position." Himstead, a graduate of the University of Illinois, earned LL.B. and J.D. degrees at the Northwestern University School of Law in 1921 and 1924. Also in 1924 he earned an M.A. in political science at Northwestern. The directory of teachers of the Association of American Law Schools lists him as having received an S.J.D. from Harvard Law School in 1929. "I received my Doctor's Degree at Harvard Law School in Public Law," Himstead wrote in 1938, after he had left Syracuse to become general secretary of the American Association of University Professors. Himstead had taught business law and debate at Cornell College from 1919 to 1922 and was a professor of political science there when Dr. Flint recruited him.

Others were asked to express their views on the law school, including Dean Pound, whose services were obtained, Dr. Flint was to write later, "after considerable consultation and negotiation." Roscoe Pound (1870–1964), the son of a judge, was dean of the Harvard Law School for twenty years during its "golden age." His vast erudition included all phases of law and jurisprudence as well as the classics, foreign languages, and scientific subjects. He was a member of many scientific societies and wrote widely on technical, legal, and botanical subjects.

All involved concluded that the Syracuse curriculum was cluttered with unnecessary courses aimed at preparing students for the state bar examinations. Moreover, Syracuse students carried more class hours than those at better law schools but they had fewer electives. The evidence also showed that Syracuse students did less well in the examinations. Himstead said: "The facts are that the best and only real preparation for the bar examinations is the development of a legal mind, the power of legal analysis, and this can only come after a thorough grounding in the fundamentals of the common law and jurisprudence."

These skills, Himstead continued, should be acquired by the inductive and scientific approach in methods of study. The textbook and lecture program, based largely upon memory, should in most instances be replaced by the casebook method. This implied that each student owned a casebook whose contents had been selected and edited, and in which each case was supported by majority and minority opinions. Thus a student would realize that law was something to be studied and understood, not learned by rote. "This situation is lacking . . . in our law school," Himstead wrote. The fact that all schools except Syracuse belonging to the Association of American Law Schools "use the casebook method raises a powerful presumption in its favor." Himstead deplored the fact that some of the part-time faculty members were amateurs as practitioners and certainly amateurs as teachers. "Their career does not lie in the school and they are indifferent to its problems," he said, concluding that the school's future depended on more full-time professors capable of commanding respect as instructors and students of law.

Dean Pound was in general agreement with Himstead's conclusions, but his report offered a more penetrating review of the faculty that included reasons why some should be retained and others dismissed. The Harvard dean grouped American law schools into three categories. The first, consisting of the older colleges, enjoyed a national status that drew students from all parts of the United States and taught law from a national point of view. These schools prepared students to practice in any jurisdiction based upon the English common law. "As things are today, this more and more proves in the long run to be the best training for local practitioners... hence the tendency everywhere is toward the national school." The second group was primarily local. It taught local law and local practice, from the standpoint of the general law and in the manner of a national school. The third category was purely local, preparing candidates almost exclusively for the local bar. Such schools were likely to "insist overmuch upon details of procedure" and the anomalies of local decisions. Pound said Syracuse fell into the last category. He particularly noticed a certain listlessness in the classes, indifferent if not poor instruction, inadequate examinations, unsatisfactory grading, and the absence of moot courts. Nevertheless, the institution might easily move into the second group and meet the needs of upstate New York. In his proposal for reorganization Pound suggested that the college function within that area by teaching New York law from a general or national point of view. Furthermore, a law review and a legal aid bureau should be established. The faculty should consist of a dean and at least four full-time professors and one instructor. The students should give up all general extracurricular activities.

Pound sketched in detail a revised curriculum and teaching load and stressed the need for improved instructional methods, examinations, and moot courts. Finally, he proposed certain budgetary improvements that included salary increases and larger library appropriations.

Chancellor Flint responded quickly. He arranged for physical improvements in the classrooms and increases in the library budget. A more significant result, in keeping with Pound's report, was the retirement of seventy-two-year-old Dean Walker. Appropriately, the dean received special recognition and a retirement allowance for his long service to the University.

Recommended by Pound and selected to be the new dean was Paul

Shipman Andrews. He had been born in Syracuse on August 2, 1887, the son of William S. Andrews, who had served on the State Supreme Court and the Court of Appeals. His grandfather, Charles Andrews, was one of the University's founders and in 1873 was one of a committee of three trustees named to help decide whether there should be a College of Law. Chancellor Winchell and George F. Comstock were the other two members. When in 1894 the board of trustees approved establishing a law school "at as early a date as practicable," Charles Andrews helped organize the curriculum and faculty. Paul Andrews graduated from Yale in 1909 and earned his bachelor of law degree from Columbia three years later. Returning to Syracuse to practice, he joined the law school as a part-time instructor in contracts. He married Hannah S. Sessions, granddaughter of Frederick D. Huntington, first bishop of the Episcopal Diocese of Central New York. During World War I, Paul Andrews served overseas as a captain in the 151st Field Artillery.

After the Andrews appointment Chancellor Flint said in a memorandum "to the teaching staff of the College of Law" that the board of trustees had accepted Dean Pound's recommendations and that "we are endeavoring to reorganize for this coming fall in spite of the late date of our decision to effect the general change."

He continued in the memorandum dated June 22, 1927: "In general, all teaching will be done by full-time teachers, discontinuing, as is now general among the best law colleges, teaching by practicing attorneys. We may not be able to reach this goal absolutely the first year, but will come as near as we can.

"The attitude of the present staff toward the change has been most gratifying and helpful. I bespeak your cordial backing for Dean Andrews in his difficult task of reshaping the curriculum and securing the new staff for this next year.

"I must clear the way for him, as you see, and as, I am sure, you will agree, by announcing that all plans and arrangements for part-time teaching are cancelled, except as he may find it necessary to make temporary arrangements later."

Dean Andrews reorganized the college with the help of Judge Clarence N. Goodwin and Louis Marshall. Andrews dropped the part-time instructors and when the college opened in the fall of 1927, the faculty consisted of himself and Professors George Cheney, George Grey, Ralph Himstead, Willis Sargent, and Victor Levine. Of these Levine was a newcomer; a graduate of Harvard College and Harvard Law School, he had practiced in Boston and New York City and had served briefly in the Department of Justice in Washington. With the

Paul Shipman Andrews, dean, College of Law, 1927–1953.

exception of Himstead, who taught a course in constitutional law in the Maxwell School, and Grey, who temporarily retained a limited private legal practice, and the dean himself, all were full-time members of the law faculty. Andrews divided his days between the college and his law practice, an arrangement he frankly admitted was "radically wrong."

The faculty had been augmented earlier by the appointment of a future dean of the law school (1953–66), Ralph E. Kharas, as an assistant professor. Kharas, like Himstead, had taught at Cornell College, of which Dr. Flint was president. Unlike Himstead, Kharas was also a graduate of Iowa's Cornell, with a law degree from the University of Chicago.

With the cooperation of the faculty, the casebook method was quickly introduced, and the required class hours for students were adjusted to a more satisfactory level. The number of electives was increased and the curriculum thoroughly revised. Certain old courses were dropped and new ones added, and a system of moot courts was started for the first time in the college's history. Academic standards in examinations and grading were raised, and admission of students in mid-year was abolished. Except for Syracuse students registered in the combination courses in Liberal Arts and Business Administration, those seeking admission to the college were required to have bachelor's degrees; previously only three years of college work had been necessary. Finally, the combination of a bachelor's degree and the law degree, formerly restricted to Syracusans, was opened to those from other institutions having similar programs. The various improvements raised the rank of Syracuse University students taking bar examinations.

The dean and his staff were unwilling to stop the reorganization at this point. Although they knew the new admission requirements would cause a temporary drop in enrollment, they believed the University should raise faculty salaries, as the Chancellor had promised, commensurate with those of other law schools, add to the faculty, and broaden course offerings. In this hope they had the backing of the Pound report and the support of such men as Judge Clarence N. Goodwin, a graduate of the law school who in the fall of 1929 proposed that the University advance money from its general funds for salary increases. The judge also recommended that the salary scale of the law school be distinct from that of the other schools and colleges of the University. Andrews had been pressing Chancellor Flint to do this since 1927. In one instance he bluntly stated that unless salaries were raised within a reasonable time he would recommend that "the law college be closed." Three years later he reminded Dr. Flint of his promises and said: "It will be necessary to make good on that promise ... on most salaries." The increases the Chancellor did provide never satisfied the dean, the professors, or interested alumni and friends. His stated policy for the law school was that he was ready to raise the salaries of worthwhile instructors and to appoint new staff members, but he was not willing to give raises to those of lesser competence.

There continued the unsolved problem of a part-time dean. Presumably Andrews had accepted the position on the understanding that he would continue his remunerative law practice. In 1930 the Chancellor discussed the delicate matter in a letter to a friend, saying "more than he [Andrews] realizes, the school is suffering from the divided relation." Dr. Flint believed Andrews should devote his full time to the deanship or stop being an "acting dean." Andrews learned of the Chancellor's feelings, but nothing changed.

Because Dean Pound's study of the College of Law was so recent, the Commission on Survey of Educational Institutions of the Methodist Episcopal Church did not deal with the law school in its comprehensive study of 1930 (the so-called Reeves Survey).

The Chancellor returned to the problem from time to time. In the fall of 1934 he sought the advice of Judge Goodwin and trustee George Bond, as well as of several deans and faculty members of other law schools. One reply urged the appointment of someone who would be willing "to devote 16 hours a day to the job, if necessary." Bolstered by such counsel, Dr. Flint was ready to bring the issue to a head, but he had scarcely begun his search for a full-time dean when he became ill and the problem again went into abeyance.

In December 1935 Professor John M. Maguire of the Harvard Law School inspected the Syracuse law school for the Association of American Law Schools. Maguire focused on the Flint-Andrews situation along with other matters, and the association forwarded copies of the report to the Chancellor in January 1936.

The Harvard professor acknowledged a debt to the Pound report of 1927 and spoke well of improvements that had been made in the meantime. He said he had found the situation much better than he had expected. Yet he felt that the college had lost more than it gained by its location on Montgomery Street; he thought it should be moved to the campus—a change that he knew was impracticable unless there was "an unexpected windfall of funds."

To Maguire, the law school library was somewhat deficient and the admission procedures for transfers from other schools faulty; but these and other minor items, he believed, could be corrected without much difficulty. As to the salary scale and curriculum, they did not suffer by comparison with the other colleges of the University. There was, however, a serious deterrent to the scholarship among the faculty caused by the system of alternating courses each year. This forced the staff to devote considerable time to study in order to keep abreast of normal developments in the courses. Accordingly, he strongly recommended the addition of two more full-time faculty.

Maguire then came to the matter of the deanship. He said he had found faculty morale suffering from the existing arrangement. "The faculty are not unanimously confident that the college can long be continued at all," he wrote. "Some of them live from year to year, not daring to make the domestic commitments which depend upon permanency of employment and certainly thinking in long terms of the future of the institution for which they work. They feel themselves in a position of economic peril. At the same time they see their dean not taking the full risks to which they are perforce exposed."

The Harvard professor had high praise for Dean Andrews: "Personally charming, he is versatile, energetic, intelligent, and patient of criticism. He has human sympathy and can get the best out of his associates. He loves the college, rejoices in his own connection with it, yet so far has not felt in a position to tie himself to it exclusively. Hence, he says, Chancellor Flint is fully aware of the necessity of changing deans and of the willingness of Dean Andrews to make way for a full-time successor. Dean Andrews has been equally outspoken to his faculty of the matter. It would seem, though, as if Chancellor Flint had mistaken frank recognition of the problem for its solution, since he has delayed action year after year. I have termed the change not only imperative but urgent. It has been made urgent largely by the fresh recognition of its necessity. ... Too many people have almost been offered the deanship, or think they have. Too much talk about the college has got going in the law school world. A feeling is growing that its difficulties cannot be met, or at least will not be met, and that it is destined to drag out an existence—perhaps not very prolonged—as a second-rate humdrum institution."

Maguire went on: "My report shows that I do not share this feeling. But in the practical affairs of life false damaging beliefs only too often contrive to harden themselves into disastrous facts."

A list of ten conclusions and recommendations came at the end of the single-spaced, twenty-two-page report. The final paragraph said: "I find it urgently imperative in the best interests of the college that a full-time deanship should be substituted for the present part-time deanship."

At this time, according to the report, salaries in the College of Law were "on a par with, possibly in some instances higher than, corresponding salaries in other colleges or departments of the University," and Dean Andrews's salary for part-time work was $5,750. Maguire said Andrews was of the opinion that he gave somewhat more than half his time to the college and had been forced to give up trial work, maintaining only a consulting and appellate practice with his firm, Andrews, Andrews, and McBride.

Despite Maguire's strongly worded recommendation, Andrews continued his part-time status for the rest of Dr. Flint's stay at the University. It was not until early in the Graham administration that arrangements were made with Andrews, who thereafter devoted full time to his position as dean.

The Maguire report brought existing weaknesses to light, but outweighing them were elements of strength that indicated a prosperous future once the matter of the deanship was settled. In this conclusion Maguire was seconded by the Chancellor, Andrews, and the college faculty. Thus the University administration had reason to be pleased when Maguire stated as the first of his conclusions: "I find, and recommend that the executive committee [of the AALS] approve my finding, that the Syracuse University College of Law satisfactorily complies in all substantial respects with the requirements of the Association of American Law Schools."

His commendation for past improvements and encouragements for future growth prompted Chancellor Flint to increase the size and reputation of the faculty. In the fall of 1936 there were brought to the law school Theodore F. Bowes, who gave courses in sales, corporations, and insurance, and Joseph Cheadle, a Harvard Law School graduate who became the first holder of the Chester Agate Congdon Professorship of Public Law and Legislation. The chair, given by Mrs. Congdon in honor of her late husband, a graduate of the Syracuse Colleges of Liberal Arts and Law, was established to develop the functioning of lawmaking in the American constitutional government, the administration of national, state, and local legislation, and the comparison and standard of such legislation. The appointment of Cheadle was occasioned in part by the resignation of Himstead, who moved to Washington to become executive secretary of the American Association of University Professors. Himstead may have been one of those who had "almost been offered the deanship." Chancellor Flint wrote to a friend in May 1935: "I am inclined to think if Himstead had been somewhere else during this period, I might be seeking him as dean of our law school."

The faculty changes and establishment of the Congdon Professorship came in the closing months of Dr. Flint's administration.

During his years at Syracuse he had struggled against many odds and financial restrictions to build the law college into an institution of much higher standing and reputation. He never solved the problem of the deanship to anyone's satisfaction, but his interest in and efforts on behalf of the college were manifest. Among other things, he recognized the imperative necessity of a full-time faculty, raised salaries, promoted a sounder curriculum, backed a better system of admissions, and stimulated faculty morale and better relations with the local bar in Syracuse.

Chancellor Graham continued to build on these foundations. But when Joseph Cheadle resigned in 1937, undoubtedly because of salary differences, attempts to fill the vacant Congdon Professorship failed—largely, Dr. Graham asserted, because the University could not afford a salary that would attract the right man. The Congdon chair was not filled again until 1948. Offsetting the loss of Cheadle were the additions to the staff of associate professor John W. Hansen and assistant professors William Lloyd and Robert W. Miller. Miller was to be acting dean and dean from 1966 to 1971.

By the fall of 1940 the college was feeling the impact of the war in Europe. National defense cast a long shadow over the campus, and retrenchment was the order of the day, especially when enrollments declined. A short time after Pearl Harbor Syracuse University was on a war basis. Andrews, Bowes, and Miller obtained leaves for government or military service. Kharas was named acting dean during this period. The decrease in staff reduced the number of courses offered and caused a staggering of required and elective work beginning in the fall of 1942. Meanwhile provision was made to accelerate the program by admitting students in February, June, and September and conducting classes throughout the calendar year.

A comparison of the curriculum of 1941 with that of 1922 shows how the college had enriched its programs. Gone were courses that had accumulated during the Day administration and, while the courses were fewer in number in 1941 than at the earlier date, their quality was materially better. The entrance of the United States into World War II retarded the growth and expansion Dr. Flint, Andrews, and the law faculty had initiated, but Dr. Graham maintained the foundations during the war years to set the stage for a remarkable growth of the college after 1945.

12

The Graduate School

Grades were important, but more significant was the student's ability to comprehend and solve specific problems and master them by contributions to knowledge.

William L. Bray, dean of the Graduate School from 1918 to 1943, once said his school was in fact a college. He noted that most of its students had graduated from liberal arts colleges, in the classical tradition. Of these, most were preparing to teach in secondary schools. Others went into the ministry or became faculty members at colleges and universities. A few who studied in the liberal arts tradition planned professional careers, although the Graduate School did not offer instruction in medicine or law. Early graduate work was confined to liberal arts and education courses.

Bray, a botanist who had been the first head of the College of Forestry and its acting dean in 1911, during his long tenure with the Graduate School was to expand it to attract graduate students in political science, public administration, fine arts, engineering, and many other fields.

There is no unanimity on the question of when or whether a clearly defined graduate faculty existed, or even, as a future Chancellor was to observe, what graduate education includes.

For the record, the *Bulletin* for 1922–23 said the Graduate School was organized as an "independent faculty consisting of a dean and

William L. Bray, dean, Graduate School, 1918–1943. Photograph © Bachrach.

those professors and instructors of the University who give instruction in courses approved for graduate credit." It added: "This faculty is the legislative body of the Graduate School."

The 1941–42 *Bulletin* did not define a graduate faculty as such but listed University faculty members who taught at the graduate level. It also printed a list of the twenty-three members of the Board of Graduate Studies headed by Chancellor Graham, Acting Vice Chancellor Charles Lee Raper, and Acting Dean William L. Bray.

At any rate, in the early years of the Flint administration financial problems hung like a pall over graduate study. The Graduate School, in existence since 1912, had no separate faculty, buildings, library, or endowment. It had only a few classrooms and its budget was microscopic. The presence among the so-called graduate faculty of instructors without advanced degrees was further evidence that academic standards were lax.

The new Chancellor did what he could to enrich the school by bringing in a few able professors, and 1924 saw the birth of the School of Citizenship, whose faculty enhanced graduate work at the University. Dr. Perley O. Place, the professor of classics who was associate dean of the Graduate School from 1923 to 1926 while Dean Bray was on leave as acting dean of the College of Liberal Arts, spoke of the increased quality of instruction and examinations, rising registration, the influx of better students, and the growing national prestige of the school.

Several University scholarships established in the fall of 1923 also contributed to the school's growth. In 1926, when Dean Bray returned to the school, the number of scholarships had increased to sixteen. In his report for 1926–27, Dean Bray stressed the importance of the "nonprofessional or as, we may say, 'cultural' study leading to the higher degrees of Master of Arts or Science and Doctor of Philosophy."

Admission to the Graduate School in 1922 was open to all graduates of Syracuse and of other institutions with similar requirements for the baccalaureate degree. In addition Syracuse seniors who at mid-year had met the requirements for a bachelor's degree or who had completed 117 of the 120 hours of credit needed for graduation might be admitted. In general, however, the school gave no credit for work taken in the senior year unless the dean approved, and then only for certain graduate courses. All applications had to be approved by an executive committee, and a graduate of another institution had to submit an official transcript. Most of the requirements remained substantially the same through the academic year 1941–42. For a brief period selected Syracuse juniors might elect graduate work, but no credit was given for it. In 1931 the stipulated 117 hours were dropped. Between 1932 and 1939 those with degrees approved by the Association of American Universities were admitted. There were certain other exceptions. Admission to the Graduate School did not automatically make a student a candidate for an advanced degree. In 1923 candidacy depended on approval of a program drafted by a major professor and the dean; the recommendation of a minor professor was added in 1927. In that year candidacy for the master's degree required completion of one semester's work, and candidacy for the doctorate required four semesters. In 1940 a student had to apply for candidacy two months before the degree was expected.

Another requirement involved residence. Except for teachers and others engaged in professional work within metropolitan Syracuse, graduate students had to attend classes at least three days a week. Those seeking master's degrees had to complete a minimum of one year of study amounting to 22 semester hours, not counting a thesis. In some cases a half year might be spent in the field or at some approved institution; this provision was discontinued in 1940. There was no mention of a foreign language requirement for a master's until 1928, when every candidate for an advanced degree was required to have training in a foreign language: "The prospective candidate must satisfy the specific requirement of his major department in this regard." This requirement disappeared from the *Bulletin* in 1941. Those working for doctorates were required to live on campus for three years, but instructors, graduate assistants, and fellows on part-time teaching or assistance schedules had to stay longer. In estimating residence, four summers or one regular semester and two summers were the equivalent of a year's residence. For someone seeking a master's degree, an additional summer session might be needed.

In 1923 the University stressed the fact that graduate work differed materially from undergraduate study. Grades were important, but more significant was the student's ability to comprehend and solve specific problems and master them by contributions to knowledge. A "B" average was needed. Failure to pass a course made a student ineligible for a degree in that year. No grade below "B" was accepted in certain political science programs and in the College of Fine Arts.

The *Bulletin* for 1922–23 reveals that most of the courses listed were open to undergraduate and graduate students. Of the seventeen courses in history, only two were limited to graduate students; in Latin, only three of thirteen; in physics, four of ten; and in mathematics thirteen of twenty-six. Some of the courses were not offered regularly, but it seems clear that many upperclass courses were open to candidates for advanced degrees. Graduate students were usually expected to do extra work through special assignments, but there was no machinery to compel the fulfillment of such requirements.

A candidate for the degree of master of arts or master of science elected 16 hours in a major department and 6 in a minor. With the approval of the department chairman, the student might take four of the sixteen in an allied department. The candidate also submitted a thesis, for which he or she normally received 4 hours' credit. On completion, a bound copy was turned over to the University library. Master's candidates had to pass an oral examination on the thesis and the courses taken. There was also a written examination. In 1931 the requirements were changed to a schedule of 24 to 30 hours including a thesis, to be in a single department or in supporting courses in related fields; the term "minor department" was dropped. After 1937, 30 hours, including a thesis, were required. The degree of master of science in business administration conformed to these standards.

In the College of Fine Arts, applicants registered for work leading to master's degrees in architecture, painting, and music. Students might matriculate in the College of Applied Science in mechanical and electrical engineering. Master's degrees in forestry, city forestry, and science were given in the New York State College of Forestry at Syracuse University.

Only in the Colleges of Liberal Arts and Forestry were there programs at the doctoral level. A doctoral candidate in Liberal Arts was admitted if he or she had a baccalaureate degree in arts, science, or philosophy from Syracuse or another approved institution of higher learning. A reading knowledge of two modern languages besides English was required. The candidate had to spend three academic years in residence, the last of which had to be at Syracuse during the regular session or in summer school. All graduate study, wherever taken, was subject to examination; anyone with a master's degree from Syracuse might count those credits toward a doctoral program. Each doctoral candidate chose a major subject requiring not less than 36 semester hours of course work. At least 24 more hours were to be divided into a first minor, chosen from the same group but not from his or her department, and a second minor approved by the dean and the student's major professor. Starting in 1940 the plan was modified to define the two minor subjects as "supporting" study to strengthen the total program. In addition, there was the research for and writing of a dissertation based on original study and constituting a contribution to knowledge. This dissertation, more than any other part of the student's work, was deemed an important index of scholarship and largely determined recommendation for the doctoral degree.

In preparation for a Middle States evaluation team visit in 1956, Dean Carl Bye reported on a self-evaluation that included a summary of developments in the Graduate School. The report said that until 1935 the Ph.D. was the only doctorate offered by Syracuse University. It could be earned in such areas as the humanities, science, the social sciences, and education. Since the 1930s the Ph.D. program had been expanded to include chemical engineering, romance languages, history, geography, geology, international relations, biochemistry, Germanic languages and literature, home economics, electrical engineering, communications, and solid state science and technology. In 1935 the University authorized the awarding of the Ed.D. in education, in 1943 the D.P.A. in public administration and, in 1945, the D.S.S. in social science.

A 1923 requirement was that fifty copies of the thesis were to be placed in the library. There was a provision, however, that allowed an abstract of the thesis to be published with one thousand copies put in the library. Only in a few instances were the stipulated number of theses or abstracts to be found in the library. Various other rule changes took place. In 1941 the candidate had to deposit two bound, typed copies of the thesis; later fifty printed copies were required, although a satisfactory abstract, with a $50 deposit "to cover publication of this abstract, *if such publication seemed desirable,*" might be substituted. So far as is known, the requirement of a deposit and publication was not enforced.

To promote graduate work and research, the University had established ten fellowships worth $500 each. Fellows—students working for a master's or doctor's degree—were expected to devote half time to study and research and the other half to assisting in their major departments. All fellows were exempt from the $100 annual tuition charge, but they paid the $5 matriculation and $10 diploma fee.

For several years there was little change in the Graduate School. Modifications that were frequently suggested involved additional funds, and since they were not available the executive committee limited its attention to existing programs and requirements. It cost nothing, however, to talk about better standards, and there was discussion of grades and credits. Mere coverage of subject matter was viewed as futile. What really counted was the depth of study and the need of the school to extract maximum creative power from the student with a minimum of material. Should a year's work entail 30 semester hours or the then existing 28? Dean Bray favored an increase, but others, like Professors William Smallwood and Ralph Harlow, thought credits should be forgotten to let the student focus on specified groups of knowledge. Those working in the field of medieval history, for example, might read and study not only history, but such allied subjects as medieval art, philosophy, law, and science.

Because graduate students engaged in full-time teaching or other employment could register for only 6 semester hours a year, the executive committee found it necessary to set a time limit for completion of graduate work. The *Bulletin* of 1927–28 informed candidates for master's degrees that they "must" finish their study within five years or within four of six summer sessions. Later all candidates for higher degrees were warned that their programs could not be prolonged "indefinitely."

In 1927 those seeking doctorates were asked to pass their modern language tests before taking other required examinations. In evaluating the quality of the master's program the Chancellor and the Graduate School were convinced of the University's and departments' ability to direct it. At the doctoral level a less optimistic note was sounded. This was reflected in the candid language of the *Bulletin,* which said not all departments were prepared to offer doctoral programs. In the history department, for example, it was unanimously agreed that the size of the staff was inadequate and that library facilities were much below standard. At a committee meeting in 1929 there was vigorous discussion of the need to raise the size and quality of the faculty, to reduce the graduate teaching load, and to have larger appropriations for library and equipment facilities.

The 1930 Reeves Survey of the University, undertaken at Chancellor Flint's request, noted other shortcomings. It found that the Graduate School, judged by the contributions of its students to society, functioned chiefly as a training ground for prospective teachers and administrators at secondary schools and colleges. The school also educated men and women for positions in business, industry, and government, the survey said, adding: "If in actual practice the research output of its graduates is not immediately significant, the presence of such a chosen body of students aids in creating the atmosphere and inspiration for productive scholarship on the part of the faculty. Thus the intellectual life of the University is intensified."

Elsewhere in its report the Reeves group said: "It is difficult to see how a strong program of graduate work can be maintained with more than one-third of the course work being taken in classes whose enrollment is predominantly freshman, sophomore, and junior."

Among the graduate faculty an opinion circulated that although there were obvious defects in the school, the Reeves Survey lacked substance and was prone to generalization.

By November 1934 Dean Bray was able to report to the Chancellor that for some time Syracuse graduate work had had a par rating among American graduate schools in terms of credits and degrees. "In 1933 the University was for the first time, I believe, given direct if qualified official recognition in respect to graduate work," he said, when the Association of American Universities invited Syracuse to send observers to its annual meeting at Princeton. In the spring of 1934 a committee of the American Council on Education had published its findings on graduate study in the nation. Although its report listed Syracuse as a school for doctoral study in only three of thirty-five fields, Dean Bray said, this was a vantage point from which additional gains might be expected, especially in chemistry, zoology, and geology-geography. He added: "Syracuse is in a position to welcome the most searching analysis as to its facilities for graduate work up to the master's degree in at least 20 fields and up to the doctorate in at least 10 fields."

William Pearson Tolley, Chancellor from 1942 to 1969, recalled:

> When I came in 1942 we had modest programs in the Ph.D. in chemistry; we had them in biology under Smallwood, and Bray before him. We had a fair program in physics, not distinguished at that time, and of course we had a big program of graduate education in education.
>
> That always raised some questions because you're talking about M.A. candidates who were getting ready to teach, and it's doubtful to think of that as graduate education. Even the number of Ph.D.s in education was enormous. We were one of the biggest schools of education in the country, and it probably was more than half our graduate program. As a matter of fact, the Graduate School of Education was not a part of the Graduate School; it was separate.

The rank of graduate assistant, established by the Chancellor in 1931, joined those of graduate scholars and university fellows. Students appointed graduate assistants were expected to do part-time work in laboratory and quiz sections. Their stipends depended on previous training and teaching aptitude. A graduate assistant had to spend two years in candidacy for a master's degree.

In the years that followed graduate assistants received financial aid that ranged from $100 to $850, depending upon the teaching load they carried, and were exempt from all or part of their tuition. By 1941 tuition had risen to $375 a year.

Also by 1941 the ten University fellowships were limited to candidates in the several departments of Liberal Arts. All received free tuition but no stipend. In the Maxwell School ten fellowships in public administration were by then available, paying $500 and allowing free tuition; four fellowships in political science provided the same financial assistance, as did a single fellowship in social psychology. Twenty scholarships in public administration and four in political science paid tuition only. In the School of Education there were two half-time instructorships yielding $800, plus free tuition for a half-time schedule of class work. Four graduate assistantships paid $600 and free tuition on a half-time program, and ten scholarships provided tuition only. When the Office of Dean of Men was established a system of resident advisers began, and the dean of women offered a number of graduate assistantships in the student deans program.

Although the graduate faculty realized, as did the Chancellors between 1934 and 1942, that these various grants had increased the number of graduate students, they also were aware, especially within the College of Liberal Arts, that there had been a decrease in stipends. Financially, a fellow was not as well off as a scholar or assistant, a situation that must have discouraged applicants as well as the departments affected. Dean Bray's efforts to overcome this handicap were fruitless. A proposal to set up a budget for the school resulted in Chancellor Graham authorizing a small expense account, chiefly for clerical work, which amounted to less than $4,000 in 1937. Thus was the poverty of the graduate program clearly shown.

Graduate work at Syracuse had grown significantly in the two decades after 1922, as enrollment figures attest. During the academic year 1922–23 a total of 217 students were enrolled, and it was not until 1931–32 that the figure rose above 300. In 1936–37 it was 421, and stood at 768 in 1940–41. The following year it dropped to 653, probably because of the impact of World War II. The gradual increase may be attributed in part to a larger and better qualified teaching staff. Moreover the administration, aided by the faculty, had raised academic standards, enriched the library resources, added better laboratory facilities and, through scholarships and fellowships, brought new life to the school.

13

The School of Journalism

There are some 542 institutions which offer instruction in journalism in the United States. . . . By common consent I think there are three at the top—Northwestern, Minnesota, and Syracuse.

—William P. Graham, 1942

THE SCHOOL OF JOURNALISM was born as a department with four aging typewriters, two instructors, and eighty-one students. That was in 1919 when the school that was to become the S. I. Newhouse School of Public Communications began life in the newly established School (later College) of Business Administration (now the School of Management). In a sense the department of journalism was a cooperative venture between the University and Syracuse newspapers—the teaching staff was drawn largely from the city's working press. In addition, for the first four years of its life the department's advisory council was composed chiefly of representatives of the newspapers.

The first courses were part of a four-year program in newspaper work that led to the degree of bachelor of science in journalism.

When Dr. Flint became Chancellor, journalism was being taught by Associate Professor George C. Wilson, head of the department since its founding, and four other faculty members, Harry K. Skerritt, Howard T. Viets, Arthur J. Brewster, and John O. Simmons, plus the city librarian, Paul M. Paine, and John H. Howe of the Syracuse *Herald.*

Before he died in January 1924, Wilson had developed the department to the point where it was rated Class A by the American Association of Schools and Departments of Journalism.

Most of the department's courses were in liberal arts and business, but 32 of the 120 credit hours were given in such subjects as News Writing, Law of the Press, Newspaper Practice, Criticism, News Reporting, Magazine Writing, Applied News Writing, and the History of Journalism. The department, housed on the fourth floor of Slocum Hall, also offered a two-year sequence known as the short course; it consisted of 60 hours of work in journalism, liberal arts, and business administration, but this was discontinued in 1923.

Simmons became acting head of the department on Wilson's death, and the curriculum did not change materially for several years. Student interest in the program flagged, and the teaching staff dwindled to three—Simmons, Paine, and Samuel Cahan, an instructor.

A concerned Chancellor Flint in the 1928–29 academic year mailed a questionnaire to journalism graduates, asking for a frank evaluation of the department. His questions included: What are the weaker elements of the course? Are you satisfied or disappointed with the course? Would you enroll in journalism if you were reentering college? How would you change the course? What suggestions for general reorganization would you make?

The dean of the College of Business Administration, Charles L. Raper, first learned about the questionnaire from the Syracuse *Journal* of January 21, 1929, in an article headlined "Hill Course is Being Probed." The dean regarded it as a "nasty shot" both at journalism and his college and said in a letter to the Chancellor that the writer had the "reputation of kicking against other courses" besides those in journalism. The dean asked whether those who received the questionnaire were qualified to give intelligent answers.

Dr. Flint replied that his questionnaire had been confidential and that the writer of the article had been guilty of a breach of ethics. The Chancellor also told the dean:

> I have been deeply interested in our Journalism situation, as you know, and have received suggestions in regard to it quite frequently during the past five years, both from newspaper men who were interested and from graduates in the course. I feel we should be looking around in every direction for two things: (1) for that rare article, a man who is qualified both from a faculty standpoint and from the newspaper standpoint with the necessary personality to promote work in this field beyond the stage that we have reached; (2) for individuals or organizations who would be interested in giving us either annually a sum for current support or an endowment for the development of this work.

In 1930 the American Society of Newspaper Editors (ASNE) released a study of journalism in American colleges and universities. A copy was sent to Vice Chancellor Graham in April 1930 by J. Roscoe Drummond, a 1924 graduate of the University who was to become a nationally syndicated columnist. Drummond underscored these statements in the study, made by an ASNE committee:

> The calling needs more journalists and fewer newspaper men;
>
> Systematic study of societal relations, of history, of economics, the basic sciences, languages, and a keen appreciation for cultural values is difficult at the close of a ten-hour day of reportorial leg work; and
>
> Shop practice . . . can be acquired in a year amid the rush and turmoil of a newspaper office.

The ASNE study went on to say: "It seems a mistake to push trade or school subjects into the academic work. Your committee thinks this is a point of paramount importance, transcending the urge for classification of existing departments of journalism." The report said twenty-one schools or departments of journalism had been examined by the ASNE committee. It listed Syracuse as having fifteen journalism majors and a total of ninety students registered in one or more courses. (Records of the registrar show that in the eight years since 1922, Syracuse University granted seventy-five journalism degrees.)

In his accompanying letter to Dr. Graham, Drummond wrote: "I should like to add that my experience as a student and as a practicing newspaper man conforms entirely to the recommendation of this report." The Vice Chancellor's answer was: "It has always seemed to me a pity that time and energy were wasted in such a school. and particularly that of Syracuse. I hope I may have the opportunity to make effective use of the report."

The ASNE report became a controversial one. *The New Republic* in its October 29 issue quoted Professor H. B. Rathbone of New York University as stating: "One is only able to say of this report that while in itself it was not definitely unfavorable to the teaching of journalism in colleges, remarks made after the report was submitted received rather widespread publicity and were somewhat distressing to those engaged in the teaching of journalism."

Wesley C. Clark was more blunt. Writing to University historian W. Freeman Galpin on February 20, 1958, when he was dean of the School of Journalism, Clark described the ASNE report as "a planned attack on the schools of journalism, like Missouri and Wisconsin, and aimed at advantaging the Pulitzer School (a graduate school at Columbia)." Clark added: "For years the report was a scandal and a joke in the profession and perhaps a decoration for Dean Ackerman, of Columbia, who wangled and lobbied for its substance."

By chance, in the same month that the ASNE document reached Syracuse the Reeves survey of the University was getting under way. The Reeves report devoted a page and a half to journalism. It said that at the time of the survey the department at Syracuse offered nine courses and a seminar, "all given by two of the younger faculty members ... and a course on the history of journalism given by an outside lecturer."

The report went on: "The survey staff found a considerable amount of criticism on the part of the University faculty regarding the standards of work that are maintained in journalism." It said the professional courses were "inferior in quality and largely devoted to the learning of routine and mechanical things that might much better be left for the newspaperman to pick up after he has entered the profession."

There was "a great deal of repetition in the courses that are now spread out over four years," it added. In conclusion, the Reeves group made these suggestions:

> 1. The head of the work should be a well-trained man with experience in the field of journalism,
>
> 2. The work should be made a school in the College of Liberal Arts, or an independent school. In either case it should not take students before they have reached their junior year. This will mean that the work in technical journalism will not begin before that time.
>
> 3. The staff as a whole should be strengthened as rapidly as is practicable considering the availability of funds and of properly trained men.

Elsewhere in their report the Reeves investigators were strongly of the opinion that the financial condition of the University did not warrant establishing a separate school unless it had an endowment of between $750,000 and $1 million.

Dean Raper refused to accept all of the Reeves criticism, but he admitted that the journalism department needed an improved staff. He vigorously opposed a transfer of the department to the College of Liberal Arts, where he said journalism would suffer.

Whatever the merits of the ASNE and the Reeves reports, there is no doubt that Chancellor Flint was influenced by both, as well as by the counsel of Vice Chancellor Graham and Burges Johnson, who came to the University in 1927 as director of public relations. Events moved slowly, however. The University trustees approved a major in journalism in the College of Liberal Arts in 1931. In the spring of 1932 steps were taken to discontinue the department of journalism in the College of Business Administration within two years.

Despite the Depression and larger classes in the department of journalism, Professor J. O. Simmons was able to report that in 1932 a greater proportion of students got jobs in their field than in the previous year. Probably one reason was that Simmons and his assistant, Samuel Cahan, sent students throughout Syracuse to gather news and write it up. Unless a certain amount of it got into print, the fledgling reporters were not eligible for graduation.

The Depression had another effect on his classes, Simmons said. As far as possible he dispensed with the use of textbooks, using current periodicals in their place.

And to keep himself current, Simmons spent part of his vacation taking a course required of all journalism majors, municipal finance.

Finally, in December 1933 the trustees agreed to the founding of a school "as an experiment in that division of education" (journalism), provided the executive committee approved, which it did in February 1934, saying however that the expense of a dean and new instructors in the proposed school must come from outside sources, not from regular University income.

Before the month was over M. Lyle Spencer was named dean of the new School of Journalism, with Burges Johnson as associate dean. Dean Spencer, born July 7, 1881, in Batesville, Mississippi, received his A.B. and M.A. degrees from Kentucky Wesleyan College, and his Ph.D. from the University of Chicago in 1910. He taught at Kentucky Wesleyan and other schools and worked on the Milwaukee *Journal* as reporter and later chief editorial writer, before becoming director and then dean of the School of Journalism at the University of Washington from 1919 to 1927, when he was named president of that university. He held the presidency until 1934 when, he said later, "I resigned to keep from being fired." Washington state politics were at work each time. In 1927 a Republican governor took office and fired first the trustees and then the president of UW. In 1934 the Democrats regained power in the state, and the new governor fired the trustees. Dean Spencer recalled: "I saw the handwriting on the wall and offered my resignation. It was gratefully accepted."

Johnson, born in Vermont, graduated from Amherst in 1899. After several years as a reporter on major newspapers including the *New York Evening Post,* he held editorial positions on the staffs of *Putnam's Magazine, Harper's,* and *Judge.* He turned to teaching in 1915 as a professor of English at Vassar College, where he was also director of public relations and wrote several books of prose and poetry.

Today Burges Johnson is perhaps best remembered on the campus for his role in perpetrating the "Saltine Warrior" hoax, which had many Syracusans believing the remains of an ancient Indian brave were dug up on the campus in 1931. He was capable of lending verisimilitude to a fictional but convincing narrative by digressing to mention a mythical Professor Hornswoggle who left Syracuse to join the forestry school at the University of Wisconsin, "where he is professor of tree climbing and barking up trees."

Johnson was endlessly inventive. In the same excavation that yielded up the Saltine Warrior, he told the *Daily Orange* in a straight-faced statement, members of the geology department discovered "the dinosaur teeth that now border our campus lawns." He added: "Too little has been said about that, and there has even been an absurd rumor abroad on the campus that they are meteors. Even a freshman must realize that meteors never fall in such regular arrangements, whereas dinosaur teeth are invariably in regular rows."

The first *Bulletin* of the new School of Journalism listed its original staff. In addition to Spencer and Johnson there were Leslie A. Nichols, assistant in journalism, and Paul Paine, lecturer.

When the University opened in the fall of 1934 the school was in Yates Castle, which also housed offices of various University and student publications. The school's philosophy was stated in the *Bulletin:* "The prescribed studies in the arts and sciences and the professional courses in the School of Journalism have three major purposes: to provide the broad cultural training that must be the possession of educated men and women, to offer instruction in standard newspaper practice on both the editorial and the business sides, and to present current journalistic problems in the light of their origin and development."

As the school grew there was a marked increase in its offerings: twenty-three courses were listed in the 1934–35 catalog, more than forty in 1941–42. Most of the increase resulted from the introduction of special four-year sequences in Advertising, Newspaper Management, Teacher Training, Editorial Practice, Radio, Magazine Practice, and Business Management. The school was accredited in 1934, and in 1938 graduate degrees, master of arts and master of science, were awarded for the first time.

Students seeking admission were told when interviewed that efficiency in study and success in practical newspaper work rested on sound preliminary training; this foundation required two years of college work with at least a "B" average. Thus the two degrees the school granted, bachelor of arts and bachelor of science, entailed considerable study in English, social sciences, and foreign languages during the freshman and sophomore years.

Dr. Frank Graves of the New York State Education Department deplored granting journalism students the bachelor of arts degree, saying in a January 16, 1934, letter to Chancellor Flint: "This degree is about the only evidence we have left of the survival of a broad cultural college course not leading to any profession. I strongly urge that highly specialized vocations and professional courses should not enjoy this time-honored degree." But the University continued to award it, firm in its belief that a journalist should have a broad cultural background.

Of a total of 120 hours needed for graduation from the School of Journalism, including the 60 hours required for admission, 32 to 34 were in journalism. These consisted of such specialties as Journalism as a Profession, News Writing, Principles of Journalism, Reporting, Copy Reading, Principles of Advertising, Typography, Law of the Press, History of Journalism, Newspaper Administration, and Editorial Writing. Electives included Community Newspaper, The Press and Public Affairs, Radio Publicity, Creative Writing, Magazine Writing, and Principles of High School Journalism.

Improvements in the curriculum were matched by new resources in the school, including the Frederic W. Goudy Typographic Laboratory, named for the internationally known designer of type who made a gift to the University of the type used in his laboratory in Marlboro, New York.

Beginning in 1936 the school housed the offices of several press organizations, adding much "to the prestige and usefulness of the school," as Dean Clark put it. The groups included the New York State Publishers Association, representing the daily newspapers in the state; the New York Press Association, representing 300 state weeklies; and the Empire State School Press Association, an organization of 200 to 300 high school publications advisers. Dean Spencer and Professor Douglass W. Miller founded ESSPA, which still meets in annual convention and workshop at Syracuse and is credited with being a fruitful source for recruitment. For the newspaper publishers, the residency at Syracuse was to continue for nearly half a century.

The school also housed the New York State Society of Newspaper Editors and the Advertising Managers Bureau of the state dailies.

Dean Spencer's review of the first year of the school showed 181 students, a record number and one he considered an auspicious beginning. He added, however, that it might be "almost too auspicious"—increased registration at the junior and senior levels would require large investments in equipment and faculty. These were imperative if the school was to maintain its prestige, he told the Chancellor in his report for 1934–35.

Along with its academic responsibilities, the school had other duties assigned to it by the administration. Among them were supervision of student publications and the Office of Public Relations. Some thought the basic reason Burges Johnson was brought to the campus in 1927 was to put him in charge of publicity and public relations, although at the time Dr. Flint said little to him about the duties of that office.

Johnson made his own policy. In general he was responsible for all relations between the University and the outside press, for editorial and publication control over official University publications, and for dealings with student publications. As his office grew, new duties were assumed and some old ones dropped or transferred. Soon the Office of Public Relations became a clearinghouse for what Johnson called a "steady procession of small items and inquiries." Kenneth G. Bartlett, one of Johnson's successors-to-be, described his own 1960s position as vice president and dean of public affairs as "vice president for everything else." In that way not much had changed in forty years.

Among Johnson's major tasks were editing and publishing the general University catalog, seventeen college bulletins, and the student directory. He also handled the University's advertising and compilation of a University calendar, and he provided news stories and photographs to the press. He kept in touch with alumni, students, and faculty, as well as with prominent or influential people and institutions throughout the city, state, and nation. His itinerary included rounds of dinners and receptions. He wrote a monthly column for the *Alumni News.* It was clear that the office would be unable to continue without eliminating some duties or increasing staff, and in June 1934 Burges Johnson resigned, partly because he failed to get additional staff and partly because of an attractive offer from Union College. Thus the University lost a man of talent, charm, and wit.

Among others who helped the school grow were J. Leonard Gorman '29, like Nichols an assistant in journalism; Bartlett, who taught radio from 1939; Clark, the future dean who joined the staff as an assistant professor of journalism in 1941; Goudy, who lectured on typographic design from 1939 to 1942; and Miller, who was acting dean during Spencer's absence in 1937 and two years later was named professor of journalism and assistant to the dean.

A 1934 journalism graduate, Arlene LaRue, columnist and former women's editor of the Syracuse *Herald-Journal,* deplores use of the word *communicators* for newspaper reporters and editors, authors, radio, television, public relations, or advertising people and, in general, those who use words professionally. But what other single word is there for men and women in such classifications? Says Miss LaRue: "I was, I am a reporter—or a columnist, if you will. A communicator? Never!" Nevertheless, many a noted person in the world of words is a Syracuse alum. Graduates from the Flint-Graham era fanned out from the campus to join newspapers, magazines, and wire services, write books, or otherwise make distinguished careers for themselves in public communications.

One of the earliest to gain national fame was (James) Roscoe Drummond '24, who became a syndicated Washington columnist after a long career with the *Christian Science Monitor.*

Drew Middleton graduated in 1935 but did not receive his degree until 1941 because he had failed a typing test. Despite that handicap he joined the Associated Press and later rose rapidly on the *New York Times,* serving as Moscow and Berlin correspondent among other major assignments.

Robert R. Booth '25 became treasurer of the Associated Press.

Frederick G. Vosburgh '25 went from the Syracuse newspapers to the Associated Press to the *National Geographic,* rising through the editorial ranks of that magazine and into a place on the board of the parent National Geographic Society.

Cecilia Barber Martin '26 went from commercial to combat photography. In 1941, before the United States entered World War II, she won a George Arents Pioneer Medal. "You were the first woman photographer to be on the scene of battle in England," her Arents citation read.

Ellis M. Haller '37 worked on Syracuse and Watertown papers, then became White House correspondent for the *Wall Street Journal* and assistant managing editor of *U.S. News & World Report.*

Kalman B. Druck '36 headed the Harshe-Rotman-Druck public relations firm in New York City.

Chester B. Hansen '39 became an aide to "the soldier's general," Omar N. Bradley, who credited the former *Daily Orange* editor with helping him to write his World War II memoirs, *A Soldier's Story* (Holt, 1951), which drew on Hansen's 300,000-word wartime diary.

Jess Stearn '36 is the author of popular nonfiction books.

Stanley Edgar Hyman '40 was a noted literary critic. His wife, Shirley Jackson '40, was the distinguished writer of short stories and novels.

John D. MacDonald '38 is the prolific author of the Travis McGee books and other suspense novels.

The list is long and, as the School of Journalism grew and evolved into the Newhouse School, was to get much, much longer.

Daily Orange staffers learn what "going to press" meant in earlier days as Dean M. Lyle Spencer, right, observes. The students, from left, are Barbara Pritchard '38, Estella Holdsworth '37, William Evans '37, and Kalman Druck '36.

Dean Spencer reorganized the public relations area as the Bureau of Public Information, familiarly known as BPI, in the fall of 1934 and directed it himself. Miller, who had taught journalism at Ohio Wesleyan and was in charge of the news service there, took over BPI in 1937.

The bureau became an efficient news and public relations organization, but even the best of shops stumbles now and again. BPI's blunder was a classic, involving Chancellor Flint and two other distinguished churchmen.

On December 8, 1935, a Sunday, the University awarded honorary degrees to Ivan Lee Holt of St. Louis, president of the Federal Council of Churches of Christ in America, and Dr. Richard Roberts of Toronto, moderator of the United Church of Canada. BPI duly sent out a press release to mark the event, at which one of the men received a doctor of letters degree and the other a doctor of sacred theology.

Unfortunately that is not what the release said, as was pointed out by James R. Joy, editor of *The Christian Advocate,* a national weekly. The news release said Roberts received a doctor of *scared* theology. Joy wrote to Dr. Flint: "This is a new thing in honorary degrees, but I think it is a very proper idea."

The Chancellor readily forgave the public information people the typographical error; he called that "blundering, not the truth—not for the gentlemen concerned this time—but it's a suggestion for some we know."

Dr. Flint, however, could not overlook a second, more embarrassing error. He added in his note to the editor: "I am peeved to find they mixed the degrees in sending the item." It was *Holt,* not Roberts, who received the sacred theology degree.

The Chancellor also let BPI know of his displeasure. Dean Spencer replied to the Chancellor's memorandum with one of his own. In the course of it he did not hesitate to give Dr. Flint a lesson in press relations and a reminder that a news bureau should be taken into the confidence of the administration and should have a role in planning a major event. The dean wrote in part:

> You told me confidentially last summer about this particular convocation. I remarked at the time that it offered opportunity for widespread and invaluable publicity for Syracuse in national religious publications. But that was the last and only word I had about the convocation until Friday afternoon, when the Vice Chancellor telephoned me that the most important convocation of the year was to be held the Sunday following. . . . If L. or I could have had the story a week before, we should have sent it to the New York papers, the *Christian Science Monitor,* and to every religious publication in the United States. . . . As it is, the degrees have been granted, this week's papers are on the press, the news cannot get in until next week, and at that time it will be worth only a few lines.
>
> L. is so depressed over the whole affair that I find his resignation on my desk this morning, a copy of which I see he has sent to you. I do not think he really expects me to accept it. But his action indicates something of how he feels, that the administration has not shown enough confidence in him to give him the advance news and is in effect expecting the Bureau of Public Information to make brick with an insufficiency of straw.

The forthright professionalism Dean Spencer exhibited in his note to the Chancellor was evident in many ways. Another was in the shirtsleeves attitude he took in workshops for future journalists. He taught a number of classes, including magazine article writing and magazine editing and publishing. One such class, in 1937, served as the editorial board for *The Syracusan* magazine. Members met for two hours each week to solve editing and production problems without benefit of textbooks, making suggestions and criticism in a professional but informal atmosphere. Dean Spencer told the first meeting of the workshop: "We are meeting not as student and instructor but as an editorial board for *The Syracusan*. Smoke if you want to. Take off your coats. Put your feet on the table. I'm interested not in appearances but ideas."

Also in 1937 he went to Egypt and established a school of journalism at the American University in Cairo. While there he studied Middle East communications and taught for five months.

He was the author of two standard textbooks on journalism, *News Writing* and *Editorial Writing*. In the latter he deplored "the swivel-neck editorial writer who expects salary or recognition in return for daily utterances of silken sayings he thinks his employer wants."

The tough-minded concern for quality Dean Spencer brought to the fledgling school raised it to national eminence. By 1942 the School of Journalism was among the top three of its kind in the country, according to Chancellor Graham. He reported to the board of trustees on June 5 that year: "There are some 542 institutions which offer instruction in journalism in the United States and out of that number 32 institutions have been admitted into the American Association of Schools and Departments of Journalism; and our school is one of that number. By common consent I think there are three at the top—Northwestern, Minnesota, and Syracuse."

Dr. Graham listed a number of distinguished graduates of the school and concluded: "Some of us were rather skeptical when the School of Journalism was first talked of, but I think the way Dean Spencer has organized it and carried it on has removed all doubts and questions that we ever had. It is one of the strongest units now in the University."

14

Home Economics

Eu-then-ics n. from the Greek, plenty, prosperity, well-being. The science of bettering the environment or living conditions, as for improvement of the race.
—*New Century Dictionary, 1948*

EUTHENICS, ALTHOUGH LITTLE HEARD TODAY, was a word to be reckoned with in the second quarter of the century, when Canadian-born Annie Louise Macleod was dean of what is now the College for Human Development.

Miss Macleod joined Syracuse after fourteen years at Vassar College, where she had been professor of chemistry and euthenics. On March 1, 1938, a decade after she became dean, her faculty honored her at the annual Orchid Dinner of the college by establishing the Annie Louise Macleod Euthenics Fund. Edith H. Nason, professor of foods and nutrition, reading the citation that went with the award, noted that in 10 years enrollment in the college rose from 161 to 402 and that the number of faculty grew from 6 to 20. Dr. Nason went on: "We realized that of more value to you than a personal gift would be one that would advance the arts of living as expressed by the word *euthenics*. About the first thing a freshman hears from you is a definition of euthenics. ... One of your former students has written of you 'Dean Macleod has given her students a design for living. She has shown them the joys and deep happiness to be gained from a life that has many worthy interests.' We of the faculty agree with this representative student. We find in you the best illustration of euthenics. You are Euthenia par examplar."

Dean Macleod herself had defined the word at the first Euthenics Conference, held at Syracuse University October 15, 1928. It is the science of efficient living, she said, and "directs attention primarily to the study of the controllable environment and the need for, and the possibilities of, its adaptation for the improvement of the individual and of the race. It places culture in its proper perspective as a means toward the enrichment of life, not an end in itself."

To modern ears this has a more acceptable sound than the opinion expressed by William Nottingham, a staunch but old-fashioned supporter of home economics. Dr. Nottingham, an 1876 graduate of the University who earned his Ph.D. the following year, a trustee from 1892 to 1902 when he became a member of the State Board of Regents, and a prominent Syracuse lawyer, had helped plan the home economics program and had this to say about it: "I should like to require every young woman in the University to pursue this course for at least one year. There would be more happy homes and fewer divorces." Dr. Nottingham did not live quite long enough to see the program become a full-fledged college. He died in January 1921.

The college was born in the fall of 1918 as the Department of Home Economics in the College of Agriculture with Florence E. S. Knapp as director. In 1919 and 1920 Chancellor Day referred to it variously as the School of Domestic Economy, the School of Home Economics, and the School of Domestic Science, according to minutes of the board of trustees. Then on April 29, 1921, the board's executive committee recommended "that the name of the School of Domestic Economy shall be changed to the College of Home Economics." On June 10 the full board adopted the recommendation and approved Dr. Day's nomination of Florence Knapp as dean.

The college was described at that time as "the only institution of its kind in the state chartered as a college by the Board of Regents."

Dean Knapp, an honors graduate of Cortland (New York) Normal School, did postgraduate work at Cornell and Columbia universities. As principal of the Fairmount School west of Syracuse, she introduced courses in domestic science and manual training. She drafted a resolution from the New York State Grange asking the legislature to provide for the teaching of agriculture in public schools.

She and her husband, Philip Schuyler Knapp (they married soon after her graduation from Cortland) were from historic stock. He was a descendant of Philip Schuyler, a Revolutionary War general. She was descended from Ebenezer Hancock, librarian of Harvard University and brother of John Hancock, signer of the Declaration of Independence.

Home Economics was first listed in the *Bulletin* as a college in 1921–22. The description said in part: "Through its connection with the regular work of the College of Liberal Arts, the College of Fine Arts, Teachers College, the College of Agriculture and the University Hospital, it offers practical and professional courses in vocational instruction for women. Women regularly enrolled in the several colleges of the University may elect special work in Home Economics as part of their chosen course."

The *Bulletin* in a parenthetical description as late as 1930–31 referred to "A College for Women within Syracuse University" and defined its purpose as threefold:

> First, to provide a broad liberal education for young women, with a view to their peculiar responsibilities and dominant interests, to the end that they may live effectively and joyously, and so contribute to the welfare of the race.
>
> Second, provide training in those professions which offer women the widest opportunities, and in which an intimate knowledge of the needs of the home and of women and children are necessary background, such as institutional management, certain branches of public health work and organized social service, certain lines of business merchandising, journalism, advertising, educational work for public utilities and manufactures, banks and insurance companies.
>
> Third, to produce progressive-minded teachers who have added to a scientific and cultural background an understanding of the problems of modern society and who are fit to assume leadership in the field of women's education.

Fulfilling these laudable objectives was no mean task, particularly for a college founded in wartime and in a field in which such rapid progress was being made. Over the years there were changes in the curriculum to meet the broadening scope of the college.

Admission to the college in 1922, when Dr. Flint became Chancellor, required 15 units of high school credits—three each in English and foreign languages and one each in elementary algebra, plane geometry, history, and science, plus five electives.

Until 1929 students seeking the degree of bachelor of science followed approximately the same course of study. The freshman program consisted of 6 hours of English, 8 of chemistry, 3 of botany, 3 of zoology, 6 of cookery, 6 of clothing and design, and one each of hygiene and gym. The sophomore year entailed 6 hours of English or a foreign language, 6 of organic chemistry, 6 of sociology, 6 of cookery, 6 of clothing and design, 3 of home economics botany, and 3 of physiology.

Upperclass students specialized. In the general home economics program, called Group A, juniors had courses in history, economics, bacteriology, psychology, nutrition and dietetics, and clothing and design. Each was a 6-hour course except bacteriology, which was 8. The final year consisted of 6-hour courses in pedagogy, senior seminars in food and clothing, and household management, 2-hour courses in house design and decoration, architectural appreciation, business law and accounting, a one-hour course in elocution, and 2 hours of electives.

The inclusion of subjects from the Colleges of Liberal Arts and Business Administration reflected a conviction that the students should have a well-rounded education. From the beginning there had been close and reciprocal cooperation between Home Economics and other colleges on the campus, enabling hundreds of women students from other parts of the University to elect Home Economics courses, as Dr. Nottingham had wished.

Juniors in the program in institutional management and dietetics—Group B—took courses in history, economics, bacteriology, psychology, institutional cookery, nutrition and dietetics, nursing practice and theory, and cafeteria practice. Seniors took physiological chemistry, chemistry of foods, institutional management, advanced nutrition and dietetics, a seminar on food and clothing, cafeteria practice, and 4 hours of electives.

Dressmaking and millinery, a program designated Group C but dropped as a special group by 1926, offered juniors history of fine arts, economics, bacteriology, psychology, textile chemistry, and children's clothing and design. Seniors took elocution, nutrition and dietetics, seminars on food and clothing, shoproom theory and practice, elementary millinery, and 4 hours of electives.

In the teachers course, Group D, juniors took history of education, principles of education, economics, bacteriology, psychology, nutrition and dietetics, educational psychology, seminars on food and clothing, household management, practice teaching, and elocution. A graduate in this program received a B.S. degree plus a teaching certificate.

By the end of 1924 Dean Knapp reported that the college was no longer in the experimental stage. Its graduates were in demand as teachers, cafeteria managers, dietitians, interior decorators, and textile experts. Not one was earning less than $1,200 a year to start.

Mrs. Knapp had long been interested in politics. In 1911 she was elected district superintendent for schools for Onondaga County, the only public elective office then open to women, and served for five years. During the first world war she was an associate director of food conservation for the state. With the adoption of women's suffrage she became increasingly involved and was a delegate to the 1920 and 1924 Republican national conventions. In 1924 she campaigned for secretary of state of New York and, at age forty-nine, was elected by a plurality of more than 130,000. The following January 1 she was sworn in as the first woman to hold an elective position in the state government.

Florence Knapp kept the title of dean and planned eventually to resume full-time direction of the college. But after she completed her two-year term as secretary of state (1925–26), charges of misuse of state funds were brought against her, and she was convicted on a count of grand larceny. She served a 30-day term in the Albany County Jail after her sentencing on September 4, 1928. She had resigned as dean in February of that year. Sentencing was delayed several months, reportedly for health reasons. On October 26, 1949, she died in Marcy State Hospital, near Utica, at the age of 75.

Chancellor Flint took semipublic notice of the Knapp case in separate memoranda to the Home Economics students and faculty on February 13, 1928, the day the executive committee of the board of trustees accepted her resignation as dean, but he referred only to "Mrs. Knapp's absence in Albany." In resigning, she had written: "In full knowledge of my own integrity, and in justice to the University, I place my resignation in your hands until such time that my good name is fully cleared before the world."

To the students Dr. Flint said, in part: "The past few months have been somewhat distressing to all of us. ... Our present plan is to considerably enlarge and enrich the program next fall."

To the faculty he wrote: "May I suggest that you be unusually attentive and helpful to the students, who, like yourselves, have been upset by the past few months' experience, following up Mrs. Knapp's absence in Albany. Keep them cheered up; promote the esprit de corps; encourage them; suppress anything discouraging or disconcerting, and promote confidence and enthusiasm. Let us close the year triumphantly."

The executive committee authorized Dr. Flint "to complete negotiations with Miss Annie Louise Macleod, and in September of 1928 she began her twenty-year tenure as dean of the college.

Miss Macleod was born in Economy, Nova Scotia, and earned her bachelor's, master's and Ph.D. degrees at McGill University, Montreal. She taught chemistry at McGill, Barnard, and Bryn Mawr before she joined the Vassar faculty.

She was the author of three books, *Chemistry for Nurses* (1920), *Vital Factors in Foods* (with Carlton Ellis, 1922), and, after she joined Syracuse,

Annie Louise Macleod, dean, College of Home Economics, 1928–1949. Photograph © Bachrach.

Chemistry and Cookery (with Edith H. Nason, 1929). She had become a consulting editor on euthenics for the McGraw-Hill Publishing Company in 1924 while at Vassar and continued that association at Syracuse. In 1934 she was elected a fellow of the American Association for the Advancement of Science.

Within a year of her arrival Dean Macleod outlined her philosophy about the College of Home Economics. This was that students in the freshman and sophomore years should take fundamental courses in English, psychology, economics, sociology, and public speaking, with possible electives in language, a natural science, or citizenship. Such a program paralleled to some degree that of the College of Liberal Arts but with a different approach. Home Economics students would use the knowledge obtained to apply to problems of the home. For example, a course in chemistry would help a person become a better cook, and physiology was related to nutrition and health. The upperclass years would be devoted to specialization in such areas as child care, household management, and applied arts, but there would still be time for electives in other colleges on the campus. The social sciences were suggested as electives, with a focus on social adjustment of the individual in the family and the community.

In a letter to Chancellor Flint dated December 19, 1928, which included her recommendations for reorganization, Dean Macleod said:

> There has been no notable advance in the education of women during the last 50 years. The colleges for women occupy themselves with the cultural development of their students on the assumption that what I may call their sociological development, preparation for home and family responsibilities, is adequately provided elsewhere, though where else it would be difficult to say. An equally pernicious assumption made at the same time is that study of the practical problems of life is not cultural. If this educational tradition is maintained how can we expect successful homes, and without successful homes what of the future of the race?
>
> The departments and schools of home economics ... have concentrated almost entirely upon matters of physical well-being, forgetting apparently that the life is more than meat. There has been too often a certain tenuousness about their intellectual atmosphere that failed to attract the great body of students with at least a pretense of desire for culture. Even in the high schools we find a certain social distinction clinging to the 'college preparatory course' as opposed to the home economics courses which is disastrous to the latter. The result in school and college alike has been to divert the most alert and ambitious girls from any consideration of the household as a suitable field for study and research. Indeed the progress in home economics (and there has been

> tremendous progress) has been due almost entirely to the vocational motivation given to the subject and the inspiring example of the successful home economics women in business.
>
> A new education for women must be developed, which will take account not only of the great cultures of the past but also of present-day conditions and of the fact that young women of this generation will be the mothers and teachers of the next.

Putting her philosophy into practice, Dean Macleod gradually reorganized the existing group programs and introduced others.

The first step was taken in 1929 with four restructured and renamed programs. The first was Applied Arts, in which general courses were given in the selection of clothing for the student and her family from an artistic, social, and economic point of view: where and how to buy; the relation of the clothing budget to other expenses; and the relation of clothes to good appearance. Students seeking professional training would supplement the general courses with more specialized instruction in techniques of clothing construction and design.

Foods and Nutrition was reorganized next. This program dealt with the science and technique of food selection and the care and preparation of meals. At the advanced level it provided professional training for teachers, hospital dietitians, and nutrition and food specialists.

Institutional Economy, the program in charge of the cafeteria in the basement of Slocum Hall, prepared students for managerial positions in tea rooms, hotels, cafeterias, clubs, college dormitories, hospitals, and other types of institutions.

A new area, Household Techniques, aimed at giving basic courses in fundamental laws of physics, with emphasis on their application to household problems.

The University cafeteria was organized in 1919, when the college was still a department in the College of Agriculture. Dean Knapp said of it later: "The object was to develop the spirit of hospitality by making every student realize that the training received would fit her to perform the duties of a hostess in her own home. Efficiency in service, she was taught, was not only a part of her class problem, but a real mark of culture."

By 1931, under Florence Quast, assistant professor of institutional economics, the cafeteria was feeding 550 student meals a day. It also served other members of the University community.

Those were hard times, and it seemed appropriate that the members of the board of trustees, after a meeting at which they often

College of Home Economics Advanced Food Laboratory, Slocum Hall.

heard discouraging news about the University's budget, adjourned for lunch to the cafeteria in Slocum Hall instead of to more sumptuous surroundings.

Miss Quast, who earned her master of science degree at the University of Washington, described how she and her staff—many of them students—during "the emergency of this present economic depression" provided meals that were "not only scientifically adequate but cheap and attractive." She said: "We have been studying our average customer, and find that breakfast costs him 20¢, lunch 37¢, and dinner 42¢." A penny less than a dollar a day.

For reporters she listed the quantities of food the cafeteria served during the school year, September to June—ten tons of fresh meat; twenty tons of fresh vegetables, including twelve tons of potatoes and two and a half tons of onions; nearly 2,000 cans of vegetables; a ton and a half of butter; more than 3,000 dozen eggs; 1,200 pounds of cheese; 7,000 gallons of milk; 1,200 gallons of ice cream; forty barrels of flour; 250 pounds each of prunes and raisins; sixty gallons of pickles; 3,000 loaves of bread; 8,000 tea bags; 1,200 pounds of coffee; a ton of salt, and three and a quarter tons of sugar. Her customers used about 160,000 paper napkins.

The word *euthenics* kept popping up. In 1930 the team headed by Floyd W. Reeves of the University of Chicago that surveyed Syracuse took note of Dean Macleod's curriculum changes. Its report said: "The curriculums have been completely revised recently so that the program now represents the point of view of the present administration which is relatively new." But the Reeves group questioned the implications of the legend, "A College for Women Within Syracuse University," saying it was not entirely clear. Quoting the first paragraph of the statement of purposes of the college—"to provide a broad liberal education for young women"—the team said: "This can hardly be interpreted as the statement of the function of a professional college. The survey staff is of the opinion that this would be more appropriate as the aim of a college of liberal arts than of a professional college in home economics."

The Reeves report then went on: "The curriculum in euthenics appears to have much to commend it. In the opinion of the survey staff it should be a part of the program of the College of Liberal Arts. The College of Home Economics may well find its largest opportunity in Syracuse University in making this course possible."

In an article in the April–May 1938 Issue of the *Alumni News* Dean Macleod wrote:

> In the plainest of terms, euthenics is to living what eugenics is to breeding. The euthenicist agrees that good inheritance is of vast importance, and then says given whatever inheritance we have, how can we make the most of ourselves? How, to use a good old-fashioned phrase, can we better ourselves? Also, how can we better our families, our community, our race? It is a big word, euthenics, and a big conception, measuring progress in terms of human lives.
>
> In terms of education, euthenics is a program of studies, not a single subject. It covers all that the arts and sciences have to contribute to the improvement of living conditions and, by this means, to the improvement of mankind. There is scarcely a subject in a liberal curriculum which has no contribution to offer, but since right living, like charity, begins at home, euthenics might reasonably begin with that body of subject matter now commonly assigned Home Economics.
>
> The Home Economics of the present day has gone a long way beyond its old limitation to the skills connected with food, shelter and clothing. The skills have their place—what art can be divorced from its technique?—but standards are more important than skills. The emphasis on Home Economics today is on the understanding of basic facts on which standards may be formed. Knowledge of child care, of the management

College of Home Economics Clothing Laboratory, Slocum Hall.

> problems of a home, of how to buy food, textiles, clothing, and equipment economically and satisfactorily are more necessary in these days of economic uncertainty than they were in the comparatively stable lives of our grandmothers.

In the University archives is a copy of a circular Dean Macleod sent to high school principals about 1934 listing home economics students she recommended as being ready to teach. Her covering letter said it was significant "that many more high school teachers active today in New York State, outside the metropolitan area, were trained at Syracuse University than at any other New York State college or university." The principals were referred to the University's Teachers Placement Bureau for further information.

The potential teachers were not named but were described in such phrases as: "Tall, slender, dark hair ... A stimulating and convincing teacher" and "Gently bred, well mannered. ... Exceptionally skillful in design and clothing construction" and "Sparkling brown eyes, well built, gracious and poised . . . capable in art and clothing." All of them, one might be sure, fitted the description of "progressive-minded teachers" with "an understanding of the problems of modern society," as outlined in the college's statement of purposes.

Dean Macleod and Chancellor Flint corresponded frequently, judging by examples in the archives, and when Dr. Flint left to become a bishop she continued that tradition with Vice Chancellor (soon to be Acting Chancellor and then Chancellor) William Pratt Graham. Michael O. Sawyer, whose student days overlapped the last of the Graham years, remembers the late Chancellor as an austere presence, erect and dignified in black coat and black homburg, polite but remote, making his way magisterially across the campus. Dr. Sawyer, as Dr. Graham did, moved from the ranks of student to faculty member to Vice Chancellor. He said his recollection was that one did not *speak* to Dr. Graham. Even if one were more than a student, he said, one *wrote* to him, and Dr. Graham replied. More often than not he drafted his reply with a worn-down pencil and in slanting angular script, and his secretary later typed it.

A 200-word letter to Dr. Graham dated August 8, 1936, illustrates the caution with which one dean spent a dollar in those Depression-wracked days. Dean Macleod wrote that her secretary was going on vacation and that a half-time substitute could be hired for one week at a cost of $12, "if you agree." Dr. Graham, then Acting Chancellor, replied, "by all means employ her."

Sometimes the Chancellor wrote first, and it is clear that the spunky Dean Macleod didn't hesitate to give him back as good as she got. It also appears from their exchanges that just beneath the words lay wit, good humor, and mutual appreciation.

Two examples from 1939 show Annie Macleod replying spiritedly in the matter of a forbidden bridge party and the question of whether it was safe to eat what was served in the cafeteria.

On March 8 Dr. Graham wrote:

> My dear Dean Macleod:
>
> A few weeks ago you held a bridge party in Slocum Hall for the purpose of raising money.
>
> When the matter came to my attention, plans had gone so far that I did not wish to cause embarrassment by raising a question.
>
> Now that a reasonable time has elapsed, I wish to point out that the holding of bridge parties in any of our buildings is contrary to University policy.

> On page 10 of the Student Desk Book you will find rule #5. "No sales, tag days, or other forms of 'fund raising' activity are permitted in the University buildings or on the campus."

Dr. Graham signed the note to Miss Macleod "Yours very sincerely" and at the bottom listed four other deans to whom copies were being sent. One might almost suppose it was at someone else's urging that he had raised the matter.

Dean Macleod replied promptly on March 9:

> Referring to your letter of March 8th I am much distressed if the University ruling has inadvertently been broken.
>
> I was aware that students might not carry on any money making activities in the buildings but the bridge party to which you refer was entirely an alumnae activity, and I did not realize there could be any objection to their using this space on Saturday afternoon. The question of money was very much subordinate to our desire to encourage friendly feeling among the alumnae of having them meet here. On the other hand, a party of that sort involves so much labor that it would not be possible to carry it on without charge.

A little more than two months later Dr. Graham had occasion to address the dean again, saying on May 19:

> Complaints have been made relative to the Cafeteria which touch the care used in preparing food and more particularly the attitude with which complaints are received.
>
> Particles of glass have been found in the food. Crawling things have been found in the salad. Complaints are received with an indifferent or hostile attitude. Conditions at Syracuse are contrasted with those at Cornell to the disadvantage of our College of Home Economics.
>
> How serious the situation is I, of course, do not know. But I felt that you should be told that complaints have been received.

Dean Macleod replied, not as promptly this time, on May 27:

> I wish to thank you for your letter of May 19th, with regard to the cafeteria. It is always wholesome for us to know that there are a few complaints to balance the many compliments that we have received—otherwise we might be in danger of being too smug.
>
> I was unaware that any one was able to make an unfavorable com-

> parison of Syracuse with Cornell in spite of the fact that Cornell has the advantage of running a cafeteria which is chronically in the "red."
>
> I had heard that a single aphid had been discovered on a lettuce leave [sic]—a fact that was very much regretted by everyone concerned. I was not aware that we were incorporating ground glass in the food. Complaints such as these are unquestionably very serious. It seems to me that the whole matter should be referred to Dr. Hickernell as a matter of importance in the general health of both students and faculty.

Presumably no threat was found to the health of the cafeteria's customers who, it must be remembered, included members of the board of trustees. At least there is no record of further complaints at the Chancellor's level.

Another indication of the dean's sense of humor could be seen in the names of her two English bulldogs, with whom she sat for an informal portrait in 1939. She called them Cherry Bounce and Drinkmore Martini.

Throughout the thirties Dean Macleod reorganized courses and introduced two new sequences. Her cherished euthenics program, and a more modern version of the earlier Home Economics program (Group A), continued to provide a cultural education for the general student. Chemistry, cookery, clothing selection, design, euthenics, child care, social adjustment, nutrition, physics, and household technology were the major required courses. Electives, chiefly from Liberal Arts, included English, literature, psychology, and the social sciences.

A new Group B was the teacher-training sequence. Among the required courses were child hygiene, home nursing, household management, foods or clothing, child psychology, Liberal Arts electives, and the courses in education needed for eventual certification for teaching.

With varying requirements but with basic Home Economics subjects were Group C (Institutional Economics); Group D (Foods and Nutrition); Group E (Home Economics in Business); Group F (Applied Arts); Group G (Pre-Professional Social Work); Group H (Child Care); Group I (Journalism); and, by 1941, Fashion Design and Merchandising.

Thus by the end of the administration of Chancellor Graham, Deans Knapp and Macleod had put into operation curricula that kept pace with the increasing demand by women students for an education both specialized and cultural that also widened opportunities for women seeking business careers. One result of their work was a steady growth in enrollment, particularly after 1930. When Chancellor Flint became head of the University, the still-young college had 292 students. The Depression brought a decline, and in 1930 a low of 126 was reached. Thereafter enrollment increased steadily, and in September 1941 stood at 467. The total does not include the many students from other parts of the University who elected the increasingly popular courses in the college.

A skilled faculty also contributed to the prestige that the college was gaining locally and nationally. In 1922 there were twelve on the teaching staff, all instructors. When the United States entered World War II, Dean Macleod headed a faculty of twenty-six including Anne Bourquin, professor of nutrition; Edna Bryte, associate professor of applied arts; Frederica Carlton, associate professor of home economics; Evelyn Herrington, professor of home economics education; and Ethel Trautman, professor of clothing.

Dean Macleod retired in June 1948. Ten years after that the Annie Louise Macleod Euthenics Fund came full circle when the committee administering it unveiled an oil portrait by A. Henry Nordhausen, a New York artist who painted many prominent Syracusans. Students, alumnae, administrators, and past and current faculty members attended the unveiling at a reception in Slocum Hall. Miss Macleod's health had not been good when the fund commissioned the portrait in 1947, so Nordhausen went to Sarasota, Florida, where she was living in retirement, to complete his study of the dean in her academic robes.

But his improvised studio at the New Terrace Hotel had no suitable place for her to sit. Later artist and subject were amused to recall that Nordhausen, aware of the dean's pride in her Scottish ancestry, had rigged a dais for her from empty Scotch whisky cases found in the cellar.

The portrait is in the Syracuse University collection.

15

The Maxwell School of Citizenship and Public Affairs

I have been intending [for] some time to establish a chair of "United States Citizenship" in Syracuse University. The need of endowment, however, is so pressing now that I have decided to enlarge the gift to $500,000 and found and endow a "School of Citizenship."

—George H. Maxwell to Chancellor Flint, October 11, 1923

THOSE WHO ENTER MAXWELL HALL BY THE EAST DOOR see on the wall behind a statue of George Washington these words inscribed in gold:

> We will ever strive for the ideals and sacred things of the city, both alone and with many; we will unceasingly seek to quicken the sense of public duty; we will revere and obey the city's laws; we will transmit this city not only not less, but greater, better and more beautiful than it was transmitted to us.

These sentiments, from the oath of the Athenian city-state, reflect the aims and purposes of the Maxwell School's first dean, Dr. William E. Mosher. Many have said the quotation also fits the academic objectives of Syracuse University, recalling that Dr. Daniel Steele, the first ex-

George Holmes Maxwell, portrait by Stephen Seymour Thomas.

ecutive of the University, had pledged the faculty to train and graduate "American citizens competent to discharge the duties of citizenship."

George Holmes Maxwell, a Boston attorney and financier and an alumnus and trustee of Syracuse University, first met Chancellor Flint in 1922. Dr. Flint recalled later that at their meeting Maxwell spoke of the need for more University scholarships. Then, on October 11, 1923, he wrote to the Chancellor: "As I told you last year, I have been intending [for] some time to establish a chair of 'United States Citizenship' in Syracuse University. The need of endowment, however, is so pressing now that I have decided to enlarge the gift to $500,000 and found and endow a 'School of Citizenship'—which will gather in quite a number of subjects and hence carry the salaries of several professors and thereby relieve the University to that extent."

Maxwell, born at Woodstock, New York, April 16, 1864, was the son of the Reverend Joseph and Elizabeth (Holmes) Maxwell. The family moved to Fayetteville, New York, a few miles east of Syracuse, when the father became pastor of the Methodist Church in the village. Among George Maxwell's boyhood companions was Levi S. Chapman, whose later influence stimulated Maxwell's donations to the University. Maxwell matriculated at Syracuse in 1884 and Chapman the following year. Although they were members of different fraternities, their friendship grew stronger with the passing years. A successful attorney, Maxwell became wealthy as an inventor, manufacturer, and financier. He frequently found time to revisit his alma mater. His loyalty to the University led Chancellor Day to ask him to become a trustee, a position he held until his death September 16, 1932, in Pasadena, California.

In 1916, as his fortune grew, Maxwell founded the Maxwell Benevolence Fund and through it made grants to many charitable and educational institutions. When the United States entered World War I in 1917, his interest in good citizenship was accentuated and more and more of his philanthropy centered on training in that field.

His objective was expressed in a letter he wrote to the president of Boston University, one of the recipients of his philanthropy, in the fall of 1918: "My idea is to develop a body of leaders, especially trained in United States citizenship, who will go out through this country as educators, statesmen, financiers, business men, etc., to upbuild the foundations and bulwarks of citizenship intellectually and patriotically, so that the masses of the people may come to have a generally disseminated knowledge of the value, importance, and distinctiveness of their United States citizenship."

In 1926, after the school at Syracuse had been started, he amplified these ideas in a letter to Dr. Frederick M. Davenport. His gift to Boston University, he wrote, "was occasioned by the war which forcibly demonstrated the general ignorance among the masses of our history, the principles of our government, its aims and safeguards. The blind patriotism of the young people was pathetic. Almost every strenuous agitator found a large following. This was simply because the crowd did not have the mooring or background of actual knowledge of what we are, have been, and should stand for. So I started this Chair of Citizenship."

After he made his $500,000 pledge to Dr. Flint, Maxwell became aware of the inroads made by federal taxes on his many philanthropies. He determined to concentrate his gifts, mainly on a single institution, and asked his old friend Levi Chapman if he could form a corporation under New York State law that would avert interference with the proposed School of Citizenship at Syracuse. Chapman suggested a holding corporation, and in March 1924 the North American Holding Corporation succeeded the Maxwell Benevolence Fund. The original directors were Mr. and Mrs. George H. Maxwell, Bishop Frederick D. Leete of the Methodist Church, and Chapman. In accordance with its charter, the directors were to make grants to corporations or community chests operated for religious, charitable, educational, scientific, or literary purposes.

Spadework for the Maxwell School quickly followed the birth of the holding corporation, along with many trips and much correspondence among Maxwell, Chapman, and the Chancellor. Alert to possibilities for leadership of the new school, Dr. Flint called Maxwell's attention to Dr. Frederick Morgan Davenport, then a rising educator and prominent political leader in New York State. A graduate of Wesleyan University, Davenport had received his doctorate at Columbia University. He then became professor of law and politics at Hamilton College. Later he was elected state senator from Oneida County and subsequently served four years in Congress as Republican representative from the 33rd New York Congressional District. With the advent of the New Deal, President Franklin D. Roosevelt appointed him chairman of the Federal Personnel Board.

It was while Davenport was in the state senate that Dr. Flint spoke of him to Maxwell. At about the same time, late December 1923, the Chancellor wrote to Davenport to enlist his interest and counsel. He expressed his own view that the proposed school influence and serve all the other University schools and colleges. To achieve this objective, he said, Syracuse needed someone like Davenport who had the "right mixture of stable conservatism and sane progressiveness who could found a school which could make haste slowly." Then the Chancellor added, "I feel sure you represent what this man has in mind, although I do not believe there would be on his part for one minute any idea of control or limitation over the college he would endow."

The Chancellor was aware that Davenport had greater political ambitions but hoped he could be induced to return to academic life. Accordingly he offered him the deanship of the College of Liberal Arts, a key position whose incumbent would have the privilege of molding the foundations of the Maxwell School. And if that was not sufficient inducement in itself, there was the prospect of becoming the director or dean of citizenship. Then, for extra measure, the Chancellor intimated that the Maxwell School might number among its "divisions" the offices of the deans of men and women. Davenport replied that the offer promised a most inviting opportunity, and he would give it careful consideration. Finally, he wrote in April 1924 that in all justice to Syracuse University and himself he could not be tied to an office that excluded other personal interests. Nor, he continued, could he serve on the faculty although he would be willing to aid in the early organization of the school. Should Maxwell concur, he would talk soon with Raymond Fosdick, who exercised a voice over grants of the Rockefeller Foundation, about additional financial assistance. Maxwell agreed, and in early June 1924 Davenport assumed the role of counselor to the Maxwell School.

The inclusion of Davenport in the planning process led to a major modification of the goals articulated by Maxwell, according to an essay published for the fiftieth anniversary of the school by Peter J. Johnson, a Ph.D. candidate in history. Johnson wrote:

> Maxwell and Davenport differed in their hopes for the finished product of the school. Maxwell wanted the graduates to defend the status quo while Davenport hoped they would participate in the reform of the system. Moreover, Davenport's real commitment was to the creation of an efficient governmental bureaucracy. He hoped to utilize the school for the realization of that goal. . . . Opposing George Maxwell's original objective of simply inculcating a patriotic love of America in undergraduates, Davenport saw an opportunity for a much grander undertaking. In reply to a letter from Chancellor Flint, Davenport outlined his objective: "The core activity should be thoroughly scientific and practical, dealing constantly with the problems of government which arise in the various localities, in the state and in the nation. . . . In this respect the school should be an institute of public administration not simply furnishing a teaching force in citizenship."

In his golden anniversary essay Johnson described Maxwell, Flint, Davenport, and Luther Gulick as "the founding fathers of the Maxwell School."

The University's board of trustees in June 1924 endorsed Dr. Flint's proposal to establish "what might be called a School of Citizenship [that] would include all the work in political science, and some in history and the other social sciences gathered together under a director, to be a department of the College of Liberal Arts." The Chancellor referred to the donor as "a gentleman who is interested in the University," adding: "The money is available for establishing this school but is not available for the payment of the University debt or for anything else. The school will not be any additional expense to the University, but will relieve the present budget."

Public announcement of the gift, without mention of Maxwell's name, was made at the 1924 commencement. Not until June 1928, when Maxwell received an honorary doctor of laws degree from the University, was he named publicly as the donor.

The Chancellor and Davenport worked on plans for a faculty and curriculum, aided by Dr. William E. Mosher of the Institute for Public Administration and Dr. Luther Gulick of Columbia University. Ultimately it was agreed that the school should be "an integral part" of the College of Liberal Arts, subject to the authority of the Chancellor, and its name, with the donor's consent, was changed to the School of Citizenship and Public Affairs. It was also agreed that as counsel Davenport would pass on "major matters of policy and ... render such assistance in the organization and development of the school as possible." Mosher, who was named director, was to be responsible for the growth of the school. Mosher, born in Syracuse November 22, 1877, graduated from Oberlin College in 1899. Later he studied at the University of Berlin and received his doctorate at Halle in 1904. He was professor of German language and history at Oberlin from 1905 to 1918. He left Oberlin for a post in the Bureau of Municipal Research in New York City. During World War I he was a special agent of the U.S. Labor Department, then returned to New York City and joined the National Institute of Public Affairs, of which Davenport was a prominent member.

The original members of the Maxwell faculty included Floyd H. Allport, professor of social and political psychology, Russell M. Story, who served briefly as chairman of the political science department, and William C. Casey, an assistant professor. Recruited from existing campus personnel came Finla G. Crawford and Waldo Schumaker, professor and assistant professor of political science, respectively. Ralph G.

Himstead of the College of Law and Paul W. Ward, assistant professor of philosophy, became part-time members of the staff.

Then with a sequence of courses approved, the Maxwell School of Citizenship and Public Affairs was formally opened on October 3, 1924, with its quarters on the second floor of Slocum Hall. The guest speakers for the occasion were Elihu Root from nearby Clinton and James W. Garner of the University of Illinois. Just about a week after the dedication ceremonies, Maxwell outlined his views for establishing a firm foundation for the school in a letter to Chancellor Flint:

> My object is not to train citizens but to train teachers of citizenship, to develop lobbyists who will go out in the world and become centers of influence on this subject, each permeating his circle with the good-citizenship essentials, enthusiasms, and education. Most of the students who specialize in this course I should hope would become teachers of citizenship (in schools, community, civic centers, Chautauquas, etc.) and others would, as business men and professional men, make it part of their daily life work to inspire their communities, their associates, their employers with the same intelligent comprehension and realization of United States Citizenship.

With the help of the regular Maxwell School staff and faculty members from other branches of the University, Dean Mosher introduced the course "Responsible Citizenship," popularly known as Cit I. Of his purpose the dean wrote in an annual report: "Through having on the staff representatives of the several social sciences, it has been possible to illuminate social and particularly political problems from a variety of angles. In this respect our school has been among the pioneers."

Cit I constantly changed in content. Patience, study, and editing went into the preparation of each year's program. Faculty conferences arranged the weekly assignments and class discussions. During the first semester the student was introduced to the aims and purposes of the social sciences through weekly lectures and spirited class sections that met twice a week. In the second semester the course centered on the application of those principles to current national and international problems; both sides of an issue were presented by readings from contemporary newspapers, magazines, and other publications. Visiting scholars and public leaders of national and international standing lectured frequently. As a course required for graduation in the College of Liberal Arts and usually taken in the freshman year, Citizenship I could not escape student criticism. Many complained either that the academic standards of the Maxwell School were too high, or, particularly in later years, that the subject matter was poorly selected, or that the instructors were not sufficiently prepared. On the other hand, seniors and alumni repeatedly expressed appreciation for the course, although many of them said they might have profited more had it been given in the senior year.

Political Science 200 was a weekly seminar in political science. In it the scope and methodology of each social science discipline was critically presented and discussed.

The public administration program grew from a humble beginning into a sequence of national prominence. With the aid of the Maxwell funds and several grants from national foundations, the program expanded from one to two years. Before 1935 Public Administration centered on municipal government; thereafter increased emphasis was placed on state and federal administration. Illustrating these trends were new courses in Problems of Metropolitan Areas, Centralization, Public Personnel, and Public Administration, which embraced Budgeting, Public Revenue, Public Works Administration, Police Administration, Housing, Public Health, and many allied subjects. Supplementing class work, the students in the program served as employees of government at all levels, as well as of agencies surveying government work. For example, students worked as interns with the New York and New Jersey Civil Service commissions, the Syracuse Planning Board, and the Division of Personnel Efficiency of Kentucky, among other organizations. Their studies, plus a thesis, led to a master's degree; the degree of doctor in administration was also offered.

Chancellors Flint and Graham were both proud of the program in Public Administration, the first of its kind in the United States. Its reputation was enhanced by a strong faculty whose publications were viewed as outstanding scholarly contributions and by the splendid record of its graduates. The program not only gained reputation for its technical courses, but also for uniting theory and practice in administration.

A third objective of the Maxwell School, one dear to the heart of its founder, was a training program for high school teachers. Granted that American academic institutions had promoted this end before Maxwell's time, teaching methods and instructional materials had not kept pace with changing conditions, especially during the years immediately preceding World War I. The war showed the imperative need for change and demanded closer attention to the role education should play in improving American citizenship. Much thought was given to the problem by Drs. Flint and Mosher at the June 1924 faculty conference.

Out of this came the decision to develop a program for instructing teachers in teachers' colleges in the essentials and methods of teaching citizenship. In 1925 a summer session was devoted to the problem, led by Dr. W. C. Smith of the state education department, Professor Edgar Dawson of Hunter College, and Dean Mosher. Some forty persons attended. Other gatherings, soon opened to all the social sciences, were held under the guidance of the Maxwell School and the American Political Science Association. In addition, the Maxwell School was promoting student interest in government through such organizations as the International Relations Club, which in 1929 reenacted a session of the Pan-American Conference. Similarly, mock state and national political conventions were held.

Significant as these developments were, Chancellor Flint stated in 1934: "We seem to have been rather seriously negligent of this highly important phase of the natural work of the school." As a remedial measure he suggested having at least "one teacher of teachers, dually related to both Citizenship and the School of Education," develop a course to train teachers in the social sciences. Seconded by Deans Mosher and Harry S. Ganders, the plan was implemented in 1935 by appointing Dr. Roy A. Price as the first dual professor at Syracuse. The result was a series of integrated programs. Known as Social Studies Teaching Majors, students in this concentration met the liberal arts requirements during their first two years and enrolled as well in courses in history, geography, sociology, economics, and political science. As juniors and seniors, they took additional work in these social sciences, plus 12 hours in specialized aspects of education. A master's program was also given. Price skillfully smoothed the way for cooperation by the social science departments, whose liaison with high school principals and the education department at Albany was highly successful. Another highlight was the annual Citizenship Day, when selected New York high school students attended a conference on campus, at which they exchanged ideas, became acquainted with one another and with the school, and competed for scholarships.

The achievements made in the freshman course in citizenship, the public administration program, and the development of teacher training constitutes what has been described as one of Syracuse University's greatest contributions to American education and democracy. The gains were made in spite of limited means and the ravages of a nationwide financial depression.

In the *Alumni News* of November 1925 Mosher wrote: "Political Science forms the center of the present program," and said the faculty "has been selected with reference to this emphasis in the realities of

Political Science." Though stressing the course Responsible Citizenship, greater weight was given to political science, politics, government, and public administration.

Davenport supported the Mosher thesis in an article in *Outlook* in 1927 in which he described the School of Citizenship as "an experimental school of Political Science."

But what was George Maxwell's thinking? A copy of the school's first bulletin was mailed by him to his friend and college classmate, Bishop Leete, whose counsel Maxwell frequently sought and often followed. The bishop was not enthusiastic about the catalog, believing the aims of the school as stated needed "much correction." Specifically, there should be less of "the pedagogic Ph.D. business" and more of the practical Americanism with some "spiritual and even religious bearing." To this criticism, Maxwell, the son of a minister, said "amen," adding the comment, we have "gotten too far above the average undergraduate."

Two years later Maxwell told Davenport the freshman course was "too abstruse and scholastic." About the same time he wrote to Mosher: "I think it will be more practical in results if for a number of years it [the Maxwell School] is confined almost exclusively to United States Citizenship. That certainly is a big news subject for any young people. But Chancellor Flint introduced the subject of post graduate work and therefore I consented in broadening out that scope because post graduates would want to delve into World Citizenship." For undergraduates, however, Maxwell still wanted the school to be as practical as possible. "They are in the period requiring the laying of a foundation of knowledge and facts. The philosophizing and theorizing will come later, but unless a thorough foundation of facts is laid, they are apt to go off on a tangent of radicalism and all sorts of isms."

By 1932 Chancellor Flint had become deeply concerned over the curriculum and finances of the Maxwell School. And he was not deaf to growing criticism downtown of alleged "scholastic" and "pink" members of the Maxwell faculty. Consequently he felt obliged to "get them thinking along original lines." In part this was done through personal conversations and memoranda. More provocative were his claims that the school had exalted political science and public administration to a point where citizenship was being forgotten and Maxwell funds were being spent contrary to the donor's wishes. He also suggested the school embrace more of the social sciences and the departments of philosophy and religion, which Maxwell had favored.

Levi Chapman, Henry Philips, and Mrs. Maxwell were among others soon drawn into the controversy that gradually led to misunder-

William E. Mosher, first dean of the Maxwell School. Photograph © Bachrach Brothers.

standings and ill will between Davenport and Mosher on the one hand and the Flint administration on the other. Davenport and Mosher flatly denied the Chancellor's statements and asserted the "break" had been caused by the "precarious conditions" of University finances. Frayed tempers led to many unhappy and unseemly words. Clearly between them and Chancellor Flint a disagreement of unusual proportions had developed. Had Dr. Flint not resigned in 1936 to become a Methodist bishop, the controversy might have become a crisis.

A possible solution had existed in a suggestion made as early as 1930 about a reorganization of the Maxwell School. This statement appeared in the Reeves Survey of that year: "The staff is informed that the creation of the School is in reality a move toward a divisional organization in the College of Liberal Arts. Such a move is heartily approved." About the same time Chancellor Flint remarked that the school might become a "Division of Social Sciences." During the next few years, as tensions mounted, he mulled over the idea that he ultimately outlined in a rough draft. His plan called for giving all control of the Maxwell School to the dean of the College of Liberal Arts. To do so would be financially and educationally economical, would lessen overlapping and duplication of personnel and courses, and would reduce the "separateness" and somewhat irritating independence of the Citizenship faculty. Then on second thought the Chancellor concluded that the dean's talents lay in other fields and came up with the idea of making Mosher director of Public Administration. As for the school, it was to become an entity within Liberal Arts, directed by an executive committee of the social sciences.

Chancellor Flint held his proposal in abeyance, but it became the base upon which he drafted his "Report to the Trustees of the School of Citizenship" in 1936, the height of the controversy. In this document he expressed regret in leaving the University with the Maxwell School in so "unsettled" a condition, though he hoped the trustees would restudy his "Ten Year Report to the University Trustees," made in 1932. So far, he continued, the school had concentrated on political science and social psychology, with only an "attenuated relation" to other social sciences. This development, he believed, ran counter to national trends favoring a division of social sciences, an idea that was "strikingly in the mind of Maxwell." Syracuse University, he added, had "failed Mr. Maxwell at some points" by stressing political science and public administration at the cost of undergraduate instruction in citizenship.

A copy of the 1936 report was sent to Vice Chancellor Graham, who described it as "excellent" and said it was "heartily in accord" with his own views. He then suggested that the director of the reorganized school be the dean of Liberal Arts as well and that the faculty cease being defined as members of the school. Equally pointed was his proposal that all future appointments be made by the departments and not by the school. In making these suggestions, Dr. Graham was writing in a subordinate capacity that represented in part acceptance of Chancellor Flint's thinking. At the same time, however, they revealed an independence of thought favorable to Liberal Arts and would be meaningful for the future. This was to be shown in the fall of 1936 when Dr. Graham was named Acting Chancellor.

About this time Mosher asked Dean Leebrick of Liberal Arts to make an adjustment in the Liberal Arts budget favorable to the Maxwell School. Leebrick endorsed the request and forwarded it to Dr. Graham. The Acting Chancellor returned it with a terse "unapproved." He accompanied the rejection with a statement that reflected his earlier views and concern about the financial future of Maxwell School. He added this comment: "We are faced with a most difficult problem of properly integrating the School of Citizenship with that of Liberal Arts. Before this can satisfactorily be done certain important and fundamental questions must be settled. Pending such a settlement I am not willing to become involved in an attempt to make petty allocations of fractions of individual salaries."

In another communication, sent shortly afterward to Deans Leebrick and Mosher, Dr. Graham said that because Citizenship was "a part of the College of Liberal Arts, no expenditure for that school should be allowed unless it bears the approval of the dean" of that College. Mosher wrote later that the new administration was "reactionary" and wished to "bring us to heel."

The Acting Chancellor was disturbed again in April 1937 when the directors of the North American Holding Corporation proposed a new agreement under which the school would be "given the same dignity and standing as the other schools and colleges ... and that its head be made a dean with the same authority as the [other] deans." Dr. Graham retorted that this would not be considered even if it meant the loss of the School of Citizenship. The morale of the Liberal Arts faculty, he said, would be hurt if certain individuals in some departments received preferential salaries and privileges. Davenport said he believed Dr. Graham was "incredibly confused" over the holding corporation's proposal.

Nevertheless, financial relations between the Maxwell School and the holding corporation were ironed out in an "oral" agreement in October 1937. Among other things, the agreement restated the purposes of the school and stressed the belief that these ends could be met through selected courses in political science, social psychology, economics, sociology, philosophy, and ethics. These disciplines, it was hoped, would be coordinated with the other schools and colleges so far as Citizenship funds allowed. It was also suggested that the school would be more useful if it were reorganized on a graduate level. To implement these proposals, the University obligated itself to make a survey of the school. Though Davenport had played an influential role in drafting the agreement, he soon expressed some uneasiness over the situation. Would the University abide by its promise to consider converting the school into a graduate one while retaining increased services to undergraduates?

Davenport's doubts stemmed largely from the failure of Dr. Graham, now Chancellor, to name Mosher to the survey committee, and Davenport took it on himself to brief the committee members on the aims and sentiments of the holding corporation. The committee recommendations that resulted quickly dissipated Mosher's fears.

In June 1938 the recommendations were adopted by the University trustees, who approved the establishment of the Maxwell Graduate School of Citizenship and Public Affairs. It became a part of the University Graduate School, to which it was responsible for courses and programs. The administration of the Maxwell School was placed in the hands of a dean, who was also to be chairman of an executive committee consisting of the chairmen of the departments of economics, history, political science, philosophy, and sociology and four members elected by the faculty of the Maxwell Graduate School. All undergraduate courses of these departments—geography was added later—were to be cleared through the College of Liberal Arts before going to the University Senate. Thus the dean and faculty of the school were basically members of Liberal Arts, though faculty not giving graduate work were not of the Maxwell Graduate School. In this way a compromise was reached in the long jurisdictional dispute between the University administration and Liberal Arts on the one hand and the Maxwell School on the other.

The financial status had been cleared up by the October agreement. This provided for the North American Holding Corporation to transfer a block of securities to the New England Trust Company. The income from this source, together with the earnings of the Lacene Manufacturing Corporation, a subsidiary of the holding corporation, was to be set aside until the sum of $1 million was reached. This amount was to constitute an endowment for the school. The holding corporation was also to appropriate $75,000 annually for current expenses. The agreement was to end in November 1947.

Chancellor Graham and former President Herbert Hoover at the dedication of Maxwell Hall, November 12, 1937.

While the controvery over the composition and organization of the Maxwell School was taking place, a new building to house it was being erected. The idea of such a structure had been in Maxwell's mind since the School of Citizenship was established. Various delays ensued, however, and it was not until early 1929 that he told Chancellor Flint he was "planning for the building," with the cost to be under $500,000. The Chancellor relayed this information to Dwight J. Baum, a New York architect, with the suggestion that a suitable site would be between the Administration Building and Crouse College. Various matters—cost, the Depression, and differences of opinion over style—delayed action until July 1936 when the way was cleared for immediate construction. By October 1937 Maxwell Hall was about ready for occupancy, and on November 12 it was formally dedicated with impressive ceremonies.

College and university presidents and representatives, federal and state officials, and leaders and educators in political science and public administration came from many parts of the nation to participate.

Three symposia were held in the morning. In the afternoon there was a reception and tea, as well as a special broadcast from radio station WSYR that was carried throughout the country by the parent National Broadcasting Company. The formal dedication exercises were held in the evening in Hendricks Chapel. The principal speakers were Davenport, Chapman, Mosher, and Herbert Hoover, former president of the United States. The Maxwell faculty, resplendent in their academic robes, found irreverent amusement in watching Hoover's unsuccessful effort to stay awake during the tedious speeches that preceded his own.

Mrs. George H. Maxwell, widowed five years earlier, was among the distinguished guests. She heard Chancellor Graham speak warmly of her late husband's ideals and his hopes for the school named for him.

Dean Mosher, in his 1941 book *Introduction to Responsible Citizenship,* wrote: "Citizenship means much more . . . than participation in government or politics. The good citizen is one who in all his activities is guided by the desire to contribute to the common well-being, the commonweal. Citizenship means intelligent participation in the activities of society in their whole range, from the home and fireside to the family of nations. Its basis is the fullest possible realization of life—the abundant life, for himself, for his kin, his neighbor, his fellow countrymen, and his fellow man."

16

The Public Arts
Speech, Drama, Radio

Syracuse is on the air . . . a vast unnumbered audience is enrolled as guest students of the University. . . . As pioneers in a new field, unlimited possibilities lie before us.
—*Daily Orange,* 1931

SPEECH WAS TAUGHT from the opening of the University in 1871, when it was a course in the English department. In 1910 the department of oratory was established, and three years later it became the School of Oratory with Hugh Massey Tilroe, professor of rhetoric and public speaking, as director. Thus Syracuse University became the first institution of higher learning in the United States to award a four-year degree in the speech arts—a bachelor's in oral English.

In 1921 the school was reorganized as the School of Public Speech and Dramatic Art, with departments of speech arts, dramatic art, forensics, and speech science. Tilroe, who had joined the University in 1906, continued as director. The other faculty members were Sherman L. Kennedy, professor of debating and public speaking; Editha Parsons, professor of elocution; Harry J. Heltman, assistant professor of public speech; Grace S. Bull, assistant professor of oral English, and Rowland N. Cloud, instructor in speech.

It was a proud day in 1923 when the debate team defeated one from Oxford University. There was also pride in the well-produced plays of the Boar's Head dramatic society. Chancellor Flint provided new quarters for the school on the top floor of the Hall of Languages and approved the addition of faculty members, notably Ralph E. Kharas, assistant professor of public speaking, eventually to become dean of the College of Law, and Sawyer Falk, assistant professor of dramatics.

In 1929–30, because of Professor Tilroe's age and increasing absences due to illness, Vice Chancellor Graham exercised general supervision of the school, whose offerings were from the departments of drama, literary interpretation, oral English, private recital, and speech correction. Dr. Graham asked Professor Kennedy to prepare a report on the school's past record and suggestions for its future. The twenty-two page report, completed in November 1929, was prophetic. One recommendation was that there should be a speech art building big enough for drama also, with an auditorium for recitals and space for a radio broadcasting studio.

Of such a studio Kennedy said: "This would enable us to train broadcasters of plays, readings, story hours, debates and speeches. It would give training through work at WSYR and would enable Syracuse University to make a further contribution to 'better speech.' Obviously, the radio is one of our most powerful influences in the development of a universal standard of speech."

Most of Kennedy's ideas were not acted on because of the University's financial situation. But the Chancellor did strengthen the school by appointing two new instructors. One of them, Kenneth G. Bartlett, blazed trails for the school and the University. Through his pioneering efforts in the teaching of radio and television broadcasting, Bartlett was instrumental in the founding of the Television-Radio Center and, later, the S. I. Newhouse School of Public Communications.

Bartlett, a 1927 graduate of Albion College, did graduate work at the University of Michigan and worked in radio in Detroit before he joined Syracuse in 1929. He directed the first formal broadcast from the campus on May 5, 1931. Aired over WSYR, it consisted of musical selections and interviews with a group of University scientists recently back from a South American expedition.

Reporting the event on page one the next day, the *Daily Orange* said: "Syracuse is on the air. . . . a vast unnumbered audience is enrolled as guest students of the University. ... As pioneers in a new field, unlimited possibilities lie before us."

The first broadcast of the 1931–32 academic year, on November 9, featured an address by Chancellor Flint. Programs were scheduled to be heard every afternoon at three o'clock for an hour, in addition to evening broadcasts three times a week.

Milton Dickens, assistant coach in debate, was enthusiastic about

Kenneth G. Bartlett, director of Radio, and later, director of the Television-Radio Center, dean of University College and vice president of Public Affairs. Photograph by C. Wesley Brewster.

rekindling interest in debate through the use of radio. During the 1930–31 season Syracuse University had extensive programs aired over WSYR and WFBL, he said. In addition the University team debated with Union College over the world's largest broadcasting station at Schenectady. "We've had as many as 200 letters in reply to a single debate," Dickens said, explaining that this meant there were thousands of listeners. Colgate, Cornell, St. Lawrence, Buffalo, Columbia, Hamilton, and Albany Law School were also among opponents of Syracuse debaters. During the year the men's varsity team traveled to the nation's capital, debating along the way, and the women's team made a similar tour to New York City. At home in the community teams debated at the invitation of Rotarians, Optimists and Monarchs, and at the Labor Temple.

Bartlett was named director of radio in 1933–34 and in June 1934 Dr. Flint appointed a special radio committee and declared: "The Radio Program will be part of the general publicity program of the University." The School of Speech allowed up to 6 credit hours for radio courses. Bartlett urged the University to develop student talent in radio and to increase the size of the staff to give more time for faculty supervision of radio work.

The Syracuse University Symphony Orchestra made its radio debut April 2, 1936, over the University station WSYU under the direction of Professor André Polah from Crouse College auditorium. James E. DeLine was the student announcer for the program, which preempted the usual Thursday night interview of a campus personality or guest by Professor Bartlett. On the program were Tchaikovsky's "Fantasie Overture" from "Romeo and Juliet," "Scherzo" from Brahms's Third Symphony, and "Roses from the South," a Johann Strauss waltz.

The *Daily Orange* reviewer wrote of the pioneering concert that despite the fears of radio technicians, "the large and unexpected audience (of 300) served as an absorbing effect on the natural echoings in the hall."

In February 1939 Bartlett was named chairman of a special committee on radio policy and that June the trustees, acting on recommendations by the deans of Liberal Arts, Business Administration, and Journalism, changed Bartlett's title from assistant professor in public speaking to assistant professor in radio education.

By the fall of 1939 courses were being taught in public school radio, script writing and program production. Graduates of the radio sequence earned bachelor of science degrees.

By the 1941–42 academic year more than 150 University-produced programs were being broadcast by local stations, most of them at night. Faculty participation in the shows increased with a resulting rise in their quality. Among notable programs were "The University Singers" under the direction of Professor Jacob Kwalwasser of the College of Fine Arts, and "Ask the Scientists," which ran for several years and in 1942 received the first place award at the American Exhibition of Recorded Education Programs. Also notable were the School of Citizenship's "Perspective for War," "The Forestry Forum," "A Senior Ball," and several broadcasts of home games of the basketball team.

When Professor Tilroe retired in 1931, Dr. Graham served as acting director of the School of Speech until February 1932, when Chancellor Flint appointed Dean K. C. Leebrick to that post. This meant that administratively the school became a subsidiary of the College of Liberal Arts. That state of affairs continued when Finla G. Crawford became the Liberal Arts dean and the school's acting director.

Dramatics came to the fore with Boar's Head staging outstanding plays and Tambourine and Bones presenting musical productions, both series under the direction of Sawyer Falk.

The high quality of the plays drew large audiences from campus and community. Boar's Head productions included Lynn Riggs's "The Cherokee Night," Martin Flavin's "Sunday," William Saroyan's "My Heart's in the Highlands" and "Love's Old Sweet Song," Philip Barry's "In a Garden," and others by Paul Osborne, Zona Gale, Maxwell Anderson, Ibsen and Molière.

An active member who became president of the Boar's Head society was Liberal Arts major S. Leonard Bershad '29 who had a leading role, that of Andrew Mayo, in the 1927 production of Eugene O'Neill's "Beyond the Horizon," presented at the Wieting Opera House. The following year Bershad had the title role in "The Great Gatsby," Owen Davis's play based on the F. Scott Fitzgerald novel. In his senior year he played Pastor Manders in Ibsen's "Ghosts."

Bershad, as Sheldon Leonard, achieved professional fame on Broadway, in radio, films, and television as actor, director, and producer. He wrote in 1940: "During the four years I spent at Syracuse I was in a dozen plays or so . . . it was the equivalent for me of many years of professional experience." When Leonard returned to his alma mater in 1967 to receive the George Arents Pioneer Medal for excellence in television production he said it was at Syracuse under Sawyer Falk that "I first learned the use of stage makeup." He added that at the time he looked on this theater work as a hobby rather than the prelude to a career.

Falk also directed the Children's Theater after the 1928 graduation, magna cum laude, of its founder, Dorothy Kelley Carr, later a leader in Democratic local and state politics, executive secretary of the Syracuse Radio and Television Council, and teacher of English, drama, radio, and television at various Syracuse area high schools.

Typical of musicals presented by Tambourine and Bones were those composed by the students themselves, such as "Bring on the Music," "Life Goes to College," and "Piety Hill Billy," which was written by (Paul) Joyce Crabtree '42, chosen by his fellow students in the school as "most talented undergraduate." Crabtree's selection by 85 percent of the votes from among forty candidates won him an appearance on the Fred Allen radio show and was the beginning of a successful Broadway career.

Sheldon Leonard, left, with the principal players in the 1927 production of Eugene O'Neill's "Beyond The Horizon"—from left to right, William Michelfelder, Thomas McGrath, and Kathryn Tolbert.

Staging Boar's Head productions downtown at the Wieting Opera House and in Crouse College auditorium satisfied no one. In December 1932 a romance of the Oregon Trail, "Distant Drums," managed to please its standing-room-only audience at Crouse College because the cast overcame the acoustics. The *Post-Standard*'s critic wrote: "Sawyer Falk is to be congratulated on having trained his cast in enunciation so as to rise to the aggravating demands of the auditorium." Falk's production problems were of long standing. He wrote of the difficulties he encountered during the 1929–30 season in producing O'Neill's "The Great God Brown": "The directorial and business office of that production was located on the fourth floor of the Hall of languages; the play was rehearsed on the stage of the Slocum Hall Theater; the scenery was built in the Old Power House; the masks were made in the Observatory building; and finally, the play was presented in the Crouse College auditorium."

In 1935, and for the rest of the Flint-Graham administration, the University productions were staged at the Civic Theater on South Salina Street.

Active in Tambourine and Bones, the lively music society founded in 1911, were two men who demonstrated the talent to make theater their careers but chose other paths. They were a future member of the House of Representatives from Pennsylvania, Daniel J. Flood '24, and

Tracy Ferguson '31, who earned a Harvard law degree and returned to Syracuse to become a nationally known expert in labor relations.

Flood had leading roles in the pre-Falk Boar's Head productions "George MacFarland, of New York" and "Believe Me, Xantippe." His host of other campus activities included the presidency of Tambourine and Bones and of the Debate Union, the Glee Club, the University Forum, University Social Council, and extemporaneous oratory.

Ferguson displayed several talents in the Tambourine and Bones production of the musical revue "Time Out." The program credited music and lyrics for the show to Harold De Temple and Tracy Ferguson, but Ferguson alone had credit for the words and music to "The Long Walk" and the torch song "Lonely." Ferguson also conducted the orchestra of this Sawyer Falk production. He had a featured role with Leonard Bershad in "The Great Gatsby" (as Nick Carraway) and appeared with him again in John Galsworthy's "Loyalties," which opened the 1928–29 season. Ferguson was Julien Mervan in the Boar's Head production of the French play "Martine" by Jean-Jacques Bernard in December 1929. He was treasurer of Boar's Head in 1929–30.

A student who counted it a privilege to work with Sawyer Falk was Rietta Trimm '32 of Syracuse. She divided her talents between activities in the English department, where she edited several magazines, and dramatics, which included directing plays and working for Falk.

"I started working for him in 1928," she said. "He was one of the two great professors I had—Sawyer Falk and Leonard Brown." The same reaction came from her husband, Ray Gantter '39, during a joint interview at their Syracuse home in 1981.

Rietta Gantter went on:

> Falk's office was on the third floor of the Hall of Languages, in a cubbyhole, and there was room for his desk, one other desk, and a table and a bookcase. But the glowing light that came out of that room was incredible.
>
> He was a born teacher—probably a better teacher even than a director and he was a damn good director. ... The universal feeling about Sawyer—freshmen were absolutely starry-eyed about him—he was a perfectionist. By the second year you'd begin to hear the ones who were really interested saying "Well, he's a genius but he doesn't have to be so nasty." By the third year you recognized everything he'd given you.

Ray Gantter said:

> The genius of his teaching was that he never really lectured. He never taught you what you ought to know; he made you find it out for yourself.

He was heartlessly cruel sometimes to those who had little or no talent or weren't getting off their duffs. He could be ruthless—he could strip the flesh from your bones. He didn't tolerate stupidity. And he'd work with people in his cast to an absolute nub which is why this sequence of attitudes about him. But many of his students went on to Broadway and other professional areas in the theater. I've never known one who didn't say, "I owe it all to Sawyer." He made them understand what perfection was and why it was worth staying up all night.

"The Depression really knocked holes in a lot of things," Rietta Gantter added.

One of the things—and we share this with many people—is the bitterness that Sawyer never got anything that was promised to him and never anything he deserved. It was always hand-to-mouth about the cost of putting on plays that were better than a lot on Broadway. Undoubtedly he was one of our really great people, known, ironically, all over the country as one of the truly great people in academic theater. Well, everywhere but here, so we never had a theater. He always put on plays in holes in the wall. Plans had been drawn up, promises had been made, but I don't think the University ever meant it. Really! We owe great debts to him.

One of the people who knew Sawyer Falk best is Gerald F. Reidenbaugh, who studied under Falk, who later was his colleague, and still later was a successor to him as chairman of the drama department. Reidenbaugh, B.S. '49, M.A. '51, Ph.D. '67, professor in the College of Visual and Performing Arts and former associate dean, was interviewed September 30, 1981, in the Mayfield Room of Bird Library. His recollections of Falk illustrate the methods used by an unorthodox and memorable teacher who built a fledgling drama department into a remarkably effective laboratory of the theater.

Q: Gerry, you knew Sawyer Falk, and I wish you would talk informally about him—what kind of man he was, what kind of influence he had, whatever occurs to you.

GFR: He came here in 1927 as a full professor in the School of Speech and Dramatic Art. He had a tremendous ongoing fight with the speech people because they always saw drama as a branch of speech, while he always saw a very clear division between them. They were not the same. Indeed, I don't think they are either. As a matter of fact, I'd say that in the 1980s the potential for speech and drama growing together, achieving some sense of unity, is better now and clearer now than it was during the 1920s through the 1940s when what they taught was diametrically opposed, contradictory to each other.

Q: Are you talking about elocution or therapy?

GFR: We're talking about elocution and speechmaking and interviewing and role playing and all those things. Some of those things are more and more coming into the lexicon of the new theater theories, and speech can make that adjustment and be much more unified with drama than it has been in the past. We're talking about all those things. There's almost a common language that has not existed since the classical Greek times, a new language developing that is common to both of them, and it makes it easier for them to live side by side, like brother and sister. In the 1930s and 1940s there was just no hope of them ever being the same thing because they were interested in different things, they dealt with the human psyche in different ways.

My favorite story about Falk at that time is the following: Norman Vincent Peale used to be the minister of University Methodist Church, and Sawyer was a die-hard Methodist, and he went to church every Sunday—well, most Sundays. One time as he was leaving the church Peale said to him, "Sawyer, I haven't seen you in church lately. You haven't been to hear any of my sermons," and Falk replied, "Well, you haven't been to see any of my plays."

There's a whole wealth of philosophy in that, and I think that's what made him a great teacher. He taught from that particular point of view, that drama was a way of saying something about the human condition that was of equal import and had equal impact with religion or a sermon or any kind of philosophical statement. Falk worked from that base, so there is a philosophy in his riposte to Norman Vincent Peale, and they always had that kind of thing going on.

A great teacher. He came here in 1927. I remember they offered him $1,800 and a full professorship and a theater. And at that time he was in a little college in Michigan called Hillsdale, and proudly—he used to boast and laugh about this—he said, "I told them I wouldn't come for anything less than $2,000." Well, they gave him the $2,000.

Q: They never gave him a theater, though.

GFR: They never gave him a theater. That came about, by the way, shortly after his death. Money had been put away for a theater, earmarked for it. Before they ever got around to spending it for Falk he died, in 1961, and Chancellor Tolley, as a way of memoralizing him, said it, quite openly, "I did not build a theater when Sawyer was alive. I will do it now." And that's how that theater came about—Tolley released the money that was there.

Q: Was that the [J. Robert] Rubin money? [Syracuse-born J. Robert Rubin '04 graduated from the College of Law in 1906, was awarded the George Arents Pioneer Medal in 1941 and the honorary doctor of laws degree in 1942. He was a movie industry pioneer and instrumental in the formation of Metro-Goldwyn-Mayer. He became a University trustee in 1936, and when he died in 1958 he made a bequest to his alma mater. The will designated that a J. Robert Rubin Theater be built on the campus.]

GFR: That was the Rubin money. Rubin left a lot of stock, over a quarter of a million. It wasn't nearly enough to build that theater—[the 200-seat Experimental Theater on Irving Avenue built as an addition to the old Regent Theater, now part of the Archbold theater complex]. We built it for a little less than a million, but his [Rubin's] money was the seed money that got the whole building started. Dr. Tolley released that money. One of the things that still bothers me twenty years later—Tolley's purpose in releasing the money was to create a theater for Falk, and nobody has made any effort to name it or anything in the theater connected with it after him. Last year I did get some of the alumni moving, hoping we could get a plaque honoring him, a plaque with his name and face.

I think it's a shame that nothing around here memoralizes him, one of the greatest teachers that Syracuse ever had. When he walked into a classroom everybody became quiet. He was a phenomenon. No prof ever walked into a classroom and the class went quiet, and nobody does it today, but they did it when he walked in, automatically went hush, and they sat hushed until he finished talking. One of the lovely things about him is the way he knew how to teach. He knew that fifty minutes was a limit of any young person's attention, and this whole thing now of shortening semesters and hour-and-a-half periods and fifty-five-minute periods and three-hour classes he just thought was so educationally stupid that he wouldn't get involved in it. He wouldn't permit it in his own department. The longest class he ever taught was two hours long—it was playwriting, and he taught it once a week. But there a play was actually read and there was no way you could break that up. He'd be quite an antagonist, quite an outspoken critic of the contemporary forms of time used in education if he were alive today. A brilliant lecturer.

Q: Did he ever direct you?

GFR: Oh yes, a number of times.

Q: Could you talk about him as a director?

GFR: The tough thing about him was I never knew how good a director he was because I rarely sat in the audience to see the problem. He always had me on the stage doing the damn thing. I know as a teacher he was probably the greatest theater teacher in the country. There was a group of them in the 1920s and early 1930s who were very great—Alexander Drummond at Cornell was one, Falk was one, Koch at North Carolina was one, and Samuel Selden at North Carolina. These were great theater teachers. They were the ones who forced the drama and theater into the college curriculum. Up until then it was just an extracurricular activity; they made an academic regimen out of it. Falk was one of the titans who did that. I refer to them as titans—they were great, great men, and the esteem they held him in I think was pretty clear in the fact that he was president of the National Theater Conference for twelve consecutive years. He quit himself saying, "I don't want to do this any

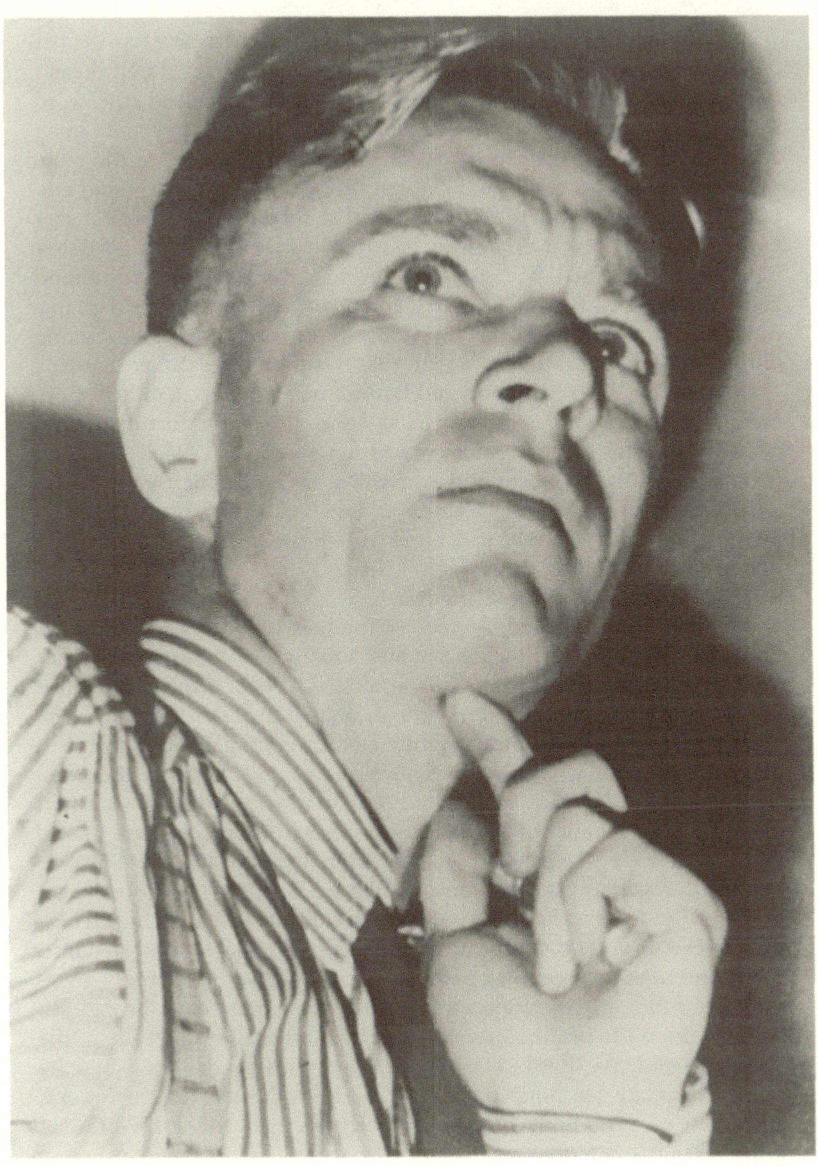

Sawyer Falk.

more." Since that time the National Theater Conference has a new president every year, and they've had some big ones. They've had Norris Houghton and John Houseman and so on, but Falk for twelve years. They just kept putting him back in there because he was such a brilliant man of the theater.

Another thing—they never referred to the departments as theater departments; those boys talked about the drama. Today it's all theater departments, which suggests there's no literature involved, the word theater. Those guys worked from a literary base, and yet they knew more about the craft and the mechanics of the theater art! One of the main subjects they always taught was theatricality. They would stress and emphasize theatricality, but they always talked about it from the point of view of literature and how the literature became theatrical. In this regard they were great, great men. There's an old saying about Falk and Drummond being the two best that we used to laugh about. Whenever they'd go to a conference they played Cabot and Lodge. You know, the Cabots talking only to the Lodges, and so on. And that was the saying there, that Falk would talk only to Drummond and Drummond would talk only to God. Believe me, that's the way it was. And I was one of the fortunate guys because I was so close to Sawyer. I was a student of his. He used to beat on people generally, browbeat and everything else. And then eventually I joined his faculty as a graduate assistant, finally as an instructor, and then on from there, so I knew the man and I trusted the man and I could talk to him because we shared this Syracuse basis.

Q: How did he fit into Broadway?

GFR: He was trained by some of the best Broadway men around. Louis Calvert was his acting teacher, and nobody at that time was a better actor than Louis Calvert nor, as Falk would say, a better acting teacher. He was trained in the appreciation of the drama by Brander Matthews, one of the great scholars. Brander Matthews was teaching at Columbia, and he kept taking him to the theater. This is where he got to know [the critic] George Jean Nathan, and he thought Nathan was an idiot. He was taught by the best. As a matter of fact Falk got a scholarship to Columbia, got his baccalaureate degree in mathematics, and then got his M.A. degree because they gave him an assistantship to teach English. That's how he got in with Brander Matthews. He never took a drama course in his life. He didn't need to, and he'd laugh at all the courses they have today. First he'd laugh and then he'd get mad because things today are machinery, trade things. To him an education was far more than that. What he did was teach in the trade in the rehearsal. He did not teach in the trade in the classroom and give them course credit. The rehearsal hall was where he put the dramatic teaching to work. To do that today you'd have to work, you'd have to spend hour upon hour upon hour with students. Professors don't do that any more.

Q: Can you distinguish the way he taught from the way other professors of drama taught?

GFR: When you worked with Sawyer on a play he started from class, which he called Styles of Acting and Directing. He started the readings of the play in there, and from that he would deal with its history, with its criticism, with its historical place in things, so you knew what you were doing, what kind of play you were doing, and how it fitted into things when you hit the rehearsal. Once you hit the rehearsal hall he dealt strictly with the mechanics of acting.

One of the things that he did I always liked to do; I took it as part of my own way of doing things, but I have known very few other directors who do it. He spent hour upon hour in the rehearsal hall writing down the words you were saying that he did not hear or understand, and it was not uncommon for you to get 150 of those in a night, per actor. The lead actor could get 150 of those. "I don't get this word, I don't get this phrase, I don't hear this, you're garbling this." He kept coming down to words all the time in getting that literature across. He wanted to make sure that everybody got it, that the audience got it.

They don't do that today. Today they give you voice exercises to give you the ability to speak a consonant or to express a vowel. That's nonsense. It has nothing to do with the literature at all, and it has nothing to do with diction. What Sawyer was teaching you was the diction of that particular writer, his style, his arrangement. He was teaching you this because the only way you'd get it was the way he'd make you take the words apart to get your articulation clearer. And he would differentiate between articulation and diction, so he was teaching you the style of that playwright all the time.

Q: When he was teaching a Shakespeare play, for instance, would he go over the meaning of a particular word?

GFR: Both. He'd start there, and his marvelous way of dealing with that was, "I don't know what you're talking about, I don't know what you mean," only if you were so thick you couldn't get it on your own. What he would do is drive you back to the text, that was his way of teaching. He drove you back to the text, and you had to go back and say, "What does it mean if he doesn't know what I mean? Well, it means ... " and then you would have to bring it out. It's a beautiful way of teaching because you are learning and teaching yourself at the same time. That's what he had you do, and in a rehearsal hall he spent an awful lot of time, but he was relentless, relentless on that kind of thing. I remember doing "All My Sons," which was my first major role up here. I had a speech that was two and a half pages long.

Q: What part did you play, Gerry?

GFR: George. That was its first performance after Broadway, by the way. Karl Malden played George on Broadway. We got it right off Broadway and played it up here. And Sawyer foresaw already what Arthur Miller was going to do with "Death of a Salesman," break the proscenium arch, he saw that. He could never do a production if he had already seen it and didn't think he could improve on it, which is why he never did "Oedipus Rex." He said, "I could not improve on what Tyrone Guthrie and Laurence Olivier did with that play so I will never do it. I could only do it less." He foresaw that Miller was breaking the proscenium arch in "All My Sons," and out came "Death of a Salesman" thereafter and that's what he had done, he had breached it right through.

I remember that two and a half pages. It was easy enough to memorize, and I did that thing every night and all Sawyer would say was, "It needs work." We had eight weeks of rehearsal, and after the second week he would no longer say, "It needs work." He'd just shake his head. And I would go home after having rehearsed until 12 or 1 A.M. and work on that speech for another two hours. I'd come back the next night and he'd shake his head.

Q: Did you know what he meant when he shook his head?

GFR: Yes, when he shook his head he meant, "It's not interesting, you're not getting your meanings out, emotionally it's not holding together, intellectually it's not holding together, it needs work." I didn't work the first two weeks that way, but for six weeks I did, every night come home to the fraternity house (I was a Kappa Sig), go into the cellar, and for two hours I'd work on that speech. And the next night I'd look out and he'd shake his head no. Finally in desperation one night about a week before opening he came up and he said, "Let me show you how it's put together." Well, he went down, giving me readings, putting everything together. I took profuse notes. I went home that night and worked until dawn. And I came back the next night and he said, "Well, it's better."

And for a solid week I worked on it and I still couldn't get it. He still would shake his head. Opening night he said, "Well . . . " We did that play for about three or four weeks here, and then we revived it in the summer, and that speech was still driving me out of my mind, and then we revived it again in the fall, down where the Hoople Center now stands, where we used to have a theater in the old nurses' recreation room. And the second night of that performance, the whole thing fell into place. One night it just fell into place, and I left the stage, I didn't even take a curtain call. I left the stage and ran to the telephone and called him and said, "I got it, I got it. You've got to come back tomorrow night. I'll prove to you I got it." And by god he was there.

Q: You knew it.

GFR: I knew it, I knew it. He came back the next night and he sat through the speech. It ended the second act and I didn't go back in the third act. He came back stage, he looked at me and he smiled, and he said, "That's it," and left. That is a teacher. I learned. I learned more on that speech than I could have gotten out of 150 plays with lesser instruction. I learned it because I had to do it.

Q: And you learned to be a teacher from him, too.

GFR: I sure did, and I'm a good teacher. I'm a good teacher of acting. I know it, and that's how I know it, that's who I am, and I had that kind of teacher. He was a great, great teacher. Funny, you know, he was such a great teacher of acting, but he never turned out a lot of actors. He turned out producers.

Q: Who were some of those actors and producers?

GFR: Paul Crabtree and Dorothy Loudon, Phil McAneny, John Larson to a degree. But there should have been more actors to come out of there. I think it was because very few people were going into the theater in those days. He never really had a big drama department until after World War II when the vets came back. Paul Crabtree, of course, turned to directing after he didn't want to act anymore; John Larson gave up acting for directing. Dorothy Loudon you know from "Annie." There were others. He never had much respect for Peter Falk's acting, and he wouldn't today. They didn't like each other because Sawyer would tell Peter the truth.

Q: They were not related, were they?

GFR: No, no relation at all. He didn't like Falk's style. He thought Falk had potential, but Peter never got away from that delivery he still uses, Columbo. Whatever you see Peter do, it's Columbo, and Sawyer always resented his playing Gonzalo or something from "The Tempest" like Columbo.

Q: Newell Rossman said the other day Sawyer Falk had one play on Broadway, and he was satisfied that he had done the big time. Could you talk about that?

GFR: Sawyer had to prove within himself that he was a Broadway man. It was a play called "Live Life Again," and that's where his animosity toward George Jean Nathan started because Nathan gave him such a bad review. Sawyer had hit Broadway; the play was there, and the play failed because the writer had run out of steam. Falk knew it before he opened, there was just so much he could do as a director. He took an awful beating from George Jean Nathan—the year I think was 1941. He called him an academic, and oh that made Sawyer mad. However, Sawyer got his name up in lights. Everybody knew that that was in Sawyer's craw. Jerry Leider ['53] was producing a play called "Archy and Mehitabel" with Eartha Kitt, and Sawyer was called in. The play was dying in rehearsal, and Leider was desperate so he came to ask Falk what to do, and finally he hired Falk to come down and be a play doctor, and "Archy and Mehitabel" ran far longer than anybody ever gave it credit for running. Anyway, the thing was opening in the winter—it ran right through to the summer and died because of summer audiences—and Falk at that time asked and got Leider to put his name up on the marquee, "Directed by Sawyer Falk."

I'm sure that was the happiest moment of Sawyer's life. Eartha Kitt thought he was just great, that the sun rose and set on him. At that time she bought him a watch to say thank you which he always wore. He almost became a father figure to her, and he wore that watch until the day he died. She loved him dearly. So he was successful, he got what he wanted, he proved he was a professional.

One of the things he always drove into his students was "You've got to do this the way a professional does it, you've got to learn how the professional goes about his job." Yet while he did that he was still teaching the literature, the esthetics, the criticism. The beauty of it was he was a man for all seasons, quite a guy. Tough, he showed no mercy. Take his class in Styles of Acting and Directing—if you got through the year without crying you felt he was indifferent to you. You felt you were a failure if he didn't vivisect you.

I recall three compliments that he gave me as an actor. The first was when we were doing "The Tempest." I was doing Prospero and that was rough; I had never done Shakespeare in my life. We rehearsed for about three months. After about two months had passed, talking to him after a rehearsal I said, "It's driving me crazy. I know I'm not doing it well and I'm worried." And he said, "You're getting better." That was compliment number one.

The second compliment was when I did the lead in O'Neill's "Desire Under the Elms," a compliment which he never gave directly to me. It was during the performance one night and there wasn't a big house. He turned to someone who later came back and related it to me and said, "Look at that lousy house. And that guy up there is giving a hell of a performance. They won't see one like this anywhere else, and nobody's coming to see it." The third compliment he never gave me personally either, and that was for "Othello." We finished the play and they interviewed him—he was sixty, I guess. In the room was a reporter for the *Daily Orange* and one for one of the downtown papers, and he told them that what I was doing as Iago would be acceptable on any stage in the world. So those were the three compliments that I got from Sawyer, one of which he gave me—"You're getting better." The other two he never gave me.

Q: In all your years. How many years were you associated with him?

GFR: I came here as a student in 1946 and he died in 1961. That's fifteen years.

Q: Three compliments, two second-hand.

GFR: Right, two second-hand.

Q: Was there some other way that an actor or student might get to feel good about having worked with Sawyer Falk, other than compliments?

GFR: He didn't give compliments. He gave you jobs, and he helped you. He spent hours and hours with you, and you felt if you didn't do something you were letting him down because he gave so much of his personal time. And then when he'd call you in and say, "Do you want to do so-and-so?" you knew he had some respect for you. That's when you knew, when he asked you to do another one. But he wouldn't tell you you were good. If he wanted to he'd pass the word somehow, like those two second-hand compliments. You learned how to work, though. You broke your back for him.

Q: Newell Rossman said that there were certain eccentricities about Sawyer Falk, that he never signed a check in his life; he left all that to his wife.

GFR: Oh, I'm sure he did.

Q: And that he never shaved in the morning; he shaved in the evening before he went to bed.

GFR: Because he wanted to be clean-shaven when he went to the theater. That was his pattern. He got into that habit as a young actor. He always shaved before he went on stage, and so he wouldn't shave in the morning. He was a great believer in his art and the decorum that went with the art. People have often called them eccentricities, a lot of things, but he had a reason for them, there were strong artistic reasons for many things. He'd never let an actor, for example, come out of the dressing room in makeup and costume and speak to the audience when the audience was leaving. He thought that ruined the whole artistic illusion, and I've seen him throw people out of the cast for doing that, defying him. He had those principles and he stuck to them.

Q: Was Falk a formalist in the sense that he wouldn't change a play, whereas today directors will instruct the cast to come down into the audience, for example?

GFR: No, he was pretty eclectic. Sawyer was not a purist; he also was not a mouth-foaming liberal. He read a text, and he taught me to read a text, with a sense of feeling for this dramatic fare. You respected the playwright, respected him very much, and you didn't play around with his words, and if you did make changes you damn well better have a good artistic or intellectual reason for doing it.

When he made any kind of major change he'd always write to the playwright and ask him, if the playwright was still alive. No, he was not a purist. When he hit a bad play he'd say, "Here's a bad play," and he'd call Maxwell Anderson, for example, and say, "Max, you know so-and-so in 'The Eve of St. Mark.' That's a lousy scene you wrote. What the hell am I supposed to do with it? Would you mind if I alter it a little?" And Max would always say sure, so he used to rewrite some stuff. It was always kind of stilted when he wrote it, but structurally it was always sound.

Eccentricities. Oh, I know one marvelous thing about him—he never bought a hat or a pair of rubbers in his life, and that was because he always found extras at the theater that people had left. He used to boast of that, and to this day I still wear a pair of rubbers that Sawyer's wife gave me after he died. They still work, too. Old-fashioned rubbers, and I know where he got them. He picked them up at the theater one night because somebody left them. I still have them, I still wear them.

Q: So you're following in his footsteps, almost literally.

GFR: Yes. Sawyer was almost godlike to students, and in many ways he was almost godlike to some professors because intellectually he was so superior to them. One of my own favorite students tells a story—this kid had come out of Case University, Western Reserve University, as an electrical engineer, and he decided that he wanted to check out the theater, and he heard about Falk, heard that this guy was so tough but that everybody thought he was godlike. We were over in Machinery Hall at the time. The kid always tells this story. He was sitting there, pretty cocky, sitting there in a chair with his feet up on the wall and he heard somebody downstairs at the bottom of the steps say, "Good afternoon, Professor Falk." He had been waiting for days to see this guy, he wanted to see what this man was like. He said that up the stairs came this little guy in an overcoat, with his hat crooked, his hands in his pocket, padding along. He turned the corner at the stairs and walked by him and the kid said, "Good afternoon, Professor Falk." And Sawyer said, "Get your goddamn feet off the wall," and kept walking into his office.

Q: There's a wealth of material on Sawyer Falk here in the library. There are five linear feet of class and lecture notes from 1919 to 1961, and there's a section in his notes on the cinema devoted to censorship.

GFR: He was a great one on that, censorship. Sawyer was against censorship of any kind. He maintained that an audience would do its own censoring, and he took that same position that I heard Supreme Court Justice Potter Stewart take later. Sawyer had always taken that position, that censorship is an admission of a country's fear of itself. Sawyer took that position, but he never talked about censorship without accompanying it with the subject of good taste, and what he was driving into you was never let them censor you because it's impinging on your freedom of speech, your artistic freedom, the rights of the artist. But he also said that by the same token you have a reciprocal obligation to exercise the best possible good taste you can. He always talked about good taste in relation to censorship. Good taste is the artist's responsibility, censorship was the audience's responsibility. And he used to talk about it in terms of specific plays, saying things like, "You know, they banned 'Strange Interlude' in Boston." He always used references to this kind of thing, how they closed down a couple of other plays. One had to do with a homosexual, the first play on homosexuality, by reference; and he laughed at the way the Europeans used to try to censor Ibsen. He gave you the history of it, but he was just dead set against it. He said, "I don't care how bad it is. If they're stupid enough to do it, the audience can censor it themselves if they want it censored. And when they don't want to do this themselves, when they want to ban it as pornographic, then you've got to worry about your society." He might well take a position like that today. He thought censorship was the audience's responsibility, that the best censor in the world was the box office.

By 1942 students and alumni of the School of Speech and Dramatic Art, its many friends and the University and community had ample reason to be proud of the school's accomplishments over two decades. In 1922 Chancellor Flint had found it a small school with an uncertain future, and there were times during the next six years when the administration questioned whether it should continue. In 1930 the Reeves Survey, carried out for the Chancellor, criticized overlapping courses between the school and the College of Liberal Arts and suggested that the former might be made part of the latter. But in that same year there was an upturn in the school's fortunes; enrollment rose, especially in its division of forensics, drama, and radio, and a more permanent faculty grew with the increasing number of students. In the depths of the Depression there was another drop, but in the late thirties enrollment again rose past the 100 mark. It did not reach the peak figure, 120, of the early thirties but mere numbers had never given the school the special qualities it possessed.

Chancellor Graham paid the school a high compliment in his report to the trustees on November 18, 1939. He recognized Kenneth Bartlett's contributions when he mentioned the University's work in radio as one of "the outstanding educational developments at Syracuse ... in which we can take particular pride." He added: "Our radio work ... is coming to be a model, and I think that fact has been recognized by the national government."

Dr. Graham spoke next of "a rather remarkable man in the School of Speech by the name of Heltman," adding: "He is a most outstanding leader in speech education so far as it relates to speech defects and their correction. I find that Columbia would like very much to get Professor Heltman. We are not going to let him go."

Harry J. Heltman stayed. He served as acting dean of the school from 1939 to 1945, then was dean from 1945 to 1950.

In 1941 the name was formally changed to the School of Speech and Dramatic Art, a deletion of the word *Public.*

The School was to retain its particular individuality for many years to come. Eventually radio would evolve into television-radio and become a major component of the S. I. Newhouse School of Public Communications, and speech and drama would become departments in the College of Visual and Performing Arts.

But that was in the future.

17

The Summer and Extension Schools

Summer School was losing its reputation as a sort of penal colony where delinquent students were punished for having failed during the regular academic year.

SYRACUSE UNIVERSITY FOUND MANY WAYS TO HELP as many people as possible earn a college education. Important among the ways were the Summer and Extension schools, which grew amazingly during the Flint-Graham era in both student registration and the number of courses offered. Some observers attributed the remarkable growth to a belief after World War I that a college education was essential to economic and cultural success in the United States. But many Americans could not attend the regular academic sessions because of the need to earn a livelihood, to take care of household responsibilities, or because they thought they were too old to compete with people of traditional college age.

Furthermore, summer school was losing its reputation as a sort of penal colony where delinquent students were compelled to go as punishment for having failed subjects during the regular academic year, or as a means of giving athletes with more brawn than brains a chance to become eligible for varsity teams in the fall by taking snap courses in the summer months.

Instead, summer school was more and more regarded as an excellent opportunity for graduates of two-year teacher-training programs who were teaching full time from September to June to obtain their baccalaureate degrees and permanent teaching certification; for graduate students to complete their advanced degrees; and for undergraduates to accelerate their college work. Similarly, extension work enabled a public school teacher to obtain certification by devoting several evenings a week or Saturday mornings to continued schooling, and provided a way for a high school graduate who had to work in the daytime to get a college education.

At Syracuse, the faint beginnings of the Summer School were found as far back as 1876, when the College of Fine Arts offered a few summer courses in music. Evidently there was not much interest for nothing more was done until 1898, when the Summer School of Sociology was conducted under Professors John Commons and James Hamilton. Four years later the College of Liberal Arts expanded its summer offerings to include more disciplines with the approval of the board of trustees. Other areas of the University gradually fell in line, although there was no central administration; each college supervised its own program. By 1910, however, Dean Frank Smalley of Liberal Arts was listed in the Summer School *Bulletin* as director of the Summer Session, an indication of a greater University-wide effort. Student registration increased as more courses were offered, and they became broader in scope instead of concentrating largely on teacher training.

When Chancellor Flint came to the campus in 1922 the director of the Summer School was Loren C. Petry of the botany department. He was followed in 1926 by a committee consisting of Ross Baker of chemistry, Finla Crawford of political science, and Ernest Reed of botany. By 1928 and continuing through the administration of Chancellor Graham, Reed was the only director; he also served as acting dean of the Graduate School during the summers.

Each succeeding year after 1922, more colleges offered more courses to meet the growing demand of more students from an ever-widening geographic area. In 1923, the first Summer School under Dr. Flint, 774 enrolled. There were consistent increases until 1932, when 2,287 took summer courses. The full effects of the Depression then hit the Summer School, and in the next few years enrollment declined to a low of 1,398 in 1935. An upswing started again in 1936 to reach a total of 2,473 in 1939.

Chancellor Graham expressed Syracuse University's philosophy of summer school in November 1939 when he told the trustees: "Our Summer School is one division of the University that has been very

Ernest Reed, director, Summer Sessions 1928–1952, and assistant dean of the Graduate School.

successful, and continues to be. A number of institutions made the mistake of regarding the Summer Sessions primarily as a means of adding to University income. That we have not done. We try to set the Summer School on an educational plane as high as that maintained during the regular session. The result is we have attracted a very desirable class of students, mostly mature students, a large number of teachers."

By 1942 the impact of the international situation and the entrance of the United States into World War II brought summer attendance down to 2,127.

The size of the Summer School faculty kept proportionate pace with student enrollment. The teaching staff was recruited not only from the regular University faculty, many of whom taught to supplement their salaries, but also from institutions throughout the country and from abroad. In 1927 there were 100 on the faculty, including 15 visiting professors, offering some 200 different courses: in the summer session 10 years later there were 215 faculty, of whom 54 were from other institutions, teaching a total of 450 courses.

Reed was not only an able director; he was a good publicity man as well. The *Bulletins*, the *Alumni News*, the downtown press, and special brochures—some summers there were twenty or more—played up the innovations for each summer's increasingly diversified programs. Each succeeding summer saw more courses and course concentrations introduced. For example, curriculum workshops, usually limited to twenty students each, gave an excellent opportunity for a better exchange of ideas and methods. English, social studies, science, mathematics, art, guidance, adolescent study, home economics, and family relations were some of the areas featured in the workshops.

Demonstration classes constantly grew in number. Those in social studies, for instance, illustrated modern teaching techniques and methods, using silent and sound films, film strips, slides, recordings, radio materials, books, pamphlets, maps, cartoons, newspapers and other source materials, and improved courses of study.

Special conferences also proliferated. Thirteen were scheduled in 1941 in such fields as the teaching of English, public affairs, education, health and physical education, home economics, radio and education, visual education, and modern foreign languages.

The Maxwell School often conducted what it called integration seminars where instructors in political science, history, economics, sociology, philosophy, and anthropology commented on important current events.

Professor Perley Place of the Latin department gave a popular series of lectures on the great men of the Roman period and other classical themes. The science departments regularly offered programs explaining the newest techniques in their fields. Fine Arts held symposia on such subjects as "New Points of View in Music Education." The School of Education sponsored convocations at which leading pedagogists spoke. A highlight was the annual J. Richard Street Lecture, delivered by an outstanding member of the faculty.

An innovation was made in 1936 with the establishment of Maison Française. Its objective was to stimulate interest in the teaching of French in the schools of New York State. Under the supervision of the department of romance languages, Maison was directed by native French teachers for a limited number of selected students. Only French was spoken in the house, French plays and entertainment were staged, French films were shown, and talks were given on French life and culture.

At various times the geography and geology departments conducted camps in the Catskills for actual field training in their particular disciplines. Forestry and Applied Science had similar and compulsory summer programs for their students.

To make Summer School attendance more attractive as well as to broaden the cultural aspect, the English Club held many gatherings on the campus that combined literary readings with a social hour. Concerts conducted by such members of the College of Fine Arts as André Polah, Jacob Kwalwasser, and George Mulfinger made for pleasant evenings. The College Players, consisting usually of graduate students in the School of Speech under the direction of Sawyer Falk and supplemented at times with professionals, offered a series of plays and one-act skits for Summer School audiences. Faculty members gave illustrated lectures on their recent trips to other parts of the nation or abroad. Sidman Poole of the geography department conducted trips to Niagara Falls, the Thousand Islands, Howe Caverns, and the Onondaga Indian Reservation, explaining to the touring students the geographic, geological, and historical background of the particular site. Picnics and films rounded out the recreational benefits of the summer term.

Thus, in the twenty-year period of the Flint and Graham administrations, Summer School made vast strides in scope and appeal. There were some complaints that it was dominated by the School of Education and that the majority of those who attended were public school teachers, but a comparison of the Summer School Bulletin of 1922 with that of 1942 shows that the later course offerings were numerous and diversified enough to fit the needs of students in every category of advanced education.

Ernest Reed said in 1927: "Most of those taking summer work are school teachers and students from other institutions. However there is a large percentage of Syracuse students taking advanced work and making up deficiencies." This was true of virtually every summer session.

Closely associated in purpose with Summer School was the Extension School, originally referred to as the Evening Session or the Evening School, later as the School of Extension Teaching, then as the School of Extension Teaching and of Adult Education, and now as University College. Founded in 1918, the school's director when Dr. Flint became chancellor was Floyd F. Decker, professor of mathematics at the University. Extension School headquarters were then in the College of Law building at South State and East Fayette streets.

According to the Extension *Bulletin*, the objective of the school was "to extend the facilities of the University to the people who, while unable to carry other courses in the institution, are in a position to devote a part of their time to the work. These courses exemplify the desire on the part of the University to make its resources of the utmost use to all whom it may be able to serve. The drafting rooms, the laboratories, the machine shops, the gymnasium, all are used."

From the beginning, the school opened its doors primarily to three types of students:

1. those who wished to take courses leading to a degree, but who, for some reason, could not attend the regular University sessions: for them to obtain college credit they had to meet the requirements of the particular college they sought the degree;

2. those who wished to begin a business or technical career immediately after leaving high school or who were already employed during the day and wanted to obtain a thorough training while so employed: ultimately they might receive a certificate after completing the equivalent to two years work on the Hill; and

3. those who merely wanted to study particular subjects for individual pleasure or profit.

The Extension School was heartily endorsed and supported from its outset by Syracuse public school officials, the chamber of commerce, the local chapter of the American Institute of Banking, the Onondaga Health Association, the Americanization League, and, among many other local organizations, the Technology Club. The various civic groups realized the great contribution the school could make to adult and continuing education for the residents of the city and of Onondaga County. With few exceptions throughout the Flint-Graham era most of the students in the Extension School, as in Summer School, were women.

In 1922 about 1,000 people were enrolled in Extension School, taking evening or Saturday morning classes in the law college building or on the main campus. The most popular subjects were in liberal arts, prelaw, predental, chemical engineering, general business, accounting, secretarial science, journalism, and general college entrance courses. The faculty members were recruited from the regular University staff.

As in Summer School, the increase in enrollment led to more and more courses being offered by the colleges and departments. As a result, by 1930 a full-time director was needed, and D. Walter Morton was appointed. Originally trained for the ministry, Morton had become a certified public accountant with experience in Wisconsin, California, and New York. Under his guidance the Extension School broadened considerably. Morton died on July 5, 1941. The dean of men's affairs, A. Blair Knapp, served as acting director until he entered military service.

In the belief that a service institution must provide as wide a program as possible, extension centers were established first in neighboring communities and, as the demand for adult education grew, in various parts of the state. Morton worked on the theory that if potential students could not go to Syracuse, the University would go to them.

Thus in the decade of the 1930s the Extension School established centers at one time or another in Auburn, Broadalbin, Canajoharie, Cazenovia, Chittenango, Cortland, DeRuyter, Earlville, Endicott, Fayetteville, Fort Johnson, Fulton, Glens Falls, Hannibal, Johnstown, Little Falls, Mohawk, Mexico, Newark, Norwich, North Creek, Oswego, Poughkeepsie, Port Leyden, Rochester, Rome, Skaneateles, Saratoga Springs, Solvay, Utica, Watertown, Waterville, and Waverly.

The most ambitious of the centers was at Endicott, where the first classes were held at the high school in 1932 at the invitation of Superintendent Herbert H. Crumb '37. About fifty students attended. By the late thirties the Endicott center had grown so big it required a full-time director. Benjamin Hopkins-Moses '34 became the resident director and did such an outstanding job he was often described as "Mr. Syracuse University in the Southern Tier." The number of students quadrupled to 200 by 1940 and in 1946 the University established Triple Cities College to serve Endicott, Johnson City, and Binghamton. In 1950 Triple Cities was transferred to the state to become Harpur College and later the State University of New York at Binghamton.

In 1933, a year after the Endicott center was established, Syracuse University responded to many requests and started an extension teaching center in Utica. The first classes were held at the Plymouth Congregational Church and in a building provided by the city. By 1945 about twelve hundred people had been educated in the evening extension program which in 1946 became a two-year branch college and later the four-year Utica College of Syracuse University.

In Syracuse, the move of the law school to Hackett Hall caused the Extension School to transfer its headquarters to the University Block on Washington Street by 1935. Downtown classes were then held in both that block and in the new law building. Soon those quarters were outgrown, and in 1939 the Extension School moved to 309 South McBride Street, a building vacated by the College of Medicine.

Like the Summer School, the Extension School constantly sought ways to provide more and varied choices in the field of adult education. One of these was the alumni reading course, a program that encouraged people to broaden their knowledge by reading twenty books from a list of about ninety classics in diverse fields. Those enrolled in the noncredit program discussed what they had learned with University faculty members.

Maxwell was one of the several University schools that provided lecture series conducted by faculty members and, for example, those connected with the citizenship program gave weekly talks on contemporary issues. The American Institute of Banking furnished instructors for accredited AIB courses. The School of Education, through its department of teacher-in-service, simplified registration for those taking education courses leading to certification and streamlined the curricula for people already in the field of professional education. The Bureau of Educational Research was set up to help improve educational training.

Nelson M. Blake, professor emeritus of history, Syracuse University, recalled in 1982: "From my own experience I can testify that one important function of both Summer School and University College was to provide opportunities for underpaid professors—particularly those in the lower ranks—to earn enough extra compensation to get a living wage. This also served the interests of the University in holding faculty during these years of financial stringency."

Attendance at the Extension School tended to follow the business index—it gradually increased when times were good. There were 1,481 students in 1927 and 2,323 in the early thirties. The depression caused a downswing, but in 1942, despite the war, 1,501 were attending evening classes.

18

Faculty

With the University hard pressed for funds, a promotion in rank did not always mean additional compensation. As one dean expressed it, the practice of "dry" promotions was common.

A UNIVERSITY HAS BEEN DEFINED AS A COMMUNITY of scholars devoted to the promotion of learning and the development of intellect. Such a definition mirrors the role a faculty plays in the annals of a college or university. It logically follows that what a faculty does—in teaching, research, publication, and administration—largely determines the academic standing of an institution of higher learning.

Dr. Flint's concern for the welfare of the faculty was shown after he arrived on the campus of 1922. Generally the faculty members found him sympathetic to their needs, in contrast to the view many of them had of his predecessor, that of a strong-minded administrator who often forced his will on the teaching staff. Among those who risked the disapproval of Chancellor Day were the founders in 1915 of the Syracuse chapter of the American Association of University Professors. The more active members of the AAUP at Syracuse were Professors Eaton, Graham, Place, Bray, Tanner, Flick, Richardson, Pattee, and Hargitt. At their meetings discussion centered on the aims and potentialities of the association, the relation of vocational education to higher education, and graduate study at the University. At that time the attitude of the administration was not particularly favorable to the

AAUP, and the rank and file of faculty for varied reasons ignored the organization.

Its prospects brightened when Dr. Flint became Chancellor. His role in establishing a retirement plan through the Teachers Insurance and Annuity Association and his sympathetic expressions toward the AAUP encouraged the local chapter, whose membership rose from twenty-eight to sixty-three during 1925–26. The president of the national association congratulated the Syracuse unit and said: "I wish to add a word of appreciation on the very satisfactory increase of membership in Syracuse University, and to hope that the success of your chapter . . . will be marked by further growth."

The chapter initiated studies of its own problems and its relations to the administration. One of these concerned leaves of absence. Although no statement of policy had been enunciated by Chancellor Day, the University did grant some such leaves, and it was one of sixty-two institutions listed by the National Science Foundation in 1919 as granting sabbaticals. Six years later, Vice Chancellor Graham stated: "We have no definite regulations concerning sabbatical leaves nor any published requirements. A member of the faculty who has been with us for several years may apply for a leave of absence and, if leave is granted, he is allowed one-fourth salary for that year. There is no contract, although it is understood on both sides that there is an obligation on the part of the instructor to return to Syracuse. If an instructor would receive a very desirable offer while he is away, the University probably would not oppose his accepting it, but we might raise the question as to whether he would be ethically entitled to retain the sum which he had received during his leave."

Dr. Graham went on to say that if Syracuse were financially able, it might allow an instructor one-half of his salary or possibly more. Occasionally a leave was extended beyond one year, although no salary was given after the first year. Leave was also granted on an exchange basis, subject to certain conditions. No leave was given for the purpose of being employed elsewhere unless special arrangements were made. The AAUP chapter at Syracuse wanted a firmer statement of policy on leaves.

In October 1927 an article by Professor Allan Lemon of the College of Puget Sound in the *Journal of Educational Research* listed Syracuse in a group of American universities and colleges that granted leaves of absence. Most of the institutions required seven years of service before leave was allowed for a period of one year. Of the eighty universities surveyed, twenty-three gave a half-year's salary.

Shortly after Professor George T. Hargitt, president of the Syracuse chapter, read the report he appointed a committee to study the situation at Syracuse. The committee found that leaves of absence were closely related to the twin problems of salaries and teaching loads. It reported:

> Any system of sabbatical leave would require quite an outlay of money annually by the University unless the work of the absent professor were distributed among his colleagues within the department. Since the teaching load at Syracuse is already at its maximum, it seems inadvisable that we should advocate any program which would increase the teaching load of the professors. In most of our departments under any scheme of sabbatical leave, there would be someone absent on leave almost all the time, with the result that the teaching load would be increased because of the distribution of the work of the absent member.

Teaching loads varied in the departments and colleges. During most of the 1922–42 era instructors taught at least fifteen hours a week; those of professorial rank taught twelve. Department chairmen might teach nine.

The committee recommended that the chapter list as its first demand an adequate salary scale; second, an optimum teaching load; and, third, a policy for leaves with pay. Dean Moon of the College of Forestry and Professors Tanner and Porter were among those who discussed the report at length at a chapter meeting late in 1927.

The realities of the situation, according to Chancellor Flint, were that the University's financial condition could not meet these costs. Nevertheless, early in 1930 he announced the first official program for leaves at Syracuse University. Beginning on July 1, 1930, those of professorial rank having six years of continuous service might apply for a leave for one year at half pay or for a half year at full pay "so far as the work of the department and so far as the number of applicants in a year would permit." Everyone who received a leave was to return to the University for at least one year of service.

In the academic year 1930–31 five members of the faculty received leaves, two of them for a full year. Their duties were taken over by other members of their departments or by outside faculty brought to the campus.

The AAUP, local and national, was also concerned with faculty appointments. Selection of new personnel was the subject of a query from the national organization to Vice Chancellor Graham in 1928. It asked how the AAUP might "render the best services in facilitating the selection of competent teachers ... and in assisting the right sort of candidates to secure suitable appointments or transfer." The association also asked the Vice Chancellor's opinion of the value of existing teacher agencies.

He replied that the agencies scarcely touched on the most important aspect of recruiting faculty—obtaining useful information about prospective candidates—and for that reason the University avoided dealing with agencies as far as possible. Dr. Graham said the best way to get reliable information was through the recommendations of experienced teachers who knew the candidate and the university where he was employed.

At Syracuse appointments at the full professor level and for department chairmen generally were carefully screened by the departments concerned, and critically weighed by the deans. The applicants were often interviewed by members of other departments and frequently passed upon by the Chancellor in person.

Much the same procedure was followed in reviewing appointments at lower professorial ranks. Appointments at the instructor's level were usually settled by agreement between the department and the dean. Among criteria used in making appointments were general scholarship, inspirational power, social culture, teaching efficiency, specialized knowledge, originality in thought and method, degrees earned, and health. Naturally much depended on the University's ability and willingness to meet salary demands. No firm policy was established, although these practices were followed throughout the Flint and Graham administrations.

With the University hard pressed for funds, as it was during these years, salary increases were difficult to obtain. Exceptions were made when the University felt justified in raising salaries to keep valuable people on the faculty. But a promotion in rank did not always mean additional compensation. As one dean expressed it, the practice of "dry" promotions was common.

Other criteria for promotion were the candidates' degrees and general competence. The problems were more acute in Chancellor Flint's years than in Dr. Graham's, largely because of debts inherited from the Day administration and the financial doldrums of 1929–33. For example, Dr. Flint, in a letter to Dr. Graham in June 1923, regretted having to rule out promotions because of lack of funds. In several cases he saw no reason for promotion because candidates had neither master's nor doctor's degrees. In one instance he noted that an instructor who had no master's had been made an assistant professor in 1922 and said a request for advancement to associate rank was clearly impossible. In some cases, too, the rank and salary scales in certain colleges were so out of line with the rest of the University that the Chancellor questioned whether any promotion should be made before greater equity was attained.

But there was no unanimity. In September 1927 Dean Raper of the College of Business Administration said promotion from one professorial rank to another generally was made after three or four years of service. To be a full professor one should have a doctoral degree or advanced technical skill or training. To hold a lower professorial rank one should have a master's degree or advanced skill and experience.

Some of his faculty questioned these criteria, but the dean assured them his statement coincided with those of Chancellor Flint and the policy of the University senate. A year later Vice Chancellor Graham stated the issue somewhat differently: "We have no fixed time, either maximum or minimum, for serving in any rank, but in general an instructor will not be advanced to a higher grade in less than three years nor is he expected to remain as an instructor for more than five. Certain departments require the doctorate before advancing to the grade of assistant professor. Others do not require this. In general, the department recommends for promotion, and promotion would in no case be given without the approval of the department."

Early in 1938, after he became chancellor, Dr. Graham insisted that appointments and promotions were the result of custom rather than legislation. Recommendations for promotion went from the dean to the senate and then to the trustees. A departmental chairman might give his staff a voice if he wished, but this was not required. If a vacancy existed, a good man already on the campus would usually receive the promotion, but in many instances the University might prefer to go outside. Dr. Graham added: "Unrestrained faculty action often expresses itself in queer and even absurd ways. Faculty desire is frequently very unintelligent." Some exceptions were made in this promotion procedure but the general principles were in force when Chancellor Graham retired in June 1942.

During the Flint-Graham years, although the administration and the campus chapter of the AAUP had a number of differences, no serious problem arose despite the economic sacrifices caused by the Depression. Retrenchment became the order of the day. In the latter part of the 1929–30 academic year all employees agreed to give back 10 percent of their pay; the voluntary contribution to the University continued in the next year.

Supplies were curtailed and expenses trimmed wherever possible. One of the most difficult tasks facing Chancellor Flint was that of limiting promotions and of avoiding appointments that were not absolutely necessary. More difficult was the decision to reduce the number of University employees. Student assistants and recently appointed young instructors were let go, a policy that involved considerable soul-searching by the Chancellor, the deans, and the departments.

The Syracuse chapter of AAUP understood the need for drastic economy measures but expressed the hope that the administration would not encroach on academic tenure. The position of the national association, unchanged since the mid-twenties, included these points: all terms and expectations of every appointment should be in writing; any termination of a permanent or long-term appointment should require action by both a faculty committee and a university's governing board, except for gross immorality or treason when summary dismissal might ensue; in all other cases, and especially where the facts were in dispute, the accused teacher should have the opportunity to face his accusers and be heard by those who were to pass judgment; when the charges were those of professional incompetence, testimony of scholars both on and off campus should be obtained; and termination of permanent and long-term appointments because of financial reasons should not be made until every effort had been taken to meet the need in other ways and to find the teacher other employment in the institution.

But conditions had changed, and in April 1931 the national AAUP decided to restudy the matter of tenure. A series of questions was circulated to all institutions accredited by the American Council on Education. Chancellor Flint replied at once. He said Syracuse had no written appointment contracts and did not deem them advisable. Nor could he recall any dispute over such a matter since he joined the University in 1922. As to the length of appointment, no instructor or professor of any rank received a definite statement of his period of appointment although in all cases, except for instructors, there was presumption of permanency. As to removal, the Chancellor added that Syracuse had a definite procedure, and that provision existed for notice of charges and hearing, as well as for faculty participation in such removals. The system of tenure at Syracuse was based on usage, not any law, rule, or resolution of the trustees. Finally, Dr. Flint said, although the AAUP provisions had not been "formally adopted" they were "adhered to in practice."

Despite complaints about low salaries and poorly defined policies on appointments, promotions, and leaves of absence, the Syracuse faculty was probably treated as well during the Flint-Graham years as were those employed in comparable institutions. The administration professed good intentions and took gradual steps toward reducing teaching loads, granting leaves, recognizing rights of tenure, and providing retirement benefits. If the faculty's relations to the administration and the students were sometimes strained, this tension was no more than was normal in American universities.

19

Radiant Young People

Student Deans and Resident Advisers

Eunice Hilton told her student deans that even to walk across campus they had to wear hat and gloves and carry a purse.

It was September 1931.

Twelve young women, all college graduates, arrived at the Syracuse railroad station with freshly marcelled hair, knee-length suits, close-fitting hats, and a look of anticipation. They collectively were the first student dean class about to register for a graduate training program in personnel work.

By taxi or street car each found her way to the office of Acting Dean of Women Eugenie Andruss Leonard to claim her assistantship which had been awarded the previous spring by the University's board of trustees.

When the tenth anniversary of the course was celebrated in 1941 it was conceded that the experimental phase was past and that there was now on the campus of Syracuse University a nationally recognized training program in educational personnel work. Other leading universities had studied the program and set up similar ones on their own campuses; to national conventions and to placement bureaus were coming specific requests for Syracuse-tested persons; and applications for assistantships had steadily increased in number.

And on the twenty-fifth anniversary of the course in 1956 the account above was published in a booklet that listed the program's leaders and participants over the years.

One of them was Mrs. Frank P. Piskor, who as Anne Calder had been a student dean from 1938 to 1940 and was on the dean of women's staff for five years after that. At her home in Canton, New York, in the summer of 1981 she looked back to those times. It was her last week as First Lady of St. Lawrence University. Frank Piskor, who was in the dean of men's office under A. Blair Knapp, when his wife-to-be was a student dean under M. Eunice Hilton, was about to retire after twelve years as president of St. Lawrence University.

The Piskors supplemented each other's recollections in a joint interview.

Anne Piskor said:

"It was the graduate program that brought us here, Frank to the Maxwell School and I to the student dean course. Eunice Hilton, as dean of women, and Marjorie Smith, as assistant dean, ran it. That's what brought me from Mount Holyoke. My first assignment was as head resident of Vernon Cottage, which was the first sorority house in America. It was torn down for Newhouse I."

Vernon Cottage was formerly the home of Alpha Chapter of Alpha Phi. The national women's fraternity was founded at Syracuse University in 1872 and the home of its first chapter was built at 17 University Place, facing the main campus, in 1886. Alpha Chapter later moved to its present home at 308 Walnut Place.

Miss Hilton was a student herself when the program began in 1931.

"The student dean course was the only one of its kind in the country," Frank Piskor noted. "Others focused on the training of deans of women or personnel officers, but this course stressed practicum and theory simultaneously. You had to live in residence to get into the course. You had to be affiliated with the dean of women's office as a head resident to get into their seminars, and it was approved as a graduate seminar on that basis."

"I came to get my master's," Anne Piskor said. "They had all age groups, but I was one of the few right out of college."

"In fact, you were an experiment," her husband said. He explained to the interviewer: "That was the first time they took freshly graduated students into the program. Most of the time they took school teachers or people who had had a range of experience in vocational or other kinds of counseling before that."

As director of activities for city women after completing the student dean course, Anne Piskor "worried about" the women students who lived off campus. "It was a big group, and we were trying to make them feel a part of the campus," she said. Later, as social director, she was in charge of overnight permissions for women. She recalled the strict rules: "You had to be where you said you were going to be or you were out."

Frank Piskor said: "And your place had to be approved, unless it were home."

"Yes, and there were only certain places you could stay in New York City. Or if you went to West Point you had to stay at the Hotel Thayer."

"If you went to the Biltmore in New York you stayed on a certain floor," he said.

"Did that hold for men, too?" their interviewer asked.

"No," he said. "There was always a double standard."

She said: "You had to sign in and sign out, and you had to be where you said you were going to be."

"Yes, that was a double standard, and another was in drinking," he said. "Women could not drink in private or in public, whereas men had a different rule."

"Women couldn't drink, period," Mrs. Piskor said.

The office of dean of women came into existence in 1909 when Chancellor Day appointed Jean Marie Richards to head it. Miss Richards, who had taught English at the University since 1895, became a full professor in 1903. As dean of women she found her range of duties limited by the overpowering personality of Dr. Day, the relatively small number of women students, and by the fairly uncomplicated problems of the women of the era. Basically she was responsible for vocational guidance, supervision of conduct at social affairs, management of living centers, and some teaching. In years to come Miss Richards' successors handled increasingly complex duties.

In the fall of 1923, a year after Chancellor Flint succeeded Dr. Day, Marguerite Ellen Woodworth '18 was appointed assistant dean of women. She had been general secretary of the campus YWCA. When Miss Richards retired in 1924. Miss Woodworth was named acting dean and two years later associate dean, but was hampered in her work by a staff limited to two, herself and a secretary.

At about this time Chancellor Flint hoped to interest Mrs. Clara Bradley Burdette, an 1876 Syracuse graduate and a longtime trustee, in women's affairs at the University. Early in 1925 he talked to her about endowing a women's building, but she intimated that such an undertaking was beyond her resources. She remained open to suggestions, however, and in March Dr. Flint sent her a long letter saying in part:

"My investigations and observations are leading me to increasingly emphasize the importance of the dean of women not only on account of the service to all phases of women's life and work, but indirectly, nay directly on the men also. The tone of the woman makes the tone of the man."

He then asked her to relate the "generosity of your plan for Syracuse to the endowment of the deanship—of the individual dean or of the department of women's welfare—or the whole deanship organization for women." The endowment for a "Clara Bradley Burdette Deanship of Women," he said, might entail $80,000 to $100,000.

In another letter he told her he had recently visited Goucher College where he had met Mrs. Iva Lowther Peters, a 1901 Syracuse graduate with a master's from Columbia and a doctorate from Clark University. Dr. Peters was a professor of economics and director of vocational guidance at Goucher and had a national reputation in women's work as scholar and administrator, particularly in vocational guidance. In an age when there were few well-qualified women deans, Dr. Peters was a rarity, and Chancellor Flint was determined to bring her to Syracuse.

Relaying his enthusiasm to Mrs. Burdette, he mentioned $6,000 as a fitting salary for Dr. Peters and hoped Mrs. Burdette would meet it in whole or part. He added: "I fully believe her coming would mean, almost *at once,* a new intellectual, social, and general cultural atmosphere for Syracuse women. I feel her ideas, ideals, and interests would greatly please you." Mrs. Burdette was slow to reply, but the Chancellor, after several interviews with Dr. Peters, prevailed on her in February 1926 to join Syracuse at a salary of $4,000, plus the use of a suite of rooms.

The following June, with Mrs. Burdette present, the trustees approved Dr. Peters' appointment. During a recess Mrs. Burdette handed the Chancellor a note that said: "I have not had a chance to talk with you, but I will assure the $4,000 salary for this year and the next if she proves her value." The next year she increased her gift to $5,000, of which $1,000 was for office expenses. She continued to give $5,000 a year until June 1935.

Dr. Flint informed Mrs. Burdette that Dean Peters would concentrate at first on personal and educational matters while the associate dean, Miss Marguerite Woodworth, dealt with personnel, social, and religious matters. Dr. Peters, in an article in the January 1927 *Alumni News,* wrote of her national commitments, her membership in learned societies, addresses to various meetings, her teaching duties in the Maxwell School, and her general activities as dean of women. Despite her many obligations she had time to continue her research in the problems of women. Chancellor Flint and Mrs. Burdette expressed satisfaction with what she had accomplished at the close of the 1926–27 academic year.

During 1927–28 Dean Peters reorganized her office and delegated certain duties to her assistants. Mabel C. Lytton was put in charge of the religious program. Mabel C. Rhoades was responsible for compiling statistical data and drafting personnel forms that helped the director of admissions and Margaret B. Brockway, the social adviser. But now illness and family responsibilities began to keep Dean Peters away from the campus. In addition to her own illness, her mother died, and her husband became ill and died.

The dean's extended absences were a problem, but Dr. Flint told a friend it was too soon to draw any clear conclusions about her overall effectiveness. He endorsed what she had accomplished thus far, especially in organization.

As Dr. Peters convalesced at Newfoundland, New Jersey, she had every intention of returning to Syracuse but was not certain she could resume her full responsibilities as dean. She wrote to the Chancellor: "I have thought of myself becoming perhaps an alumna adviser." In response Dr. Flint praised what she had achieved and hoped she would soon resume her duties. He added: "Progressively, as this is accomplished, you will naturally become more or less an alumna adviser and also be called upon to fill more engagements in a large field." During the academic year 1929–30 Associate Dean Florence Nicholson, Assistant Dean Lytton, and others ran the dean's office.

Dean Peters spent several weeks in the South in early 1930, still uncertain what she would do. She told the Chancellor she might leave the University after training someone "on whom she could let the campus deanship rest." Later she repeated this intention to Dr. Flint and told others of her general intentions. In this dilemma, and on the advice of Dr. Peters, he interviewed Eugenie Andruss Leonard, the widow of a former professor of education at Columbia University. Dr. Leonard had graduated from the University of California in 1920 and, after her husband's death, earned a doctorate at Columbia in 1930 in religious education. She was a close friend of Dean Peters and had visited the Syracuse campus in 1929 to study the cottage system for undergraduates, a feature she incorporated in her doctoral dissertation.

Eugenie Leonard expressed interest in the Chancellor's proposal. During his absence on vacation in Europe academic matters were handled by an administrative council which, among other problems,

Eugenie Andruss Leonard, dean of women, 1932–1936.

was called on to settle the question of Dean Peters' successor. After interviewing Mrs. Leonard and conferring with Dean Peters, the council late in March 1930 instructed Dr. Graham to cable the Chancellor for authority to appoint Dr. Leonard acting dean of women. Dr. Flint gave his consent, and board of trustees approval followed.

An unpleasant situation faced Dr. Flint soon after his return in June. A letter from Dr. Peters questioned him about the relative spheres of authority between herself and Dr. Leonard. Apparently no clear division of authority had been established at the time of the Leonard appointment. Mrs. Burdette, unhappy at the prospect of losing Dr. Peters, thought it a mistake to have named Dr. Leonard acting dean. As "vice-dean" she could have handled the dean's work while she was absent, fitting herself for the deanship on Dr. Peters' departure. It was obvious there had been no unanimity about what the two deans were to do.

Increasingly Dr. Peters believed she was being forced out. She expressed herself vividly in her June letter, claiming Dr. Leonard was taking over "the administration of the dean of women's office entire. My relationship becomes advisory; that is, I act only upon invitation. Mrs. Leonard takes the personal relation with you; she understands that she is your dean of women, taking her directions from you and administering on that basis." Later, in a note to Professor Burges Johnson, she said she carried the rank of dean of women only "by courtesy."

The situation was becoming a campus issue. A worried Dr. Flint, writing to Mrs. Burdette, said he had hoped Dean Peters "would for several years maintain and direct control of the work here. When I found however she desired to be foot-free in order to give more time to visiting other institutions, attending conventions, writing books and papers etc., I reconciled myself to the idea of having her secure or train others to do her general relationship to us and use this as a base for her other work. I shall hope this may be consummated."

The upshot was that Dr. Peters left the University for good in June 1931. Despite the problems, she had endeared herself to many alumnae, and the women students generally found her most gracious. Her role as a teacher in the School of Citizenship was noteworthy. She had assumed the deanship at a critical time in the financial life of the University, a factor that sometimes limited her administration. All things considered, her deanship was not "wasted," as she declared in 1935, and Chancellor Flint and Mrs. Burdette always spoke of her in complimentary terms.

Nevertheless, they believed the arrival of Dr. Leonard in the fall of 1930 would bring a renaissance in the management of women's affairs. During her first year she busied herself learning the many tasks she would face when she became dean in her own right at the opening of school in 1931. Her report for 1931–32 shows how active she had been—supervising women's living centers, vocational guidance, tutoring-advising, social affairs, and student activities generally. Dr. Flint was pleased with her record.

But so was the dean of education at Columbia University, who tried to entice her back in 1932. She sent a copy of his letter to the Chancellor with this penciled note: "I should like to refuse this offer unless you advise me otherwise."

Presumably Dr. Flint was not eager to face the prospect of having a second new dean in two years. He told Dean Leonard the University was highly satisfied with her work and would take "reasonably good care" of her. Accepting this as a vote of confidence, Dean Leonard decided to remain at Syracuse.

The student dean program grew out of conditions that arose during Dr. Peters' tenure. Housing for women students had become inadequate by the fall of 1926. Haven, Winchell, and Lima halls were reserved for upperclass women. The freshmen and sophomores were distributed among thirteen living centers in the care of individual chaperons who, under the dean, advised, counseled, and supervised the younger women. At first many of the chaperons were recruited from among graduate women who planned to study in various University departments. As chaperons they received free room and board. But some had difficulty dividing their time between their responsibilities to the students and their own course work toward advanced degrees.

These conditions plus Dr. Peters' own experience at Columbia and Syracuse merged into the idea of a teaching internship. At Columbia she learned about Paul Monroe's pioneering work in courses for deans in administration and counseling and studied under Professor Sarah Sturtevant, who stressed training women students to assume the duties of deans.

When Dr. Leonard visited Syracuse University in 1930 she talked to Dean Peters about the suggested program and during Dr. Peters' leave of absence discussed the project with Chancellor Flint and others. It was agreed to establish a course in the Graduate School titled Advisers of Girls and Deans of Women. Dean Leonard's plan was that every living center "shall have a mature young person as chaperon and that these chaperons shall consider themselves on the staff of the dean of women with the distinct duty of developing the highest type of character in the individual students under their care." As Margaret C. Wells said in her 1950 doctoral dissertation, "By combining Mrs. Peters' plan of using graduate students as dormitory head residents with the Columbia idea of giving them specific training in personnel work, Mrs. Leonard laid the foundations of the now nationally recognized student dean training program at Syracuse University."

This "deanette" program was publicly announced in the spring of 1931. To underwrite the cost, graduate assistantships were given to a limited number of women. The grants covered room, board, and tuition. On finishing the course the student deans received the degree of master of science in education. Course work was supervised by Dean Leonard, with the assistance of Professors Floyd Allport, Herbert Shenton, and Louis Hickernell, Deans Ganders, Mosher, and Powers, and the staff of the dean of women. In announcing the new program Dean Leonard made it clear that it was not one in the theory of becoming a dean, "but a laboratory course in deaning." She added: "The dormitories filled with radiant young people are the laboratories."

The first year's trial was a success, and in the fall of 1932 the term "chaperons" was changed to "student deans." The program became widely known in American educational circles, especially at state and national conventions of women's deans.

Dean Leonard's report to Chancellor Flint for 1934–35 spoke of "the high quality both of the academic work of the student personnel, and successful placement of graduates." She said this resulted in more than "10 application-inquiries for 1933 and of nearly 200 for 1934–35. Twenty-three received appointments in 1933 and of the 62 completed applications of 1934, 32 were appointed or reappointed, including two for co-operative houses and three for sororities."

In addition to her regular course and laboratory work, each student dean did extensive research in such subjects as the Chairmanship of Tutor-Adviser Program for Women Students, Transfer Students and Their Problems, and the Social Adjustment of College Women Students. More faculty members cooperated—Professors Elizabeth Manwell, Ross Hoople, Ralph Strebel, Ernest Thelin, Harry Hepner, Katharine Sibley, and Gladys Allis. Authorities in specialized fields came to the campus to lecture. The student deans attended a three-day institute each fall for orientation in their work. They made visits to other colleges and to state and national meetings of deans of women.

Despite the success of the student dean program and Dean Leonard's other achievements, there was increasing tension between herself and the administration. In her annual report of June 1934 she complained of misunderstandings about her work and her authority. She urged the Chancellor to spell out her duties in the University bylaws to give her power over all women students regardless of their relationship to other deans or directors. She believed she should be next in authority to the Chancellor, and at least equal to the Vice Chancellor, in the power structure.

Dr. Flint, saying he could not grant her request, asked her to try to adjust to what he and others in the administration considered the limits of her authority. This was a blow to Dean Leonard. Those close to her indicated she had believed Dr. Flint considered her services indispensable and would do anything to keep her. But soon she learned of an opening at a junior college in San Francisco and in May 1935 tendered her resignation.

Rather than make the resignation final, Dr. Flint offered her a year's leave of absence if she would let him know by January 1936 whether she would return. As an alternative he proposed a year's leave, at half salary, during which she could study and rest.

Dean Leonard replied that her decision to leave the University was not sudden and added: "I shall be interested in returning to Syracuse only if working conditions were so changed as to give full authority to the dean of women to carry out the functions for which she is responsible. This is, of course, only what I have requested during the four years that I have been dean of women." She then agreed to withdraw her resignation and suspend her ultimate decision until January 1936. A few days later she submitted suggestions for managing the office during her absence, then left for California. In due time Dr. Flint wrote and asked whether she intended to return. In her abrupt reply she said she would remain where she was.

When Dean Leonard first offered to resign she suggested Helen Moreland, then dean of women at Albany State Teachers College, for the post of acting dean for 1935–36. Before anything could be done about this recommendation, one of the first student deans, now a member of Dean Leonard's staff, M. Eunice Hilton, announced she was about to accept a deanship of women elsewhere. Dean Leonard then told the Chancellor she had changed her mind and now believed Miss Hilton was a better choice. After some hesitation because of Miss Hilton's "youth"—she was thirty-five—the Chancellor named her acting dean for 1935–36, intimating that the appointment would be reviewed in the spring of 1936 if Dean Leonard did not return. But Miss Hilton's year of probation proved more than satisfactory, and the board of trustees made her dean of women without a formal review as of September 1936.

The new dean received her bachelor's and master's degrees at the University of Nebraska in 1922 and 1926. She was dean of women at McCook Junior College in Nebraska for five years before she enrolled at Syracuse as a graduate student in the deans program. At first in charge of Annable Cottage, in 1932 she became vocational director. For the next two years she was assistant dean in charge of residence, at the same time completing her Ph.D. in education.

As acting dean in 1935 Dr. Hilton, in addition to the general management of women's affairs, had direction over classes for the

M. Eunice Hilton, dean of women, 1936–1949.

student deans and handled as much personnel counseling as time allowed. Joining Syracuse University that year as assistant dean of women was Marjorie C. Smith, who assigned the rooms in the living centers, directed personnel problems there, and did some teaching. The vocational director, Virginia Keller, was responsible for the social calendar and chaperoning and was secretary of the social committee. Margaret Brockway was director of social education for freshmen women, advised the student deans, and also taught.

Three future Syracuse deans were on the dean of women's staff in the 1930's—Martha Eunice Hilton, Bernice Huff Meredith '29, and Marjorie C. Smith. When Miss Hilton became dean of the College of Home Economics in 1949, Miss Smith succeeded her as dean of women. In 1964 "Bunny" Meredith, then Bernice M. Wright, became dean of Home Economics (later the College for Human Development).

Others on the dean of women's staff after 1930 were Florence Partridge, Marie W. Wilson, Bess and Jean Templeton, Sarah Lutes, Julia E. Reed, Opal Berg, Ruth Paul, Hazel King, Mary Gilmore, Sarah Healy, Elizabeth Broad, Ethel Armstrong, Nancy Lewis, Ellen Peterson, Maude Stewart, and Anne Calder.

Anne Calder Piskor, looking back from 1981, said that when she became a student dean "I was told that even to walk from Vernon Cottage, which is where Newhouse I is, up to the administration building I had to wear a hat, gloves, and carry a purse. And if I had ever gone downtown without them, that would have been the sin of sins. As the president's wife up here [St. Lawrence University] I don't even own a hat; I never wear a hat."

"Wouldn't that apply to the men?" she was asked. "Did they have to wear jackets and ties?"

"No. I think this was a standard Eunice and Marjorie set because they wanted their student deans to be a little bit apart. And probably the fact that I was younger than some of the girls who lived in my dormitory made them think it was necessary in my case."

Notable during Dr. Hilton's deanship was the changing nature of graduate work. By 1937 the student deans were registering for the course Advisers of Girls and Deans of Women, for a seminar, the Philosophy and Techniques of Student Personnel Work, and a course in Problems in Educational Research. By 1940 Student Housing was added to the curriculum.

Dean Hilton prepared a syllabus with suggested readings for several of the courses. She began the practice of letting the students assume some duties of her office. She gave them the option of writing a thesis or taking a comprehensive examination for a master's degree and excused them from advising undergraduates when their studies demanded. More and more the program concentrated on the techniques of counseling, and there was a marked decrease in the number of lecturers from other departments of the University and from outside.

The University was housing increasing numbers of undergraduate women and year after year Dean Hilton pressed the administration for bigger appropriations and the maintenance of academic standards in the student dean program. "We have been drawing about the limit in number of good student deans we can secure and the load with respect to their study program is as heavy as we feel we can carry," she wrote to Chancellor Graham in May 1941.

That Dr. Graham was proud of the program was clear from his report to the board of trustees at the end of that month: "We are celebrating in June the tenth anniversary of the establishing of the deans' training course. . . . The course now has a national reputation. It is one of the best things Syracuse University has ever done so far as advertising value goes, and so far as educational value goes."

Closely identified with the student dean program but separate from it were the senior guides, who were active in Orientation Week events attended by all entering freshmen. The guides introduced new students to the campus, and in 1933 the system became a feature of University life. Junior women were invited to arrive on campus early in the beginning of their senior year to receive special instruction by the dean and her staff. Each senior was assigned to a freshman house where she greeted the incoming women. Under the guide's supervision the house elected officers and established rules for self-government. The senior guide counseled her charges on all phases of college life. Later, under Dean Hilton, the guides took a two-hour course in the principles and techniques of personnel work. At about the same time the Women's Student Government initiated a program of junior guides who were assigned to the various living centers and to groups of city women students.

One of the more important subjects studied by the student deans was vocational guidance. Dr. Peters was nationally known for her work in guidance at Goucher College. On joining Syracuse she formalized work in the field. Her successors continued the program, which centered chiefly on student counseling and placement. Eventually the program consisted of advising freshmen and sophomores on their academic schedules, particularly the fields they planned to major in.

Many students asked the help of the director of vocational guidance in finding employment in business and the professions. She arranged interviews between the young women and firms seeking employees, but her work did not end there. The director also considered it her duty to counsel the students on marriage as a career or to discuss a combination of marriage and a career.

A major reason for the success of the office of the dean of women was the devotion of the staff to the deans, particularly Dr. Hilton whose thirteen-year tenure was greater than the combined terms of her two immediate predecessors. She often praised the cooperative spirit of her assistants. But Dean Hilton's colleagues in the administration noted it was she who provided the vision and had the faith in her program and policies that made the office function so well. Her leadership, built on the groundwork of Deans Peters and Leonard, was largely responsible for earning the University national prestige as a training center for future deans and advisers of women students.

The office of dean of women had been in existence since 1909, but it was not until thirty-one years later that a similar office was set up for men.

From the early stages of his tenure, however, Chancellor Flint expressed interest in student welfare and that new phenomenon in education known as the "personnel movement."

The first real evidence of this at Syracuse was a system of faculty advisers established in the College of Liberal Arts in 1923 to help students select courses and otherwise counsel them individually. Some of the advisers took these added responsibilities less than seriously, and the program deteriorated to the point in February 1927 when Dr. Flint created an all-University committee on scholarship to plan "an adequate advisory system."

Religious and ethical ideas permeated the Chancellor's thinking, and he envisioned the personnel movement leading to a day when "our mechanistic system of credits, with stilted stimuli and crude measurements, will give way to a system of assignments, case-methods, problem-methods, research methods which will naturally stimulate to initiative, self-supervision, and self-testing, and to a system of measurement of attainment, achievement, and attitude of a totally different and more delicate type."

At the time Dr. Flint named Iva Peters dean of women, in 1926, he appointed Mark A. May director of personnel for men. May soon left the University and was succeeded by Donald B. Watt, formerly a research associate at Yale University's personnel department.

Watt devoted most of his time to improving the system of student scholarships and loans and running the placement bureau, then, in 1930 he was put in charge of the broadened University employment office for men and women students.

The men's personnel department was discontinued in June 1931 because the Depression made it impossible to finance it any longer. Before Watts' departure he had the satisfaction of knowing that a proctor system for Sims Dormitory, to which he had contributed, would be continued by Ernest S. Griffith, dean of the lower division of the College of Liberal Arts. The dean introduced a pioneering tutor-adviser system in 1930, holding that older methods had failed because of lack of adequate organization and because the burden of administration had fallen on the faculty. Since little had been required of the students, fewer than half of those who entered the University graduated. Of those who did, not all made the most of their opportunities. In Griffith's words, "The real tragedy ... is this waste of human possibilities."

Under the Griffith program the advisory system was voluntary and about 500 freshmen enrolled each year through June 1935. The lower division dean saw his mandate as covering all matters affecting curriculum, faculty, and students. This often resulted in conflicts of jurisdiction with other agencies. Yet Dean Griffith was convinced that his work deepened faculty-student relations, promoted individual attention to education, provided better planning of course work, and let the tutors help their advisees more efficiently. The system sought to stimulate student preparation for tutorial sessions and to acquaint each advisee with a knowledge of campus problems, including study habits, religion, athletics, self-support, racial questions, and the maze of student government and fraternity life. Dr. Griffith did not let the program drift into a routine of teas and parties. At first each adviser had one or two students. Later, under A. Blair Knapp, it averaged three. Dr. Griffith was aware, however, that some students did not prepare for their conferences and that at times some faculty members lost enthusiasm for their work. It was his hope that the administration would reduce the regular teaching load of professors who showed an interest in the program and ultimately increase their salaries. He also believed that in time the University would appreciate the merits of the students.

In any event, Dr. Griffith was able to take pride in the fact that Syracuse was the first American university to introduce the tutor-adviser program.

His efforts were criticized by some faculty members who believed the results were negligible and the effort misplaced, but others praised them highly. The tutor-adviser system was only for men, because Dr. Griffith thought they needed it more than the women students, but the dean of women, Dr. Leonard, was among those who spoke well of it and hoped funds could be obtained to broaden it.

Chancellor Flint tried to raise an endowment fund for the system, and a number of departments in Liberal Arts published brochures on how to study. Professor Burges Johnson of the English department called it an unqualified success and complimented Dean Griffith for his chatty *Handbook for Student Advisers.* Knapp, then teaching in the Maxwell School, also praised the program and particularly the faculty advisers, noting that they received no added compensation for this work.

The success of the tutor-adviser system led to the establishment of resident and fraternity adviser programs before Dr. Griffith left the University in 1935. A subsequent survey of student life found overlapping jurisdiction and confusion over authority with too many committees at work.

Chancellor Flint decided to reorganize the entire program. He set up a Council on Men's Affairs headed by Arthur Blair Knapp, a 1926 graduate of Syracuse who received his M.A. two years later. At the time of his appointment to what was to become the office of the dean of men he was an instructor in American government.

In the framework of the Flint directive, the Council on Men's Affairs was an experiment with modest budget and its first year was primarily one of observation. The Knapp innovations were still to come.

Knapp said that in the following year he proposed to correlate all informal activities that would develop a sound educational objective—training students in "responsible citizenship." Without such schooling for them, he said, the democratic form of government would fall short of its aims and responsibilities. Campus life as well as the classroom, he believed, should serve as the laboratory for such training. A second major objective was to help students with their personal problems—finances, religion, health, and morality. A third was to promote the scholastic welfare of the students. Borderline students and those of average ability would receive special attention, and exceptional ones would be encouraged to find "independent adventure in the field of scholarship."

Chancellor Flint, pleased with Knapp's program and initial efforts, soon moved him to the Administration Building.

When Dr. Flint left the University the responsibility for continuing the program fell to Chancellor Graham, whose confidence in Knapp's ability was shown by his frequent compliments in reports to the board of trustees.

An insight to the functioning of the tutor-advisor system is found in the *Handbook for Tutor Advisers* for 1935–36. In his introduction

A. Blair Knapp, dean of men, 1940–1943, and head of Council on Men's Affairs, 1935–1943. Photograph © Bachrach.

Knapp said student conferences averaged about eight a year for each advisee, most of them during the first semester. Generally they were at the tutor's office. Subjects discussed were methods of study, difficulties in course work, fraternity matters, and the student's choice of profession or occupation. Other topics were athletics, finances and self-support, use of leisure time, campus activities, religion, housing, cultural reading, national and international problems, drinking, the other sex, health matters, and racism. In most instances the tutors were able to help the students directly but sometimes referred them to doctors or ministers better qualified to advise them.

The handbook reminded the adviser that the program was essentially a cooperative one. "Basically, it is a relationship between two individuals," it said. "The student has asked for the assistance of a more mature mind in his adjustment to University life and methods. The tutor has responded to this, presumably in part influenced by the desire to assist the student in realizing the full possibilities of his university life. Such individualizing calls for flexibility, for the recognition of the seriousness of purpose of each student, and for mutual cooperation in meeting his peculiar needs."

Knapp reorganized the resident and fraternity adviser systems, which expanded rapidly. Gordon Barclay was put in charge of the advisers and was assisted by such men as Clayton Shay and Benjamin Hopkins-Moses, along with graduate students living in Sims Hall, seven fraternity houses, and the approved houses for men.

These advisers were carefully selected from among graduates of Syracuse and other universities. They received financial aid in the form of room, board, and tuition from either the University or the fraternities. After an orientation week just before the opening of classes, at which the advisers were introduced to the University and the nature of their work, they met weekly in Knapp's office. There he warned them against being "one of the boys," although he urged them to mingle freely with the students. Because of the daily contact with their students, they had an opportunity to strengthen moral and religious attitudes.

There were occasional problems in adminstering the program. One was that resident advisers sometimes dated undergraduate women, a practice frowned on by the dean of women.

But in general the program worked well with the result that in 1940 Knapp was rewarded for his all-around services by being appointed the University's first dean of men. His new duties consisted of coordinating all personnel services, promoting citizen education through student government, and other matters referred to him by the

Chancellor. Among his assistants were Professor Lewis Crawford, who continued in charge of fraternities, and Benjamin Hopkins-Moses, who administered the resident advisers. Named to help in the important work of counseling students were Arthur Boulter, John Gough, Bernard Horowitz, William Jones, and Frank P. Piskor. All had served apprenticeships as resident advisers.

Hopkins-Moses later headed the Syracuse University extension program and became the first registrar of Triple Cities College, now the State University of New York at Binghamton.

Frank Piskor went on to become dean of men and later Vice Chancellor and Provost at Syracuse, and then president of St. Lawrence University.

One of Dean Knapp's first innovations, in the fall of 1940, was a program of Orientation Houses. It grouped together certain tutor advisers and the resident and fraternity advisers. The plan worked so well that the following May at the Gridiron banquet Chancellor Graham presented the Orange Beret award to Knapp as the faculty member who had done the most for Syracuse University in the previous year. Later Piskor was put in direct charge of the Orientation Houses program.

Soon the University was preparing for the impact of World War II. Campus life changed. Male enrollment declined. Most of the fraternity houses temporarily closed their doors. More and more Dean Knapp confined himself to wartime concerns. He became the campus representative of all branches of the armed forces. He and his assistants advised students on service-connected problems and helped recruit men for various military reserves. One day in June 1943 Dean Knapp himself was sworn in as a captain in the Army Air Forces. Mustered out as a major, he joined Temple University in 1946 as dean of students, later a vice president. In 1951 he became president of Denison University. The same year Syracuse University awarded him an honorary doctor of laws degree.

Frank Piskor, who was named acting dean when Captain Knapp left and who became full dean three years later, had high praise in his 1981 interview for the man he succeeded, for the dean of women, and for the way their offices worked together. He said he hoped the University history would recognize "the tremendous qualities Blair Knapp represented" and brought to his job. Almost single-handedly, for instance, he developed the grant-in-aid system.

"The grant-in-aid was a way in those days not of supporting athletics, but of supporting the poor youngster who was a Depression casualty," Dr. Piskor said. "It was a device under which you really extended what a student needed to get through Syracuse University, with the understanding that it wasn't a gift scholarship. There was the assumption of a moral obligation to repay what you could of that grant sometime in the future to the extent that you could. That was as broad a credit system as you could establish, in the discretion of one man, to provide equal opportunity and help for the people.

"In my early days, even as a director of freshman counseling, I had to make a lot of those decisions; that is, make the recommendations to Dr. Knapp and have him act on them. And even today people will come with their children to a place like St. Lawrence and reminisce about that bit of credit they got, and assure me that they have repaid it three or four times over, as I'm sure a lot of them have."

Not only was the repayment factor very good, Dr. Piskor said, but later, in the Tolley years, "you actually had more coming in than you were passing on."

Dr. Piskor paid tribute to Knapp's role in developing and expanding the resident adviser system to a point where it paralleled the highly successful student dean course for women. "Blair Knapp recruited graduate students on a competitive basis from many areas, but because Maxwell was one of the larger graduate school components in the system, the bulk of them were the Maxwell School," he said. "That helped undergraduates and the campus undergraduate life stay closely and consistently knitted together. There was a friendly rivalry but basically an effective cooperation between Blair Knapp as dean of men and Eunice Hilton as dean of women, and policies for men and women started being integrated more effectively."

As Blair Knapp himself once said: "Institutions now feel a positive responsibility for the social, physical, civic, cultural and religious development of their students. It is not simply a matter of 'exposing' the students to a set curriculum of lectures and assignments; still less is it a simple process of teaching a professional skill with which to earn a livelihood. The emphasis upon scholarship alone is no longer the whole program. The ultimate objective is the full realization of the potentialities of the human personality and character which is the raw material of the process."

20

Religion

Students don't come here any more because Syracuse is a "Christian university." They come because it's a good university.

—Professor D. B. Robertson

SYRACUSE UNIVERSITY has always been something of a paradox. Founded by leaders of the Methodist Episcopal Church as a "Christian university," it has been nonsectarian from the start. Supported financially by members of the Syracuse local community, it is not a municipal institution although national media sometimes refer to "the University of Syracuse." Graven in the red Longmeadow sandstone over the front door of Crouse College (which is not a college) are the words "The John Crouse Memorial College for Women," but Syracuse University from its inception has been coeducational.

Although founding father Jesse T. Peck, a bishop of the church, declared as president of the board of trustees in his address at inaugural ceremonies in 1871 "We are ... devoted to the promotion of Christian learning," he also said "We propose no narrow-minded sectarianism on one hand nor infidelity on the other."

And the first chancellor, Alexander Winchell, declared in 1872: "The University is not sectarian. It is an institution founded in the interest of truth, which knows no sect, no sex, no color, no contrasts."

Long before the word ecumenical became fashionable that concept was practiced at Syracuse University:

Senator Francis Hendricks, circa 1918.

The first chairman of the religion department had been converted to Christianity from Judaism by a Lutheran minister in Berlin.

The donor of Hendricks Chapel was a Presbyterian and the long-time secretary to the first dean of the chapel was Jewish.

When a prominent Jewish merchant endowed a lecture series in Judaic studies at the University, it was first administered by the Willard Ives Professor of the English Bible, a Presbyterian.

As the fourth dean of Hendricks Chapel was being installed he took off his shoes "to join with those of the Islamic faith who practice this ritual when they worship."

He then pledged to implement a vision of the ninth chancellor, a Methodist who believes there should be a welcome at the chapel for those not otherwise affiliated. The dean said: "We will emphasize the churched as well as the nonchurched."

From its beginnings the great majority of Syracuse University students were Protestants, and most of the Protestants—faculty and students—were of the founders' faith, Methodist. That religious pattern did not change materially during the University's first half century, and the heights on which it was built became known as Piety Hill. Probably the nickname originated on newspaper copy desks—the words Piety Hill, with fewer and skinnier letters than Syracuse University, take up less space in a headline.

Thus until the early 1920s the University not only reflected the impact of Methodism, but it also stimulated a religious program and chapel that were Wesleyan in spirit and action. At the same time non-Methodists were urged to practice their religions as they wished and, as the University grew, there was a gradual increase in the number of students who were not Methodist.

There was also a weakening of chapel's influence on campus life. Furthermore, Syracuse had grown in size and wealth, and there was rising interest in or concern with organized athletics, student housing, the demands for student government, and abuses in the fraternity system. It appeared to some that Syracuse was becoming more like a big business than an academic institution, and those who felt that way deplored loss of the bond they believed had existed between themselves and the Chancellor and members of the faculty. World War I also had a divisive influence on campus religious life.

The 1922 report of the Methodist board of visitors recognized these trends. It urged the churches to forsake their parochialism and undertake a Christian crusade among the students. The board did not mention it, but many campus observers felt that the major reason to continue chapel exercises was not to instill religious values, but rather to unify the student body socially and for the convenience of the administration.

During the first years of the Flint administration, chapel and the University's religious program remained virtually unchanged. The University *Bulletin* of 1925, for example, continued to carry this statement:

"The chapel exercises, held every day except Sunday—9:50–10:10 a.m.—consist of singing, responsive reading of the Scriptures and the Lord's prayer. Students are expected to attend regularly the Sabbath church service of the denomination to which they belong. In several of the colleges, convocation is held once a week. The Young Men's Christian Association and the Young Women's Christian Association are flourishing and effective organizations."

By 1926, however, Chancellor Flint had introduced a series of changes. In January services in the old chapel on the top floor of the Hall of Languages were abandoned in favor of a voluntary chapel convocation for all University students, held in Crouse College auditorium at noon each Tuesday and Thursday. The gatherings, arranged by a joint student and faculty committee, consisted of formal lectures, talks on current issues, musicales, and dramatic readings. Attendance was better than at chapel service.

Many alumni questioned the new order, but most seemed to realize that the University was following national trends toward secularized higher education. The trends were measured in great detail on the Syracuse campus in 1926 by David Katz, a Ph.D. candidate, and Floyd H. Allport, professor of social and political psychology in the Maxwell School. The opinion-samplers asked 1,502 Liberal Arts students to make one of seven choices about a deity. The choices ranged from orthodox belief in an "infinitely wise, omnipotent Creator" through progressively less orthodox beliefs to agnosticism, atheism, or materialism. Of the 1,321 who answered the question, 21 percent believed in an omnipotent creator, and 43 percent believed in an "infinitely intelligent and friendly Being, working according to natural laws through which he expresses his power and goodness."

Thus 64 percent took the two most orthodox positions on the seven-item scale. About 13 percent chose the agnostic attitude that existence of a supreme being was neither proved nor disproved. About 9 percent were at the far end of scale toward atheism and materialism.

In summarizing these and other data Katz, who later joined the psychology faculty at Princeton University, and Allport concluded that while there was no danger of the Syracuse students lapsing into atheism, liberalism and skepticism about institutional worship were increasing.

About eleven hundred of the students who replied to the Katz-Allport survey of 1926 responded to a similar study in 1970. These alumni, grown older, were called "the grandparent group" in a comparison of their attitudes then and forty-four years later. A report on the so-called replication said: "The grandparent group shows decreased acceptance of orthodox conceptions of God ... compared with their positions as students in 1926." The newer study also said the percentage of respondents not attending any religious services more than doubled from 1926 to 1970, rising from 9 to 22 percent.

The Katz-Allport findings of 1926 made Chancellor Flint realize that Syracuse, like other universities, was facing a new age. Accordingly, he was ready to break with the past where necessary to guide the

University to what he considered its proper place in religious education. Dr. Flint questioned the value of the Christian Associations—the YMCA and the YWCA—about which many religious leaders, students, and faculty alike, had reservations. Some were ready to drop the organizations, feeling they had outlived their usefulness.

The Chancellor, in his report to the trustees in November 1927, sketched a dismal future for the YMCA and implied that a thorough overhaul of the University's religious program was overdue.

Among the ideas he favored was that of a University chaplain, an office being created at other Universities. At Syracuse the University chaplain was to become the dean of Hendricks chapel.

In February 1928 a Student Church, supported by many students and faculty members, was established. It met in Crouse College, monthly at first and then twice a month. The Student Church embodied many of the key elements that were to come in the chapel.

Marjorie Bronner Pierson '31 recalled in an interview during the fiftieth anniversary year of Hendricks Chapel how the Student Church developed. She and her husband Theodore Pierson '30 were the donors in 1981 of the small chapel within Hendricks Chapel named for their late daughter Rena Pierson Dankovich.

Mrs. Pierson said:

> In the fall of 1927 there was no truly organized religious program on campus, as there had been in the early days. Daily chapel had quietly died. The churches in the university area had various programs for students and met with differing responses. On campus the YWCA and the YMCA were still organized and performed a number of activities. But for all practical purposes there was no interdenominational or interfaith program, which a few religiously oriented and sensitive students began to be concerned about. In a pre-ecumenical time they were interested in a religious organization that would transcend the limits of any one denominational or faith group.
>
> That fall Gordon Halstead, a senior at the University, was concerned about this and talked to the Reverend Norman Vincent Peale, then the young minister of the University Methodist Episcopal Church. They gathered together a group of faculty and students including Iva L. Peters, dean of women, Mabel Lytton, her associate, and Ruth Stafford, Helen Honsinger, Dominic Rinaldo, and John Leininger, all students, and discussed the possibility of worship services under the complete direction of the students.
>
> Some of those on the committee had attended the Student Volunteer Convention on their Christmas vacation where, as one committee member expressed it, "The drive of the convention was no longer to Christianize the world, but to bring all religions together in a process of

shaping, by which the best elements of each should be made available for all." With this the committee abandoned any idea of establishing a denominational church as being too restrictive, and chose the Crouse College auditorium as a place not associated with any single denomination.

Early in 1928 others were recruited to share in this emerging program. They included Wilton Chase, Ivan Gould, Nathalie Herman, Phyllis Leonard, Margaret Crossby, Marian Diamond, Mary Gilmore, Rolland Chaput, Howard Fuller, and Willard Salter. This entire committee planned the first service of Sunday evening, February 12. Before the end of the academic year four other services were held. The next year biweekly services were introduced at 11 o'clock Sunday morning, and a widespread group of speakers representing various denominational and faith groups came to address the Student Church.

Added features were a Sunday afternoon discussion with the speaker and a meeting of interested persons each Monday evening. Various committees were established to do the work of planning services and engaging in social outreach. It is interesting to note, in light of subsequent developments, that at one of the meetings of the Student Church committee the appointment of a chaplain was recommended.

In the spring of 1929 a statement of purpose was formulated by the committee. It read: "The Student Church is an experiment in religious unity. While many groups have been discussing this problem, here a definite attempt has been made to provide a service at which members of all races and creeds could forget the differences which have separated them and come together in a common worship of God in whom they all believe."

Marjorie Pierson said:

> So this group of students struggled on. Lacking in experience in conducting religious worship, they made up for it in study and hard work. Worshipping in a place hardly ideal for services, they made it as attractive as possible. Curtailed by less than adequate funds for their programs they made do, and their offerings were now and again assisted by a few generous gifts, until the University, after the program was established, began to give some financial help.
>
> The Student Church laid the foundation for three important aspects of the Chapel program that was to follow—practical interdenominationalism and interfaith cooperation, a dynamic interpretation of religion in contemporary terms, and voluntary and active student initiative and responsibility.

The Student Church did not end the weekly convocations, but attendance at them declined. Another campus tradition, however, was not to survive much longer.

The leaders of the YMCA and the Chancellor met several times to discuss the matter, but soon after classes began in the fall of 1928 it was clear that there was no place in the administration's program for the men's association. Events moved fast. The Chancellor's reorganization plan, because it related to an existing student group, was submitted to the Student Senate, which endorsed it. That action was followed by the voluntary resignation of the governing board of the YMCA. Thus the Young Men's Christian Association, which had played an important role in student life since 1870, came to an end at Syracuse University. The Young Women's Christian Association functioned until 1933, when it merged with the new Women's Association of the Hendricks Chapel Board.

It was clear that the new religious program at the University, to be successful, needed the support of the Jewish, Protestant, and Roman Catholic societies. Professor George Wilson of the Bible department endorsed that concept, saying, "The Hill has long suffered from religious anemia."

The most important single factor in the renaissance of religious life on the campus was the gift of state Senator Francis J. Hendricks, former mayor of Syracuse, who bequeathed the University $500,000 for a chapel in memory of his wife, Eliza Jane. Senator Hendricks, long a friend, benefactor, and trustee of the University, had died in June 1920, and within a year the executive committee of the board of trustees discussed preliminary plans for a chapel. But it was Chancellor Day's opinion that Hendricks had not committed himself to a building solely for religious activities and that therefore the funds might be used for other purposes, such as a suitable structure for commencement.

Accordingly, Professor Earl Hallenbeck of the College of Fine Arts was sent to Ann Arbor to study Hill Auditorium at the University of Michigan. In informing Edward Krause, an alumnus of Syracuse and later dean of the College of Liberal Arts at Michigan, of Hallenbeck's visit, Dean Peck wrote: "Understand the idea is to use the Hall of Languages as a front mask, opening up the old German Recitation Room, No. 207, as a hallway with the history room overhead and then building the auditorium behind the Hall of Languages." But with Dr. Day's retirement in June 1922 a fresh start was possible, and the University was spared what could have been an architectural monstrosity.

Realistically, little could be done before an understanding was reached on the future building needs and program of the University. Besides, work on a chapel depended on actual receipt of the Hendricks legacy. By April 1928 the estate was settled and a campus plan and development program, with specifications for a chapel, had been approved.

About $600,000 was allocated to cover the cost of clearing the site and construction of the building.

Donald G. Wright, who was a freshman at Syracuse University in 1928, recalled how the site was cleared. "During the course of that year the old building, the women's gym, was lifted up on blocks and moved a distance to the south in the direction of Archbold Stadium, where it remained for some years until finally it was torn down. This move cleared the site at the west end of the Old Oval, as it used to be called, for the erection of the chapel."

During construction the Student Church and Convocation continued to function, and Chancellor Flint looked for a University chaplain. He found William Harrison Powers, one of Syracuse's own sons, class of 1914, and persuaded him to leave the First Methodist Episcopal Church in Ithaca where for seven years he had also been on the religion faculty of Cornell University. Before that Powers had been pastor of the James Street Methodist Church in Syracuse. In 1925 his alma mater had awarded him the honorary degree of doctor of divinity.

Powers returned to the campus in August 1929 and, on January 8, 1930, with the Chancellor's endorsement, announced formation of the Hendricks Chapel Board. It consisted of the Chancellor, the university chaplain (Powers), the denominational pastors (chaplains), representative faculty members, and student leaders, and was given general control of all chapel and religious work on the campus. Hendricks Chapel absorbed the Student Church and was able to provide a more varied program. In addition, a counseling service was offered by the chaplains as well as Dean Powers and his staff. The unifying fact behind all these activities, Marjorie Pierson recalled fifty years later, was that the board had among its members students and chaplains from all the major religious groups on the campus and regarded itself not as *non*-denominational but *inter*denominational. Dr. Powers had put it similarly in a September 1939 *Daily Orange* article when he said that "probably the most significant feature of Hendricks Chapel is its interfaith (not nonsectarian) character."

A history of Hendricks Chapel written in 1979 said: "The makeup of this board is indicative of the thinking that Dr. Powers projected in terms of distribution and status of those who were to be in leadership roles." The author, the Reverend Donald G. Wright '32, noted that Chancellor Flint, an ex-officio member of the board, was an ordained minister of the Methodist Episcopal Church, that two of the four faculty members were graduates of the Boston University School of Theology, that among the students were two representatives each from the men's and women's senates, the governing student bodies of the time, and that others were student leaders in high-level positions on campus and in class honor societies. Wright added that one or more of the students held leadership positions in these organizations: athletic governing board, convocation committee, editorships of the *Daily Orange* and *Onondagan* (yearbook), Student Union, International Relations Club, Panhellenic Association, Boar's Head dramatic society, Sociology Club, YWCA, Syracuse-in-China, and the Student Church. In addition, many of the students were members of prestigious social or academic honor societies.

Students and administrators hailed the board and its efforts. The *Daily Orange* said "the way is now paved for a coordinated and definite program which will greatly extend the opportunity for religious life on the Hill." The administration attitude was expressed by Vice Chancellor Graham, who said: "No matter how much academic training a university provides, if it does not give with it religious and spiritual training it fails in its duty; when it does give that religious emphasis, even if it fails in everything else, a university has succeeded in making the most worthwhile contribution to humanity."

The cornerstone of Hendricks Chapel was laid in June 1929, and the Georgian colonial building itself was dedicated June 8, 1930, as a highlight of commencement. Representatives of Roman Catholic, Jewish, and six Protestant faiths attended the ceremony and each received an honorary degree. Dr. Wright, the chapel historian, recalling the Methodist beginnings of the University, said: "Hendricks Chapel was given by a Presbyterian who was appreciative of the interfaith traditions of the founding and wanted to see them expressed." The historian noted in an interview that his late wife, Bernice M. (Bunny) Wright, former dean of the College for Human Development, was on the staff of the chapel during the first five years of its existence. Then Bernice H. Meredith, she was a member of the group that chose the verses that adorn the frieze around the interior of the chapel.

An electric moment at the dedication came in the filled auditorium when the Syracuse minister chosen to read the Scripture, the Reverend Bernard C. Clausen, stepped back from the lectern, looked up at the foot-high letters in the frieze and said: "Ye shall know the truth, and the truth shall make you free" (John 8:32).

Again, that evening, all 1,450 seats in the new building were filled as Chancellor Flint installed Dr. Powers, whose original appointment was as chaplain to the University, as first dean of Hendricks Chapel. The Chancellor said in part: "You will provide out of your own intellectual and spiritual life, and out of the inner life of inspirational leaders of all denominations, messages which will enlighten the minds and stir the

The congregation leaves Hendricks Chapel after the first regular Sunday service, September 21, 1930. Chancellor Flint preached the sermon.

souls of the students, to the end that the highest things, the things that are external, may have their due place in the life of Syracuse University."

During the 1930–40 decade the number of students participating in chapel programs increased to more than twelve hundred.

With the departure of Chancellor Flint to become a bishop of the Methodist Episcopal Church, a significant and formative era in the life of Hendricks Chapel came to an end. Wright, who as a student had been present at the beginning of that era, wrote in his history:

> To be sure, the program would go on and with strength, but it must always be remembered that it was under the guiding hand of Chancellor Flint that Hendricks Chapel had achieved what it was to this point. As a committed Christian minister, he had located the chapel building at the 'heart of the campus' and made it central to the life of Syracuse University. ... As the years unfolded, it would become apparent that Chancellor Flint's vision and guidance in using the generous gift of Senator Francis

> Hendricks made both a creative and lasting contribution to future generations of Syracuse University students—who probably would never realize truly how much they were in his debt for the contribution of the chapel and the influence it would make in their lives as students at Syracuse University.

At the 1936 commencement Syracuse University conferred on Charles Wesley Flint, by then resident bishop of the Atlanta area, the honorary degree of doctor of laws.

When Dr. Graham succeeded to the chancellorship, he continued the strong support his predecessor had given the chapel board. Although Dr. Graham was only the second Chancellor who was not an ordained minister (Alexander Winchell was the first), he was a faithful member of the University Methodist Episcopal Church. In May 1937 he ruled that on Sundays before 1 P.M. there was to be no University activity on campus that was not religious. Daily and Sunday services were the most evident features of the post-Flint religion program.

Every Sunday in the year a regular morning worship service was held, open to faculty, students, and friends of the University regardless of faith. Generally it was led by the dean or a chaplain, but visiting speakers were not uncommon. The hour was spent on congregational singing, anthems by the chapel choir, a scripture reading, prayers by the minister, and a sermon. Most of those present were Protestants, and the auditorium was usually full. It was also the custom each Sunday for a different group such as a Greek letter society or a living center to attend in a body.

Daily chapel, a twenty-minute service each weekday except Saturday, was usually led by a student. This was less formal and was more sparsely attended. The speaker was generally a member of the chapel staff or of the faculty, but occasionally an off-campus minister or layman officiated. On some days the service was confined to devotional music.

Another feature of the chapel program was group discussion, such as Freshman Weekend conferences and Sophomore Continuation sessions. These consisted of reports and debates about personal and social problems on the campus, marriage, the home, and human resources for a Christian life. Growing out of these meetings and contributing to the basic aims of the chapel were sixteen committees. Among other activities, these related to interfaith matters, world relations, Syracuse-in-China, public relations, and publication of a magazine, *Chapel News.*

The Syracuse-in-China program brought many Syracuse graduates to the city of Chungking in West China for the purpose of establishing a three-fold mission of "medical, evangelical and educational work."

The Syracuse-in-China High School, circa 1933.

Beginning in 1921 the SIC staff, under the leadership of Doctors Gordon Hoople and Leon Sutton, renovated and operated an abandoned missionary compound that contained a church, hospital and high school. The Methodist Church owned the compound which had been neglected since the end of the first world war. However, through the diligent efforts of the SIC unit all three facilities were rejuvenated, and by 1938 the mission had reached a peak in its development. Unfortunately this success was short lived. The Sino-Japanese war and the second world war brought the project to its knees as most of the buildings suffered direct hits. The bombing of Chungking began in 1939, but it wasn't until 1943 that the last unit member left the city. That same year the university regained its Chinese association when it became the 'sister' of West China Union University in Chengtu.

The chapel also provided counseling services for the many students who came to it for help and guidance. Closely identified with the counseling program and playing an important role in the University's religious life were the pastors to students (chaplains), selected by individual city churches. They served the Methodist, Protestant Episcopal, Presybyterian, Jewish, Roman Catholic, Lutheran, Baptist, and Christian Science faiths. The churches involved supported the ministers; the University provided office space and other rooms in Hendricks Chapel.

The first pastor to Methodist students, assigned in 1928 by the Central New York Conference of the church, was Reverend Webster

Melcher. At the University Methodist Church, 1085 East Genesee Street, he led a Sunday evening fellowship that often drew 150 students. His fellow preacher at the church was the pastor, Norman Vincent Peale, who was to marry Ruth R. Stafford '28 and become nationally famous as pastor of the Marble Collegiate Church, New York City.

The duties of Melcher and other chaplains included directing student religious clubs. The oldest was the Kolledj Klan, a Sunday School class founded in 1908 by Minnie Mason Beebe '90 of the Syracuse University history faculty. Some of its members were Martin Hilfinger '14, Gordon D. Hoople '15, and William Pearson Tolley '22. In 1925 it was reorganized as the College Club. Two years later Kolledj Klan was revived and lasted until 1933, when the Friendship League was founded. Another society, founded during the Day administration, was St. Paul's Episcopal Club, sponsored by St. Paul's Church. In 1931 a Students Club was formed by Grace Episcopal Church; the following year it was reorganized as the Seabury Club, which held vesper services for students at Grace Church and promoted the Episcopal Mission at the Onondaga Indian Reservation. There were also the Lutheran Club, the Westminster Club for Presbyterians, and the Christian Science Club. Other Protestants such as the Congregationalists and Baptists maintained religious centers for students of their faiths, as did the Jews in neighboring temples. The Oxford Fellowship was a national professional fraternity for the training of ministers of all denominations.

The Newman Club, formerly the Bronson Club, for Roman Catholic students, moved from St. Mary's Hall on Montgomery Street to the Theta Phi Alpha sorority house at 604 Comstock Avenue, and the students joined in Hendricks Chapel activities. For a time the nurses recreation room in the University Hospital was used for Catholic religious services, but soon those quarters became too small and in 1937 Chancellor Graham made the auditorium in Slocum Hall available for masses.

In 1939 the Reverend Gannon Ryan announced establishment of a St. Thomas More Foundation on private land adjacent to the campus to give the Roman Catholic students a center for their religious observances and activities. Wright described this in his history of Hendricks Chapel as probably the strongest indication of a religious pluralism that was asserting itself at Syracuse University and would continue to do so. "Yet at the same time an attempt was constantly alive to have understanding and cooperation between the religious groups," Wright said. That same year, he noted, the interfaith committee of the chapel board sponsored a series of meetings whose purpose was "to come to understand the beliefs and practices of the various religious faiths represented in the chapel program." Among those who took part were the Catholic, Jewish, and Christian Science chaplains.

Earlier in the decade concern had been expressed about the decline of Methodist influence at Syracuse as shown by the relative increase in enrollment of students of other faiths. Chancellor Flint responded by saying: "I thoroughly believe a large university can remain true to its Christian origin and to the purpose of its Methodist founders not by formal or official legislative requirements or restrictions but by inner loyalty and wisely adopted methods—the method of the Kingdom—the leaven in the meal."

There was no question that other denominations and faiths were challenging the numerical supremacy of the Methodists. Religion censuses were not routinely made at Syracuse Universit, but there were enough of them over the decades to document the downward trend. In 1881, 61 of the 132 students who responded to a poll in the College of Liberal Arts—46 percent—listed themselves as Methodists. In 1929 the number of Methodists in the total student population was 25.5 percent. Had they been able to look ahead half a century to 1979, the Methodists would have seen that percentage shrink to 4.1.

But on November 14, 1931, Chancellor Flint could report to the board of trustees: "The religious preference or distribution of the student body varies but little from year to year. With very slight fluctuations above and below, the Protestants register about 70 percent of the total, the Catholics about 18 percent, and the Jews about 12 percent.

"The distribution of the Protestants, with similar fluctuations, includes Methodists 26 percent, Presbyterians 13 per cent, Episcopalians 9 percent, Baptists 7 percent, Congregationalists 4 ¾ percent, Lutherans 3 ¾ percent, etc."

Dr. Flint also had a few words about nonbelievers: "The decline of the total of avowed atheists and agnostics, from three students in 1929–30 to two in 1930–31 and to zero this year, may be ascribed to the Depression, or to any other cause you may prefer!"

Syracuse University embraced a mixture of traditionalism and enlightenment in its attitudes toward religion in the years between the world wars. In some ways the campus clung to orthodoxy, but in others it was in the mainstream of change.

On one hand, the University had in Dr. Flint a Chancellor who sent the class of 1935 out into the world from Piety Hill with Billy Sunday-style rhetoric when he paraphrased Browning in his baccalaureate address, saying: "My last official word to you is—whatever your world assignment, whatever else you may or must do—'Stand erect! Catch at God's skirts! Pray!'"

On the other hand there was Ismar Peritz, whose modernism as chairman of the religion department often collided with the views of more traditional members of the Methodist church.

In 1895 Ismar John Peritz was founder and first chairman of what was then the department of Semitic languages and archeology. He was born in Breslau, Germany, in 1863 and in 1881, at Berlin, was converted from Judaism "through the tutoring of a Lutheran minister," according to a history of the department. Later he attended Drew Theological Seminary and Harvard University, where he earned his Ph.D. in 1898 after studying seven Semitic languages—Hebrew, Arabic, Assyrian, Aramaic, Syrian, Phoenician, and Ethiopic. Before that he had served a number of Methodist pastorates in New York State and in 1889 was designated a deacon of the Methodist Church and in 1891 an elder. All of Peritz's formal academic career was spent at Syracuse University except for a year's leave of absence in 1912–13. He retired in 1933 at the age of seventy and died in 1950.

The Reverend Charles Bollinger '21, who had studied under him, said that for years "sparks flew" whenever Peritz's name came up at a meeting of the Central New York Conference of the church. In fact Bollinger was not unanimously accepted into the conference by the examining board for ministerial candidates because of his association with Peritz.

Professor D. B. Robertson, recounting this incident in his history of the religion department, wrote: "The virgin birth and physical resurrection seem to have been special stumbling blocks. Peritz held to a 'spiritual resurrection,' and it was this particular interpretation which almost prevented Bollinger from becoming a 'reverend' in the Methodist Church. Dr. Peritz told Bollinger in later years that he was happy to have lived to see the day when most of the educated clergy had come to embrace views for which he had been attacked in years past."

As a student Bollinger, of Liverpool, New York, was a circulation manager and managing editor of the *Daily Orange* and graduated cum laude. Eventually he became a Methodist-nominated trustee of the University and served in that capacity from 1937 until his death at eighty-seven in 1979.

Mrs. Elizabeth Bradley Tilden '25 of Syracuse, another student of Dr. Peritz, said his Biblical criticism "was widely condemned by his contemporaries among clergy and teachers," and "he was given much unpleasant treatment."

William Pearson Tolley '22 regretted not having studied under Peritz but said his brother Harold, a 1916 graduate, had. Elaborating in a 1981 interview, Dr. Tolley said: "Harold caused thunder in the household when he came home from Syracuse with all these wonderful new theories about the Bible. The Methodist Church was not terribly liberal in its views. Father was a trustee of the church, Mother was a soloist in the choir, and both taught Sunday School. They were extremely traditional and didn't want to hear what Harold had been taught by Dr. Peritz. My brother Earl [class of 1921] and I had an easier time. The fireworks had died down by then."

Dr. Tolley added: "Most people were more parochial in those days. Some parents believed Peritz was undermining their children's faith, harming their souls." But if the parents were suspicious of the professor, his students were not. "He was an immensely popular teacher," Dr. Tolley said. "The students treated him with great veneration. Professor Peritz was a man ahead of his time."

The so-called modernist-fundamentalist controversy that involved Peritz went back a long way and became tense at several points, Robertson said. In a 1981 interview on the eve of his retirement as professor of religion he added: "Peritz trained at Harvard in the most modern scholarship, and it would have been strange if he hadn't had a different view from that of people who trained at places like a theological seminary. He was a scholar, and at that time most ministers attended seminaries with a specific emphasis on pastoral training. Anybody associated with a university-trained person was almost inevitably subject to some suspicion."

Apparently Peritz was personally a bit abrasive and didn't hesitate to speak out boldly. He was "off and on in trouble with the church," Robertson said.

James Roscoe Day was chancellor when Peritz joined the Syracuse faculty. Dr. Day had been Peritz's pastor in a Methodist church in New York City and knew there would be objections from Methodists when Christianity was studied in the context of a new department where the Bible was subjected to higher criticism—that is, studied as a collection of human documents, not divine revelation. Dr. Day was prepared to defend Peritz and frequently did. On January 21, 1911, the Chancellor wrote to the Reverend J. B. Sweet of Binghamton, New York, about the Methodist board of visitors: "I do not understand that the visitors have for a part of their functions and duties the passing upon the scholarship of the University or the efficiency of our teachers in their classes."

Peritz himself recalled that Day once gave him a letter from a woman who complained about the "evils" of Biblical criticism and suggested that classes be turned into prayer meetings.

Professor Robertson said that from the time of Peritz on, the religion department had a feeling that chaplains on campuses were not qualified generally to teach Bible in a scholarly fashion. "That doesn't mean that scholars were anti-Bible," Robertson said. "It's just that they felt that the pastor had a special vocation and the professor had a different one, and that was to deal with Biblical tradition, history, literature, and language within the context of an academic community—and to deal with it as honestly as with any other academic material or data. There is a difference, we think, between teaching religion and the preaching function of the chaplain. We don't say one is superior or inferior to the other; we just say they're different."

Asked to contrast the "Christian university" founded by the Methodists in 1870 with the modern institution of 111 years later, Robertson said: "I think that for a long, long time we've not been a religious university by any means. Certainly by the 1920s there was already a great deal of erosion in the devotion of the student body to the traditional chapels when visiting preachers came to the campus. So I think the identification of the University as Methodist and therefore Christian in that sense has been eroded for a long time—fifty years or more. That doesn't mean that individual chancellors have not been interested in maintaining religious instruction with a scholarly sort of department. But students don't come here any more because Syracuse is a 'Christian university.' They come because it's a good university."

Asked how the department itself had changed over the years, Robertson said:

> The great shift has been from linguistic studies and archeology, which was in the original title of the department, to the study of Biblical literature, with heavy emphasis on the study of the Bible, and to a much wider study of religion in general, and in the last ten or twenty years to studies of non-Christian religions.
>
> Even when Peritz was chairman there was beginning to be a tendency to expand away from the strictly Biblical. Certainly Dwight Beck went in that direction, to a study of religion in general with emphasis specifically broadened to study particularly non-Christian religions. One of the strengths of our department now is the study of Oriental religions.

Dwight Marion Beck '18 joined the department in 1930 and succeeded Ismar Peritz as chairman in 1933. In the 1932–33 academic year it had become the department of bible and religion, a change from the department of biblical languages and literature.

Professor Beck remained as chairman until his retirement from the University in 1959. He said in a 1981 interview at his Syracuse home: "I never would say we had what you would call a 'Christian' university. The religious founders were Methodists, and the help from the city fathers provided some funds, and it seemed to me there was a good spirit of cooperation here.

"Administrative support was strong both for the chapel and for the department of bible and religion, as I wanted it called. They dropped 'bible' after I left, widened it, and simply called it the department of religion. I had inherited from Dr. Peritz the concept that the study of the Bible, its languages and literature and theology, was a good university study. That's a traditional position, of course, and long past."

Asked whether the department had any particular interest in training clergymen, Dr. Beck said: "We didn't make any special attempt to set up our curriculum for ministers. We set it up for the average college student who wanted to know something about the Bible and his religious tradition and heritage. We felt he should be informed about his religious inheritance or tradition or background, but we didn't try to go into the field of training, such as you get in a theological school. We didn't pretend to be a theological school. There never has been one here."

The former chairman, describing his predecessor, said his recollection was partly based on what Dr. Peritz himself had told the faculty. "I think it's important to remember that Dr. Peritz was born an Orthodox Jew in Germany," Dr. Beck said.

> He had a Lutheran tutor when he was seventeen or eighteen years old and somehow his study with that tutor turned him to Christianity. Of course from the standpoint of Judaism that's a bad, bad move. No Jew believes in forsaking his faith and turning to any other. Nevertheless, in his teens he became a Christian. He went to England and married a Protestant woman, a typical English lady. Then he came to this country, continued his studies at the theological school at Drew University, and went to Harvard and took his Ph.D. He represented what we would call a modern, educated, Biblical scholar, and not simply a traditionally minded man. So when he came to Syracuse and founded the department, he came as a scholar, but he also came as a converted Jew, and the result was that he got fired at from both sides. The Jews fired at him because he was a renegade, and the traditional Christians fired at him because he represented a modern attitude, reflected especially in his Harvard graduate studies. But he was a good, well-trained scholar, and he did for the University what we needed done. He set up a department of Bible and its languages and literature and theology at an academic level. He never had a large enrollment of students, but nevertheless he did lay the foundations, and they were solid ones.

Commenting on the unsettling effect Dr. Peritz's teachings had on the Tolley family, as recounted by the former chancellor, Dr. Beck said:

> You have to remember that the church is one of the most conservative institutions in the world, and it doesn't move quickly and rapidly. In certain states your schools have the teaching of creation alongside the teaching of evolution. That's an illustration of the continuing effect of a traditional viewpoint. I don't think you have any business teaching the book of Genesis in a public school, as if that were the explanation of the beginning. "In the beginning"—the first three words in the Bible—there was no man there; no one knows what the beginning was. I wouldn't use the Biblical explanation alongside a scientific doctrine of evolution and say these are two equally good viewpoints. I would take the Bible teaching for what it is intended to be, a mythical story teaching certain great religious truths. The Bible is not a scientific book at all, even if it does deal with certain matters that are scientific.

Dr. Beck said that, as chairman, in his many years of hiring faculty members most of his interest was in their academic backgrounds. "We had them come to teach on the basis of what they were as scholars, primarily, and what they were as men, which we established in personal interviews."

He summed up by saying: "I'm greatly pleased by the fact that the religion department has prospered over the years, and that we have splendid scholars here teaching, and that it has moved from a small, noninfluential department to a strong, well-developed one with a strong faculty. I'm greatly pleased that it has done so well across all these years."

A. Leland Jamison, who succeeded Beck as chairman in 1959, looked back on the 1920s as a period of growing theological liberalism. Leading thinkers of that time said it wasn't necessary to take the Bible literally. Some things must be reinterpreted—the virgin birth, the resurrection, miracles.

Jamison said in an interview that the fight then was between fundamentalists and modernists, and today there is a carry-over of that struggle in the controversy between creationists and evolutionists. Jamison, Willard Ives Professor Emeritus of the English Bible, considers himself a moderate.

"More important than whether one should take the Bible literally is the continuity of Christianity, which might deviate at some points from literalism," Jamison said:

> People who hold this view see the Bible as the foundation of the Christian faith. As Harry Emerson Fosdick put it, the Bible contains "abiding truths in changing categories."
>
> Take Heaven and Hell. Should they be taken literally? All religious language is metaphorical. Heaven is a metaphor, in a way, for some kind of fulfillment of divine purpose. Hell represents the opposite of that.
>
> The Methodists, Presbyterians, and Congregationalists were groups to whom liberalism came as early as the 1890s. Peritz and Beck were in that stream of liberalizing Methodism even though the Methodist church was still fundamentalist. Very early in the history of this University its founders and their successors placed themselves in the mainstream of liberal and progressive thought. This is illustrated by the motto of Theta Chi Beta, the religion honor society founded at Syracuse University—'Progressive Revelation.'

The society, established in 1915, is the first of its kind in the United States.

Jamison saw the study of religion at the University as having evolved into one element in a general program of the humanities. "It is a humanistic discipline alongside such others as English literature and history," he said. "It has broadened from Bible study to the study of other religions and cultures." And in Hendricks Chapel he saw "an arena in which the student can examine and practice the various religious options in our society."

Jamison said a good example of the continuity he'd mentioned was a meeting of Theta Chi Beta on the evening of April 9, 1981. It was attended by five of the six chairmen of the religion department. All but the first, Ismar Peritz, were present—Dwight M. Beck (1933–59), A. Leland Jamison (1959–64), T. William Hall (1964–72), Ronald R. Cavanagh (1973–80), James B. Wiggins (1980–).

"Professor Peritz was there in spirit," Jamison said.

21

Student Government

The Maxwell School used student government as a laboratory for citizenship training. Theoretically and potentially it was the extracurricular activity that offered the greatest opportunity for developing leadership among students.

THE CONCEPT OF STUDENT GOVERNMENT at Syracuse University matured during the Flint and Graham administrations, although an organization called the Senior Council had some responsibilities during the Day regime. In 1910 the board of trustees recognized the council to the extent of adopting a series of resolutions that body submitted. They pertained to the council's financial problems. The organization was one that seemed to exist at Chancellor Day's pleasure and which in 1919 he abolished temporarily.

Chancellor Flint, early in his administration, asked Vice Chancellor Graham to search the minutes of the board of trustees and its executive committee to learn if any rights of government had ever been given to the Senior Council. Dr. Graham found nothing. He reported: "The bylaws of the University are explicit in stating where authority is lodged. There is no provision in these for student government."

The Student Council was for men; its constitution said its purpose was "to safeguard customs and traditions of Syracuse University, to form an executive head for the student body, and to create a close and more harmonious commonism of interests between the students and the faculty." The council consisted of seven seniors elected by the men students, and twelve ex-officio members, including the presidents of the student body, the YMCA, and the Interfraternity Conference, the head cheerleader, and the athletic managers of the major sports. It was expected to supervise all men's affairs, except fraternities and athletics, to govern class rushes, to be in charge of student celebrations, mass meetings, and excursions, and to regulate class and college elections, except those handled by the Athletic Association.

In practice the council mostly enforced campus traditions such as the wearing of class caps, standing during the singing of the Alma Mater, and removing hats on passing a member of the faculty. It supposedly enforced a ban on the wearing of high school insignia and the rule that only seniors could wear derbies and carry canes. Actually, however, the council did little, as this comment by a member indicates: "We spent most of our time trying to figure out what we might do that would be of some importance. We passed resolutions, which the men studiously disregarded, and for many years the most important job of the Senior Council was to see to it that there was a successor government."

The constitution was amended in 1924 but not significantly. In 1927 the council drafted another constitution that sought to unite the council and the Women's Student Government Association (WSGA) in the interest of better government. Chancellor Flint supported this effort, and in May 1927 he attended a banquet that nominally marked the end of the Senior Council and the formation of a Men's Student Senate, which was given the "final authority to settle any disputes or misunderstandings that might arise in relation to student government." The WSGA refused to join the new organization at the time, seeing more value in its independent existence. A year later, however, the women accepted the new constitution without losing their own separate organization.

The Chancellor was pleased with the developments, believing that with the change the University had risen "above the outmoded juvenile idea that there is an inherent clash of interest between faculty or administration on one hand and the students on the other, and since theoretically their aims and purposes are one, some method could and should be worked out for practical relationships and cooperative functioning." The *Daily Orange* declared: "Yesterday, March 1, 1928, will be emblazoned in Syracuse history as one of the venerable days in the history of the University."

According to a new constitution, all legislative power was in the hands of a Men's Student Senate and a Women's Student Senate. Members of the former were to be chosen from the junior class by the male students of the various colleges, and the women senators were elected or appointed on a merit basis. In cases affecting both men and women, the senates met in joint session, and in matters involving either senate and the administration, an executive board, consisting of the officers of the respective senates, two faculty representatives, and one official of the administration, made the decisions. Judicial power was lodged in each senate.

One of the first actions of the Men's Senate was to establish a Men's Student Court in May 1928. It consisted of a chief justice, two assistant justices, and nine associate justices, elected annually by the retiring senate. Conceived as the guardian of Syracuse lore and tradition, it reviewed and ruled upon all infractions of the senate's directives.

During its first year of operation (1928–29) the new student government could not be called successful. Both the *Daily Orange* and the dean of women complained of improper coordination and ignorance of proper procedure. There was considerable improvement the following year. The dean of women said the senates had learned to work together, and that "the possibilities for growth in student responsibility and effective control are very far reaching."

Vice Chancellor Graham was more reserved in his opinions. He viewed the constitution as overambitious, believing there were some matters the "senate can at most approach by petition," such as the use of buildings and grounds, the length of holidays, faculty rulings, and athletic events. The Vice Chancellor insisted that rules for student conduct be laid down by University authorities; he said there would be "serious misunderstanding" if the senates claimed jurisdiction over such matters.

By March 1930 the *Daily Orange* was losing some of its original enthusiasm for student government. In one issue it declared that student elections continued to reflect past practices rather than fulfilling the high hopes of those who had conceived the new government. The last election, it said, had been a quiet and uninteresting campaign. "There is more excitement over the election of a May Queen than there is for an office in the men's or women's slates."

Over the next three years the newspaper devoted considerable space to the problem of self-government. In 1931, for example, it urged students to follow their convictions and not their emotions in voting for candidates to the senates. At another time it deplored the fraternity influence it said had been instrumental in keeping qualified men out of office, particularly aspirants for athletic managerships. But the *Daily Orange* failed to arouse much student interest, and the winning candidates were those backed by the social or honor societies.

In 1932 the student daily, echoing the views of some students, criticized what it called the indifference of the Men's Student Court to its responsibilities. The issue reached a crisis when Collin Williams, chief justice of the court, declared his bench to be stagnant. The Men's Senate, he insisted, had so restricted the court's authority that it ruled chiefly on violations of university traditions. Williams said the senate should enact new legislation to widen the powers of the court, to define its authority, to establish less formal procedures, and to require the keeping of accurate records. If these remedial actions were not taken, the court should be abolished. Herbert Ross, president of the student body, heartily supported the suggestions.

The issue was raised again in the fall after formation of a Women's Student Court. When the new senate failed to act on the chief justice's earlier proposals, Williams questioned the constitutionality of the court, and he again proposed that it be abolished. The *Daily Orange* reported meanwhile that the court had ruled on only two issues—it found a class president and a social chairman guilty of mismanagement of an all-university dance. In both instances, according to the newspaper, officers of the senate had sat with the court. The impact of these and other charges finally led to abolition of the court in 1933 and the return of all judicial power to the senate.

Up to that time the constitution of the Men's Senate had been changed only in minor ways. But with the elimination of the court an amendment permitted creation of a Men's Administrative Commission. This consisted of a chairman from the senior class, five junior commissioners, and at least fifteen sophomores as aides, to carry out such duties as the senate might direct; it was not, however, to serve in a judicial capacity. The *Daily Orange* regarded it as a successor to the old sophomore vigilance committee and said its chief responsibilities appeared to be to regulate smoking in campus buildings, the wearing of "lids," and student seating at athletic events.

Seating rules were soon changed. For years it had been traditional for men and women students to sit in separate sections of Archbold Stadium. Then in the fall of 1935 the director of athletics announced that a third section would be available for optional seating. It was a popular innovation.

But the matter of freshman caps was still a stormy one. The freshmen were divided on the matter, and there were lengthy disputes. The Men's Senate finally dropped attempts to enforce the wearing of the caps, although the *Daily Orange* expressed a hope that the young students would continue to do so out of respect for tradition. The disputes continued, however, and in December 1936 the commission had to step in to prevent those advocating abolition of the tradition from publicly burning their caps.

By this time the Council on Men's Affairs had been created and its director, A. Blair Knapp, announced that one of its aims was to organize all existing informal activities into a "well-rounded educational program." The Maxwell School, where Knapp taught, was to use student government as a laboratory for citizenship training. Dean Mosher of the Maxwell School endorsed Knapp's idea.

To Knapp and others the need for student government was self-evident. Theoretically and potentially, it was the extracurricular activity that offered the greatest opportunity for developing leadership among students and promoting a sense of personal responsibility. But in actuality, Knapp said, "student government has never fulfilled this promise either on our own campus or elsewhere." He added: "Colleges and universities have tolerated student government within a very restricted sphere and have never utilized it as an educational device or opportunity."

There were several reasons for the failure of student government, Knapp said. One was lack of a representative character in its organization, a defect that robbed it of contact with student sentiments and ideas. Another was a lack of continuity in personnel; leaders had graduated by the time they were familiar with their duties. Many officers were selected through political manipulation that often substituted mediocrity for ability, destroying student confidence in them. Finally, Knapp believed, college administrators had not bothered to guide these students into worthwhile channels or to stimulate student government to fulfill its obligations.

The Council on Men's Affairs now drafted a new constitution for the new organization called Men's Student Government. There was a separate women's organization.

Features of Men's Student Government included a Men's Student Assembly of more than 100 members representing living centers and other areas, and a Student Civil Service. The latter was a nonpolitical agency, set up under a merit system to help other branches of the student government perform their duties. Civil service apprentices, students in their sophomore year, attended a seminar that concentrated on developing skills in committee work, parliamentary law, the history of the University, and the limitations of student government. Through the civil service, according to Knapp, his office hoped to counter "fundamental weaknesses of student government, such as lack of training and experience, lack of continuity of personnel, and dominance of campus politics."

In October 1937 elections were held under the new government, and the Men's Student Senate went out of existence. William Lambert, former president of the student body, became head of the new organization.

By November 1937 Dr. Graham, now Chancellor, told the trustees that "greatly to my surprise," Knapp's plan of student self-government was showing itself to be successful.

But then, in March 1938, Lambert used his veto for the first time and raised an uproar on the campus. The men's and women's student governments both had approved a petition recognizing the American Student Union, a national organization formed in 1935 that claimed twenty thousand members on high school and college campuses across the United States. Lambert justified his use of the veto by declaring the Union to be a "pink" communist organization. His veto was sustained. Contemporary views of the ASU varied widely. Harold Lord Varney, writing in *The American Mercury* of August 1938, said: "this undisguisedly Communist-directed movement steadfastly maintains the fiction that it is a Liberal organization." Bruce Bliven, Jr., in the *New Republic* of January 11, 1939, said the organization supported trade unions, favored New Deal aims, was for civil liberties and against racial or religious discrimination. He added that delegates to the ASU's national convention in New York City during the 1938 Christmas break "have confident, brash opinions about what should be done and their faith in Democracy is fervent."

At Syracuse, signs of internal strife began to appear in the Men's Student Government. Campus politics infiltrated its workings. At the same time apathy set in, and the Men's Student Assembly was unable to function because a majority of its members stayed away. That was in May 1938.

The situation was no better the following year despite efforts of the chief civil service officer, John Olver '39. He wanted to study the reasons behind the veto in the matter of the American Student Union but was opposed by the *Daily Orange* and others, the newspaper declaring: "Regardless of the better-government motives of Mr. Olver, he has exceeded his position as an administrator in ordering the investigation."

Late in 1938 a reorganized assembly, meeting in October, again refused to recognize the American Student Union and authorized an investigation of the junior honor societies, Corpse and Coffin, Monx Head, and Double Seven.

As head of the student civil service, Olver led the investigation of the organizations, which had turned over to him their scholastic and financial records. The records showed that the thirty-six members of the three had a scholastic average slightly better than "C," with none in the "A" category. There was also a public hearing, after which the civil service reported that the junior societies had been lax in fulfilling their duties and had no program of genuine worth.

The *Daily Orange* questioned the fairness of the report and said it was the civil service that needed to be examined. Nevertheless, the civil service began a sweeping investigation just before Christmas 1938 of fifty-eight honor and professional societies with some fifteen hundred members.

In February 1939 the assembly voted unanimously to abolish the three junior societies, and three months later a new society, Orange Key, dedicated to service to the University, was formally organized with John C. O'Byrne as president.

Otherwise during the academic year 1938–39, Men's Student Government surveyed the need for a student court, lifted a ban on radios in Sims Hall, proposed publication of a campus "Congressional Record," and suggested a revision of the University curriculum to make it more valuable to the "average" student.

The *Daily Orange* described that record as catastrophic. It noted that of 110 elected assemblymen, 32 were dropped for nonattendance at meetings or for poor grades.

Nor was Blair Knapp happy with the record, although he was by no means discouraged. He reported to Dr. Graham: "If this office were to perform no other function than to guide a student government to a successful development, we believe its existence will be justified." And the Chancellor reported to the trustees in June 1939: "Four or five years ago we set up... the Council for Men's Affairs.... That experiment I feel has been fully justified, for the change of attitude of the men students is one of the surprising developments of recent years. So I feel that in the educators' sense the quality of our work, judged by the reaction of the students themselves and the graduates of recent years, indicates that we are on the right track."

Many years later—as he was about to retire from his post at the United Nations as an assistant secretary-general—John Olver spoke of "the tripartite that was Men's Student Government" and "the civil service prong of that three-cornered organization."

Olver reminisced at a 1981 Syracuse dinner honoring his classmate Newell Rossman '39. He recalled that one of his responsibilities as chief of the student civil service had been to compile a directory of student organizations.

"Chancellor Graham called me in to express concern about leftist organizations on the campus," Olver said. "He knew I was making a list of student groups. I was head of the bureaucracies."

The Chancellor suggested that they compare lists. "Dr. Graham went to get a copy of his information for me," Olver said. "He kept it in his office safe."

Referring to student government as it was practiced then, Olver said. "I guess it was a failed experiment, but I learned to grapple with government."

During the rest of the Graham administration the story of Men's Student Government was one of continued apathy on the part of the student body, an apathy that deepened as the prospect of America's entrance into World War II became more real. The student government officers, now and then, suggested procedural changes in the conduct of elections, but the student body paid little heed to a problem that apparently had little meaning to them. On another occasion there was a flurry of interest when it was claimed that student government could survive only if a party system were introduced. Thereupon the "Fundamentalists" and the "Unicrats" emerged, but their platforms and ideals were restatements of past aims and purposes and sparked no resurgence of student interest.

Among the several projects that student government did promote was a survey of the growing traffic problem on the campus and its environs. The rapid increase in the number of automobiles not only made parking difficult, but resulted in injuries to several students. As a consequence, a student vigilance committee was established to police the danger areas, and the administration placed stop signs at major intersections. On another occasion there was a proposal to discuss a revision of the curriculum, and later the annual Flour Rush was abolished.

With the coming of war, Men's Student Government rapidly declined in importance and activity. In January 1942 the *Daily Orange* said it seemed best "to turn the corpse of what was once the leading men's function on the campus over to the coroner before rigor mortis set in, whose verdict would be, 'death from lack of initiative at the committee level.'" As for the assembly, despite its valuable work in promoting military defense, it was a "mere vestigial organ," whose overall record for five years was nothing short of failure, the newspaper said. But at its spring banquet, Chancellor Graham nevertheless praised the student government, saying: "MSG had solved the problem of capturing sentiment and the cooperation of those governed."

It would be wrong to blame the comparative failure of Men's Student Government solely on the student body: the faculty and the administration shared some of the responsibility. Most of the faculty gave it scant attention, and some may have been unaware of its existence. In the administration, Chancellors Flint and Graham generally favored student government and allowed it to impose sanctions on student offenders in some instances. But neither was willing to admit that it could handle certain matters better than the University. The Chancellors might have been more consistent in their policies and less prone to wait until issues had arisen to exert authority, while the students should have known that their own experience could not match that of the administration.

But there was also the Women's Student Government Association. WSGA's prime objective was to foster "the true college spirit" and carry on "the ideals for which the University stands." All women students were automatically members of the organization; those who paid a small annual fee could vote and hold office. In order to be a candidate, a woman had to pass a physical examination and maintain a "C-plus" average.

A Large Board, consisting of all house presidents, representatives of minor groups, and delegates elected from the smaller University houses, comprised the executive and legislative branch of WSGA. It met every two weeks. All rules passed by this board, however, had to be approved by a Small Board, which included the women's editor of the *Daily Orange,* the presidents of the YWCA and the Women's Athletic Association, and the chief woman officer of each of the four college classes. The Small Board also served as a trial jury for all indictable offenses against the association.

WSGA supervised certain women's activities, such as the Middy Party, the May Morning Breakfast, and the Big Sister Party. It was also a branch of the Women's Intercollegiate Government Association, a nationwide organization.

Among the WSGA rules generally in force between 1922 and 1928, fourteen governed absences from all houses for both ordinary and special occasions, overnight and out-of-town permissions, and the entertainment of guests. Permissions to enjoy such privileges were issued either by the dean of women, the WSGA president, or the house presidents. Attendance at dances was under the jurisdiction of the dean of women, whose influence must have affected the association in many other ways. During these years and in accordance with the wishes of Chancellor Flint, a new campus organization, the Men's and Women's Student senates, came into being; WSGA at first refused to join, but had a change of heart in March 1928. The women's senate, although it faced many problems, operated more smoothly than the men's. Between 1929 and 1938 several minor changes were made in regulations affecting women. A fall orientation course was required of freshmen to acquaint them with all phases of college life, and each woman was assigned to a small group that held weekly meetings during her first month on the campus. In 1931 a freshman dance was instituted to promote fellowship among the members of the incoming class. In the same year an Off-Campus Association, composed of women students not living on the campus, was formed. A student loan fund was established for women who were financially hurt by the Depression. During 1932–33 a senior student adviser was appointed to each freshman house to help the women in scholastic and personal matters.

In 1936–37 the new dean of women, M. Eunice Hilton, noted considerable progress in and a better understanding of student self-government. She said gallant leadership by Joan Crumb and Geraldine Seidel had stimulated panel discussion groups, supper meetings, and weekly sophomore gatherings, as well as a revision of the constitution to eliminate possible campus political influences and to provide for a merit system for office holding.

The new constitution became effective in the fall of 1937. It authorized an enlarged governing board of the women's senate, as well as an increase in the number of officers. Misconduct or incompetence in office could result in impeachment and removal. Among other responsibilities, the president, at a convocation of all entering freshmen, explained the nature of the women's senate and the University traditions. She attended staff meetings of the dormitory and sorority chaperones, as well as those of freshman house presidents. Duties assigned to other officers consisted of attendance at sophomore discussion groups, supervision of all overnight permissions, and, in the case of the social chairman, conducting all social affairs of the women's senate.

The senate maintained close relationships with the Women's Chapel Association, the Women's Athletic Association, the Panhellenic Association, the City Women's Club, and the Senior Guides. It also had general authority over all women's affairs, judged the qualifications of all women seeking office, voided student elections conducted contrary to University regulations, formulated rules for student conduct, and arbitrated controversies brought to it by individuals or groups. The first president under the new constitution was Catherine Long, who was singled out by Dean Hilton for her exceptional leadership.

In the fall of 1933 the women's senate had provided for a women's student court of eleven members. In commenting upon its work, Dean Leonard remarked in 1935 that the court had aided materially in the development of cooperative morale among the students and had increased their appreciation of their citizenship responsibilities in campus life. "As an educational venture," she declared, "I have felt it to be really valuable," although she admitted there was a danger of allowing the court the same degree of publicity that other women's groups enjoyed. To the dean the court worked best in an unobtrusive manner.

In 1936–37, however, Dean Hilton informed the Chancellor that she believed the need for a court had definitely passed. Accordingly, the next year a select committee of the women's senate, consisting of the dean of women and several student leaders, handled such matters that heretofore had been the court's responsibility. Although the committee continued to function in 1937–38, the results were none too successful, probably because of the irregularity of its sessions.

The story of Women's Student Government Association during the Flint-Graham era lacks the turbulence and notoriety of the Men's Student Government; having escaped the excessive publicity and criticism heaped on the latter by the *Daily Orange,* its achievements were more outstanding and lasting. WSGA was generally a strong and influential force on the campus. The dean of women used it in a legitimate way to regulate the life of women students socially and in the living centers. The initial reluctance of WSGA to join with the men in the 1920s did not stem from any weakness or desire to withdraw from controversial issues; it was because of a firm and sincere conviction, shared by the dean of women, that WSGA had a "good show" which might be downgraded by affiliating with a men's group that had been relatively impotent. And it was the opinion of Blair Knapp that Women's Student Government "was by all odds more important and more significant to the campus than any comparable agency for the men."

22

Student Publications

The humor is clean, if characteristically undergraduate.
—Burges Johnson

THE *Daily Orange* WAS READY TO GIVE UP THE GHOST IN 1922. This was not the first time the student newspaper, founded in 1903, had been in financial trouble nor would it be the last. The problem this time was the failure of students to support the daily. Its salvation was a complicated one.

The Orange Publishing Company printed most of the University bulletins, programs, office stationery and student publications, including the *Daily Orange*. It was a private company, but many of its stockholders were alumni and the close relationship sometimes embarrassed the University. Now the situation was compounded by the fact that Dr. Flint was about to assume the chancellorship.

The *Daily Orange* had ended its publication year with a deficit of more than $3,000. There had been times in the past when the newspaper went into the red, but the company had found it worth swallowing that loss to have the University's other printing business. This time, however, company finances were in worse shape, and the principal stockholder, Henry Curtis, asked the University for a sizable mortgage. Vice Chancellor Graham questioned the feasibility of such a step, whereupon Curtis offered to assign his stock in the company, free of encumbrances, to the University. This would give the University working control of the printing firm. The idea was appealing, Dr. Flint

Burges Johnson, director of public relations, 1927–1934.

agreed, and Dr. Graham headed the new board of directors of the company. The advantages of having its own print shop included the academic one of providing a laboratory for journalism.

From owning 40 percent of the company stock when the deal was made, the University increased its holdings to two-thirds by 1934. The Orange Publishing Company became a valuable and profitable part of its assets. Now the Chancellor was chairman of its board of directors; the dean of the new School of Journalism, M. Lyle Spencer, was another director, with the responsibility for running the company.

Having solved the financial problem when it gained operating control, the University was ready to deal with the matter of running the student newspaper. Editorial control and business management were delegated to four students, two men and two women, who were given salaries and the right to name their successors.

When Burges Johnson joined the administration in 1927 as director of public relations, his office became responsible for all student publications. Johnson told a reporter from the *Alumni News* about his attitude toward student publications: "I am interested in them whether I have to be or not, though personally I don't believe much in censorship."

Johnson apparently was the person who established new rules governing publication of the *Daily Orange*. There were five rules, constituting a cooperative agreement between the University and the student editors. A stipulation was that the students could not change them unilaterally. The rules were:

1. The newspaper would come out daily with enough copies to meet campus needs.

2. Advertisements would be limited to one-third of the space in the paper; any that clashed with the University interests would be prohibited.

3. After consultation with the proper authorities, editorial criticism of the administration would be permitted "if, with full knowledge of the facts, the editorial board still maintains its position."

4. Libelous or indecent matter would be prohibited. If such material appeared, the administration might impose sanctions in keeping with established newspaper practice.

5. The University would have no control over the newspaper's managerial duties nor would it interfere with distribution of the salaries allotted by the administration unless editors were deadlocked on such decisions. The newspaper would provide space for all University announcements.

The rules were restated in February 1928, when Johnson said relations between the *Daily Orange* editors and the administration were relatively satisfactory; neither party wanted to assume the "obligations and responsibilities of the other." It had not been necessary "for your administrative partner" to force his views on the editors, he told students. He added, "I have heard it stated that there is not a free press here (but) there is no censorship of the student press at Syracuse. Censorship means a submission of material before publication ... with power to edit or destroy it. Obviously the University authorities possess such a right, but they do not care to exercise it and have no desire to do so."

There were differences of opinion over the years, with *Daily Orange* and other student editors convinced that the Chancellor hid strong hands inside kid gloves and looked on all student papers as obedient agents of the administration.

But no serious difference arose, and the cooperative agreement was observed. Dr. Flint himself once said: "I have leaned over backward to guard against even the appearance of 'control.' I cannot recall a single instance ... in which I have either forbidden publication of a particular article or on a particular subject, or in which I or my colleagues have disciplined an editor of the *Orange* in such connection."

After Dean Spencer assumed supervision over the newspaper he declared that the editor of "a college paper, like the professional editor, should have freedom, not license," to publish anything he wished, but that the staff of the *Daily Orange* should view its duties as laboratory work in journalism, subject at all times to direction in such matters as editing and business management.

Dean Spencer, acting under new rules in 1935, put administrators on the editorial and business boards of the newspaper. The Chancellor had drawn up a plan affecting all student publications. As approved by the executive committee of the student government, it called for an eight-member board including five students plus the journalism dean, a representative of the Orange Publishing Company, and a faculty member elected by the University Senate. The board, headed by Dean Spencer, then chose the editors and business managers of all student publications. There were protests but, with slight modifications, the new rules were in effect during the rest of the Flint and throughout the Graham administrations.

Despite earlier denials by Dr. Flint, he did exercise a form of censorship in late 1935 after the *Daily Orange* printed advertisements for "drinks of all kinds," "wine and dine," and "legal beverages." The Chancellor, a noted prohibitionist, declared "I am covered with shame, confusion, and humiliation," and banned such ads in future issues of student publications.

Chancellor Graham also was disturbed by questionable ads and certain editorials but was less volatile than his predecessor. Asked in 1938 by *Daily Orange* editor Chester Rondomanski '38—later editor and publisher of the Fulton, New York, *Patriot*—for his views on censorship, Dr. Graham praised freedom of the press but said it must be freedom and not license. He believed, he said, that a reasonable policy might rest on past standards and traditions, enforced by the good judgment of the editors. A year later in 1939, when an alumnus became irate over a story in the newspaper Dr. Graham replied: "In view of the present world situation ... it would set a very poor example for the University to censure its publications, beyond seeing that they conform to accepted standards of decency."

The most enduring of all student publications at Syracuse is the *Onondagan*, published annually since the 1884 number came out in March 1883. Like the newspaper, the yearbook had financial problems, especially in the Flint era. Often the costs of publication, generally met through advertising, exceeded income as succeeding editorial boards sought to make their books bigger than those of previous years. Some editors felt the Chancellor's wrath when they failed to meet obligations, and Dr. Flint got the bills for their debts. Finally, after declaring the University not liable, he channeled receipts and expenditures through the treasurer's office. Burges Johnson took over responsibility for the *Onondagan* when he joined the University in 1927; later Dean Spencer assumed it.

There were various squabbles over the *Onondagan* in the thirties—questions of selection of the editorial and business staffs, whether every junior should be required to buy a copy, whether there should be a less expensive annual. By the fall of 1933 there was a genuine crisis; the administration appeared ready to suspend publication, refusing to recognize a new editorial board or sanction a 1934 edition. Johnson blamed poor business practices and mounting debts but denied rumors of a scandal. "There is nothing scandalous about it," he said. "Outworn and outgrown machinery has at last broken down." This was true at other institutions as well, he said.

The junior class, hoping to salvage the situation, expressed continued confidence in the *Onondagan* and suggested that juniors again take control. Before 1930 the yearbook was managed and published by the junior class; from 1930 to 1933 the seniors controlled it. Finally the 1934 *Onondagan* was published by the juniors on terms acceptable to the Chancellor.

There were three other annuals—*The Empire Forester* and *The Camp Log,* published by the College of Forestry, and the freshman handbook, which until 1927 was published by the YMCA as the *University Hand Book.* This was taken over by the director of public relations who in 1929 renamed it the *Student Desk Book;* after 1936 the registrar was responsible for it.

Many student publications came and went during the Flint-Graham years. There was the *Phoenix,* begun in 1920 as a magazine for poetry and prose. In 1922 it opened up to sports, other student activities and events, and campus opinion, as well as to literary work. It was supported by the English department until 1924, when its title became the *New Phoenix* and the department connection ceased.

The first issue of the reborn periodical featured a short story, "Rain," by Frederick G. Vosburgh, who was one day to be editor of *National Geographic.* The color cover showed a young woman with curly hair, rouged cheeks and painted lips—a typical flapper—over the legend "Touching Up the Old Oval." At 35 cents only 750 copies were sold, and in future issues the editors featured more and more humorous material. Sales went up, but so did the eyebrows of the administration, which failed to appreciate the *New Phoenix's* brand of humor.

Chancellor Flint and Vice Chancellor Graham talked separately at different times with the editors of the *New Phoenix* under that title and again when it was reborn as the *Salt Shaker.* The magazine continued to publish material that distressed the administration, then died in 1926.

Meanwhile an English department publication, *Green Leaf,* edited by students but guided by a departmental committee, had begun life in 1925. It featured poetry and prose by freshmen and some faculty members and lasted until 1932. *Green Leaf* was closed to outsiders, a policy that favored the birth in 1928 of *The Crystal.* This was an experiment of the Crystal Literary Society that published some creditable articles before it expired in 1929.

The *Chap Book* came along in 1928 and lasted about three years.

Rietta Gantter '32, then Rietta Trimm, had some things to say about literary magazines and her effect on them: "The market for a purely literary magazine was not great. I was editor of half a dozen. I'd get to be an editor, and they'd promptly die. The *Chap Book* failed; it was purely literary. I had been working with Jerry Mangione on that. Then they decided to start *Sparks,* which was part literary and part issues of the day—controversial. Jerry graduated and I became editor, and it limped along for just that second year and it died. I felt like a murderess. It died partly because we were now in 1931–32, and there wasn't any money to do anything with."

Sparks, described by its editors as "an experiment as a semiliterary campus magazine," first appeared in November 1929. It featured serious articles on such subjects as rushing, student government, and athletics, and poetry by Rietta Trimm. Other editorial staffers were Edward C. Reifenstein, Jr., Helen Barnette, Ivan Gould, Edward Obrist, and Elizabeth Pyke. Among *Sparks* contributors were Burges Johnson, discussing a Carnegie Corporation report on college athletics, and Sawyer Falk on a projected campus theater.

From the *Chap Book's* ashes and those of *Green Leaf* in 1933 came *Argot,* an ambitious literary periodical with high standards and some powerful backing—one of its patrons was Johnson, Dr. Flint's public relations man. Professor Leonard Brown of the English department helped guide its fortunes, and it continued to publish significant articles by students and faculty.

Argot survived with distinction until 1935 when the administration, in a move that was difficult for many to understand, merged it with the rambunctious *Orange Peel* and produced *The Syracusan* (in the process reviving the name of a campus magazine of the nineteenth century). This action bitterly disappointed friends of *Argot,* who failed to see why that respected magazine had to die to satisfy the administration's avowed desire to see the creation of "a fairly balanced magazine."

The *Orange Peel,* originally founded as a humor magazine in 1913, had a long and troubled career that included being banned by Chancellor Day. Revived in 1927 by the journalism society Pi Delta Epsilon, it was published on Moving-Up Day. Its thirty-four pages offered fiction, essays, poetry, humor, and illustrations. Norris Johnson, the editor, kept his promise to make it mirror a cross-section of student life. Over the next few years the comic content grew. Burges Johnson, the administrator, said "The humor is clean, if characteristically undergraduate." But by 1935 the administrators decided that the humor had deteriorated too far and they banned the sale of the February issue on campus.

No record can be found to pinpoint the material deemed objectionable. The offending article could have been a satirical one headed "Shirley Temple for Dictator." It showed the Hollywood starlet dressed as Napoleon and said "Fuhrer Temple remains the hope of world!" It added that her platform consisted of such planks as "the razing of Radio City" and "the razzing of Rudy Vallee."

More repugnant than this feeble jape was a cartoon by the magazine's art editor depicting a little boy kneeling at his bedside in pajamas, praying: "And, dear Lord, please see to it that I sleep with Shirley Temple. ... Amen."

But the most likely offender was something else on the page with the cartoon. It was an anecdote purporting to be about an unnamed former dean of women. An *Orange Peel* columnist said the incident might not have really happened but the story was that several years earlier the dean addressed freshman women "on the advisability of keeping themselves on the virtuous path—with no detours." The dean of women reportedly concluded: "Above all, girls—please, *please* don't sacrifice honor and decency and all these things for only ten minutes of pleasure!" And the columnist concluded: "One demure looking freshman leaned over to her neighbor, so the story goes, and whispered: 'My God! How does she make it last that long!'"

Whatever the objectionable material was, the student senates declared the issue "not representative of the campus." Editor Kermit Kahn resigned. The administration combined the *Orange Peel* and the *Argot* into *The Syracusan,* and the first issue appeared in the fall of 1935. Its editor, Ellis Haller, pledged to keep the magazine balanced. He and his successors did so through the end of the Graham administration in 1942, when *The Syracusan* died.

Shirley Jackson '40.

More puzzling was the reason for the reported administration banning of *Spectre,* an ambitious literary quarterly published by the English Club. *Spectre* first appeared in 1939. All four issues were edited by Shirley Jackson and her husband-to-be, Stanley Edgar Hyman, Hyman became a respected literary critic and Miss Jackson first earned fame as the author of the memorable short story "The Lottery." Later she wrote macabre novels and rollicking nonfiction about her four children.

Each issue of *Spectre* was crammed with fiction, articles, criticism, art, commentary, poetry. All fifty-plus pages, including the cover, were mimeographed, permitting publication of much more material than if the magazine had been set in costly type. It sold for a dime.

The contents included fiction and poetry by Miss Jackson and others plus artwork and articles by Hyman, faculty members Leonard Brown and Floyd H. Allport, jazz musician Muggsy Spanier, and a diversity of other contributors.

In their final issue "We the Editor" paid tribute to Brown, a professor of English. The editorial said: "Whatever there was good in the magazine came out of Leonard Brown. What we learned from him about writing (and, more important, about reading) almost made the four years we spent up here worthwhile."

In addition to a serious concern for world issues and the human

Stanley Edgar Hyman '40.

condition, there was an air of wit and whimsicality about *Spectre.* A sometime poet who hid behind the pseudonym Meade Lux (from boogie woogie pianist Meade Lux Lewis?) wrote "Lines for a Memorable Day" for the Spring 1940 issue—two lines that read

> Thompson and Thomas, Thompson and Thomas
> The first was a lick and the second a promise.

Dorothy Thompson '14, the columnist, and Norman Thomas, the Socialist party leader, had spoken on the campus on the same day, March 11, 1940.

It is difficult to believe that University administrators would ban a magazine like *Spectre* today, in the eighties, if indeed they did ban it in 1940, and not merely cut its budget. Still today, in the eighties, a school district has banned a Shirley Jackson book because it contains "The Lottery."

June Mirken, who was on the editorial staff with Shirley Jackson and Stanley Hyman and would have been editor if there had been a fifth issue of *Spectre,* wrote in the fall 1940 issue of *The Syracusan:*

> To criticize student writing because it shows a tendency towards preoccupation with social problems, evinces distrust and questioning of

> traditionally accepted values, or even goes so far as to mention a "dirty" word, is to criticize almost all of modern thought and art. . . .
>
> Within four days after the announcement of the "suspension of publication" of *Spectre,* over 700 students and faculty members signed a petition protesting against its suppression.

Years later her alma mater wanted to give Shirley Jackson an Arents Medal, but she was too ill to travel to the campus to accept it. She visited later, in April 1965, and read from a story she was still writing at the time of her death in August of that year.

Many other periodicals appeared during the Flint and Graham years. Few lasted long. They included *The Main Spring, Hill Echoes, Hill Monthly,* and *Record* (no relation to the weekly Syracuse University *Record* of the 1970s and 1980s), *Battle Cry, Gadfly, The Syracuse Student, The Threshold, The Freshman Lid,* and *Tempo.*

23

The Fraternities

The physical consequences of Hell Week were much in evidence. The infirmary showed a marked increase in the number of patients.

On the day classes began in the fall of 1922 Chancellor Flint spoke to students and alumni in Archbold Stadium. His subject, "Partnership Together in a Common Enterprise," was designed to stimulate his audience to "spiritual purity, for earnestness of purpose and broad vision." To attain these objectives, he urged abandoning any notion of a continuing conflict between faculty and students. He declared: "Syracuse University is yours. I want you to take possession of your property. The faculty is yours. They have not been engaged for the pleasure of the Chancellor or the trustees, but for your benefit. The administration is yours all the way down and including the Chancellor."

Dr. Flint made it clear, however, that laggards would be asked to make way for those who really wanted an education. He was anxious to see the return to Syracuse of the "popularity of hard work," and he warned against the snares of college and city life.

The new Chancellor was appealing to all who were interested in their own welfare and that of the University, but his remarks were particularly applicable to members of fraternities, whose influence on the campus had been apparent from the founding of Syracuse in 1870. For many decades after that, the administration's attitude to the fraternities was generally one of laissez-faire. As long as the Greek letter societies identified their aims with those of the University in advancing intellectual development, there was no need for University authorities to govern or sit in judgment on the secret societies. But in the early years of the twentieth century the national fraternities found they had allowed the local chapters too much self-government, widening a gap between the University and themselves. As in the rest of the country, members had glorified athletics, social affairs, and student government, and were giving lip service to intellectual pursuits.

In 1914 Chancellor Day tried to correct the situation by founding the University committee on fraternities. Two years later he welcomed the creation of an Interfraternity Conference of Syracuse University, popularly called the Interfraternity Council, whose members represented several local chapters. The aims of the council were to promote the interests of the University and the fraternities, and to insure cooperation among the societies and the University, so as to improve the condition of the fraternities and their relations with University authorities.

The undergraduate members of the council were not happy about their impending loss of self-determination, but they had no choice except to weather what some of them viewed as a passing squall. For the duration of the first world war fraternity problems seemed relatively unimportant, and during the rest of Dr. Day's administration the University concerned itself little with fraternity affairs.

Chancellor Flint's stadium address in 1922 alerted the campus to the return of a strong administration policy toward fraternities, and from time to time he reminded them of his concern, declaring on one occasion that they were not outside the pale of official supervision because their social, moral and, political activities, if not properly directed, might damage the University.

The University committee on fraternities, meanwhile, favored raising eligibility standards for membership in fraternities and promoting scholastic ideals. It was significant, the committee added, that of the eighteen sororities, fourteen had a higher standard for initiation than required by the University; the example set by the women should urge the administration and fraternities to adopt better requirements for membership.

The committee also reported on drinking in the chapter houses and other matters. It said there had been little drinking in the houses and the members were no worse than the independents about frequenting city hotels and downtown taverns. Living conditions at the houses were superior to those in the dormitories, thanks to the way they were organized and to support from alumni and national offices. Unfortunately, the report said, this caused some people to view the fraternities as a superior and favored element on a campus where democratic ideas should be uppermost. The committee also believed the administration sooner or later would have to face the problem of discriminatory practices by some houses in matters of race, creed, and color.

Professor William Smallwood, the committee chairman, discussed these and other matters with Chancellor Flint during the first semester of 1922–23. He believed many fraternity members would not graduate unless they showed a marked improvement in their studies. Among the freshmen, he noted, women were doing better scholastically than the men. He also said Chancellor Flint might have to decide whether Syracuse should recognize more Jewish, Italian, and Roman Catholic societies. Specifically he asked if Dr. Flint was ready to recognize three petitioning organizations, Tau Epsilon Phi (Jewish), Phi Iota Chi (Catholic), and Alpha Phi Delta (Italian). He noted that the power to permit the founding of new student societies had once rested with the fraternity committee, but more recently Dr. Day and his staff had exercised this authority.

Probably the issue that most plagued the administration and the fraternities themselves was that of rushing. When Dr. Flint joined Syracuse there was unrestricted rushing, although most of it took place during the opening days of school and at the start of the second semester. There were no limitations on how much a fraternity could spend on dinners, parties, and other rushing expenses and none of the entertaining of prospective members had to be held in the chapter house. This had distinct advantages for the fraternities, the rushees, and the University.

Naturally, the fraternities, with a heavy financial overhead, wished to rush and pledge early in the fall. This reassured the alumni that current expenses could be met and that the national organizations would receive the dues that helped maintain their headquarters. Early promotion of fraternity ideals and full chapter houses were other benefits.

From the point of view of the rushee, it was a thrill to be pledged early, enabling him to flash the pledge pin that signified eventual membership in a select group. It also allowed him to board at the house and have a place for social activities. In some instances he might even live in the house.

As for the University, it was relieved of a housing problem, and the Chancellor noted with satisfaction the mounting loyalties that fraternity men had for their alma mater.

But few could ignore the unfavorable aspects. The University bemoaned the presence of a competitor that demanded so much of the student's time, took him from his studies and classes, and surrounded him with an environment sometimes detrimental to his own best interests and the reputation of the University. Poor students clogged the academic life of the campus, and the loss of many at the close of their first semester because of low scholarship often produced financial burdens during the second semester. Nor did all of the students like the system. House after house had too many one-year men. An improved method of selection, based on intellectual capacity and ability to meet fraternity life and costs, was needed.

Conscious of the new Chancellor's attitude and prodded by the committee, the Interfraternity Council, which consisted of representatives of the Greek houses, made rushing the chief topic at many meetings. In November 1923 the council proposed several new procedures but the following April 15 houses voted against them and only five were in favor. The *Daily Orange* said Syracuse would continue to operate under unrestricted rushing, known in campus slang as "cut-throat" or "sandbag" rushing.

A year later another proposal was made to tighten the rules, and certain amendments were adopted. The situation improved briefly, but by the spring of 1927 illegal pledging cropped up again. The reform spirit soon spent itself despite concern that most fraternities expressed over the situation.

Chancellor Flint appointed a special faculty-student committee to study the problem in January 1930, and in the spring its compromise plan received the approval of the administration and the council.

The rules of 1930 set up a rushing committee consisting of the Vice Chancellor, the president of the Interfraternity Council, and one man elected by the council. Violation of the rules by a fraternity or a freshman could mean loss of social privileges by all members and pledges; placing the group on probation; declaring the personnel of the offending house ineligible for all activities for the remainder of the college year; a University recommendation to the national headquarters of society that its charter be withdrawn; and a provision that freshmen who violated the rules could not affiliate with another fraternity and might be subject to further discipline by the rushing committee.

There was discontent among some active and alumni members about the new rules. Some insisted the regulations would either kill the chapters or force them to rush covertly. A *Daily Orange* questionnaire in December 1930 showed about 20 houses strongly disapproved of the rules. Although unwilling to accept their position, Vice Chancellor Graham, believing Syracuse had so many fraternities that it would eventually have to disband some, told Dr. Flint there was a serious defect in the rules. He said that in the past the fraternities had been "one of the most productive recruiting agencies" and had brought "a rather desirable type of students" to the campus. The new rules had disrupted the process, and he believed some restrictions might be changed.

The Greek societies debated the problem, but when in March 1931 a motion was made at a council meeting to return to the old "cutthroat" methods, only four of twenty-three houses voted to do so. Later that month the council approved the limitation of formal rushing to five days, beginning three weeks after registration. All prospective pledges were to attend a fraternity convocation in the week before rushing, where all aspects of fraternity life and organization would be presented and discussed.

In the weeks before classes began in the fall of 1931 a new administrative committee on fraternity conduct and discipline discussed the situation. Disciplinary problems were to be handled by another committee headed by Vice Chancellor Graham. Professor Lewis Crawford, named fraternity adviser, supervised rushing and guided the fraternities on pertinent issues. He also cooperated with the dean of women on matters of University parties, dates, and chaperons.

In the wake of these decisions and before rushing started, the Interfraternity Council approved of the Open House Plan—for three hours on the Sunday night before rushing prospective pledges were free to visit any number of houses to help them make their choices. The *Daily Orange* cautioned freshmen not to "dash madly" from one house to another, and suggested the fraternities should adopt a "hands off" policy during Open House hours. Generally speaking, in spite of a violation or two, the new rushing system was considered a success.

Dr. Graham kept a watchful eye on the fraternities. He was a fraternity man himself and firmly believed that, with guidance, the societies could fulfill their own purposes and render distinct services to the University. Concerned by the impact of the Depression on the fraternities, he wrote to Chancellor Flint in May 1932 that their lot would be worse during the next college year. Their supporting membership was declining and they were having increasing difficulties in meeting their financial obligations and responsibilities. Their value to Syracuse in attracting good men to the campus and in providing housing for students was self-evident. Therefore he suggested lifting the ban against freshmen living in fraternity houses, though not at the expense of University dormitories, which must be filled first.

Meanwhile, fraternity opposition to deferred rushing, resulting from a reduction in the number of prospective rushees caused in turn by the Depression, steadily mounted. No one was surprised, therefore, when in September 1932 the Interfraternity Council voted to return to an earlier rushing period with every freshman and transfer student eligible for pledging. Commenting on the new program and reviewing events since 1930, Dr. Graham said the University Committee on Fraternities had tried to deal "with a complex situation without the aid of previous experience. ... The administration has never attempted to dictate or even advise the details of rushing. The students have been told separately, 'Keep rushing out of the first week of college. Otherwise do as you please.'"

A "do as you please" policy, however, did little to improve the basic shortcomings of the fraternity system. Nor did it stop illegal rushing. The Columbia University *Spectator* advocated the abolition of fraternities on several counts including what it called their political machinations in campus elections. In Syracuse, David Brewer, secretary of the Interfraternity Council, denied the existence of any overt influence by the local societies. But he said no system could be devised that would prevent some evil practices by the fraternities.

A. Blair Knapp, appointed chairman of the Council of Men's Affairs in 1935, had this to say on the subject:

> The fraternity is an institution and a force of primary importance in the extracurricular life of the University. Directly associated with the whole history of Syracuse, fraternities condition and determine the morale, morals, attitudes, and aspirations of their members in a powerful way. Since they are human institutions, they have not been immune to the changed conditions of life on and off the campus. Conceived as active agencies for the cultural, moral, and intellectual advancement of young men, they have in many cases lost sight of old ideas and ancient traditions. They have become ends in themselves rather than splendid means toward the goals of University life.

Knapp and his colleague, Professor Lewis Crawford, tackled the problems of Hell Week, housing, rushing, and scholarship. One of their major steps was to schedule an Interfraternity Conference in December 1936 with the theme "The University and the Fraternity." More than a thousand undergraduates, alumni, national fraternity officers, and representatives of neighboring colleges and universities attended, and all aspects of fraternity life were discussed. Knapp told the delegates a university based its fortunes on intellectual foundations, tempered by a personal interest in the social and moral life of the student. "This is where fraternities come in," he said. "They must justify themselves as a part of this education or the University has only two alternatives—integration or liquidation." By integration he meant joint efforts by all houses with the University in pursuit of the common good. Fired by these and other speeches, the conference approved recommendations urging the Interfraternity Council to become more active, exchange smokers and dinners among the houses, schedule meetings of pledge masters, and promote scholarship. The delegates also favored a richer cultural life, fireside chats by businessmen, a resident adviser system, and reform of campus politics.

The *Daily Orange* called the meeting a "notable achievement in fraternity-administrative understanding" and praised the work of Knapp, who reorganized the Interfraternity Council in May 1937 so it could act as a deliberative and legislative body with power exercised by an executive secretary-treasurer chosen on the basis of merit.

The administration's policy toward fraternities was predicated in part on the scholastic standing of the chapters. In 1922 eligibility for initiation into a fraternity depended on successful completion of 12 hours of work taken in residence during the first semester. Those lacking these hours might be initiated at the end of the freshman year. No change was made in the regulations until 1939, when what had been inherent in former requirements was spelled out for the first time—that intitiation was dependent on a "C" average. (In 1938 the Interfraternity Council, by an eighteen-to-thirteen vote, had rejected a plan that would have raised the requirements.)

The scholastic standing of fraternity members had long been a matter of dismay far beyond Syracuse. In 1934 the National Interfraternity Conference published figures showing that the fraternities at sixteen colleges in New England and New York had grades so low they were largely responsible for a three-year decline in national averages. In the three years ended 1933–34 the Syracuse fraternity average was never higher than sixtieth place on the list of 166 colleges in the United States. In two of those years it was below 100th place. In the opinion of Knapp and others the chapters had only themselves to blame for their low academic standing. In general the alumni did little but render lip service to scholastic matters; they were chiefly interested in the business aspects of fraternity life.

Hoping to stimulate the houses to better study habits and raise the scholastic level, the administration devised a plan of rating the chapters according to the grades their members received; the ratings were published in the *Daily Orange* and the *Alumni News*.

In 1935–36 the administration sponsored what was known as the

In 1933, at the 100th anniversary convention of Psi Upsilon fraternity, nine members—three from Syracuse University—posed for this photograph at Union College, Schenectady, New York. In the group the three Syracusans, all members of the class of 1886, stand third, fifth, and eighth from left. They are George P. Wadsworth, Herbert G. Coddington, and John Ingham.

Resident Alumni Adviser System supervised by Dean Knapp and Professor Crawford. Each adviser enrolled in the Graduate School and carried a full class schedule. He was appointed to his position as adviser by his fraternity, which gave him living accommodations in the house. The University paid his tuition and part of his board. Although the number of such advisers decreased in later years—there were only five in 1940–41—the advisers themselves believed the program benefited the fraternities and the University.

Among his duties, the resident adviser tried to de-emphasize Hell Week, often known as "informal orientation." Whatever its name it was something each pledge endured in the week before formal initiation. During the first few days the novices cleaned the house, trimmed the lawn, and ran errands for the active members. Occasionally the pledges waited on tables at sorority houses where they sang songs and recited poetry, much to the amusement of the women. This part of Hell Week was generally considered fun by the pledges, nor did they complain about being taken some miles out into the country with each pledge paddled by his brothers-to-be. Each blow was supposed to erase demerits he had accumulated during his first semester in the chapter.

Some chapters forced their neophytes to eat concoctions that were, to say the least, disagreeable.

The physical consequences of Hell Week were much in evidence. The pledges either slept during classes or were absent. The infirmary showed a marked increase in patients. The administration frowned on the entire procedure as being beneath the dignity of the fraternities and the University. By 1929, therefore, some attempt was made to tone down the system. It was proposed that a "uniform Hell Week" be instituted—that is, that all houses conduct initiations at the same time. But it was not until 1934 that most of the houses adopted such uniformity, in return for which Dean Leebrick of Liberal Arts announced that his faculty would lessen assignments and give no examinations during that week.

The following year the National Interfraternity Council, meeting in New York City, went on record as favoring the abolition of the "brutal" aspects of informal initiation. In spite of this position and local remedial measures, Hell Week remained a serious problem at Syracuse, and in December 1935 the Syracuse Interfraternity Council declared it did not approve of such hazing. Specifically it wanted Hell Week renamed Orientation Week and actually limited to a weekend. All phases of "orientation" were to be confined to the houses, except for one night when "a long hike under the guidance of an alumnus of that chapter" was allowed. Because of fraternal secrecy, it is not known to what extent these recommendations were followed.

Late in 1936 Dean Knapp returned from a meeting of the National Interfraternity Conference with the assurance that it would support any action taken locally by the University and fraternities. No clear improvement followed, however, so in 1938 Chancellor Graham met with the local council and informed it a change in procedure was necessary. Then, at a meeting of deans and directors, Knapp was commissioned to advise the council that sufficient time had elapsed for the elimination of Hell Week and that unless appropriate measures were taken by the fraternities, the University would step in. Knapp passed this information on to the houses themselves, intimating that Hell Week was an abomination and that remedial steps must be taken at once. The council set up new rules, with fines for violators. Belatedly the fraternities fell into line; most of them officially abolished Hell Week and established a Freshman Orientation Week in its place, as Knapp had suggested. Thereafter the novices were drilled in fraternity ideals and principles. From time to time there were rumors of senseless hazing, but as Chancellor Graham's administration drew to an end conditions were far better than they had been in 1922.

When Freshman Orientation Week was being planned Dean Knapp asked Frank Piskor of his staff to review the problem of redefining the training of fraternity pledges. Piskor found that the houses centered such training "quite exclusively" on fraternity ideals, history, ritual, and social behavior, especially "with respect to boy-girl relations." In his opinion, Piskor said, adequate training should have been "less parochial," including University ideals and traditions and the responsibilities of the houses to the University and to their alumni associations.

Perennially there was criticism of the fraternities for other reasons. There were complaints of extravagances in fraternity life; many parents said their sons were subjected to increasing expenses. It was not true that some houses were fitted out like "sumptuous hotels," but they were better equipped and more comfortable than the living centers. By 1933 virtually every chapter owned its own house, with the title usually in the name of its alumni association, acting as a holding corporation for the active members. All active members and pledges paid dues covering the cost of maintenance and repairs.

In 1933 freshmen paid an average of $125 for dues and initiation fees. In 1941 the handbook of the Interfraternity Council said:

"The costs of the freshman year may be as low as $40 and as high as $200, the average being $125. Above the freshman year, the cost of fraternity includes membership dues, social taxes, and, in the case of men not living in the house, a house tax. These costs range from $15 to $120, the average being $54. Room and board figures run from $300 to $450, the average being $350."

The cost of room and board in Sims Hall at a comparable time (1940) was $400.

Men who were fraternity members in the years 1922–42 had pleasant memories of life in their chapter houses. There they were rushed, pledged, and finally initiated into a brotherhood that was a vital factor in their time at the University. Few recalled misunderstandings between them and the administration. At alumni gatherings they reminisced about the fellowship they had enjoyed; the fun and pranks remained uppermost in their minds.

Most of them also remembered that they had sought to bring honor and recognition to their houses by their part in athletic, literary, and journalistic activities, or through membership in social or religious organizations. Their vitas in the *Onondagan* reveal the variety of such positions. They could have done better scholastically, although some won high honors, but generally they remained on the same academic level as their nonfraternity classmates. Writing in August 1940 with the acute international situation in mind Dean Knapp said: "we must be

In the summer of 1929, on the eve of the Depression years, the *Alumni News* published these photographs of some stately fraternity and sorority houses on the Syracuse campus.

increasingly intolerant of substandard activities. Fraternities with chronic records of poor scholarship or poor conduct must be eliminated after fair warning. If an aggressive personnel program is necessary, it would include a more arbitrary attitude toward individuals or groups which destroy morale."

Many fraternity alumni recalled their chapters' interest in social and welfare work. Sometimes freshmen were assigned such tasks as cleaning and painting rooms in the city churches. Often a chapter sponsored a Thanksgiving or Christmas party for underprivileged children or made donations to charitable organizations. The annual Interfraternity banquets and balls and commencement ceremonies were fresh in their memories, and when they returned to the campus they divided their time between their Syracuse friends and their fraternity houses.

They were loyal to both and showed their gratitude to their alma mater with gifts and contributions—Chancellors Flint and Graham knew fraternity men could be relied on to support University fund drives and to help recruit students.

Speaking to the trustees in June 1938, Dr. Graham said: "one reason for the increase in attendance . . . is the increased interest of the alumni of the University and pride of the alumni in the University. They are all boosting now. They tell the young people 'Go to Syracuse.' That hasn't always been the case in the past. So thanks to the cooperation of the alumni, and I like to think 'Thanks to the reputation which the University is making for itself,' I believe the attendance will be as large as we want it to be."

24

The Sororities

The women enjoyed living in congenial groups that fostered pleasurable experiences.

LATE IN 1934 CHANCELLOR FLINT APPOINTED A COMMITTEE of the University senate to study the rushing system as it applied to women. His action was prompted by the confusion and disorganization resulting from the practice. Many an administrator and faculty member believed, as one said, "it is utterly impossible to go about the University's business during the rushing season."

Reporting on its investigation, the committee said that the past six semesters had seen steady increases in the scholastic averages of entering women students. Six of the biggest colleges at the University recruited up to 90 percent of their freshmen from the upper half of high school classes. Furthermore, the University had created a favorable environment for good scholarship. But, despite this, during the same six semesters sorority and nonsorority women, including freshmen, had lower scholastic averages in the first semester than in the second. The investigators blamed fall rushing.

The senate investigating committee also said, in spite of its finding that rushing interfered with classwork, that any revision of the rushing rules should be done by the twenty-two sororities themselves.

There was some agreement with a view that the sororities had served their purpose and no longer had an effective message for the women. In earlier years at Syracuse the Greek letter houses had exerted influence in matters of housing, scholarship, and social programs—activities the University, in Dr. Flint's day, was better qualified to direct. This was the view of the dean of women, Eugenie Andruss Leonard, in her 1933–34 report to the Chancellor. She said it was understandable that the women enjoyed living in congenial groups that fostered "pleasurable experiences." But there was danger "in remaining in competition with the administration rather than in striking out in new fields of culture and idealism that will give them leadership and inspiration."

Thus Dean Leonard criticised the Panhellenic Association which with the Chancellor, the dean of women, and the sororities shared responsibility for the problems of rushing, pledging, and initiation at the twenty-odd houses. The problems were now so involved, she said, that Panhellenic, founded in 1904, probably never would be an effective agency.

Dean Leonard's opinion of Panhellenic was not always so harsh. In fact, during her first few years as dean of women, from 1930 to 1933, she had seen a revitalization of the organization. There was increased pride among sorority members. Several chapters cooperated in attempts to raise scholastic standards. A code of ethics, drafted by former Dean of Women Iva L. Peters, was stimulating the sororities to better ideals and conduct.

It was against this background that Dean Leonard on November 21, 1932, took as her theme for the association's annual banquet "What Next in Panhellenic?" and predicted that on the basis of her experience with them, Syracuse sorority women would be among the moral, cultural, and intellectual leaders of their generation.

The dean told an audience of 800 in the ballroom of the Hotel Syracuse that the sororities had been of invaluable service to the University. She cited their scholarship and contributions to student government. As for things cultural, which the sororities fostered, she said that here Syracuse was a step ahead of all other institutions.

The president of the Panhellenic Association that year was Virginia E. Wartman '33 of Philadelphia, a member of Zeta Tau Alpha studying journalism in the College of Business Administration. She was also president of the Intercollegiate Panhellenic Association of Urban Universities and therefore was referred to in a press account as "titular head of most of the Greek-letter women in America."

Thus it could be expected that issues larger than those affecting the women of Syracuse University would be discussed at the banquet. And they were, by another speaker, William M. Smallwood, who said the women of that day faced a crisis of confidence.

Professor Smallwood, head of the biology department and for

fifteen years chairman of the faculty committee on sororities and fraternities, had been addressing the annual Panhellenic dinner meeting for many years and knew its problems well.

All women were living in a period of swift change, he told the sorority women, including those honored as the top five of the past year, Elizabeth Decker of Alpha Phi, Glenna Worth of Alpha Delta Phi, Doris Milton of Chi Omega, Pauline Wiley of Alpha Xi Delta, and Dorothy Timm of Kappa Alpha Delta. He cited the contributions to society of Frances Willard, Susan B. Anthony, Alice Freeman Palmer, and others he said had "opened up the whole realm of human endeavor to women." Then he asked in the accent of a westerner greeting a tourist: "Are ye jest travelin' or are ye goin' somewhere?"

In his own voice Professor Smallwood went on, "As long as tradition shaped the lives of women, they had a definite objective.... There has not thus far been revealed to modern women any common worthwhile objective."

He described his hearers as a generation whose confidence had been shaken—their confidence in history, in the church, in the home—but said: "There are probably some things that are worthwhile that have come down to us. To what are you going to pledge your loyalty? When tradition shaped, it was easy to choose. Your own choice must be made in an era of swift change. The great frontiers of women's emancipation have been taken; now there is to be a process of stabilization. You are going to establish traditions. What? If good, they will endure. If not, they will swiftly pass."

A humorous answer to Professor Smallwood's question could be seen in a skit presented by Kappa Delta, contrasting life in 1832 and 1932. The husband unquestionably was the boss of 1832; a century later the aggressive wife went out and enjoyed herself while the man stayed home and cooked.

Humor alone was a poor weapon against another problem of the era, one that affected not just fraternity and sorority life but cast a pall over the entire country. That was the Depression. Dean Leonard had spoken of its effects in an interview, praising young people for the way they were facing up to it. She told a reporter from the Syracuse *Post-Standard:* "One is just overpowered by their willingness to accept the situation and buckle down to very hard work. Their courage is something to make one work late at night and get up early in the morning to work again in order to help them find a way through."

She said she was particularly pleased with the sororities; under stress they were showing their mettle.

"In times like these, sororities do fine work attracting loans and grants to the University," Dean Leonard said. "Also they carry voluntarily a goodly part of the load by giving extended loans and grants to girls."

"There is scarcely a chapter on the Hill that is not carrying one or more students. Each sorority has written innumerable letters this summer. ... As far as we know, every qualified girl who wanted to come to college has been, or is being, placed."

The dean spoke thus as school began in the fall of 1932. The Depression did not go away—it got worse. As the holidays approached Dean Leonard told the *Daily Orange:* "Many students have expressed their intentions of remaining at home after Christmas because of lack of finances and we are anxious to get in touch with them before they do so." The dean said her staff was willing to find help for all who needed it. She particularly wanted to talk to any senior woman who might be in financial trouble. She listed as sources of help various alumni groups, local and national sororities, women's professional organizations, and the student emergency loan fund.

That was in 1932. Two years later, Dean Leonard suggested that reforms were in order and that Panhellenic's officers should initiate them.

In the years that followed many minor changes were made until, in 1938, a quota system for pledges was put into effect under Dean M. Eunice Hilton. This specified that no house could pledge more than twenty-two women, including freshmen and upperclassmen. It was hoped the plan would bring about greater uniformity in the size of the houses and that none would have more than fifty-five members. Houses that did not fill their quotas might rush during the rest of the school year.

By 1942 practically all of the sororities were housed in buildings owned by their alumni associations, which kept a close watch on the finances. What it cost a young woman to belong to a sorority before 1939 is not known, but probably it was not much more than the charges at the fraternity houses. Whether a potential member was informed of the comparative costs of the several sororities that rushed her is a matter of conjecture. In 1934 Dean Leonard complained that the houses withheld such information from her office, criticized the lack of uniformity in financial operations, and said parents and daughters were in a state of utter confusion. Starting in 1939 the Panhellenic *Handbook* carried a generalized statement. A sorority member living in her chapter house paid about $500 a year. Depending on the house, pledges were taxed from $75 to $120, which included the initiation fee.

Records of scholastic standards and achievements in the sororities before 1935 are incomplete, but from then through 1942 the averages ranged up to the equivalent of a "C+." Although this was somewhat higher than the fraternity and the all-University average, the administration had cause to wonder why the Greek women did not do better, considering that the majority of freshman women with better high school grades entered sororities.

Obviously some houses maintained higher scholastic averages than others. One of them, Alpha Epsilon Phi, was a consistent leader.

There were fifteen national social sororities on the Syracuse campus in the fall of 1922. The oldest (1872) was Alpha Phi. The others, in order of founding, were: Gamma Phi Beta, 1874; Kappa Kappa Gamma, 1883; Kappa Alpha Theta, 1889; Pi Beta Phi, 1896; Delta Delta Delta, 1896; Delta Gamma, 1901; Alpha Gamma Delta, 1904; Alpha Xi Delta, 1904; Sigma Kappa, 1905; Alpha Chi Omega, 1906; Chi Omega, 1911; Alpha Omicron Pi, 1914; Alpha Epsilon Phi, 1919; and Phi Mu, 1920.

During the Flint-Graham years seven new sororities made their appearances. Theta Phi Alpha had its origins in a local group known as Chi Sigma Theta, founded in 1920. Chi Sigma Theta became a chapter of Theta Phi Alpha in 1923. Zeta Tau Alpha started as a local, Pi Delta Kappa, which probably was formed in 1922. It became a chapter of Zeta Tau Alpha in 1923. Kappa Delta (1923) prior to its installation was known as Delta Xi, which has been founded in 1922.

Delta Zeta (1924) was formed from Lambda Delta Sigma, which was established as a local society in 1923. Delta Zeta became inactive in 1937. Meanwhile, in 1923, another local group known as Delta Epsilon Phi was founded. Later it became a chapter of Beta Phi Alpha. In 1941 Beta Phi Alpha amalgamated with Delta Zeta when the latter was revived at Syracuse.

Phi Sigma Sigma (1927) was formed from a local society known as Delta Nu Delta, established in 1924. The last of the seven to be established was Iota Alpha Pi, which stemmed from a local group, Phi Kappa Epsilon, formed in 1939.

"The sororities and fraternities were really essential for housing" in the late 1930s when she first came to the campus, said Anne Calder Piskor, who earned her master's in the student deans program in 1940. There were only two dormitories for women then—Haven and Winchell.

It was "earthshaking" to a freshman woman then if she didn't join a sorority, Mrs. Piskor added. She said in a 1981 interview that of twenty women in a living center, about sixteen pledged a sorority—a ratio comparable to that among the men. She went on: "The students

From the flapper era, two Delta Gammas, one paper beast, and one vintage car.

thought it was much more essential to be in a fraternity or sorority in order to be a campus leader and have as much social life as they wanted. Thank heavens now there's no feeling of pressure."

Despite their generally poor scholastic showing, all twenty-two sororities were active in charitable services, public activities, and scholarship aid in the twenty-year period before World War II. The tradition of this interest had been established earlier. Some had its genesis in the religious and sociological programs instituted by the Hendricks Chapel Board, the faculty, and certain benevolent societies on the Hill.

The programs ranged from furthering overseas missions, such as Syracuse-in-China, to less remote efforts like helping people in the slums of Syracuse. The spirit and enthusiasm of the sorority women were widely applauded. Individually or through their national offices the sororities supported drives to promote the welfare of the blind, of orphaned or destitute children, and of the aged in various homes or centers. They cooperated in sending children to nearby summer camps and in sponsoring Christmas parties for the needy. They visited the city hospitals. Some raised scholarship funds to help students attend Syracuse or to promote study on the campus.

The sororities urged their members to participate in student politics and government, athletics, university clubs, and honorary societies, to work on the *Daily Orange* and other student publications, and to help the University by donating their services during Freshman Week, public receptions, and at registration. During the summer sessions the chapter houses were often used as living centers for special groups of students.

Like the fraternities, the sororities became an integral part of University life. There were times when they tended to overlook the importance of scholastic achievement among their members and sometimes they were prone to promote their own interests above those of the University. Nevertheless, their record was better than that of the men's organizations. This may be explained in part by the ever-watchful eye and guiding hand of the dean of women and her capable staff. On the other hand, the fact that the University regarded itself as the substitute parent of women students since the time of its founding was an important factor in the existence of the sororities. Assisting the administration and the deans of women were the sorority alumnae, who also must have calmed chapter ire and animosity on more than one occasion and insisted that the undergraduate sisters mend their ways. In the last analysis, however, the sorority women were more sensitive and responsive than the fraternities to their duties and responsibilities to their parents, themselves, their chapters, and the University.

25

The Campus Teapot

Norman Thomas, the Socialist presidential candidate, was more popular on the campus in 1932 than the Democratic candidate, Franklin D. Roosevelt, according to an October poll in the *Daily Orange*. It showed that 737 people favored Herbert Hoover, the Republican, 297 favored Thomas, and 231 Roosevelt.

Campus unrest in the 1960s and early 1970s had its parallel—on a smaller scale and with less intensity and violence—during the two decades that followed the end of World War I. The situation at Syracuse University during the period 1922–42 was typical of those at other universities. Most of the Syracuse students were generally indifferent to the social changes ushered in by the first world war. To them "the war to end wars" had been fought and won. "Normalcy" had been restored, and the world was safe. Moreover, they saw the retirement of Chancellor Day and the coming of Dr. Flint as a happy interlude and a harbinger of better relations between the administration and themselves. Otherwise they were deeply concerned with intercollegiate athletics, the fraternity system, and other nonacademic matters. As long as they had a passing grade—many were content with a "gentleman's C"—they were satisfied. In their spare time they went to the movies, had "bull sessions," dated, and danced.

Now and then they were aroused from their complacency, particularly after 1934, by the thought of war, but they soon crept back to their sheltered campus lives, comforted by repeated assurances that the tragedy of World War I would never happen again. They hailed, even as late as 1940, the appeasement program of some European and American leaders. Meanwhile the local ROTC (Reserve Officers' Training Corps) sought to stimulate increased military preparedness, obviously convinced that if war came, American college students would shed their lethargy and flock to the colors.

On the other hand, two minority groups on campus, designated here as conservatives and liberals for the sake of convenience, were constantly concerned with the social, economic, and political issues that agitated the academic world after World War I. The differences between the two blocs were not always clear. Frequently, a fervent protagonist on one side moved into the opposite camp on a particular issue. An illustration of this is the case of a Syracuse dean of normally emphatic liberal views, who, in conversation with a member of his faculty, pounded his desk in defense of American isolation, saying, "Europe can fry in its own fat."

Generally, the conservative group favored retention of the traditional status quo. Its members honestly questioned the drift toward internationalism and found lasting values in "isolation," "nonentangling alliances," "laissez-faire," and the U.S. Constitution. Politically they followed the voting patterns of their Republican or Democratic parents and looked askance at organized labor, socialism, communism, free thinking, birth control, and unrestricted immigration. And far to the right were some who praised Hitler and Mussolini.

Smaller in number were the campus liberals. They included those, regardless of political affiliation, who reacted favorably to ideals and proposals calculated to advance the commonweal. They were vaguely international, friendly to the League of Nations, sympathetic to the Christian ethic of peace, and frowned on rampant nationalism that smelled of imperialism and colonialism. Like their conservative opponents, they often acted without precise or adequate information, easily accepted prevailing stereotypes, and were bountifully supplied with the milk of human kindness. Socially minded, they sought to promote goodwill among men, but there is little evidence that their brand of liberalism, or socialism in some cases, stemmed from a knowledge of *Das Kapital.* Most of the liberals, had they been asked, would have admitted they knew of Karl Marx only from second-hand sources. They were quick, however, to defend a college curriculum that stressed British and Jeffersonian democracy, and to resist criticism by religious and political organizations that held it heresy or treason to study and discuss controversial issues in the classrooms.

Of bona fide radicalism there was only a trace among the liberals, and those few found it more congenial to join organizations such as the American Student Union, which consisted of a hard core of radicals who leaned toward Marxist socialism. Lacking strength in numbers, they were misfits in the liberal camp and were often under administration surveillance. Unhappily, in the view of some political scientists, Chancellors Flint and Graham were not always able to distinguish between liberalism and radicalism.

Clashes between liberals and conservatives were frequent during the two decades of the Flint-Graham administrations. They sometimes involved academic freedom, at others the founding of a student cooperative society, and on more than one occasion tempers flared over administrative censorship of student activities and publications. The ROTC and the peace issue were almost constant causes of bitter differences. And, finally, sharp lines were drawn over the supposed infiltration of socialism, communism, and fascism into the intellectual life on the campus.

Although everything seemed calm when Chancellor Flint came to the campus, there were evidences of a new life and attitude beneath the surface. They attracted little attention at first, so that neither Dr. Flint nor the general student body saw anything sinister. Thus when a consumers league of the College of Liberal Arts announced a lecture program in 1922 that included such topics as "Child Labor" and "Waifs," it was thought to be both normal and proper. Somewhat later, the Oxford Club discussed "Fundamentalism vs. Progressivism in Religion" without stirring a furor, and, when the College Women's Congress was formed in March 1923 to whet student interest in current issues of a political, social, industrial, and religious nature, Vice Chancellor Graham gave his approval and recognition. Also during that year a Current Problems Club was formed under the sponsorship of Professor Edwin P. Tanner of the history department. One of the first speakers the club brought to campus was Paul Blanshard, then a socialist and labor union organizer, who spoke on "The Challenge of Labor to College Men and Women."

These activities evoked no serious comment. On the other hand, Chancellor Flint reacted strongly when the Ku Klux Klan reared its head on the campus. Although this organization vanished as quickly as it appeared, he used the event as an occasion to announce that he would not grant campus recognition to any society unless it had been sanctioned by the Senior Council. Meanwhile, Dr. Flint may have paved the way for future controversy when he condemned and prohibited gambling at football games and outlawed smoking and drinking on the campus.

Other signs of an impending conflict appeared early in 1924 and centered on the centuries-old problem of war and peace. War, some affirmed, was a sin; it separated man from God and violently contradicted the teachings of Christ, the prince of peace. Those who truly walked in His way must never cease to oppose war. Moreover, it was a travesty for the University to declare itself a Christian institution when the campus echoed to the marching feet of the ROTC. At first these friends of peace were largely recruited from the YMCA, the YWCA, the Student Volunteers, and other religious groups. They soon included others who condemned war on political, social, and economic grounds. Tangible evidence of the growing strength of the movement was shown by the peace gatherings on the campus in January 1924. During that month the merits and demerits of the Bok Plan for Peace were debated, and a student poll showed 645 in favor of the proposal and only 105 against it.

The Bok Plan was the popular name of the American Peace Award endowed in 1922 by Edward W. Bok, the Dutch-born author. His autobiographical *The Americanization of Edward Bok* had won a Pulitzer Prize in 1920. Bok, editor-in-chief of the *Ladies' Home Journal* from 1889 to 1919, offered $100,000 for the best plan to establish world peace. The winner was Charles H. Levermore, secretary of the New York Peace Society, whose plan provoked wide and often heated discussion pro and con. Bok himself noted, in his memoir *Twice Thirty,* that at one point the U.S. Senate formed a select committee to investigate allegations "of propaganda being used to influence legislative opinion." The committee reached no conclusions. Bok added that his plan had accomplished its purpose, "to bring about a wide discussion of peace by young and old." Among the Syracuse faculty supporting the Bok Plan were Alexander Flick and Finla Crawford.

In the wake of these events came outside speakers, among them Levermore and Dr. Paul Jones, one-time Protestant Episcopal bishop of Utah and secretary of the Fellowship of Reconciliation. A Syracuse University Peace Council was formed in March 1924. Pledged to the outlawry of war, the council, a student organization, denied it advocated radical aims or purposes. Its members included Everett Partridge '25, Lucie Gerard, E. Lockwood Drew, and Harold Swales. Partridge was to become one of the world's leading authorities on the treatment of industrial water. The Reverend Harold S. Swales '28 had been a minister for forty years at his death in 1968, with pastorates in the Syracuse area.

Among other things, the Peace Council condemned with reservation the presence of the ROTC on the campus. The military organization quickly defended itself, noting that it was not only a recognized department of the University, but had an official spokesman in the Chancellor, who in May 1924 accepted a commission as colonel in the United States Army Reserve. Dr. Flint justified his decision on the ground that even though he was "An Apostle of Peace," he firmly believed war was sometimes approved by God. The world, he told his trustees, could not exist solely upon the doctrine of nonresistance. In opposition was the voice of Charles Carleton, general secretary of the YMCA, proclaiming that war was incompatible with Christianity. Meanwhile, the *Daily Orange* was filled with letters in praise or condemnation of the ROTC.

In the fall of 1924 the issue of militarism was overshadowed by the national presidential campaign. The recently established School of Citizenship helped to stimulate interest and activity through discussions in Citizenship I and by sponsoring student clubs supporting the Republican, Democratic, and Progressive presidential candidates. Of these the most vocal, in spite of small membership, was the La Follette Club, which outdid itself in advocating a program closely akin to socialism. And when Oswald Garrison Villard, editor of *The Nation,* appeared in support of the club, the *Daily Orange* commented, "If Mr. Villard is a radical, then we like to listen to radicals."

At this point Chancellor Flint clarified his position on such forms of political action. He said the University in all its departments was nonpolitical, and although faculty and students as individuals might participate in politics, address gatherings, and form clubs, they were not to identify the University with their activities. Partisanship in the classroom was also to be avoided. As for campus political meetings, which normally were permitted, they were deemed "inexpedient" in an election year because there was abundant opportunity for such gatherings downtown. This policy of neutrality was reasonable and apparently caused little criticism on campus; consequently, the presidential election of 1924 caused little flurry on the Hill, and the three clubs disbanded once it was over.

But, unlike the others, the La Follette group was reorganized in late November as the Liberal Club. Meetings were held at the Cosmopolitan Club, and rumors spread that the new society would soon affiliate with the National Student Federation. In an attempt to stir up interest, several public meetings were held, with talks being given by several members of the faculty, as well as by such outside speakers as the Reverend John Sayre, editor of *The World Tomorrow,* Scott Nearing, Harry Elmer Barnes, and Villard. Encouraged by the interest shown, the Liberal Club sought University recognition in the spring of 1925.

The club stated that its purpose was to arouse and stimulate thought and debate "affecting community well-being and the general public welfare." To do so it would sponsor discussions, informal talks, and lectures; it would publish reports of such meetings and would also contemplate printing *The Speckled Bird,* a literary magazine. Finally, it promised that all its activities would be supervised by faculty advisers. Professors Floyd Allport, Edwin P. Tanner, and William Knickerbocker were the advisers. There were thirty-three members.

Drs. Flint and Graham gave the request close scrutiny. Clearly, they stated, the Liberal Club was nondepartmental, nonpolitical, and nonfraternal in either purpose or nature; moreover, it was not a public or private organization designed for social and cultural ends. But, they asked, was there need for such an all-University society? Did not already approved groups meet these objectives? Furthermore, was it wise to permit another student paper? Would it set a precedent? And should any voluntary group of students be allowed to use the University's name? "It is not a question of freedom of speech or thought," the Chancellor answered; "it is a question of donating the influence and name of 'Syracuse University' for gaining publicity." Ultimately, the administration withheld its approval of *The Speckled Bird,* refused to recognize the organization itself, but did permit meetings to be held in chapter houses and college buildings. By the end of 1925, the combination of lack of University endorsement and flagging student interest had killed the Liberal Club.

During the next few years there were many skirmishes between the conservative and liberal elements on the campus. The national election of 1928, like that of 1924, led to the formation of student clubs in support of favorite parties and candidates. One of these was the Norman Thomas for President Club, among whose faculty members were Floyd Allport, Horace Eaton, Freeman Galpin, Edwin Tanner, and Candace Stone. Thomas, the Socialist candidate for president, was invited to visit the University to address a student convocation. The turnout for this gathering, according to contemporary reports, resulted more from the desire of the curious to see and hear Thomas than from popular support of his candidacy.

Far more significant were the revived brushes between the war and antiwar blocs, whose activities filled the columns of the *Daily Orange* and drew the attention of the downtown press. Among the antiwar speakers brought to the campus were Villard, the Rev. John Sayre, Frederick Libby, secretary of the National Council for the Prevention of War, Mrs. Sinclair Lewis (S.U. alumna Dorothy Thompson '14), who addressed the Syracuse Forum on "The Patriotism of Peace," and Elizabeth

Brannon, a "convinced pacifist," who spoke in Lyman Hall under the sponsorship of a group calling itself the Students' Women's Congress. Meanwhile, the *Daily Orange* was reflecting various campus attitudes about the Kellogg Peace Proposals and the League of Nations. Downtown meetings of the Foreign Relations Society of Syracuse, formed in part by the School of Citizenship, attracted much attention through its discussion of important issues.

Some who addressed these organizations threw powerful thunderbolts at the ROTC, whose growth in membership had been spectacular. ROTC parades, led by the corps band, the official inspections by visiting officers from Washington, and the annual selection of ROTC queens, whose pictures were featured in the *Daily Orange* and the *Onondagan,* tended to enhance the prestige of the cadets. A chapter of Scabbard and Blade, a national military honor society, was formed in 1922. Additional endorsement came from downtown. In the spring of 1928, for example, the Rotarians presented a Rotary Club Saber to the senior cadet officer for "service to his country." Such events glamorized the ROTC, its opponents said, and showed the extent to which the "warmongers" would go to achieve their objectives. The Maxwell School sought to mediate the controversy by educating the students in the merits and demerits of war. Maxwell faculty member and 1916 alumna Candace Stone in November 1928 helped to organize the so-called Student Movement, originally the Committee of One Thousand. A mimeographed sheet, Student Movement Letter, said the "New Student" should acquire a knowledge of and an interest in all national international affairs. Scholarship and research were essential tools for developing a love of learning. Moreover, every student should be socially minded and assume responsibility for the welfare of his colleagues, promote a "fellowship of learning" with the faculty, and seek complete self-government at the University. A copy of the mimeographed letter was sent to Chancellor Flint.

Attached to it and to others that followed was a campus calendar of forthcoming events. Barnum Brown, curator of the American Museum of Natural History, was scheduled to talk on "Prehistoric Man," "Pat" Malin of Union Theological Seminary on "Religion on the Campus," and Professor T. V. Smith of the University of Chicago on "The Philosopher Looks on Citizenship." Other talks were to be given by Deans William Mosher and Harold Butler, as well as by University Professors Charles Kullmer, Burges Johnson, and Norman Whitney. In addition, Scott Nearing was to speak downtown on "Russia." Finally these letters included a bibliography reprinted from the *New Student,* the lively periodical of the National Student Forum that grew out of the Intercollegiate Liberal League and the National Student Committee for the Limitation of Armaments.

By this time Chancellor Flint was showing signs of alarm. He directed several searching questions to Miss Stone. In reply she defined the movement as being neither an organization nor a campus activity; it had no officers, no constitution, and no bylaws, and avoided publicity. Its expenses thus far, $125, had been paid by Mrs. Henry Philips, Mrs. William Nottingham, and George Bond, none of whom could be considered extremists. She added: "The Student Movement was authorized by our faith in you, nothing less. I was a student under the old administration, and speak with feeling."

Chancellor Flint may have been reassured by her spirited statement; obviously he found no sedition, conspiracy, or rebellion in the movement. Neither did his public relations expert, Burges Johnson, who defended the study of Marxist literature. It was absurd and highly dangerous, he wrote in the *Alumni News,* to cloister students so rigidly and graduate them "with no mental resistance to any whimsical breeze." He continued: "Chancellor Flint has said something of the same sort of thing when he has spoken of vaccination against extravagant theories. Any directors of university life who imagine they can control the thinking of students by shutting out this or that point of view are as hopelessly misguided as a parent who tries to direct his children's reading by pasting the label, 'Do not read this' on books in the library."

Meanwhile faculty were participating in political campaigns. In 1928 Finla G. Crawford was the Democratic candidate for mayor of Syracuse, and in 1929 Professor Robert Carroll of Teachers College ran for the New York governorship on the Prohibition ticket. Once again Dr. Flint sought to safeguard the University from criticism by pursuing a policy of "not prohibiting candidacies . . . but respectfully and urgently requesting would-be candidates to take a leave of absence during the semester in which they seek office, thus dissociating themselves from University relations and from their work during the period of the campaign and during the period of recuperation from their defeat (or victory) and of reorientation into academic activities."

Chancellor Flint showed less concern about his colleagues' political ambition than he did when he read in the *Daily Orange* that a speaker at the Student Church had been brought to the campus by the Student Movement. The speaker was Harry Elmer Barnes, an eminent historian and sociologist who had graduated summa *cum laude* from Syracuse University in 1913, earned his M.A. on the Hill, and went on to Columbia for a Ph.D. Candace Stone denied that the movement had sponsored the visit but admitted that individual members had promoted it. She added she thought this was a splendid example of the freedom of speech that existed at the University. Dr. Flint did not press the matter directly but began to inquire into the activities of the movement's headquarters at 314 Waverly Avenue. Recognized by the University as a "private dormitory" and funded in part by gifts from Mrs. Dora S. Hazard of Solvay, "314" had become a center for liberal and some leftist activity. Those who lived there were not subject to the usual rules but were supposed to observe approved principles and standards. Dean E. A. Leonard said: "If we were to put all our houses on this basis, I am afraid we would find ourselves in many difficult situations."

Of some concern was the fact that three residents of "314" had signed a petition in late 1931 asking for the recognition of the Liberal Club of Syracuse University, a petition that also had the signatures of twenty other students and twelve members of the faculty. Gregory J. Bardacke, Monroe Sweetland, and William J. Ronan were the student leaders; among the faculty signers were Dean Mosher and Professors K. M. Capper-Johnson, W. F. Galpin, E. S. Griffith, and H. N. Shenton of the School of Citizenship. The petition said the aims of the Liberal Club would be "1. To discuss social, economic, and political affairs with a view to arouse in the students of Syracuse University a more discriminating appreciation of their responsibilities as citizens, and of the ideals of cooperation and public service. 2. To gain an intelligent understanding of the inadequacies of our social system and to discuss ways and means of remedying them." The petition also said "The Liberal Club shall be affiliated with the Intercollegiate Student Council of the League for Industrial Democracy. In so doing it shall be understood that the recommendations of the national executive committee of the said intercollegiate council shall be advisory only."

Chancellor Flint and Vice Chancellor Graham interviewed the signatories to the petition. Sweetland made notes of his conversation with the Chancellor. According to the notes, which the Chancellor later acknowledged were accurate, the Liberal Club must not use the University's name; in any event there were already groups on campus supplying the needs mentioned by the club. Moreover, the Chancellor was aware that the genesis of the club came from outside the campus; the University would not permit "an outside propagandist group" to direct Syracuse policies. But because he was anxious to promote student study of current problems he did not object to off-campus organizations such as the Democratic and Republican clubs nor did he wish to censor student activities. Consequently, he said, the University was as free and liberal as any other academic institution.

Subsequently Chancellor Flint issued a special statement: "Re: Societies etc.—Confidential—Not for Publication." This is the text:

> Members of the student body or of the faculty or of both are found, along with other citizens, in many organizations for religious, political, social, intellectual etc., purposes—organizations which have no reference to the University in their name, neither expect or ask a meeting-place on the campus and whose publicity is entirely unrelated to the University; with such the University is not concerned. Indeed, it rejoices in having its students and faculty participate in all such broadening and stimulating relations.
>
> Nor is any question ever raised regarding the privileges of students to discuss ad lib subjects in which they are interested. This is wholly desirable, the more spontaneous and general such discussion, the better; individuals naturally will, and should, get together and discuss subjects of mutual interest, probably even to greater benefit when the spontaneity is unfettered by by-laws.
>
> Occasionally, however, there are groups that seek formal organization, using the name of the University, "composed mainly of University personnel," or "known as affiliated with the University," that is, understood as related to it.
>
> In all organizations of this sort, the University has an interest and a responsibility for many reasons—their financial vicissitudes frequently embarrass the University; they expect rent-free quarters, heated, lighted, and janitored; their published proceedings are associated in the minds of the public with the University and as representing its opinions; frequently they use the name of the University to secure a hearing and impetus for propaganda; outside speakers are given through them a University platform and University publicity; and frequently outside propaganda organizations find such groups easily-secured instruments.
>
> Moreover, the University must concern itself with possible over-organization, with the undue multiplication of official groups, each with its local, state and national dues, and appeals in the name of "loyalty" and "duty" for student support by time and interest.
>
> Duplication of effort and in objectives is a further concern of the University in relation to its family.
>
> The ability or the trustworthiness of a particular group aspiring to promote worthy objectives in the name of the University is a matter the latter is obliged to investigate.
>
> When any organization is openly affiliated, or still more, if it is covertly affiliated with some state, national or non-local parent body, with the milder inspiration or more militant lash of paid secretaries and, in some cases, of persistent, and occasionally fanatical, propagandists, the University has a further duty in the matter of approvals and encouragements. This consideration would apply equally to "conservative" groups as to "liberal."

> These are some of the reasons for the regulation on this subject included on page 88 of the Student Desk Book.
>
> In general, the University desires its students to give attention and interest to all subjects of public concern, to hear all sides of every question. The avowed purpose of the School of Citizenship is practically that also of the University, namely, that, while we stand for no particular party, nor cult, nor "ism," we want to know all the truth about each and all.
>
> Classroom instruction is based on this idea; so also are the public meetings and presentations of outside speakers. This policy has been followed with reasonable consistency. Representatives of the liberal side of public questions have been welcomed and given at least "an even break." They have had fully, if not more than, "approximately an equal hearing."

The Chancellor's supporters found his statement reasonable and consistent with his earlier positions, but others saw it as contrary to the ideals of the University. A copy of the statement was sent to each signer of the petition, accompanied by another document issued by the University Administrative Council. Its text follows:

> Recently a group composed of six graduate students, eight freshmen and nine others in an unsigned and undated document sought approval as a University organization.
>
> Their formulated objectives are highly commendable, being practically the same as recognized objectives of our School of Citizenship and Public Affairs.
>
> Without any reflection upon these individuals, it is our conviction, after considering the personal and various irregularities in procedure, that the promotion in the name of the University of objectives so inclusive and so significant should be committed to a much more representative and responsible group.
>
> If, in the judgment of the Student Senates and of the Director and Department Heads of the School of Citizenship, existing societies, organizations and the School do not sufficiently serve these worthwhile aims, a regrouping, reorganization or supplementing would be in order. They might study the situation either jointly or separately.

On these grounds the Liberal Club was not recognized. Nevertheless, its influence was still felt on the campus. Its members attended meetings at "314," the Men's Forum, and the University Convocations, where the 1932 presidential campaign issues were debated. Speaking at the November 2 convocation with the Chancellor's approval were Louis Waldman and Norman Thomas, whose Socialist party proposals won some applause. Thirty-six members of the faculty announced support of Thomas in a statement saying:

"We ought as citizens to see the very close connection between capitalism and war. Capitalism is using force and will continue to use force to maintain itself. Socialism is opposed to the fact that under capitalism the sanctity of human property is greater than human life."

Thomas was more popular on the campus than the Democratic presidential candidate, Franklin D. Roosevelt, according to an October poll in the *Daily Orange.* It showed that 737 Syracusans favored Herbert Hoover, the Republican, 297 favored Thomas, and 231 Roosevelt.

Within a month the University Peace Council had been established. Among its charter members were such respected names as Dean William Powers of Hendricks Chapel, Professor Capper-Johnson, a Quaker; Dr. Thomas R. Fisher, a member of the Chapel Board, and two other board members, Martha O'Dell and B. Hopkins-Moses.

The Peace Council held its first meeting on November 29, 1932. Conceived to promote a concerted drive for peace, the organization was a composite federation of such existing groups as the Christian Associations, the Chapel Board, the Men's Forum, Syracuse-in-China, Thomas for President, Liberal Club, International Relations, the Men's and Women's Cosmopolitan groups, and "314." One of the first steps of the council was to conduct a compuswide poll against war early in December. Student apathy was apparent, despite the energetic efforts of Miss O'Dell and Hopkins-Moses; only 171 votes were cast, of which 89 indicated that the balloters would not support the United States if it went to war.

By this time the administration had become worried about growing criticism of the council both on the campus and downtown and told the new organization it could not function without recognition. Apparently the chief objection was the presence in the federation of four off-campus groups, one of them the Liberal Club. The council officers were shocked by the administration's announcement, and Miss O'Dell promptly declared that "We are a cooperating committee and not an organization." Soon after that, on December 10, the clouds were dispelled and the *Daily Orange* reported that Chancellor Flint had given it University recognition. A few days later an editorial in the newspaper stated, "Student interest in politics and in unpartisan activity in discussions of international affairs mark a distinct change in the student body of America. On the Syracuse campus there have been outstanding examples of such a trend and they are to be highly commended." With this expression of opinion the administration was in agreement. Moreover, in a note to Dr. Graham, the Chancellor manifested sympathy with the council's aims and indicated he was willing to ignore certain irregularities as being merely examples of normal student behavior. Dr. Flint nevertheless added a note of warning when he suggested that the Vice Chancellor investigate whether the council had conformed to the requirements given in the *Student Desk Book.*

But the handwriting was on the wall. Early in January 1933 the council began to plan for a state intercollegiate conference on disarmament. While the preparations were in process Miss O'Dell abruptly resigned from the council. She refused to give any reason although there was some talk of administration pressure. Hopkins-Moses took over the chairmanship and, at a subsequent council meeting, barely saved the organization from self-destruction. The crisis arose over a proposal that the state conference be postponed because the council lacked the funds to support such a session. A noisy minority opposition ridiculed the suggestion, declaring that in any event it was too late to cancel. A month later, when tempers had cooled, the council dissolved itself for financial reasons.

Stepping into the breach was the International Relations Club, and late in Febrary Dean Powers welcomed delegates from thirteen colleges and universities in New York State. They listened to addresses by Pierre de Lannux of the League of Nations and by Paul Harris of the National Council for the Prevention of War. But soon internal friction arose. At a business meeting of the International Relations Club, an acute situation developed over the passage of a measure providing that all resolutions must receive a three-fourths majority vote. The Liberal Club faction immediately denounced this as unjust and detrimental to student rights. Moreover, the old rumor that the administration had dissolved the council was revived, adding more fuel to the fire.

In an attempt to salvage the situation and to silence gossip, Dean Powers denied the rumor and asked how a council could function on campus when high school students were among its members. By way of reply, Professor Capper-Johnson, then in England, cabled that the council had been dissolved as "the result of a number of personal conversations carried on with the administration." Evidently the *Daily Orange* accepted this as fact and sadly predicted the demise of all liberal groups on campus. The newspaper did not have long to wait for the next blow. Before the spring of 1933 was over the Chancellor had closed "314."

The campus divided over whether to accept the administration's statement that the building had been closed because of a prospective change in the University's housing program and policy; liberals saw it as a covert means of destroying "314."

The conservative-versus-liberal controversy was not limited to the matter of recognizing or not recognizing left-of-center organizations.

In April 1933 a small group of students demonstrated noisily against the ROTC at the corner of University Place and Walnut Place. In May the *Daily Orange* linked criticism of a scheduled ROTC review with support for President Roosevelt's call for a nonaggression pact. The newspaper said editorially "the militaristic display of the ROTC pomp and power ... is hardly in accord with the Roosevelt proclamation.... If we desire peace, we must work for peace. The way to disarm is to disarm."

But a month later the *Daily Orange* was saying that if war came, students would rush to enlist as they had in 1917. There had been a poll at sixty-five American campuses, sponsored by the Intercollegiate Disarmament Council and the National Student Federation, which revealed a strong pacifist sentiment. But the *New York Times* called the poll a "passing fad" and predicted that in a war "pacifist pledges will be mere scraps of paper."

The spring of 1933 also saw criticism in the campus and city dailies of the University faculty, with references to socialists and "pinks" on the teaching staff, especially at the Maxwell School. In the Faculty Club there were heated discussions over war and peace, the ROTC, and the freedom of speech and tenure enjoyed by the Maxwell faculty. Dean Mosher did not help the situation when the *Daily Orange* quoted him as saying President Roosevelt's leadership was "startling," that laissez-faire was vanishing, and the nation was moving more toward a new and regulated economic order than at any time in its history. Frederick Davenport, the Maxwell School's counselor, entered the picture when in a letter to Chancellor Flint he expressed regret over the "whiffs" made by some of the faculty and his hope that they would not be repeated. He concluded his warning with: "There is a certain price you always pay for reasonable liberty of thought; there are always some at least slightly unbalanced people upon college faculties, as you have cause to know." This in March 1934.

Matters did not improve when the university reopened in the fall. Early in October, Norman Thomas spoke at Central High School at the invitation of a committee that included Professor Horace Eaton and the wife of Professor John Washburne. Shortly thereafter the *Syracuse Journal* declared the University was infested with socialists and communists. This was embarrassing to Professor Washburne of the School of Education, who had made careless statements to two young men who sought his advice about registering at the University. They said they had heard of the liberal attitudes of the University, especially in the Maxwell School; actually they were *Journal* reporters. Others subjected to attack by the *Journal* for their "pinkish" hue were Professors Herman Beyle, Ernest Griffith, and Freeman Galpin.

Another storm swept the campus the following spring. There had been much talk among students of a peace demonstration, and posters appeared announcing it for April 12. Listed as supporters were the English Club, Eta Pi Upsilon, the Student League for Industrial Democracy, the Student Ministers Association, the Chapel Discussion Group, the Social Problems Club, the Young People's Socialist League, the National Student League, the Panhellenic Society, and the editorial boards of the *Daily Orange, Argot,* and the *Hill Monthly.*

On the appointed day, in Walnut Park, 500 or more students and some faculty braved a heavy rain to voice their opposition to war and fascism. The demonstration had reverberations in the city, where its supporters and opponents had their say. Chancellor Flint had made no attempt to prevent the mass meeting. His attitude, as reported in the *Daily Orange,* was moderate in tone and indicated he was neutral in the matter. He did believe, however, that the method was ill-advised and injurious to the cause of peace, as well as being undignified and unacademic, certainly not in keeping with Christian decorum. He hoped that the advocates of peace might find a better means of publicizing their objective in the future.

Dr. Flint devoted part of his baccalaureate address in June 1935 to the issues of war, peace, poverty, politics, and free speech. He said:

> There is no use trying to close our eyes to the current wave of hysteria. ... The depression tends to stimulate the jitters over communism and other economic sophism.... Too many fear and believe the worst, put the wrong construction on appearances, out of suspicion color the facts and the interpretation thereof, ridiculous even though sincere in such suspicion.... Amid all this I am proud of our Syracuse faculty members, not even a half of one per cent of whom could ever be suspected by heresy hunters or disturbed 'patriots'... all open and aboveboard in writings and other utterances; all standing firmly to preserve as well as to exercise the right of free inquiry.... I am proud of their loyalty to truth and to their task, their courage in the search, their progressive-ism and forward-looking detachment from and superiority to either the cramping status quo or to economic will-of-the-wisps, their poise and judiciousness. Gentlemen and scholars all. And the ladies no less!

Later in 1935, in collaboration with the Committee on Student Government, the Chancellor considered the creation of an All-University Committee on Peace. It did not materialize, probably because of student apathy and because its backers could not agree on fundamentals.

Criticism from downtown continued. Charles P. Morse of the Syracuse branch of the Sons of the American Revolution in a letter to Dr. Graham said a "cold chill" went over him when the "Internationale" and announcements about the Student League were heard over the loudspeaker in Archbold Stadium. The Vice Chancellor assured Morse that the music and announcements came from outside the stadium and not from the official loudspeaker.

Then, in anticipation of Armistice Day, some students announced plans for another peace demonstration. The Chancellor expressed a hope that the celebration would be held on campus and that the speakers might have a sense of propriety. Meanwhile the dean of Hendricks Chapel addressed the students on "Roads to Peace Across the Campus," and Professor Allport declared that man possessed no fighting instinct and that modern battlefields had become slaughterhouses. Ultimately, Armistice Day was peacefully observed with a chapel service, while the ROTC joined the city's annual parade downtown. Proponents of peace continued to lobby for a peace council, and the subject was featured on the campus at the Middle Atlantic Conference of International Relations Clubs held there in late November. A month later a campuswide poll on the peace council issue showed 562 favoring such an organization and 31 against. The Student Senates saw the vote as warranting such a council and sanctioned it. In January 1936 a governing board was selected. Several peace meetings followed, and the *Daily Orange* gave the movement favorable publicity, though reporting at the same time that the student body had generally become "tired of peace talk." When plans were made for another demonstration in April, the administration at once offered help. Classes were dismissed between 11 A.M. and noon and some fifteen hundred students and faculty listened to talks by student leaders and Professor Ross Hoople of the philosophy department. The *Daily Orange* summed up the gathering as a "sane, intelligent start," but for the rest of that academic year there was little activity.

Dr. Flint resigned at the end of July to become bishop of Atlanta, and Dr. Graham, as Acting Chancellor, was the top administrator when the 1936–37 academic year began. The dormant peace movement had energized itself over the summer, and there was activity on many fronts. Dr. Graham was quick to respond when one of the groups, the Young People's Socialist League, distributed literature at registration in an attempt to promote a boycott of the ROTC. He dispatched a representative to the scene and prevented further distribution of the material; official permission had not been sought or granted. Another group, the All-University Peace Association, scheduled an Armistice Day demonstration and, when November 11 arrived, a thousand students and faculty gathered in Hendricks Chapel to hear an address on American neutralism. There were no demonstrations. There was a lull until February 1937, when the same association sponsored a month-long lecture series. It sent speakers to all student living centers to discuss such topics as "Neutralism," "Freedom of the Seas," "Munition Makers," and "the ROTC." A peace demonstration was held on the library steps late in April, and in spite of heavy rain 800 attended. A week later the administration apparently played directly into the hands of the peace advocates by cancelling the showing of a film, "Spain in Flames," at the Civic Theater. It was asserted that the Americans who favored Franco Spain over the legitimate Spanish government were responsible for this form of censorship.

During the 1937–38 academic year the organized peace movement had to compete with other activities for student attention. Athletics, national and state elections, campus politics, and the quest for a student union kept students busy, and internal dissension within the peace organizations themselves worked to their disadvantage. Fortunately for them, however, the *Daily Orange* opened its columns freely to such peace-minded students as Rodney Fisher who kept that issue as well as others before the campus. Furthermore, the appearances at the University of Raymond Moley, Kirby Page, and Charles A. Beard were generously covered. Professor Philip Taylor of the Maxwell School stimulated the International Relations Club and directed a Model Session of the League of Nations. In addition, the peace organizations met frequently to discuss such topics as communism, the problem of China, and a possible boycott of Japan. Professor Norman Whitney of the English department debated with Alfred Haight, president of the Onondaga County Young Men's Democratic Club, on the issue of a "Big Navy." The history department introduced a course dealing with organized peace activities in the United States, and Dean Mosher initiated a University "Town Hall," which became increasingly significant. The year closed with a Peace Strike in April 1938, at which an estimated eleven hundred students endorsed a series of resolutions condemning militarism and urging Congress to seek peace and to embargo trade with Franco Spain.

In the fall of 1938 the *Daily Orange*, under the editorship of Chester B. Hansen, tried to stimulate student interest by devoting two columns a day to world affairs. Chancellor Graham urged national preparedness, Dean Powers prayed for peace, Rodney Fisher suggested that the student body was more interested in the Lambeth Walk, the latest dance craze, than in anything else, and a *Daily Orange* editorial on the Munich Conference declared that "Four men ... tolled the requiem for a nation." The students were showing little concern for the world around them; small wonder that the *Daily Orange* asserted the cause for peace was at its lowest ebb since 1917. The editor described the International Relations Club as an organization that hung onto the "outworn League of Nations," while the Chapel World Relations Committee brought a "futilistic sweetness and light" approach to increasing world tensions. Chancellor Graham spoke of the All-University Committee on Peace as "defunct" and recommended formation of a new agency that would be more democratic and representative. As a result of the Chancellor's suggestion, the Student Committee on Peace Activities was formed to coordinate and direct all student activity on international affairs. No peace group could function without the approval of the Student Senates and Dr. Graham. During the rest of the 1938–39 year, an Armistice Day celebration featured a talk by Professor William H. Laves of the University of Chicago, in which he criticized the United States for not having supported a recent European peace plan; the peace groups opened fire on Father Coughlin, the radio priest, who was being applauded by conservative elements; and, in a campus poll, a small majority favored recognizing Franco Spain.

Liberal-conservative battle lines were joined again when the University opened in the fall of 1939, with the *Daily Orange* heading the drive for peace. An editorial said: "Syracusans have crawled into their own comfortable rut, bounded by classes, Cokes, and dates, and there they sit, blinded by their own 'don't care' attitude." Germany invaded Poland on September 1 and World War II had begun.

With the outbreak of hostilities the American peace movement became sharply divided. According to national polls, almost all Americans wanted the United States to keep out of the war, but they did not agree on how to do this. The isolationists, particularly those affiliated with the "America First" movement, demanded absolute neutrality with no sale of munitions to either side. Opposed to them were the internationalists who regarded Britain, France, and China as the defenders of democracy against totalitarianism. They advocated an American policy that would permit the ill-prepared Allies to purchase war materials in the United States. As the Nazi war machine rolled over neighboring countries, the internationalists called for more and more aid to Britain and France, even to the point of actual entry into the war. These shifting waves of opinion crashed onto the Syracuse University campus, engulfing faculty and students.

Much sentiment was shown in favor of compulsory ROTC, despite Chancellor Graham's assertion that such a move would destroy the usefulness of the corps. "We must all of us guard against all acts which would tend to push us toward war," he said. Shortly thereafter Professor Philip Taylor, a leading internationalist, criticized the Syracuse Council of Churches for distributing at a Hendricks Chapel service a pamphlet entitled "Keep America out of War." During this time the question of continued neutrality was being debated on and off the campus. To measure student opinion on the issue, Professor Herman Beyle of the Maxwell School undertook an attitude study; it showed that slightly more than half of those polled favored repeal of an embargo on selling arms to the Allies, provided it would not force the United States into war. Soon afterward, on November 4, Congress approved a new Neutrality Act that included the repeal feature. A national poll at the time showed 56 percent in favor of the change.

Dismayed by the war, the campus peace organizations promoted an Armistice Day demonstration. The *Daily Orange* endorsed it, saying, "One hour pledged to peace out of a year is not too much to ask of 6,000 war-hating students." November 11, 1939, fell on a Saturday, and, as before, the administration dismissed classes at 11 A.M. Most of the speakers were students who said their purpose was to make the occasion a "memorial for the war dead." About 650 students attended, a showing that caused the *Daily Orange* to challenge the peace group to find out precisely what the students really wanted. One faculty member replied that they should live, not die, for America. Shortly before Christmas a second poll by Professor Beyle revealed that Syracuse students opposed America's entrance into World War II, but they did not want peace at any price.

With the reopening of the University early in January 1940, many students attended a chapel meeting at which Paul Harris pleaded the cause of peace. Before the month was over, the Young People's Socialist League declared the United States should in no way aid European states that had empires, that the U.S. government should stay out of all trade in munitions, and that Americans should oppose domestic militarism and oppression. These sentiments fell on deaf ears, and the *Daily Orange,* in April, said it saw little reason to suspend classes for the usual spring peace demonstration. Dr. Graham agreed because of what he called the "don't give a hang" attitude of most students. The peace advocates, however, refused to give up and on April 19 attracted about 350 people to hear an outdoor address by Professor LeRoy Bowman of Columbia University.

As the school year wound down, Shirley Cunningham of Theta Sigma Phi, the honor society for women in the School of Journalism, asked Professor W. Freeman Galpin of the history department, hitherto a staunch advocate of peace, to prepare an article for the society's forthcoming issue of the *Daily Orange.* His article appeared May 15 under the heading, "America Is Worth Defending":

> A few months ago, most Americans believed that Britain and France would muddle through and win the present war. Britannia ruled the waves, our coasts were secure! Recent events, such as the violation of Scandinavia and the Low Countries, have aroused thoughtful Americans to the responsibilities of the situation. The question is no longer one of British victory, but of possible German triumph. And if the latter should win, what of us? What shall we do?
>
> A totalitarian victory marks the disappearance of European democracies. I will not argue... whether France or Britain are democracies, but, if they are not, neither are we. Bad as the conditions may be in these states, they still are infinitely superior to anything found in Tokyo, Rome, Leningrad, or Berlin. I have never found in the histories of totalitarian states anything like the Magna Carta, a Bill of Rights, or government by debate in the American sense.
>
> Most Americans want to pick those with whom they live, and no one cares to associate with those like Stalin, Hitler, and Mussolini. The smug Britisher and volatile Frenchman are much more desirable. With their defeat we would be isolated in a world of totalitarianism, for South America would soon be converted into satellite Nazi and Fascist states under the disguise of South American Democracy. And Mexico would soon fall into the equally bad hands—of Stalin, Hitler's friend and fellow murderer. Thus we alone will have to police the Rio Grande, the Panama Canal, and both the Atlantic and Pacific oceans.
>
> A totalitarian victory means the loss of our foreign trade. Europe, Asia, and soon South America would fall under the economic system of the conquerors. A totalitarian victory, therefore, implies economic isolation for America. We are a rich country, but will that equal the combined economic strength of Europe and Asia? Where will we get essentials such as rubber? A totalitarian victory, in short, will give the enemy the upper hand in economic strength.
>
> We are told this is fancy and we should make our contribution by staying out of war and preserving democratic ideals. Let us show the world how democracy works. Rubbish! We know how it works, Hitler knows how it works, and Scandinavia, Finland, Belgium, and Holland know how it worked, but where are they today? And we know how totalitarianism works.... If we have studied totalitarian operations accurately, world domination is their ultimate goal and aim.
>
> What are we to do about it? Waving to one side the question of immediate entrance into the war, for there are many who think we should have done so last fall and by all means should do so now... we must face the question of defense. Far reaching military service must be imposed, and expenditures running into the billions must be entailed. Income

> taxes will amount to 50 percent and more, and college campuses will be drill grounds.
>
> There must be a slapping down upon subversive actions. No "fifth column" can be tolerated—all signs of such should be smashed completely, the Bill of Rights notwithstanding. Treason laid Norway low and is paralyzing Holland. If all this is needed to defend America and if the balances were weighted against us in a totalitarian world, what is to be done? Shall we wait, and wait, and wait? Let us prepare now and join with those who seek to rid the world of our enemy. Common sense dictates that it is wiser to do so now than later, when our friends will have been defeated. STOP, LOOK, AND LISTEN, before it is TOO LATE.

Campus reaction to his article was much greater than Galpin expected. The *Daily Orange* reported: "All roads lead to the Castle [Yates Castle, home of the newspaper] as foresters, political scientists, engineers, home economists, and artists join together in bringing replies to Dr. Galpin's much discussed article. Seldom before has the campus so vigorously expressed a desire to voice an opinion." Miss Cunningham stated: "This article was not offered as warmongering propaganda ... but rather as an educational effort to make the student see the other side of this all-important issue and help him make his own decision."

Professors Dwight M. Beck and Horace A. Eaton and many students, including Jessie Cavileer and Stanley Edgar Hyman, denounced Galpin's views. Dr. Philip Taylor also felt the sting of criticism when he attacked the "Do-Nothing War Policy" in the United States. Although a few voices were raised in their defense, the *Daily Orange* was probably correct when it said the campus disliked the talk of war. The paper, however, had this to say about the students:

> The hard pill to swallow is the realization that Syracuse is slow on the draw. Firmly imbedded in its secure niche, the campus refused to bestir itself to think and talk about peace until a month ago. There were disturbing headlines in the papers, yes, and history and political science professors were speaking of neutrality and aggression. But comics are more fun to read than war news, and professors only lecture because they think students should take notes. That peace convocation was a bother anyway, and who wanted to go? But wait, did you see the editorial in this morning's *Orange*? What is the world coming to? A wise person long ago said the pen was mightier than the sword. But a pen writing about the sword is mightiest of all.

During the academic year 1940–41, campus support for American entry into the war grew day by day. There was apprehension about

Japan. As Professor Douglas G. Haring of the sociology department, former student and teacher in Japan, said: "Watch the Far East." There was sharp criticism of those who wished to furnish food to Europe's starving people, the victims of Nazi aggression, even though this would mean breaching the British blockade of Germany. The critics asked if these humanitarians realized that such food would eventually feed Hitler's troops. And when an isolationist spoke of being "in favor of fighting the European Axis to the last Englishman and the Japanese to the last Chinaman," considerable opposition to such views was voiced. "I'm no war enthusiast," A. Blair Knapp stated, "but I do believe there are things valuable enough to fight for." Similar lines were drawn over President Roosevelt's Lend-Lease Act.

The University had scarcely opened in September 1941 when the issues were raised again. The International Relations Club debated them, and Dean Mosher, speaking at a Town Hall meeting in late October, favored an immediate declaration of war against Germany. Then, on November 7, a petition drafted by Professors Galpin and Robert Steadman and signed by thirty-six other faculty members was sent to President Roosevelt and the New York members of Congress urging an immediate declaration of war against the Axis powers.

Although only 16.4 percent of the students supported this petition, as another poll by Professor Beyle revealed, it seemed clear that American entrance into the war was but a matter of time. Before Thanksgiving still another Beyle poll showed that 85.7 percent of 400 students answering believed the United States should enter the war.

The days sped on to December 7 when Japan struck at Pearl Harbor. A *Daily Orange* headline said "It's Our Fight Now," and the newspaper reported that faculty and student sentiment was "overwhelmingly in favor" of war against Japan. When Congress declared war against Germany and Italy as well, Syracuse University, like all other American institutions of higher learning, bent its energies to help win that worldwide struggle; complete unity replaced the disputation that had divided the campus over the issue of peace for the preceding twenty years.

26

The Fun We Had

The brown paper parcel was addressed to "Comrade Chancellor Flint." It was ticking.

DURING REUNION WEEKEND 1981 Virginia Hagan '27 "escaped" (her word) from an organized campus tour and dropped in at Bird Library. On the sixth floor she saw an exhibition of Victorian costumes mounted by members of a textile conservation class, then looked into the John S. and Edith S. Mayfield Library, where she found an editor at work on the history of Syracuse University. He explained that the Mayfields had offered use of the room to the researching-editing-writing team that was preparing volumes three and four of the history. The editor said his material was long on facts and statistics but short on personal glimpses into the ways the students had amused themselves.

"You want to know about the fun we had," the visiting alumna said. She agreed to talk about her undergraduate days.

Virginia Hagan, then Virginia Treptau, was a Liberal Arts major in the class of 1927. She was a freshman at fifteen but, as it turned out, she was far from the youngest member of her class.

With my roommates, a sophomore and a junior, I lived at 909 Walnut Avenue, a registered house—registered as a suitable place for incoming students to live. It was marvelous to get away at that age. My father was an extremely protective person, and I'd had very little freedom at home.

It was the first time I had lived away from home. My parents visited

> me from Buffalo to see how I was getting along. When I saw them I was overwhelmed with homesickness, and my father would have taken me home but my roommates said "Don't pay any attention to her—she'll be all right." My roommates were right. I did get over it.
>
> This was a house with about sixteen girls. All of us became quite good friends. Norris Johnson was a classmate of mine, and he and his sister Doris M. Johnson '25 were from Jamestown. Later, as Doris Carlson, she lived in Boston most of her life.

Norris O. Johnson '27 earned his master's and doctorate at Harvard on his way to becoming an internationally known banker and economist, an alumni trustee of his alma mater, and a 1962 George Arents Medal winner.

When Mrs. Hagan was a freshman her classmates tried to find someone closer to her age for her to go out with. "There was a boy who was a freshman at the same time I was," she said. "My friends teased me and said that because I was so young I should go out with him. But he was only 11—four years younger than I. His name was Moses Finkelstein."

"Did you go out with him?"

"No. I don't think I was even in any classes with him."

"Do you know what became of him?"

She didn't. The editor said her eleven-year-old freshman classmate, a native Syracusan, was now Sir Moses I. Finley, a professor of ancient history at Cambridge University. He had become a British subject and was knighted for his brilliant scholarship. After leaving Syracuse University in 1927 with his B.A. *magna cum laude,* he had gone to Columbia University for his M.A. and Ph.D. He had been due to return to Syracuse to receive an honorary doctor of humane letters degree at commencement only a week before Mrs. Hagan's reunion but decided not to come. Sir Moses gave as a reason his political objections to the speaker, Secretary of State Alexander Haig.

"Wait till my classmates hear about this!" Virginia Hagan said. But before she went back across the campus to get ready for the evening's reunion activities she told how she met her future husband, now deceased, Frank Babcock Hagan '28, from Yonkers, a prelaw student.

> We met at the end of my junior year. Frank's fraternity house, Phi Gamma Delta, was just two doors from ours, Zeta Tau Alpha, at 744 Comstock. The sorority was putting on a show. One of my sorority sisters and Frank were jazz hounds—that's how we met. Soon we were going steady. We were together all the time. It was one of those very nice college romances.

> He had a 1916 Ford open roadster. In the fall of 1926 Syracuse played Army. Frank, his roommate, and I drove down in the 1916 Ford. We had eleven flat tires on the way. The motor fell out in West Winfield, about sixty miles outside Syracuse. We got back by bumming our way. Hitchhiking; we called it bumming then.
>
> One of the fun things we did was go out to the North Side—this was during Prohibition—and drink needle beer.
>
> I started at Syracuse as a history major but switched to German, an unusual thing to do in those days. There were not many of us; the country was still feeling the effects of the first world war. German had been taught in the Buffalo public schools, then they stopped; I had some German background, on my mother's side. After I graduated I taught for two years in Marcellus High School—German, history, whatever else was needed, for the great sum of $1,200 dollars a year. Some of my students were as old as I was—nineteen. They didn't know it.

Another resident of Zeta Tau Alpha was Betty Dumars, later Truex, who was in the class of 1931 but graduated in 1930. She recalled that when she lived at 744 Comstock two sorority sisters went with crew members. The boyfriends were scheduled to compete against Cornell oarsmen the next day. "You could have a 10 o'clock or a 12 o'clock to come in from a date," Mrs. Truex said:

> You could use them once a week. If you used them up you had to sneak out. They had very strict regulations in those days. This was Friday, and the races were on Saturday morning at Cornell.
>
> The housemother's apartment was in the back, and we were on the second story, and one of the girls thought it would be easier if she jumped out and let her boyfriend catch her. He did—but he landed in a clump of barberry bushes. It took his whole fraternity to take out the barberry thorns with tweezers so he could race with the crew the next day.

Betty Truex said she went through Syracuse in three years because "I had promised my father I would finish college before I got married, so it was an incentive." Her husband, Walter George Truex Jr. '29, "was a senior in engineering when I was a freshman. We both figure skated and skied, and in 1930 I was carnival queen, chosen on the basis of competition in skiing and skating. We had the winter carnival out at Drumlins then. It was an honor title; I didn't preside nor was I crowned, but I made my letters."

Theodore Pierson '30 said: "Football and basketball were very, very popular, and you went to the games if you possibly could. In old Archbold Stadium they'd get more than forty thousand people at one time, in the extra stands and all."

“There were two cheering sections—one for the men and one for the women—on opposite sides of the stadium.”—Marjorie Bronner Pierson.

Pierson's wife, the former Marjorie Bronner '31, said: "There were two cheering sections—one for the men and one for the women—on opposite sides of the stadium. We had what they called placard cheering: the boys would hold up placards and the girls would hold up placards, and occasionally they'd cooperate in cheers.

"There was no drinking on campus. Smoking? I don't remember because I didn't smoke. The men were never allowed above the first floor of the sorority house for any reason at all."

A dictionary of the 1980s defines "smoker" as an old-fashioned term applied to an informal social gathering for men only. On March 1, 1923, the *Daily Orange* had some ironic fun with the word in a headline that read "Smoking Not Permitted at Fraternity 'Smoker,' says Chancellor Flint." The newspaper quoted the statement Dr. Flint had made on the occasion: "Through misunderstanding, those in charge of the Interfraternity social gathering got the impression that smoking was to be permitted at their function. I am sorry to report those desiring this feature (and glad to report to those who do not desire it) that the regulation of the last few years will not be changed."

How Prohibition was observed on campus—one version from an anonymous member of the class of 1925: "The boys used to get their 'bonded wine' from a bonded winery which always had an abundance of permits from Jewish rabbis for sacramental wine. So we only drank the *good stuff* more or less legally." Even fifty-five years later, in talking about these more or less illegal undergraduate hijinks, the alum requested: "No names, please."

Newell W. Rossman '39 said: "I think it's important to point out that the drinking at football games was very much on the part of the alumni—the students couldn't afford much. They had 3.2 beer and it was just raising hell, up and down the streets, racing around. You must remember that in those days the women sat on one side of Archbold and the men on the opposite side. They weren't allowed to sit together, and we used to have cross-stadium cheers. Big deal. We thought it was a lot of fun."

The tradition of segregated seating seems to have begun in 1909 with the intention of assuring woman students of seats at football games. The arrangement was to continue until after World War II.

A tradition that lasted until the war was well under way was that only members of Delta Kappa Epsilon fraternity rang the Crouse College chimes. They probably were heard first at commencement in 1889. The first bell ringer was Charles W. Douglas, a Deke, who taught fellow members of his fraternity the art. They passed it along, brother to brother, through the years until 1943, when the men went to war and the women of Alpha Phi, their sister sorority, continued the tradition. The chimes ring after each home football game and at other times.

On July 8, 1983, before J. Leonard Gorman '29 retired as executive editor of the *Post Standard,* he recalled his days (and nights) as managing editor of the *Daily Orange.* In the interview in his office on Clinton Square he was asked: "What did you do for fun as an undergraduate?"

He replied:

> I think I went down to the *Daily Orange* every day of my four years there. In fact Ernie Bryan [Ernest R. Bryan '29], who was editor, and I made a pact in our freshman year that we'd work in competition on the *DO* and split the senior jobs, which was exactly what we did. We didn't appoint ourselves, but we worked them together—he became editor and I became managing editor. You got paid in those days in the senior year. I think I got $90 a month, which was room and board for me then. We really worked hard on the *DO.* It was fun to work in those days. It still is. I'm still working at 75.

A myth had its making in the October 1931 issue of the *Orange Peel,* the student humor magazine. The myth grew out of an elaborate hoax when faculty members connived with students to create a legend. Many took the story to be fact—even the *Daily Orange* reported it that way now and again—and the erroneous information persisted for decades.

It began with an article quoting Burges Johnson, professor of journalism and director of public relations. The anonymous piece in the *Orange Peel* said that when the old Women's Gym was being moved (to make room for construction of Hendricks Chapel) the bones of a sixteenth-century Indian were found in the excavation. With the bones was a portrait on cloth inscribed "O-gee-ke-da Ho-schen-e-ga-da," said to have been translated at the Onondaga reservation as "Salt Warrior." The portrait, reproduced on the cover of the *Orange Peel,* was signed Hibbardus Kleine, an early Jesuit explorer, according to the article. Actually the artist was Hibbard Kline, professor of illustration in the College of Fine Arts. The article itself had Johnson's distinctive style, and he later acknowledged having written it.

The *Orange Peel's* jape also said "Syracuse University now has 'O-gee-ke-da Ho-schen-e-ga-da,' the saltine warrier, Big Chief Bill Orange, with the orange feather in his scalp lock, bringing the fine traditions of his people out of antiquity down to present-day tribes of salty youngsters who people his ancient hunting ground."

The campus ate it up. The Men's Senate approved a resolution to have the head of the Indian adopted as the official emblem of the University, according to accounts that week in the *Daily Orange* and the downtown papers.

The newspapers also reported that a student committee was formed to promote the idea of having someone in Indian costume appear as the University mascot at football and basketball games. And lo, it came to pass. It became traditional for a tall junior to play the role. The class gift of 1951, the venerable statue of the Saltine Warrior, three thousand pounds strong, was more testimony to the persistence of legend.

A member of the 1931 student committee was Seaman Jacobs '32, editor-in-chief of the *Orange Peel.* Years later he was surprised to hear that the story was still being taken as fact. The story was finally put to rest in 1976 when journalism instructor Bill Casey assigned an interpretive writing class to write the history of the Saltine Warrior. The students did research in various places on the campus, including the library and Traditions Commission, but not all were informed that the legend was a hoax. The most enterprising of the students, Barbara Riegelhaupt '76, of Albany, N.Y., checked with the Onondaga Historical Association ("Total nonsense," said director Richard Wright), and the News Bureau, which located a copy of the October 1931 *Orange Peel* and gave her a list of its editors.

Jacobs, a television writer, reached at his home in Beverly Hills, California, told Miss Riegelhaupt: "We created the character. We were the springboard, and we were the first ones to have Indians dressed up at football games." Later Jacobs sent her clippings from his scrapbook, and she set the record straight in a story for the *Daily Orange.* He also sent a note: "Burges Johnson's story in the *Orange Peel* was a gentle rib, a harmless little hoax. But as you see, Bill Orange did come to life because of the *Peel.* And I'm pleased to learn he's still alive."

That was before the University abolished the Saltine Warrior as its mascot.

Much of the fun students had on campus was regulated by the Social Cabinet, which later was replaced by the Social Committee.

The Social Cabinet was established in the fall of 1922. It consisted of Chancellor Flint, six faculty members, and thirteen students, and its chief purpose was to cooperate with the administration in scheduling and supervising all social activities. It was admittedly an experiment. "Its success will depend on the cooperation of the student body," Dr. Flint said.

The *Daily Orange,* hailing it as "one of the most liberal policies effected in twenty-eight years," said the social cabinet would govern dances, smoking, gambling, drinking, and an honor system.

The newspaper took another look at the experiment, however, as it printed new rules for dances and the appointment of chaperons. Echoing student opinion, it now saw regulations as more drastic than had been expected and deplored the restrictions imposed on parties downtown. But the junior honorary society Monx Head, among others, declared support for the rules.

The social cabinet went on to make rules for winter sports. It granted permission for such activities as a barn dance, a fraternity revue, and a lecture by a "psychic analyst."

"Smoking was prohibited on the campus," Virginia Hagan remembered. "And there was a midnight curfew except for special occasions like the Senior Ball."

After 1925 the Social Cabinet gradually became dormant and was replaced in October 1927 by the University Social Committee, which functioned throughout the rest of the Flint administration and that of Chancellor Graham.

Ruth Paul, the social adviser from 1937 to 1940, defined her duties as "secretary to the All-University Social Committee, adviser to the students for all University social activities and living centers activities, instructor in social usage, adviser to chairmen of living centers, instructor in the student dean course, manager of the Student Dean Conference, and head resident of Haven Hall." She was also responsible for all social activities and the University calendar of social events. Dr. Graham, now Chancellor, made it clear there would be no appeal from a decision of the social adviser.

Fun downtown was cheap in the thirties. In April of 1932 a first-run movie and a vaudeville show at the RKO Keith's or Loew's cost 25¢ before 1 P.M. The Keith's offered Barbara Stanwyck in the movie "Shopworn" and "5—BIG ACTS—5" of vaudeville. Loew's had William Haines and Madge Evans in "Are You Listening?" plus a stage show with Dave Apollon as the headliner. Other downtown attractions were Tony Sarg's marionettes at the Lincoln auditorium and a double feature, starring Lupe Velez and Jack Holt, at the Paramount—which on Saturdays drew children with a 10-cent Kiddie Matinee.

And if you drove a car gasoline was cheap. A one-line ad in the *Post-Standard* said: "Seitz No-Knock Gas 14¢. Wolf St."

Frank A. Kanda, professor of chemistry who retired in 1981 after teaching at Syracuse since 1937, estimated that he taught about thirty-two thousand students in those years. He came to the Hill after earning his B.A. at Western Reserve University (now Case Western Reserve). "There was the typical Joe College flavor when I came here," he said. "I had commuted to college so I lacked getting any of that at Western Reserve, and here I saw in it what I always thought it would be.

"I loved the down-to-earth, fun-loving traditions, the many pag-

Winter Carnival, 1940. "Around Christmas time there was snow sculpting, and the whole city used to ride up here to see it; we had traffic jams."—Frank A. Kanda.

eants and a Moving-Up Day ceremony when a herald on horseback made it a festive affair." Such ceremonies also included colorful floats, induction of student officers, burning of freshman lids, street dancing, and the singing of the Alma Mater.

"As a graduate student I lived on the corner of Comstock and University Place where the big dorm, DellPlain, is now," Kanda said. "I lived in Mrs. Holmes' place; we called it Mrs. Holmes' Athletic Club because we had so many grad students we formed baseball teams to participate in the leagues here.

"Around Christmas time there was snow sculpturing, and the whole city used to ride up here to see it; we had traffic jams. The fellows and girls not only made these sculptures, they painted them. Oh, it was really nice. But those things are gone. I think a lot of kids miss them. Rather, they don't miss them—they never knew about them."

One of Professor Kanda's favorite stories has to do, naturally, with his own discipline—chemistry. In addition to the head-shaving and other pranks that went with the Colgate-Syracuse football rivalry, he said, there were more sophisticated doings. "One was for kids to fly over the lake on the campus at Colgate in an airplane and drop an orange dye. They used to come to the chemistry department and ask us what would be best. And that's what they used—fluorescent anthracene dyes that turned the Colgate pond a brilliant orange."

Newell W. Rossman '39 remembered that, too; "The pond at the center of campus at Colgate is where they threw the dye in, and it was orange, of course. And they would hire an airplane, a two-winger, to drop 'Beat Colgate,' and Colgate would drop 'Beat Syracuse' or 'Scalp Syracuse.' These little leaflets floated down and became valuable collector's items."

In 1925 the Forestry Club published *Songs of the Forester.* One of the ditties collected was "Song of the Frosh Forester" and went in part:

I said, "I'll go to Syracuse, Syracuse,"
  And when they asked me 'What's the use, what's the use?"
I said, "Just wait four years and see,
When I have studied Forestry."

Chorus

Silviculture I will master,
I will put out fires faster,
I will learn to use the compass and the calipers.
I'll learn the names of fish and bugs, fish and bugs,
Of birds and butterflies and slugs, flies and slugs,
And the name of trees will never bother me,
When I have studied Forestry.

Newell Rossman recalled a typical pleasant Saturday evening of his undergraduate days: "You'd walk downtown on a nice night—down Harrison or Madison or whichever street you chose—and go to the theater. Then you'd walk back to Marshall Street where you'd buy the Sunday paper. You'd go to the Cosmo or the Varsity. You'd have a Virginia Special, or coffee and a sandwich. A Virginia Special was a piece of white cake with vanilla ice cream on top and chocolate syrup on top of it—fifteen cents. Cosmo, I think, invented that concoction. It was a cheap date. The paper was ten cents, the movie twenty-five."

Theodore Pierson '30 said:

> The big date was to go down to the Hotel Syracuse; in those days the Persian Terrace had big bands and there was supper dancing. You didn't eat very much because you couldn't afford much. They had a modest cover charge. It was during Prohibition so you brought your own bottle and hid it under the table. Afterwards, or after a movie, the in place was Ginsburg's, which was right across from the hotel. That was a good delicatessen-restaurant. The kind of music played at the hotel was the Charleston and the Black Bottom and "Smoke Gets in Your Eyes"—soft music, thank goodness. We didn't do the Charleston or the Black Bottom. We were the slower dancers. This was in the late twenties. Then there were the fraternity dances. And Comstock Avenue at that time—I don't recall that it was paved.

His wife, Marjorie Bronner Pierson '31, said: "Sure it was paved. We called it the Long Walk."

"They also called it Lovers Lane, and that was where you walked with your girl."

Marjorie Pierson said: "It was before you had to be fearful of walking on the street. You were perfectly safe anywhere even without an escort."

"There was a lot of romance; some sex but nothing to keep up with today," her husband said. "At least sex was a more private thing."

"You went out with a boy several times—a good many times—before he kissed you," she said.

"The fraternity formals were really big time affairs," he said. People dressed up and you planned for them a long time—both to get a date and to have the money to pay for it. They were usually held at one of the hotels. The Onondaga Hotel had a roof garden that was beautiful. It was the finest place to go. There were strict curfews, and they were enforced."

"I lived at home," she said, "on the corner of Berkeley Drive and Stratford. Two blocks from campus."

"I lived just the other side of the campus which is now a university parking lot on Henry Street," he said. "Of course the end of the campus in those days was by the corner of Euclid Avenue and College Place. Sims Hall was the farthest building; Mount Olympus was completely wild."

A visitor noted that Chancellor Graham once had told the trustees College Place was far enough east for the University to expand.

"That was before everyone had cars," Marjorie Pierson said.

Dr. Graham was warm, beloved, conservative, and straitlaced. He also had a sense of humor, Ted Pierson recalled. "As far as the students were concerned, we didn't have much to do with Chancellor Flint," he said. "He was kind of remote, and was considered a rather austere, forbidding personage. We saw more of Vice Chancellor Graham."

Pierson recalled an occasion when Dr. Graham tempered a reproof with his special brand of humor. Pierson and other engineering students were in the big graphics room on the top floor of Smith Hall, tossing bags of water out of the windows. "It got a little out of hand at one point, and Dr. Graham, who was formerly dean of the engineering college, sent a message over. He said he was pleased to see the students studying hydraulics and the law of gravity but that they should refrain from dropping the bags of water on passersby."

The flavor of Chancellor Graham's mind could be tasted in his reports to the board of trustees, usually delivered orally. In his report of November 20, 1937, he spoke of the prospects of having a student union on campus: "The students asked for the use of Yates Castle as a student union. That didn't seem advisable . . . and it was decided that a much better place would be in Slocum Hall. A soda fountain has been installed, and a cafeteria for the students. The use of the corridors and some basement rooms have been made available for meetings and select dances. The students seem to be happy and appreciative of what has been done."

Graham's dry wit (on a dry campus) was in evidence at the next board meeting, June 3, 1938, when he gave a follow-up report; "The students have been using these quarters and apparently are very happy to have them. They have chosen what I suppose they consider a very appropriate name—the Club Sahara. That indicates the kind of refreshments being served there."

Another student during this period, Hildegarde F. Schine, class of 1927, along with her husband, J. Myer Schine, has been honored by her family. The daughter of Hildegarde and J. Myer Schine is Renée Schine Crown, herself a graduate of the University (class of 1950) and a long-time active trustee of the University. A three-million dollar naming gift has been received from the Schine and Crown families for the Hildegarde and J. Myer Schine Student Center in honor of Mrs. Crown's parents. This long-awaited project is scheduled for completion in 1985.

The All-University Social Committee gave much attention to the social calendar. To get on the calendar all groups except the College of Forestry were required to clear through the office of the social adviser, who screened each request to see that it conformed to the committee's rules. The stated purpose was to prevent overloading of events on a given day and avoid distraction from studies and examinations.

The committee watched over every phase of a dance, such as hiring the orchestra, assigning chaperons, cost, locale and duration, and the sensitive matter of moral conduct. The regulations were printed annually in the *Handbook*. Ever alert, students pored over them for possible loopholes. Student ingenuity in discovering ways to evade control was matched by the ability of the committee to plug the gaps as soon as they were found.

Another influence at social events was that of "deanettes"—women enrolled in a student dean course established in 1931. The young women gathered regularly to talk about campus problems with the dean of women. At their sessions matters discussed ranged from chaperons and tea dances to "petting, smoking, and gum chewing," according to the contemporary account. (The *Daily Orange* ran an editorial about the "atrocity" of women chewing gum.)

It was generally agreed that there were too many social events. A survey by the Social Committee showed that from 1927 to 1938 the number of such activities had virtually doubled while student enrollment remained about the same. A later tabulation, of dances only, showed that there were nearly 300 between 1932 and 1942.

Newell Rossman speaking of his classmate Chester B. Hansen '39:

> Chet Hansen thought he had to have some crusade as editor of the *Daily Orange,* which every editor feels he has to have, and his crusade was against corsages at University dances, formals. We still dressed for the dances, for the Senior Ball, the Junior Ball, the Sophomore Hop. All the fraternities had their big dances with orchestras, and everybody dressed and you always sent your girl a corsage.
>
> Hansen thought this was a very big burden on the poor guys who didn't have any money and couldn't really afford the corsage. Therefore he started "A Rose for a Dollar." For every formal dance we would sell roses in the lower rooms of Hendricks Chapel for a dollar—and the florists all got upset in the city of Syracuse. Hansen carried this thing to the nth degree, and it was at the Junior Ball or the Senior Ball that year all the girls wore red roses, and it only cost a dollar. For years afterward, every time I saw a rose I'd think of Hansen and his big campaign.

The expenses of the Greek letter societies for dances varied, depending on the financial resources of the members and the facilities of each house. Often, especially during the 1920s, formal and informal dances were held at moderate cost in chapter houses. By the outbreak of World War II, however, most formal dances were at approved hotels or clubs such as Drumlins. With these changes in location came additional costs, such as transportation, more elaborate refreshments, and the cost of booking a nationally known orchestra. Although the student body and the administration knew in general what expenses were involved, Chancellor Flint was not disposed to raise a question about the "private" affairs of the fraternities or sororities. During the early 1930s the Social Committee believed the societies should be cautioned to reduce expenses, but the Chancellor demurred on the ground that economy measures should be imposed by the chapters. Dances at living centers were generally modest affairs.

After 1939 all-University dances were limited to five a year, and the administration exercised greater control, especially because the dances were held in Archbold Gymnasium. But fees charged by major orchestras, such as the Casa Loma or Tommy Dorsey's, as the dances moved to downtown hotels, frequently surprised student managers of the events who found themselves unable to meet their financial obligations. As a result the administration took over the hiring of orchestras, determined admission charges, and ruled that no dance should be run for profit or a charitable purpose. When there were profits, they went into a special University account, either to offset deficits of other dances or returned to a class for a particular project, such as publishing a campus map.

In 1933 the Freshman and Sophomore hops were abolished as an economy measure. Instead each class held a banquet at the cafeteria in Slocum Hall. The same year the Junior Prom managers, facing a deficit that included an unpaid hotel bill, were bailed out by the administration. But in 1939, the Junior Prom was abolished for certain failures by the junior class when they were sophomores handling the Sophomore Hop. The Junior Prom was permitted again in 1940.

Difficulties arising from student and alumni indiscretions and laxity by hotel officials sometimes marred the better record of the Senior Ball, as in 1929 when Dr. Graham had to inform the Men's and Women's senates of new rules governing University dances. More disturbing were excesses that often accompanied dances on the night of the Colgate football game. Between 1933 and 1938 the Social Committee forbade all dances on that night. The committee believed, however, that permission might be granted where "a traditional Colgate night dance was a part of the fraternity program," and in 1939 the sophomores were allowed to arrange such a dance.

A frequent complaint about Colgate night fraternity dances centered on the use of the second floor at a chapter house; there were similar reports about the practice at other houses. The Social Committee acknowledged that the ground floor provided inadequate facilities for the woman guests; it permitted access to the second floor under certain restrictions. During intermission, for example, refreshments could be served there under proper chaperonage. But the situation got out of hand, and in the fall of 1931 the committee laid down rigid rules that outraged the fraternities. The Men's Senate objected with a series of resolutions pointing out that many a chapter house was too small to warrant closing the second floor. Another objection was that student self-government had been violated; that if it was unfortunate to see mature men and women censured in this way.

The indiscretions that took place upstairs included drinking, petting, closed doors, and speakeasy parties, to judge by minutes of the Social Committee between the years 1929 and 1942. Such conduct resulted in the refusal of many faculty members to act as chaperons, and in 1937 the trustees declared second floors off limits. By that time, however, many fraternities had shifted their dances to downtown hotels and clubs.

Other activities were "Gang Dates," which involved reciprocal entertaining between sororities and fraternities, and between living centers. These consisted of informal suppers followed by dancing—followed often by complaints from various sources. In some instances delinquent houses were reprimanded and placed on probation. The Social Committee forbade dances in the gymnasium after basketball games, banned parties during Holy Week, denied permission for certain dances and, in 1938, ruled out a Freshman Week dance.

Student reaction to these controls and other committee regulations were often negative and sometimes hostile. But mostly the students grumbled and obeyed. In time they accepted as normal what previously they had condemned. The problems were new to each incoming class, and the administration felt it necessary to restate its position year after year. Despite assertions by students that they were mature, their frequent peccadillos, many felt, justified the University in continuing to act, usually through the Social Committee, *in loco parentis.*

It was a laundry day at the post office, and a good crowd was present when the package wrapped in brown paper, addressed to "Comrade Chancellor Flint," arrived in the mail. "The post office was in a tiny area adjacent to the bookstore," said Newell W. Rossman '39. "I can still see the lines of young men and women standing there with their big laundry boxes."

The date was March 7, 1936. That was before there were laundromats and wash-and-wear, and postage was cheap. Rossman said:

> In those days you shipped your laundry home and of course when your mother shipped it back there were cookies or cake. That was always a great occasion—when your laundry box was returned.
>
> The package, smaller than a bread box, had a tick-tock sound. The postmaster called the local police, who became concerned and called in the federal officers, who decided to soak it in a rain barrel behind the post office. They found an old alarm clock and a lot of sugar. The architects in those days always had to have an annual project to stir the campus—and this was their project.

D. Kenneth Sargent '27, who was teaching that year, took up the tale in a separate interview. He said: "In architecture they had to work long hours and they'd pop off, and this was when they popped off." He was talking about students at their drafting tables in Slocum Hall.

> Everybody added a little bit to it. They brought stuff together out of garbage cans, literally. The clock just feebly ticked. The battery had been in the ash can, no electricity in it. There were some wires stuck in. Anybody with any intelligence would have known it was a fake. They cut a piece of tube and stole sugar from the cafeteria down on the first floor and filled the tube with sugar and stuck wires in each end. One of the reasons it hit the papers was the FBI, or whatever it was called then, doused it in water when they heard it ticking. Of course the water picked up the sugar, and they tasted the water and thought it was nitroglycerin because it tasted sweet. That's about all there was to it. It was innocent. They were just having a good time.

Newell Rossman explained why the ticking package was addressed to "Comrade" Flint. "Mary Jenkins owned the paper in those pre-Newhouse days, and its editor kept trying to find communists on campus," Rossman said.

After the story broke in the downtown papers—it was the talk of the campus before that—Lemuel Dillenback, head of the architecture department, got a phone call. The department, not yet a school on its own, was in the College of Fine Arts. "Dilly was upset," Sargent said. "He didn't know exactly how to handle it." But the dean of the college, Harold Butler, an attorney by training, told Dillenback: "You get every last student in architecture. And when the group that are charged go down, the whole school goes down, girls in the works." There were two or three women in the school, Sargent said. "So the whole bunch of them went down. It was typical."

Rossman said Arthur McKean, a graduate student in the College of

Law, represented the architecture students in court "after they had been booked as the perpetrators of this dastardly crime." McKean died in World War II when his ammunition ship was torpedoed, Rossman recalled.

The charge was disorderly conduct, Sargent said. "It was dismissed when the whole gang went down and said they were all in on it. They weren't all in on it, but they said they were. Then the attorney, the federal attorney, said, 'I think I ought to take you all out and buy you a beer.' And the case was dismissed."

Sargent added: "When they knew what it was and how foolish the whole thing was, of course there were a lot of red faces on the part of the law enforcement group. They had made these statements in the *Herald* that there was enough explosive to blow the top off the post office—ridiculous things like that."

On Monday, March 9, the architecture students airmailed a letter to Chancellor Flint, who was in Florida, apologizing for the prank and saying it had been in wholesome fun with no intention of being disrespectful. The *Daily Orange* said editorially: "Such foolish, thoughtless tricks are not worthy of idle hands, let alone busy architects."

The women architecture students—the *DO* said there were five—regaled a reporter with recollections of pranks past. The best of them had been perpetrated by future architects, who had more vivid imaginations than Liberal Arts or Business Administration students, the women claimed. Among their anecdotes:

Some years earlier, just before a Syracuse-Colgate swimming meet, a group of architects collected twenty-seven eels and turned them loose in the University pool. "The eels, we are told, won the meet," the *Daily Orange* reported.

"Architects were never popular with Chancellor James R. Day after the Palm Sunday on which several of the lads let loose a dozen frightened chickens from the beams above the organ in Crouse College while the Chancellor was pronouncing benediction."

A prankster who attached a spark coil to a telephone—instead of to a professor's doorknob—was surprised when the receiver was lifted. The spark blew out the entire University switchboard.

It sometimes happened on April 1 that a student received a message to call Chuck at 5-0225—and discovered that he'd been an April Fool. The "Chuck" with that telephone number was Chancellor Charles Wesley Flint.

When the *Daily Orange* reached the Chancellor for comment on the latest dido, his reaction belied the picture often painted of him as a staid and humorless man. Dr. Flint said: "I could think of several sins of omission for which I deserved a blowing up, but couldn't even guess which particular one merited such seemingly drastic action." The *DO* report added: "As far as he is concerned the matter is all over, it was a good joke, and he hopes the boys will settle down and do some studying for the rest of the semester."

27

Sports

Chancellor Flint noted with pride that three-fourths of the student body took part in some form of athletic recreation or supervised sport. The tradition of a good mind in a healthy body was a long one at Syracuse.

IT WAS THE ERA OF TRADITIONAL ATHLETIC RIVALRIES between schools, of great coaches whose names for decades were synonymous with that of Syracuse, of players known across the land. It was a time of pep rallies and bonfires, of high spirits and hijinks, of segregated student seating with men on one side of Archbold Stadium and women on the other.

Colgate was the chief rival and football was first among the sports. When the two ingredients combined in the annual battle between the Orangemen of Syracuse and the Red Raiders of Colgate the campus atmosphere became electric. Students from each school descended on the home grounds of the other, captured opponents and shaved their heads, smeared paint on sidewalks and buildings, dyed a campus pond with the rival's color, greased trolley car tracks.

Fever pitch was reached one Thursday night, November 3, 1938. The Colgate-Syracuse game was to be Saturday in Archbold Stadium, and nearly three thousand students demonstrated on and near the Hill. They set fires, tried to derail street cars, and generally conducted themselves in what the *Daily Orange* called "a disgraceful display of

Ray Barbuti makes a substantial gain against Colgate, November 13, 1926.

rowdyism and vandalism." Chancellor Graham canceled one of two scheduled pep rallies and warned that any student who traveled to Hamilton for a forbidden rally there risked immediate dismissal from Syracuse University.

Roy Simmons, Sr., recalled that rivalry in 1981 on the eve of his eightieth birthday October 30. He had played in three Syracuse-Colgate games. "They were tough ballgames," Simmons told a *Post-Standard* reporter. "You never knew what was going to happen in a Colgate game. If we'd come in as the favorite, they'd knock us off. If they'd come in as the favorite, we'd knock them off."

Simmons had played in the 1924 game, the last Syracuse won from Colgate before a thirteen-year drought set in. Those jinx or hoodoo years, as they were gloomily known, saw the Red Raiders beat the Orange eleven times and tie twice.

It was Simmons' senior year in 1924, and he was a team captain. "I was a better defensive player, but on that day Coach [Chick] Meehan had me running the ball a lot more than I did all year," Simmons recalled. "Colgate scored first on a field goal, then we put on a drive, and Jack McBride scored from the three-yard line to win." The score was 7–3, and that was the last Syracuse victory in the series until November 5, 1938.

The thirteen-year jinx was broken when Phil Allen made a fourteen-yard end run and scored a fourth-period touchdown. Pandemonium ensued and continued to the end of the game. Syracuse alumni embraced and wept. The Crouse College chimes pealed. The ecstatic Syracuse fans tore down their goalposts.

The *Daily Orange* told the story in a thirty-thousand-copy extra edition that rainswept Saturday. It was mailed to alumni around the world with this banner headline:

SYRACUSE CRUSHES RAIDER JINX, 7–0;
35,000 WATCH FIRST WIN IN 14 YEARS

In contrast to the behavior that had so disturbed Dr. Graham two nights earlier, the campus celebration featured much din but no destruction. Sunday morning the campus was clean. After the game members of the Alpha Phi Omega honor society picked up the litter left by the capacity Archbold crowd, and "when the Crouse chimes pealed for chapel at 10:45, the greens were clean, the Old Oval spotless," the *Daily Orange* reported.

It was an era in athletics at Syracuse unmatched by any other eastern university, said Newell W. Rossman '39. Speaking of the Flint-Graham years, Rossman said in an interview: "Syracuse was known throughout the athletic world because of the length of time the coaches of the various sports actually coached here—James Ten Eyck in crew, Lew Carr in baseball, Lew Andreas in basketball and football, Ted Webster in swimming, Tom Keane in track and cross-country, Bill Davison in wrestling and gymnastics. These were all national experts in their respective fields, and they were all here thirty years or better.

"Syracuse was an institution where they came and performed and were nationally recognized and didn't have to go on."

Recalling other great names in Orange sports, Rossman said: "Vic Hanson was famous as a three-time All-American basketball player who eventually became head football coach for six or seven years." Hanson '27 is in both the basketball and football halls of fame.

In crew, Rossman said, "a large group headed by Gordon Hoople, Ken Gallegher, and Hubie Stratton kept crew alive because it was known as a gentleman's sport. You had to be a real he-man to be a crew man. They really made use of that—selectivity, they used to call it. After Hubert Stratton died in 1978 his widow named a shell for him and gave it to the crew. It's in the boathouse at Onondaga Lake. Clifford (Tip) Goes was another famous name in the crew. He was the coxswain in his time and did a lot of the organization. Now the Tip Goes Cup is awarded annually to the winner of a three-way race among Syracuse, Navy, and Cornell."

Lynn (Pappy) Waldorf '25, who won All-American honors as a star tackle, spoke at reunion time a few years ago of a certain football game back in 1922. "We beat Nebraska 9–6, and they had beat Notre Dame's Four Horsemen," Waldorf recalled. "It was just like chiseling concrete."

Without question it was the major sports—football and basketball—that gave Syracuse its standing in the world of collegiate athletics in the twenties and thirties. The prestige was based on tradition, better coaching, larger subsidies, and wider popularity among students, alumni, and friends of the University than was the lot of the minor sports, which often had their beginnings in individual interests. The lesser sports evolved as small groups of students found others similarly motivated and went out for their activities, eventually getting encouragement from faculty members.

ROTC officers, for instance, welcomed students' interest in rifle. Professor William Davison gave personal guidance and instruction to wrestlers. As the number of participants increased, these unofficially organized efforts drew the attention of the Athletic Association.

The Athletic Association of Syracuse University and its governing board controlled all sports at the University, major and minor. The board, made up of students, faculty, and alumni, among others, also decided the status of the sports and funding it thought they deserved. The Athletic Association itself was funded by a student fee, and dues paid by alumni and other members.

But official sanction was easier to obtain than financial support. Often the coaches of minor sports served without pay; the students frequently provided their own equipment and paid their own travel expenses to compete at other institutions. Between 1928 and 1935, when University finances were low, minor sports were suspended wholly or in part. Some were revived later to function, despite handicaps, during the Graham administration.

FOOTBALL

John F. (Chick) Meehan, a 1919 law school graduate, was named football coach in 1920. In preparing for the 1922 season, his first under Chancellor Flint, he broke precedent by taking the football squad to South Bay on Oneida Lake because of "early games, condition of the stadium and morale of the team." This cost an extra $1,700, but the results seemed worth it. Only nine holdovers from 1921 were on the team, but the off-campus drills apparently benefited the entire squad. All the players were in good physical and mental condition, and they won six games, including one with archrival Colgate, and had two ties. The only loss in 1922 was to powerful Pittsburgh. But after two more better-than-average years Meehan resigned in December 1924, joining New York University at a higher salary than the $5,000 Syracuse had paid him.

The governing board of the Athletic Association chose Charles W.

P. (Pete) Reynolds '09 to succeed Meehan in January 1925. He was a former varsity player and assistant coach at his alma mater, with other coaching experience at Hobart and Hamilton. When Reynolds left for the business world in 1927, Lewis P. Andreas '21 accepted the job of head coach for three years. Lew Andreas had rejoined his alma mater in 1924 as head basketball coach and was also put in charge of freshman athletics. He said he viewed the football job as temporary, agreeing to accept it while he continued to coach basketball; he was basketball coach until 1949 and director of athletics after that.

The formidable and popular Vic Hanson '27 succeeded Andreas as football coach in December 1929. Victor A. Hanson had been a triple-threat athlete—in football, basketball, and baseball. His seven years as coach were controversial; the team's record was mediocre, if not dismal, and Colgate won seven out of seven against the Orange. In his final year, 1936, the Hanson team defeated little Clarkson but lost to each of the other seven opponents, and Hanson resigned.

Ossie Solem, a University of Minnesota graduate who had played football for that school and had wide coaching experience after that, succeeded Hanson and was coach through the 1941 season. His record generally was regarded as acceptable but not outstanding. He had become a campus idol for breaking the Colgate jinx in 1938. Syracuse also beat the Red Raiders one other time in Solem's five-year tenure, with one tie and two losses.

An earlier triumph in the 1938 season was the 19–17 Orange victory over Cornell. The hero of that afternoon in Archbold was Wilmeth Sidat-Singh '39, who threw five completed passes, three of them for touchdowns. His performance in that game and others made him one of the leading forward passers in the East. He was also a star of the basketball court. Sidat-Singh, the stepson of a New York City physician, played professional basketball after graduation with the Syracuse Reds and with the Renaissance Five, Negro world champions. Sidat-Singh was black, not a Hindu as some publicity men would have had it, and had been discriminated against because of his color in 1937 when the University of Maryland refused to meet the Orangemen with a black on their team. Sidat-Singh sat out the game in his Baltimore hotel room and Maryland won, 13–0. But at another time Hugh H. (Duffy) Daugherty '39, who played for Syracuse before going on to coach at Michigan State, and other teammates united against discrimination. A fraternity had rejected Sidat-Singh because of his color. When the players all stood together the chapter changed its Caucasian-only rules. "We all went into this house together because we thought so much of Singh," Daugherty said. Sidat-Singh was one of many students of that era who died in World War II. Lieutenant Sidat-Singh's plane crashed into Lake Huron on a training mission and, although he had parachuted safely, he drowned.

Another athlete with multiple talents was Marty Glickman '39, a star in track and field as well as a spectacular ground gainer in football. In 1936 Glickman was a member of the U.S. Olympic team at Berlin. Also in that year he and Jesse Owens were members of the American 400-meter relay team that set a world's record in London. Back home in 1937, Glickman scored both Orange touchdowns in a thrilling victory over Cornell. Cornell's Big Red was then one of the strongest college teams in the United States. Adding to the triumph was the fact that Syracuse was the only team to defeat Cornell in football that year.

Betty Truex Dumars '30 remembered Syracuse football games of her day: "It always snowed at the time of football games, but everybody went. Sam Sebo was one of our football heroes, as were Vic Hanson and Ray Barbuti. Ray was in the Olympics and won the 440, but when he ran on the football field he had the highest-rising knees you ever saw. He really drove."

Some of the other great football players of those between-wars years were John (Toots) McBride, Harlan (Gotch) Carr, Albert Van Ness, Tom Lombardi, Dick Fishel, Joe Vavra, Ed Jontos, Vannie Albanese, Jim Bruett, and Jack Hinkle.

BASKETBALL

Basketball was the second most popular sport at Syracuse, in part probably because it attracted some of the outstanding football players, particularly in the 1920s. Despite poor accommodations for the fans at Archbold Gymnasium, a good percentage of the crowds were from off campus. Edmund A. (Eddie) Dollard '08 had been basketball coach since 1911 and remained in the job until Andreas took over in the spring of 1924.

Recalling some of those days in a 1982 interview, Andreas said: "It was more or less an accident that I took over because Eddie Dollard, who had been the coach, retired in the first year I was here. Mr. Ferris, the director of athletics, asked me to take over temporarily until they could find a coach. I became coach of both the freshman and varsity basketball teams in that first year [1924]. After we had gone along for part of the season the kids got together, and they apparently asked the director of athletics to keep me on as coach."

His interviewer asked: "Were you winning some games, Lew?"
"Yes, we were," Andreas replied:

> I was very fortunate to have three football players, Vic Hanson, Harlan (Gotch) Carr, and Charlie Lee. They came out for the squad after the football season. I remember a game with St. Lawrence, who had a crackerjack basketball game in those days. Our kids had worked hard and got together as a real team. So I decided I wouldn't play Hanson, Lee, and Carr in the first half of that game because I didn't think they were in top shape for basketball.
>
> St. Lawrence was leading us by nine points in the first half, and we had to make that up in the second half, which we did, and we beat them by a comfortable margin. Because I had Vic Hanson, Charlie Lee, and Gotch Carr and a fellow named Hank Grieve ... we went on and beat St. Lawrence and then about ten straight... so there was a move in my favor, and I became director of athletics.

Asked to name the University's greatest athlete, Andreas replied diplomatically, saying: "I think each had his day. In Hanson's day he unquestionably was the greatest athlete at the University. He made All-American in football and basketball, and he was a good enough baseball player that the Yankees gave him a thorough trial. He was so quick on his feet and fast that he madc his letter easily in track. On top of that he was a great competitor and a fine leader."

During the years Andreas was coach the Syracuse basketball team played 324 games, won 252 and lost 72. His best season was the year the Orange were national champions, 1925–26, with twenty wins and one heartbreak loss, to Penn State, in an away game that Andreas, suffering from an ear infection, was too ill to attend.

In addition to his prize trio of Hanson, Lee, and Carr, known in their day as the Three Musketeers, Andreas had other stars that were the fans' delight, including a 1929–30 quintet of average size but dazzling swiftness known as the Reindeer—Ev Katz, Dan Fogarty, Ken Beagle, Lou Hayman, and Slim Elliott. Others deserving special mention were Stan Richtmeyer, Bill Eisemann, Phil Rakov, and Ed Sonderman.

There was also the 1938 starting center, Don MacNaughton, who was to become chairman and chief executive officer of the Prudential Insurance Company. MacNaughton, by then also a trustee of his alma mater, told Rod Macdonald, author of *Syracuse Basketball 1900–1975*, that most college basketball players in the Depression years were scholarship athletes who would not otherwise have had a college education. "Certainly that was true in my case," McNaughton said.

BASEBALL

Lewis (Lew) Carr, whose career as baseball coach began in 1910, led the Syracuse nine throughout the Flint-Graham years and beyond. His diamond was the Old Oval, the playing field south of the Hall of Languages, and Archbold Stadium. Hendricks Field was used after 1930.

Like other outdoor spring sports in the north, Syracuse University baseball frequently was hampered by short seasons and inclement weather. In some years spring practice was confined to the baseball cage in Archbold Gymnasium, and there were times when Coach Carr took untried and inexperienced teams south to play opponents such as Virginia, Maryland, and Johns Hopkins. To a degree these became practice games for key encounters with Colgate, Cornell, Michigan, and other rivals. Graduation, ineligibility, sophomore squads, and bad weather were obstacles to overcome. In 1923, for example, a game at Springfield, Massachusetts, was cancelled because of "winter" conditions. Financial problems, caused in part by administrative rulings and by poor support from the student body, also dogged the coach and his teams.

During the twenty seasons covered by this volume, 329 games were played. The longest season was in 1926 with twenty-three games. The shortest saw twelve games in 1942. The most successful seasons were in 1927, when Syracuse won thirteen games and lost seven, and 1941 with a sixteen and four record.

Among the many notable players on Lew Carr's nines were Vic Hanson, Art Cramer, Abe Stoneburg, John Chapman, Joe Vavra, Bill Van Langan, Vin Black, Jonah Goldman, Gotch Carr, and John Hafer.

CREW

Many declare that crew is the only real sport and consider it the only truly amateur athletic calling in collegiate life. At Syracuse the first University crew was organized in November 1873. These oarsmen were active only briefly; not until 1900 was there a revival of interest in crew. In 1903 that grand old man of rowing, James A. Ten Eyck, was named coach, a position he still held when Chancellor Flint came to the University in 1922, and which he kept until his death in February 1938.

Before 1922 Syracuse had participated in more than fifty intercollegiate races, and its record was creditable, especially in view of the cramped quarters and deteriorating condition of the boathouse at

Long Branch on Onondaga Lake and the short time available for practice outdoors because of poor weather. Matters failed to improve during the early Flint years under the Chancellor's tight-money policy. What little was done for the oarsmen was due to efforts of alumni and the athletic governing board.

Then in 1926 Clifford (Tip) Goes, a former varsity coxswain and later a member of the board, prepared an analysis of the problem which went to the trustees. The idea was to raise $70,000 to build a new boathouse. In 1927 the trustees endorsed the plan, but Dr. Flint in 1928 thought it needed more study, considering the $20,000 deficit already on the books of that sport. The implication that crew might be abolished brought sharp reaction from alumni and students, but in 1929 the Chancellor proposed "to suspend activities in crew for ... not less than three nor more than five years." He relented, however, by also suggesting an alternative. The trustees agreed, and a two-pronged fund drive was started to save crew and to support a faculty pension plan. The boathouse, known as the old barn, continued to deteriorate. An alumnus reported: "No danger of the antiquated boathouse floating down the river this year. The barn is anchored to trees in the neighboring swamp, but the rain still drips through, and a stormy wind may carry the roof to Liverpool any moment."

By 1931 only about $10,000 had been raised toward a new boathouse, and Tip Goes turned to the public works programs of the state and federal government, which eventually (in 1935) provided the extra funds needed. Construction began in 1936, and the James A. Ten Eyck Boathouse at Long Branch, just across the outlet of the lake from the old site, was formally dedicated in May 1937.

Ten Eyck, then eighty-seven, was touched by the honor and spoke of his pleasure, which was increased by the fact that his son Edward (Ned) Ten Eyck had been named assistant coach. After his father's death the following February, Ned Ten Eyck was appointed coach and held the position for several years.

The cream of eastern boats, Syracuse's included, were invited to the annual Intercollegiate Rowing Association (IRA) regattas on the Hudson River at Poughkeepsie. The varsity oarsmen of Syracuse gave excellent accounts of themselves but failed to win a race there during the years 1923–42, coming in second in 1930, and third in 1926 and 1940. The junior varsity won at Poughkeepsie in 1923, 1931, 1932, 1934, and 1939, and the freshmen won in 1925, 1929, 1930, and 1932. The varsity crew did not compete in 1933 or 1942, nor did the junior varsity in 1927, 1929, or 1937.

Orange crews also performed creditably, although rarely vic-

James A. Ten Eyck at the oars on his eighty-fifth birthday at Long Branch, with George Parsons and Tip Goes in the stern and Ken Gallegher in the bow.

toriously, in the intercollegiate races at Philadelphia known as the American Henley and had a fair number of victories in dual and triangular races. In 1932 a valiant Orange varsity crew defeated Navy at Annapolis (where the junior varsity and freshman shells also won), defeated Cornell at Syracuse's Onondaga Lake (where the junior varsity won again), and went on to beat Cornell once more, this time at Boston over a three-quarter mile course on the Charles River. The narrow victory on the Charles was achieved in eight minutes, forty-eight and two-fifths seconds—twenty seconds better than the previous time—and established a Charles River record that was to stand for twenty-seven years. The only varsity losses that year were to California at the IRA

Syracuse University varsity crew, 1940.

regatta (where Syracuse's freshman and junior varsity boats won) and in the Olympic trials at Worcester, Massachusetts, where the Syracuse boat was defeated by the Pennsylvania Athletic Club—which lost to California, which went on to the world championship by defeating Italy in the Olympic Games.

LACROSSE

Organized at Syracuse in 1917 by Professor Laurie D. Cox of the Forestry College, lacrosse became an outstanding intercollegiate activity during the Flint years. Cox's drive, personality, and skill earned the players' loyalty and brought deserved recognition to the University. During his tutelage (1917–31) Syracuse was known nationally and internationally for its success in this sport. Between 1923 and 1931, for example, the Orange lacrosse team had a phenomenal record of 91 games won of a total of 119 played, along with 5 ties. Its best season was in 1927 when it won fifteen with but a single loss; the poorest was in 1930, when the team lost eight of eleven contests. Included in the totals were practice games with the alumni, the Onondaga Indians, and a city club, the Crescent.

Similar warm-up games were played under the direction of Coach Roy Simmons, successor to Cox, who during the next eleven seasons—lacrosse was temporarily suspended in 1932—won fifty-one of eighty-one games. The best year under Simmons was in 1934, when Syracuse won ten of twelve games; 1938 was the poorest—three of five. Against specific opponents during 1923–42, Syracuse beat Penn State in eleven of sixteen games with one tie; beat Harvard eight times; beat Cornell thirteen times, tied one, and lost six.

Followers of lacrosse well remembered the contests with Canadian and English opponents. Against Montreal, the Orange won all four games, a record identical with that compiled against Toronto. But a touring Oxford and Cambridge team played at Syracuse twice and won each time. During the spring of 1923, after a successful home season, Cox took his team to England, where games were played with county, borough, and collegiate teams. Syracuse was undefeated in twelve games and came home to be hailed as international champions.

Among players deserving mention were Soft Wood, Willis Brown, Clinton Pierce, Fred Martin, Vic Hanson, Roy Simmons, William Welch, Les Robbins, Wally Jensen, and Ed Jontos.

CROSS COUNTRY AND TRACK AND FIELD

One of the country's most distinguished coaches, Thomas Keane, helped train Syracuse athletes in track and field events. Archbold Gymnasium offered opportunities for training indoors during the winter. Tom Keane also coached the allied sport of cross-country, along with Eric Faigle, who had been a notable undergraduate cross-country runner, and Les Bryan. Syracuse teams won the Cross-Country Team Championship of America in 1922, 1923, and 1925, and its runners performed well in other national and state contests.

Among notable cross-country runners were Clint Loucks, Larry Belanger, Lynn Radcliffe, Walt Dean, Charles Southard, Jessie Cavileer, and Don Everingham.

In track and field many individual performances were outstanding. This was true especially in national relay matches at Boston, New York, Philadelphia, and Buffalo. In addition, Syracuse quartets were strong in mile relays, making excellent showings against teams from Georgetown, Notre Dame, Harvard, Cornell, Stanford, and Chicago.

Syracusans won often at regional meetings, such as those of the Intercollegiate Association of Amateur Athletes of America (IC4A).

Among the intercollegiate champions were Allen Woodring, Chet Bowman, Oliver Proudlock, Ray Barbuti, Eddie O'Brien, Lynn Radcliffe, and Carl Biggs. The Orange produced two Olympic champions in the twenties, Woodring in the 200-meter dash at Antwerp in 1920, and Barbuti in the 400 meters at Amsterdam in 1928.

Others who deserve mention are Cecil Book, Robert Cross, Marty Glickman, Eldon Stuzman, and Benjamin Moses.

SWIMMING

Raymond T. Young '17 coached swimming from 1917 to 1923, Harold S. Ulen in 1924, and Gail Erwin from 1925 to 1928. Under those three from 1922 to 1928 the team won twenty-six of the forty-seven meets it participated in. Theodore Webster, who had a national reputation as a varsity swimmer during his undergraduate days, took over the coaching duties in the fall of 1929, and in the rest of the Flint-Graham era the Orange swimmers won forty-six of their ninety-seven meets. There were no swimming meets in 1932–33 because of financial cutbacks.

Among the important series were fifteen meets against Colgate; the Orange won nine of them. Against Cornell, Syracuse won seven of twelve. Navy, Brown, Army, and Yale all outswam Syracuse.

In the Eastern Intercollegiates Syracuse frequently won medals, but they were not often gold. Records are incomplete for swimming as well as for a water polo team Syracuse had in some of the years between the wars.

Some of the notable Syracuse swimmers were Oscar Blew, Al Atterbury, Melvin Morse, Ted Webster, Bill Dinehart, Win Margott, and Joseph Wohl.

BOXING

The earliest mention of boxing at Syracuse University was in October 1923 when William Davison, director of physical education, staged an informal match in the gymnasium. Two months later some forty men were being trained in fundamentals of the manly art, and in March 1924 the governing board made it a minor sport under Coach Victor Kinne. That same spring Syracuse staged its first intercollegiate match with Penn State, losing by a score of five to one. Shortly thereafter the team entered the intercollegiate tournament at Penn State; it tied for third place with Pennsylvania; Penn State won, with Navy second.

During the following season Coach Kinne's boxers defeated Colgate, but lost to MIT, six to zero. At the intercollegiates in March 1925 Syracuse again was third, behind Navy and Pennsylvania, but the Orange had the satisfaction of winning the 135-pound title. Among outstanding boxers on the early teams were Webster Rice, Joseph Leonhardt, and Roy Simmons, who was also president of the student body and captain of the football team in 1924.

In the fall of 1925 the governing board appointed Simmons boxing coach, a post he held long past 1942, despite difficulties. Appropriations were meager, and there was considerable opposition from those on campus who believed boxing had no place at a university. In 1935 Burges Johnson told Chancellor Flint: "College boxing is not far removed from professional boxing and is closely influenced by the vicious gossip in that sport." The Chancellor himself showed little enthusiasm for it, and at one time placed boxing on probation for a year.

Despite these and other handicaps, University boxers earned national distinction and drew large crowds of students, faculty members, and fans from the city to matches held in the gymnasium. Of 102 matches between 1923 and 1942 Syracuse won 67, lost 31, and tied 4.

Syracuse also did well in the annual intercollegiates. Albert Wertheimer won in the Eastern Intercollegiates in 1931 and 1932 in the 125-pound and 132-pound classes; in 1932 he also became national champion. In 1936 Ord Fink and Ray Jeffries earned national championships in the 155- and 165-pound classes. Fink was named an alternate on the U.S. Olympic team the same year. At other times Milford Fahey, John Roland, Gerald AuClair, Carl Sorenson, Peter Cordasco, Lewis Wertheimer, Arthur McGivern, John Mastrella, Loren Schoff, Joe Moran, George Negroni, Albert Gutzman, Chuck Healy, Tony Balash, Americo Woyciesjes, Joe Vavra, and "Toots" Mirabito won first honors at their respective weights. These and other team members combined over the years to win the Eastern Intercollegiates in 1932, 1933, 1934, 1937, and 1941, and the National Intercollegiate Championship in 1936.

SOCCER

Professor I. Laurence Lee of the College of Forestry was soccer coach from 1922 to 1924. He was succeeded in 1925 by his assistant, Arthur

Syracuse University's intercollegiate boxing champions, 1941. From left: Jack Roland, 120 pounds; Milford Fahey, 127 pounds; Loren Schoff, 145 pounds; Coach Roy Simmons; Americo Woycicsjcs, 175 pounds; Sal (Toots) Mirabito, heavyweight. In the foreground is the Edward J. Neil Cup for team championships; it was in competition for the first year. The small cup is a replica for permanent possession.

Horrocks, who continued as head coach through 1941. During those 20 years the Orange team played 145 matches, winning 65, losing 57, and tying 22. The best season was that of 1936 when Syracuse had six victories, tied twice and lost none. Other good years were 1931, 1935, and 1937. The worst were 1933 and 1940, when the team won only four of fourteen contests.

During these years Syracuse won most of its matches against Cornell and Colgate and, against smaller opponents such as Lehigh, Hamilton, and Rochester, was overwhelmingly victorious. But Penn State defeated the Orange in sixteen games, lost only one, and tied four; Army won eight, tied one, and lost none; and Dartmouth beat Syracuse in four of six matches. Other collegiate encounters included scattered matches with Amherst, Springfield, Williams, NYU, RPI, Harvard, and Bucknell.

Among the players who distinguished themselves were Bill Davison, Eugene Walker, Leo Luckman, Vin Black, Al Orenstein, John McEwan, and Samuel Servis.

WRESTLING

Recognized as a minor sport in 1920, wrestling was under the direction of William Davison during the administration of Chancellors Flint and Graham. He had joined Syracuse in 1921 after a successful career as athletic director of the YMCA at Springfield, Massachusetts. While there, he was co-author of *Gymnastic Nomenclature* and author of *Gymnastic Dancing*, a standard textbook in the field. He was unstinting in his efforts to produce winners for the University despite the meager financial support it gave him.

Penn State defeated the Orange in all nineteen contests through 1942, Cornell won sixteen of eighteen meets, and Army five of six. Syracuse shut out Colgate in a series of ten meets. In the Eastern Intercollegiates Syracuse never won as a team but placed third in 1931 and second in 1932.

Among the individuals who did well were Charles Okun, Jake Patterson, Bill Jeffers, Sumner Forward, John Hordines, Ken Crotty, Sam Servis, and George Hooper. Hordines was editor-in-chief of *Wrestling News*, published by the Keylock Wrestling Society. Its first issue was in 1934.

TENNIS

The fortunes of tennis at Syracuse were never bright. Financial support from the University was modest, and during the early years the teams practiced and played on city courts. Sometimes spring practice was confined to the gymnasium. Scheduled contests were often rained out, and the coaches, who received no compensation, failed to recruit many players. Student interest remained at low ebb season after season.

During the years 1922–25 Professor Albert Acheson of the College of Applied Science was tennis coach. He was followed by Charles Slater and Ted Weinheimer. Tennis was suspended in 1928 but revived on a limited basis in 1929 under the direction of Professor Percy Haskell of the English department. Between then and 1935 tennis eked out an existence. Other coaches were Don Casety and D. Parsons.

Information is scanty, but apparently most of the tennis matches were against Cornell, Colgate, Hamilton, Penn State, and Union. Marvin Brown, Ed Stafford, Bob Dixon, Jack Rogers, and George Manold were among the players.

BOWLING

Informal bowling started in the fall of 1911 when the Archbold Gymnasium alleys were used for the first time. Various telegraph matches were held in 1922, 1923, and 1924 with Yale, Minnesota, Kentucky, and RPI. In April 1925 the athletic governing board recognized it as a minor sport. That year, the *Onondagan* reported, Syracuse won twenty telegraph contests and lost sixteen. Telegraph contests were common in some sports where teams did not need to face each other physically to compete. Scores were exchanged in messages sent over telegraph wires. This method saved travel expenses.

At about the same time the University became a member of the Intercollegiate Bowling League. Financial limitations forced a suspension of bowling in 1927, and it was not until a decade later that it was revived and restored to minor status. From then until the spring of 1941, Mike Hickok coached the team. Few records exist, but some of the better bowlers were Donald Hunter, Fay Flanagan, Fred Weller, George Holland, Ralph Keller, and Ed Warren. The alleys were well used by many fraternity teams and by a faculty league.

FENCING

Little interest was shown in fencing until 1923 when the enthusiasm of Professor Gaetano Aiello of the College of Fine Arts led to formation of a fencing club. Shortly thereafter the Athletic Association provided needed equipment and made it a minor sport.

Relative success in 1924 and 1925 led Syracuse into the Intercollegiate Fencing League, and during subsequent years matches were held with Harvard, Annapolis, Hamilton, Cornell, Dartmouth, and Pennsylvania. Although fencing was suspended as a minor sport in 1927, individual enthusiasts continued to train. In 1938 fencing was restored to its minor status, but there were few participants at that time. Coaches after the 1938 revival were L. F. Ballard, M. Zepeda, and Getty

Page. Notable student participants during the 1920s and 1930s included Lester Platz, Robert Clark, John Dutton, Art Friedman, John Gorelich, Irving Herrman, and Roger Wells.

GOLF

Golf, one of the oldest of the minor sports, came under the tutelage of Professor Nelson Brown of the College of Forestry as acting coach early in October 1922. That season's record included a victory over the University of Buffalo and future prospects seemed good, so the governing board named golf a minor sport and made Brown's appointment as coach official.

Between 1923 and 1927 Syracuse was in twenty-six matches, winning seven and tying three; opponents included Amherst, Colgate, Army, Lehigh, Union, Penn State, Pennsylvania, and Wesleyan. In 1923 Syracuse placed second in the State Intercollegiates and won top honors the next two years. Larrie Sovik, Archie Thompson, and Fred Ackley were among the players.

In 1927 the administration suspended golf for financial reasons but revived it nine years later, and matches were held for the next six years. Once again there were monetary limitations, and the successive coaches, Frank Dolan, Charles (Bud) Wilkinson, and Bob Lannon, served without pay. During these years fifty-six matches were held. Prominent among the Syracuse players were Rollie Anderson, Jack McElwain, Jim Daley, Duncan Thompson, and John Ward.

HOCKEY

During the Day administration hockey had been recognized as a minor sport, but got so little support that the athletic governing board dropped it in 1914. Eight years later a student scrub team played against the local Crescent and Sedgwick Farm clubs, and in 1924 a Syracuse University Hockey Club was formed under the presidency of William Davison. At the time the governing board reestablished hockey as a minor sport, with Professor Hugh Kennleyside of the history department and Laurie Cox of Forestry as coaches. Several games were played with local and neighboring city clubs, as well as with teams from Clarkson and Hamilton colleges. The following season saw cancellation of several games because of the weather.

Ernest Paul became coach in the fall of 1925. In the next two seasons inclement weather limited practice and forced cancellation of several games. Another handicap was the fact that the team had no regular rink. At first the Old Oval was used and, when that proved unsatisfactory, the rinks at Thornden Park and the Sedgwick Farm Club were substituted. Weather conditions continued to be unfavorable. The University chose not to use the Coliseum, a sports arena at the State Fairgrounds. The sport was dropped and, except for a temporary revival in 1940, hockey disappeared from the campus.

RIFLE

A rifle club was formed in the fall of 1922 under the presidency of Robert Patterson. During the first season matches were held with Virginia Poly, Lehigh, Colgate, Pittsburgh, and Cornell. Charles Love was the best Orange marksman. In 1923 Syracuse joined the Eastern League of the National Rifle Association. Generally thereafter most of the opponents were other members of that organization, although there were some intercollegiate matches. Practice was held on ranges in Slocum Hall and the gymnasium. Syracuse won nine of fourteen matches in 1923–24 and was in fifth place in the Eastern League.

Alexander MacNab was coach and Francis Heffernan was a leading marksman. Reports of the athletic governing board show disbursements for rifle from 1922 through June 1927 ranging from $600 to $925, including a modest amount for coaching and equipment. But in 1927 the board, facing severe economic problems, suspended rifle, along with seven other minor sports. Thereafter through 1942 a rifle team was not maintained by the University. Whatever matches were held during that period were handled and financed through the ROTC. Even when there was a University team, the relationship with the ROTC was always close; the coaches were recruited from the military department, and the personnel of the two teams were frequently the same.

There was also sporadic interest among the students in rugby, handball, and, in particular, skiing, which was recognized as a minor sport in 1937.

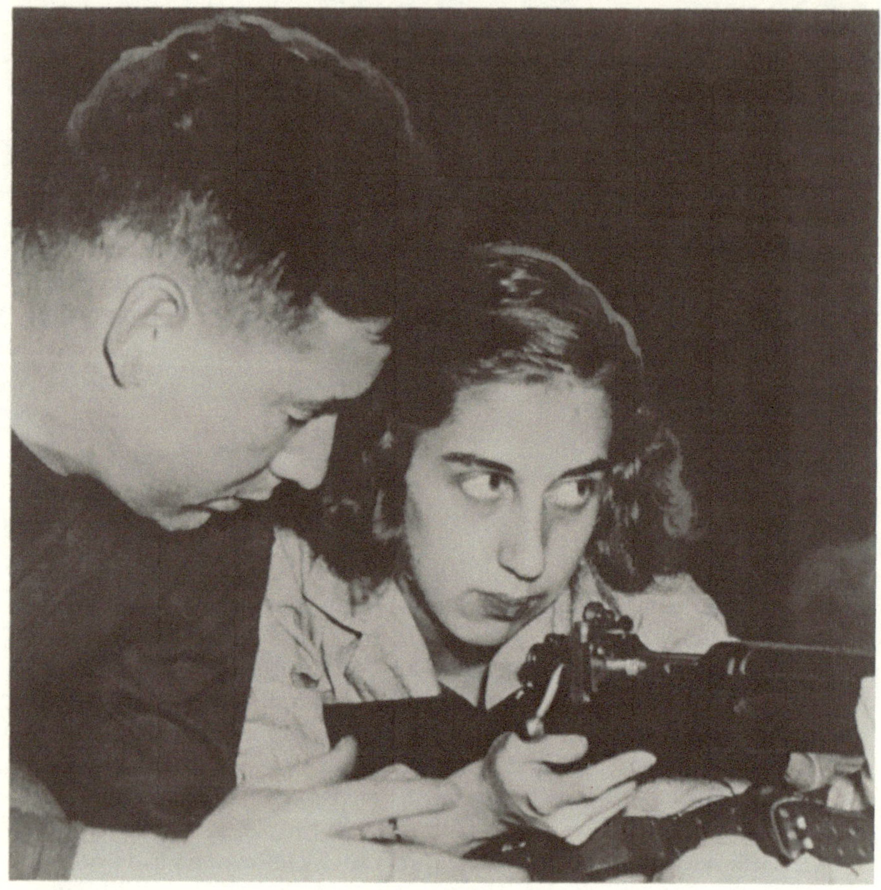

Sergeant Harry Smith and Jean W. Steckroth '42.

THE WOMEN'S ATHLETIC ASSOCIATION

The genesis of an athletic association for women was in 1904. Its first president was Katharine Sibley, whose contributions to the well-being of the University earned tributes to her as one of the University's most loyal and devoted friends. Although hampered by lack of funds, an adequate gymnasium, and limited playing areas, Miss Sibley, who was also professor of physical education and hygiene, advanced the fortunes of the Women's Athletic Association (WAA) during the Day administration.

In 1922 membership in the WAA was open to all women who paid

The archery club poses in front of the Physical Plant "Barn," now the site of the VA Hospital, late 1930s.

an annual fee, but voting rights were restricted to those who participated in athletics, managed sports, or served on the governing boards of the association. The WAA controlled and regulated all formal, informal, and intramural sports for women. It also awarded an old English "S," blouse and sleeve numerals, insignia, cups, and trophies.

Among the sports that attracted most attention were basketball, field hockey, rifle, swimming, and tennis. In basketball, the oldest and most popular sport, local tournaments were scheduled between teams recruited from the living centers and sororities; there were also interclass and intramural contests. In 1935 there were three different leagues.

Field hockey was probably organized as a sport in 1925 and within two years had grown sufficiently to warrant membership by Syracuse in the United States Field Hockey Association, which included such colleges as Vassar and Wellesley. Other contests were held from time to

Construction of the Women's Gymnasium was completed in 1891. In 1921 it was moved from its original site (where Hendricks Chapel now stands) to a site between Steele Hall and Archbold Stadium. The building was occupied by the School of Journalism in 1953 and was demolished in 1965.

time with Cornell University and Wells College. Its prominence is also shown by the fact that Syracuse was represented at Mount Pocono, Pennsylvania, which for some time was a training center for selected players from many colleges and universities.

A rifle team, formed in 1920, probably was the first such college team in the country and for a while the only sport in which Syracuse women competed with outsiders. Coached by personnel from the University ROTC with practice held in the women's gymnasium, telegraph matches were held with many colleges. Reports in the *Daily Orange,* the *Onondagan* and the city papers showed that the University was proud of its women's rifle team, which often took top honors. A women's swimming team practiced and held meets in the YWCA pool downtown.

Tennis was also an active sport, although it was handicapped before 1925 by inadequate courts, which were often monopolized by male students.

Other sports included archery, track, baseball, and soccer. Archery was introduced in 1927; at its range in front of Bray Hall, telegraph

matches were held with Cornell, Elmira, Holyoke, Vassar, Russell Sage, and Skidmore. In track most of the activity was limited to class and intramural meets. For several years it enlisted large student support but declined during the years before World War II. Baseball also had a limited following among women. The introduction of soccer in 1923, ice hockey under Professor Laurie Cox (with contests played on the Old Oval and on a rink at the rear of Crouse College), bowling, fencing, lacrosse, winter games at Drumlins, and a fairly active Outing Club lessened baseball's popularity.

The Women's Athletic Association and its guiding star, Katharine Sibley, sought to impress on the administration the need for improved facilities within and outside of the women's gymnasium. Constructed in the early 1890s as the University gymnasium, it was turned over to the women when Archbold Gymnasium was built. Located originally on a site now occupied by Hendricks Chapel, the building was moved to the rear of Steele Hall in 1928 and thoroughly renovated. The basement, for example, was remodeled to provide more overhead space, new showers, a dressing room with lockers, and an indoor range for rifle and archery. With the passing of the years, however, it became both outmoded and inadequate.

In addition to controlling women's athletics, the WAA fostered the growth of women cheerleaders and managed the annual Military Ball, an important social event in University life. It also sponsored an athletic dinner, at which women who had won distinction in the various sports received their awards from Miss Sibley. Abiding loyalties to the University resulted from the women students' many associations with Katharine Sibley and the WAA.

When Miss Sibley received the George Arents Pioneer Medal, the University's top award to its graduates, in 1945 the citation said: "Upon thousands of young women you have left the impress of your integrity, your unfailing standards, your characteristic disdain for the superficial or tawdry. Among the first to rebel against the formal exercise and routine drill that made gymnastics a distasteful requirement for many college women, you led the movement to make physical education an integral and zestful part of their general development." The award also recognized "the allegiance and devoted friendship of successive generations of students."

HENDRICKS FIELD

In 1919 Francis Hendricks, president of the University's board of trustees, deeded to Syracuse University a large plot of land bounded by East Raynor Avenue, Irving Avenue, Oakwood Cemetery and Stadium Place. He asked that the area be converted to an athletic field and provided funds for the purpose.

When news of the gift reached Katharine Sibley she urged the Chancellor to have the area set aside as an athletic field for women, and in June 1922 he suggested to the trustees that part of the land be allocated for women's athletics.

Early that fall Dr. Flint, the new Chancellor, authorized a survey of the land and as much work on it as the season would permit. Dean Louis Mitchell of the College of Applied Science was commissioned to draw plans. He discovered that three small lots on the east side of Stadium Place were not included in the Hendricks gift. Arrangements were made to buy them, but it was not until the early summer of 1923 that the University was able to do so. Meanwhile the street car loop was rerouted from the south side of the Irving Avenue entrance to the stadium to the north side. One other matter delayed action; it was necessary to reroute a right of way given by the University to the state in 1913 from Irving Avenue to the College of Forestry grounds.

On June 17, 1924, the northwestern part of the field, which had been assigned to the women, was opened. Here is a contemporary description from the *Alumni News* for January 1925: "After a year's work of clearing, grading and equipping, this extreme southwestern corner of the campus, instead of being a tangle of waste land, is now the site of one of the largest, neatest and most complete athletic fields for women in the eastern United States. The field, within its outer enclosure of 10-foot iron fencing, contains a hockey field, two basketball courts, 125-yard running track, six tennis courts, space for field sports as jumping pits, throwing stands and an additional field for the use of classes in restrictive games, croquet, quoits, etc." A full-time caretaker kept the field in immaculate condition, the magazine reported.

In 1928 a portion of the Yates Castle grounds (then used by Teachers College) west of the intersection of University Place and Irving Avenue and extending almost to Van Buren Street, was made over into a new Women's Field. Miss Sibley approved of the change, probably because it brought the field closer to the Women's Gymnasium. On this new field the WAA held many of its contests, as well as formal outdoor gymnasium training. From time to time, however, the administration was annoyed by the infiltration of men and mixed couples, who often used the tennis courts reserved for the women.

Meanwhile Dwight Baum, the architect, prepared plans for the conversion to a men's athletic field of the entire lot given by Hendricks. Designed for men students and not for varsity practice, the field was dedicated during commencement week of 1930.

INTRAMURALS

Chancellor Flint noted with pride in 1927 that three-fourths of the student body took part in some form of athletic recreation or supervised sport. The tradition of a good mind in a healthy body was a long one at Syracuse, where in the early days informal athletic activity—whether sandlot baseball, scrub football, or interclass track and field meets—overshadowed organized intercollegiate games. In recognition of this intramural athletics was formally organized in 1919, and in 1921 Professor William J. Davison became director of the men's gymnasium and professor of physical hygiene. Two years later his title was director of physical education, and he was urging greater financial support for the intramural program and bigger playing fields. Professor Davison wanted to see the administration provide space for intramurals behind Steele and Lyman halls and at the University Farm until such time as an amphitheater might be built for intercollegiate events and the gymnasium reserved for all other sports.

But little was done because of the stringent financial situation, which became so severe by 1928 that some of the minor sports were transferred to the intramural program.

The program was a success, and a special committee of the athletic governing board recommended that the University establish intramurals as an athletic department, holding that intramurals were educationally sound and financially feasible. Furthermore, it said, they provided physical and recreational benefits for the great majority of students not participating in intercollegiate sports.

Chancellor Flint liked the idea and appointed Harrison Clarke, a graduate student in physical education, to direct the new program. Starting as a Sims Hall project in the spring of 1931, it had all-campus status by the fall of that year. Aware that success of the effort would entail more than administration blessing and modest financial support, Clarke formed a Student Intramural Council to help promote and manage the program.

During Clarke's tenure intramurals increased in number and variety. Students found facilities for tennis, golf, basketball, track, rifle, touch football, swimming, bowling, indoor track, and gymnastics. Others discovered an outlet for their energies in horseshoe pitching, ping pong, softball, chess, and bridge. Of them all, touch football was most popular; there were sixty-five student teams in 1932. The *Onondagan* of 1935 referred to thirty-six different sports and said the University should be proud of its intramurals.

Clarke remained at Syracuse until 1940, by which time Syracuse had what was considered one of the most outstanding intramural programs in the country. For competitive purposes students centered their interest in fraternity and nonfraternity leagues, interclass and intercollege contests, and on one occasion pitted themselves against intramural teams from Colgate.

It was obvious to all, however, that future progress depended on greater financial support and better playing facilities, although the opening of Hendricks Field in 1930 was of great benefit. University subsidy for intramurals ranged from $623 in 1931–32, to nearly $5,000 in 1940–41, not counting stipends for Clarke and his assistants, Clayton Shay and Mark Guley. When Clarke left Syracuse he was succeeded by Shay.

The next two years saw a decline in the intramural program. This resulted mostly from demands of the war effort, but there is evidence that Chancellor Graham was concerned about some phases of the program. He believed it seriously interfered with the scholastic standing of the students and led to physical injury. Clearly his views of the program differed from his predecessor's. Nevertheless it was generally agreed that the years 1922 to 1942 were the golden age of intramurals at Syracuse.

ATHLETIC POLICY

The Athletic Association at Syracuse University, established in 1873 to promote and maintain athletics for the enjoyment and well-being of students, was deeply entrenched in the life of the University. How deeply Chancellor Flint was to learn soon after his arrival in 1922 as he studied the association's constitution, bylaws, and eligibility rules.

The organization consisted of all undergraduates, who paid an annual athletic fee fixed by the board of trustees, plus alumni and sustaining members. The last two groups paid yearly dues.

A governing board ran the association. It consisted of four faculty members appointed by the Chancellor, four alumni chosen by the Alumni Association, four students elected by the undergraduates, four sustaining members, and a graduate manager who supervised all athletics and directed the association's financial affairs. The Chancellor could veto any action of the governing board he deemed detrimental to the University's interests. The board was thus a de facto agency of Syracuse University and, as Dr. Flint said, it was impossible to dissociate it from other branches of the University.

Dr. Flint had definite ideas about athletics and expressed them to the board of trustees of the University in 1923. He believed in amateurism, which to him stood for fair play, honor, and fellowship.

He believed intercollege games had a legitimate place at the University, but he questioned their cost. He saw inequalities between an athletic budget and one for academic purposes, such as the library. He opposed subsidies for athletes simply because they were athletes; if their scholarship was such that they deserved aid, it should be given regardless of skill in sport.

To the trustees and to other audiences the Chancellor stressed that anyone who was unfit scholastically should not represent the University in sports.

Thus eligibility was one of his concerns when he considered questions of athletic policy. He found these matters in good hands—those of Vice Chancellor Graham, who was both the University's eligibility officer and chairman of the governing board's committee on eligibility. As Dr. Graham stated in 1924, eligibility was based on records kept by the registrar. Names of students on probation, and thus ineligible, were posted by deans and directors.

Although he was pleased with the strict enforcement of eligibility rules, the Chancellor was not happy with the Athletic Association's deficit, which was $30,000 when he arrived and kept going up, and in August 1926 stood at nearly $53,000.

The athletic governing board and the executive committee of the board of trustees wrestled with the debt problem at a meeting in February 1927 without finding a solution, and in December of that year Dr. Flint sent the governing board a blunt memorandum that began: "Rigid economy in all sports. Syracuse can't afford the athletic company we are in, unless we make up the difference in sacrificial economy." The Chancellor's "Suggestions," as he headed them in his memo, called for reductions in amounts spent for coaches' salaries, training table, equipment, travel, and baseball, track, and minor sports.

Three weeks later he sent another memo which included this candid comment about a budget item of $90,504 for athletic scholarships: "The University can not justify using tuition hard-earned by other students to help athletes as athletes, nor justify refusing similar aid to other students as worthy or more worthy, except on one ground—that our players are professionals and we are paying for them."

In that same December of 1927 the athletic governing board dropped minor sports in favor of intramural athletics. Student reaction later forced the board to modify this step. A year-end financial statement showed a deficit of $24,034.

Alumni and others criticized the University's athletic policy from opposite viewpoints. There were those who would have liked a return to days when students played for personal enjoyment or out of loyalty to the University and not for a coach or for a national title. Others wanted more elastic recruitment policies, more athletic scholarships, and higher salaries for coaches.

Meanwhile there was a national drift toward professionalism in college athletics and a national foundation, the Carnegie Corporation, began to look into allegations of unethical behavior. Early in 1928 the foundation sent representatives to Syracuse University, as it did to other institutions, to survey the athletic situation. Chancellor Flint welcomed the members of the survey team and answered all their questions. He saw that any University records they wanted to examine were made available.

After the team completed its study the foundation sent Dr. Flint the draft of a statement it planned to issue. Among other things this said on the subject of recruiting and subsidizing players that the graduate manager at Syracuse was allowed $14,000 in tuition scholarships and that some athletes were paid for routine maintenance chores in the gymnasium. It said that certain fraternities gave athletes financial aid and that the athletic board financed a training table and paid the travel expenses of high school athletes to Syracuse games.

But when the Carnegie report was published it was found to contain wording that differed from the draft statement—changes that the Chancellor believed reflected adversely on him and the University. He flatly denied having said, for instance, that Syracuse maintained students at secondary schools in preparation for an athletic career at the University. This allegation had not been in the draft he saw.

He said the Carnegie report might give the wrong impression about athletic scholarships—the graduate manager had allotted such grants when Dr. Flint first came to the campus, but now they were reduced in number and were awarded by a personnel committee in much the same way that Rhodes Scholarships were given. Moreover, he said, no cash scholarships had been awarded for seven years.

Dr. Flint sent these and other comments to Vice Chancellor Graham, public relations director Burges Johnson, and George Thurston. He said the information was personal, unofficial, and confidential and that the men might use it in any way they thought best but should not quote the Chancellor.

Conditions at Syracuse were no worse than at institutions the University played, Dr. Flint wrote. He added that, "while recognizing what might be regarded as certain mistakes in the report," all published replies were to be cordial. He hoped American colleges, collectively, might reform their athletic procedures. He urged his colleagues to stress that the University welcomed the inquiry, which he said had strengthened his hand in dealing with differences between himself and the athletic governing board and some alumni.

In 1931, when the Carnegie Corporation released another statement, Chancellor Flint described it as "admirably summarized, ... accurate, and satisfactory."

Continued failure by the governing board to solve financial and other problems besetting athletics led the board to set up a new committee consisting of three respected alumni, George Bond, William Nichols, and Lewis Ryan, to take an entirely fresh look at athletics. The result was that on May 30, 1931, Nichols moved at a meeting of the executive committee that a new program on which he had been working be put into effect.

The motion carried and the old Athletic Association was abolished.

Control of athletics now lay in the board of trustees. The executive and administrative officer was a director of athletics and physical education, nominated by the Chancellor, appointed by the trustees, and solely responsible to both. He and his corps of coaches enjoyed full faculty status under the reorganization.

Integrated into a single department were all forms of physical training for men and women, an intramural program, and intercollegiate athletics.

There was an administrative board whose function was advisory, although it might make recommendations to the director. It met four times a year and consisted of seven members: two alumni elected by the Alumni Association board of directors; two faculty members named by the Chancellor, one of whom was to be the chairman of an eligibility committee; a University trustee chosen by the executive committee; one undergraduate, the president of the student body; and the director of athletics. Thus the power of the Chancellor and trustees was securely entrenched.

An alumni council, chosen by the various alumni groups, met once a year, at commencement time. It disseminated athletic information and worked to cement the loyalties of alumni to the University and its athletic program.

The first meeting of the administrative board was held at the Onondaga Hotel on July 13, 1931. In addition to the Chancellor, those present were Samuel Cook and Lewis Ryan, alumni members; Vice Chancellor Graham and Dean Charles Raper, faculty representatives; William Nichols, of the trustees; Milton Weiler, president of the student body; and George Thurston, acting director of athletics pending selection of a permanent director. Thurston divided his time between athletics and his office as University plant and maintenance officer. Meanwhile the crippling Depression was felt everywhere, and debts mounted again, abetted by unseasonable winter weather during the 1932 football season that cut attendance and receipts. Syracuse athletics, like all other departments, was cut to the bone: salaries fell, schedules were curtailed, and office expense budgets hit a new low.

Not until 1934 were there signs of improvement. The Depression was easing, and there was partial restoration of spring sports. Professor Leslie Bryan of the College of Business Administration was named director of athletics in June. He held the post until 1937 when he was succeeded by Lew Andreas.

In 1936 the administrative board of athletics looked back five years. It agreed with a finding made earlier by the alumni council, that football was the most expensive and yet the most profitable of all sports.

The council had also described football as the best medium for gaining national recognition of the University and said that, financially, football carried all the other sports, whose losses normally exceeded earnings by many thousands of dollars.

The administrative board confirmed this, showing that between 1931 and 1936 net earnings from football were $134,986, offsetting the losses from other sports by $24,835. Losses were noted particularly from such activities as freshman athletics, intramurals, and the band.

But there was dissatisfaction among alumni and other supporters of athletics. In football, for instance, the Colgate hoodoo persisted, and Syracuse managed to win only one game in all of 1936. Controversy over athletic scholarships continued throughout the Flint administration and into that of Chancellor Graham. At one point Dr. Graham expressed puzzlement over the fact that the question had not been put to rest, citing a case in which the athletic board had recommended an award to a student with a poor scholastic record simply because "the man is an athlete."

In general, the two Chancellors were in agreement on athletic policy. Dr. Flint's philosophy about athletics did not change during his administration. He remained a firm adherent of amateurism, as he had told the trustees in 1923. A true amateur would not twist the rules or take advantage of an opponent, he believed. The amateur spirit stressed promotion of physical fitness, intellectual alertness, sound moral qualities, and good social habits.

Nor had Dr. Flint yielded on the matter of eligibility, continuing to take the position that mere possession of athletic skills, without a good scholastic record, was not enough to merit financial aid.

And in the Graham administration recruiting of students was kept in the hands of the admissions office, a ban on postseason games was continued, and eligibility standards were maintained.

In his last formal report on athletics to the board of trustees, at its meeting of May 30, 1941, Dr. Graham was able to say: "Athletics also seem to be in a healthy condition—no disturbances and no problems. Things seem to be running smoothly. The students seem satisfied, the faculty seem satisfied, and I think the alumni have been reasonably well satisfied."

It seemed they had reason to be. After the lean years of 1930–34, spending for athletics rose. The figure stood above $200,000 in each of the years from 1936 to 1942, with the biggest expenditure, $277,252, in 1938–39. There were salary increases, especially for football coaches, and a general rise in spending for all sports.

28

Time Traveler
The Alumni Remember

As a result of a large number of petitions on the issue, Syracuse University, with a kind of reluctant wariness, allowed a noncredit course on the subject of marriage to be held in Hendricks Chapel.

—Donald G. Wright

TRAVEL INTO THE PAST is not condoned by physicists but is practiced every day by those who browse in the historical records and other archives of the University.

Alumni and others who travel back through time are rewarded with glimpses of a gentler, more leisurely era. The patina of nostalgia settles over the past. A kind of magic invests events long gone.

"Is that the way we were?" the time traveler asks. "Was it that long ago?"

"That's the way it was in the twenties, the thirties, and a bit of the forties," the chronicler replies. "But if you let the magic work for you, it will seem to have been only yesterday."

The problem of inflation troubled Chancellor Graham in 1940—but to a different degree than today. On May 31, 1940, he told the board of trustees: "For almost ten years the country has been faced with the possibility of inflation, monetary inflation. It has come slowly. ... it is quite possible we may have to increase tuition again in the not too distant future. We may find it necessary to charge $400 instead of $375, the present figure."

"The Boys from Syracuse," in addition to being characters from Shakespeare and a New York Air National Guard Squadron, were four legendary show business figures, three of them with connections to the University.

One was Lee Shubert of the theatrical family perpetuated in the Sam S. Shubert, Lee Shubert, and Milton Shubert Chair in the Theater Arts. Arthur Storch, drama department chairman and producing director of Syracuse Stage, was named the first holder of the chair on November 22, 1977.

Another of the "boys" was J. Robert Rubin, who graduated from the University in 1904 with a bachelor of philosophy degree, earned his law degree in 1906, and became general counsel of Loew's Incorporated, the parent company of M-G-M studios. Before he entered the entertainment industry he was assistant district attorney of New York County (Manhattan) and deputy police commissioner of New York City. Rubin was active in alumni affairs and was named a University trustee in 1936.

A third was Sime Silverman, founder of *Variety,* the so-called Bible of Show Biz.

The earliest of the four was Frank J. Marion, who graduated from the University in 1890, then worked for the Syracuse *Standard* and in the advertising department of E. C. Stearns Company, Syracuse bicycle manufacturer, before entering the movie business. He worked for Thomas A. Edison with the Biograph Company in New York City and then founded, with two partners, the Kalem Company, the first film enterprise to settle in Hollywood. He was the "M" in Kalem. After the first world war Marion sold the Kalem firm, which had branches in Fort Lee, New Jersey, and Jacksonville, Florida, to the Vitagraph Company, which became Warner Brothers. He retired in 1920.

Marion is credited with being the first person to produce a film with story continuity and a battle movie. The Kalem studios made one of the earliest "undead" films, *The Vampire,* featuring Harry Millarde, in 1913. Marion was a life trustee of the University and contributed funds for a ceramic studio, which was razed to make room for the E. I. White College of Law Building.

A document dated February 20, 1941, says the first attempt to organize all women at Syracuse University—at a time when sororities were known as "Ladies Societies"—may have been the short-lived Panthugaterian Society. The previously unpublished document is among Chancellor Graham's papers in the University archives.

The "inspiration" for the organization with the multisyllabic name was Cora Dodson '94, according to the document. Miss Dodson was to become Mrs. William Pratt Graham.

The Panthugaterian Society held its "first conclave" on June 2, 1893. The program consisted of "charades, tableaux, orchestral selections, recitations, solos and whistling and comb choruses," *The Syracusan* reported three days later. Refreshments were "interspersed with witty and appropriate quotations, prepared and read by one of the young ladies." Mrs. Charles N. Sims, wife of the third Chancellor, was among the guests.

The Syracusan took note of the apparent purpose of the organization when it added: "The evening closed with promenading and merry conversation ... and as the conclave broke up it was generally understood that the 15 prime movers had accomplished their aim by creating a good fellowship among the college girls."

In its issue of November 28, 1893, *The Syracusan* dismissed the second conclave of the society in twelve lines. Two of them conveyed the gist of it: "A large representation was present. The evening was spent in playing games, etc."

That seems to have been the Panthugaterians' swan song.

The 1941 document, which looks like a draft from the development office, spoke of the Panthugaterian Society in connection with plans to raise funds for a women's building, saying, "Although this organization did not continue for a long period the call to 'all the daughters' of Syracuse to organize into a group for mutual benefit, for advantage to fraternity and non-fraternity women alike, was the first conscious effort of Syracuse women to become more articulate."

In the early thirties, when people still argued over whether there was such a thing as a curve ball in baseball, a Syracuse University teacher named Daniel Boone Lloyd demonstrated that a ball traveling a curved path is quicker than one moving in a straight line. Lloyd, an instructor in the College of Applied Science who said he was distantly related to the hero of coonskin cap fame, built something he called a katabas' kronodiaphorometer to prove a straight line is the longest distance in time between two points. He defended the name, saying he'd consulted a professor of Greek about it and had been assured that no word with fewer than eleven syllables could scientifically express what otherwise might be called a distance-time-difference measuring device.

The katabas'kronodiaphorometer, hereafter k-meter, consisted of five runways, each about three feet long from top to bottom. One was straight and the others curved in different mathematical ways. Five balls were released simultaneously at the top. The one on a cycloidal curve reached bottom first, while the ball on the straight track was still ten inches from the finish line.

Lloyd was modest about his k-meter. "There is nothing new in the mathematical principle," he said.

About that other kind of curve ball: at his fiftieth reunion in 1930 Judge Benjamin J. Shove claimed the distinction of having demonstrated to the satisfaction of a physicist that a baseball pitcher can throw a curve. The judge said when he came to the campus in 1876 as a lad of sixteen, Professor J. J. Brown was head of physics and chemistry. One day Brown "proved" to a class that a curve ball was an impossibility under the laws of physics. Egged on by classmates who had seen Shove on the mound, the future judge got Brown to agree to a demonstration. Shove said he placed the professor in a position where only a curved ball could reach him, and then threw him one. The professor acknowledged he'd been wrong, Shove said.

At least no one at Syracuse claimed it was immoral to throw a curve, an opinion that was held at Harvard according to the following item, reprinted in its entirety from *The Syracusan* of November 19, 1894: "When curve pitching was first introduced into the game of base-ball, a Harvard professor objected to it on the ground that it was intended to deceive the player at the bat."

Annie L. Macleod, dean of the College of Home Economics, said Syracuse had a better attitude than most universities toward women's voices and ways to improve them. A reporter had asked whether she agreed with an expert who said his electric voice analyzer showed that most women spoke "abominably."

Dean Macleod said she was glad the matter was out in the open. She said reasons for a bad speaking voice included carelessness, nervous tension, which tended to raise the pitch of a voice, and a herd instinct that made women hesitate to diverge from the common failings of their environment.

"Of course there are many splendid exceptions," she said in the 1933 interview in the Syracuse *Post-Standard.* But she added: "The common attitude of students is resentment at a requirement of which they don't approve, and ridicule of the idea that one should improve one's speaking voice. Here the study of spoken English is taken very seriously. Certain courses are required of all girls entering the College of Home Economics, with advanced work for those preparing for special vocations."

The Reverend Donald G. Wright, A.B. '32, Ph.D. '38, in his history of Hendricks Chapel, writes amusingly of the timidity with which the administration approached a certain course in 1935–36:

> As a result of a large number of petitions on the issue, Syracuse University, with a kind of reluctant wariness, allowed a noncredit course on the subject of marriage to be held in Hendricks Chapel.... The initial enrollment was 150, with more and more students wanting to participate; this led to the course being moved from the Colonial Room to the main auditorium of the chapel. The whole enterprise excited considerable interest and attention. Interestingly enough, when the marriage course was rescheduled the following year it had a very bland, noncontroversial title—"The Art of Living." A start had occurred, however, and at least some of the fears that accompanied this daring departure originally seemed now to have been allayed by the very tentative and carefully proper presentation of the subject matter.

Dr. Wright noted that the course received "a good deal of attention beyond the campus," including coverage by *Woman's Home Companion,* the *Toronto Star,* and the national parent-teacher magazine, and that "the academic authorities" were still wary of it. He added: "Under the repeated requests of students, however, a noncredit course was projected for the second semester under the title 'Personal Relations.' The sessions were held in Hendricks Chapel, and before it was over approximately 780 students had participated."

By 1937–38, Dr. Wright reported:

> Slowly but surely the course in marriage which was so much desired by the students was gradually making its way into the regular college curriculum.... The course was still divided, however; the men, numbering 83, met in the men's student lounge, and the women, numbering 90, met in the Colonial Room. Later in the year, a campus-wide poll was taken at which time 80 percent of 1,119 men voted in favor of the marriage course. Earlier it had been given a decisive vote of the women with 644 in favor to 44 against.

Ismar J. Peritz, chairman of the department of Semitic languages and archeology (later religion) from 1895 to 1933, never apologized for the many courses his department offered despite the fact that students rarely took them—for example, Aramaic and Assyrian. Once, replying to a questionnaire, he said that although some of the language courses were never taken, the standing of the University required them to be listed for any who might want them. Some time later he recalled proudly that he'd had one student in the course in Arabic. It was Rabbi Joseph Hertz (1872–1946) of Syracuse's Temple Adath Yeshurun who was to become world famous as a Jewish leader, author, and chief rabbi of the British Empire.

Universities endure longer than many governments, it is said. Therefore if Oglethorpe University is still in business in the year 8113 and its Crypt of Civilization is opened on schedule, the people of eighty-second century Atlanta will find a memento of Syracuse University.

It is a microfilmed copy of *American Arts,* by Rilla Evelyn Jackman, a former member of the College of Fine Arts faculty who was present when Oglethorpe closed its time capsule in May 1940. Miss Jackman taught American arts in the public school art department at Syracuse University for more than two decades.

Her *American Arts* is a standard textbook that was written at a time when "there were not many textbooks, if any, in American Art," according to David F. Tatham of the fine arts department. He added: "It's a book which is collected by scholars because it's a very interesting document of how American art was taught in the 1920s."

In 1937, with the United States locked in a Depression and the world on the edge of calamity, it was natural for the planners of Syracuse University's commencement to turn to the person described by critic John Chamberlain as able to "write rings around any other newspaper columnist"—Dorothy Thompson. The distinguished journalist and pundit was also the wife of novelist Sinclair Lewis, who had won the 1930 Nobel Prize for literature.

Thus on May 31, 1937, Dorothy Thompson became the first woman commencement speaker at her alma mater. In clear, hot weather she addressed a thousand graduates in Archbold Stadium in the first open-air graduation ceremony since the first world war.

Miss Thompson, listed formally as Dorothy Thompson Lewis, took

Alumna-columnist-pundit Dorothy Thompson (Mrs. Sinclair Lewis) addresses graduates in 1937—the first woman commencement speaker at Syracuse University. Seated is Dean William H. Powers of Hendricks Chapel.

as her theme the address she herself had heard as a graduate twenty-three years earlier on June 10, 1914—a warning against temptations of materialism, mysticism, and power. She warned the class of 1937 against "substituting for the tyranny of 'economic royalists' the tyranny of a mob." She also saw danger in the organized labor movement and urged the graduates to "make your sense of responsibility equal to your love of freedom." Miss Thompson received an honorary doctor of humane letters degree.

She was to be honored by the University on other occasions. In 1939 she received, in absentia, the George Arents Pioneer Medal. She was one of three former students selected as the first recipients of the award established by trustee George Arents. Also in 1939 she was elected an alumni member of the University's board of trustees. There is no record that the globetrotting writer ever found time to attend a board meeting.

In March 1940 Miss Thompson received honorary alumna membership in the campus chapter of Phi Beta Kappa. The president of the chapter, Dwight Beck, chairman of the religion department, presented her with the citation. Later in the evening she addressed an overflow audience in Hendricks Chapel where she declared that the fear of a "total war" by Germany's Adolf Hitler was proving unfounded. She added: "For it would seem that 'total war' is the reductio ad absurdum of war, that it becomes so costly, not only of lives but of resources that not a single nation can indulge in it." Miss Thompson then returned to Europe to continue her interpretive reporting of the world war that was not yet total.

Gordon J. Alderman and his mother, Rose Alderman, both received degrees from the University in 1935. Rose Alderman had been a teacher, on the speech faculty of Hunter College, and later (1967) was to be honored with an emeritus professorship in the Speech Assocation of the Eastern States.

As an undergraduate Gordon Alderman was active in the Boar's Head dramatic society, Tambourine and Bones, and the Radio Workshop. As a senior he wrote and directed the Tambourine and Bones musical "Bachelor of Hearts."

As an alumnus he returned to write, produce, and direct the 1940 edition of the Kum Bak Show, that perennially popular highlight of Reunion Weekend. In his years away Alderman collected many theatrical credits, including graduate work in playwriting and acting at Yale and production of two of his plays there, plus a role in the American premiere of T. S. Eliot's "Murder in the Cathedral"; summers as actor-writer-producer with the Lake Placid Club Players; other summers as actor-manager for theaters in Rhode Island and Long Island;

radio work for NBC, including a part in "Death Valley Days," and acting and writing for the experimental radio station WQXR. He appeared on stage with such stars as Jean Muir, Ilka Chase, Douglass Montgomery, Philip Merivale, Gladys Cooper, Richard Widmark, and Bela Lugosi.

At his death in 1965 he was director of programming and public service for WHEN-TV, Syracuse. In his memory the Gordon J. Alderman Award for Excellence in Creative Broadcasting is awarded annually to a student in the TV-radio sequence of the Newhouse School.

Burges Johnson, one of the University's gifted literary people, brought gentle humor to his column in the *Alumni News.* Late in 1932, inspired by a glimpse of Florence Quast, he wrote: "I always have an elusive and indefinable sense of hunger at sight of her, due, I hasten to explain, to the fact that she directs the University cafeteria.... I found that she was wondering what a cafeteria ought to feed visiting archeologists and philologists. I suggested lentils, and preserves, and dried fish and pemmican, and other mature items, such as old eggs from China; but so far as the philologists are concerned perhaps alphabet soup would be better."

How orange was adopted as the color of Syracuse University was described in June 1940 at the fiftieth reunion of the class of 1890. The chronicler was Frank J. Marion, the motion picture pioneer. Marion, a member of the class he said was responsible for the change from the colors pink and blue, recalled:

> At the end of our senior year Syracuse accepted the challenge of Hamilton College to a track meet and ... a number of us went along to cheer our team. We wore high collars, right up under our chins—cutaway coats, baggy trousers, and rolled-brim derby hats. On our canes we had ribbons of the college colors, pink and blue.
>
> Much to our surprise, we won the meet, and on the train coming home from Utica we tried to "whoop it up." What kind of "whoopee" can be made with pink and blue, the pale kind that you use on babies' what-do-you-call-thems? It just couldn't be done!
>
> So on Monday morning a lot of us went to see the Chancellor in his office and told him our tale of woe. Chancellor Sims was a kindly old gentleman, a real father to us all, and he was very sympathetic. He agreed that pink and blue were not very suitable colors.

Professor J. Scott Clark was named chairman of a committee to find new colors, Marion said. "I recall that we seniors had a sneaking idea that we might put over our class colors, orange and olive green." Professor Clark consulted Baird's Manual, then the authority on college matters, to see what combinations of orange were already taken. Orange and blue were the most popular, but orange alone apparently was not claimed by any school and was Syracuse's for the taking. It was adopted unanimously by the committee, the faculty, the Alumni Association, and finally the trustees.

Theodore Pierson '30 recalled an odd public ignorance about radio in the late twenties: "During the football season everybody went to the games. You couldn't hear them on the radio . . . there were radios, but I don't think there was very much sports broadcasting at that time. And it was unusual to have a radio."

Pierson, who had a job servicing radios, added: "Radios were just becoming popular. They were great big things, big and bulky. Generally theirs was the first radio people had, and when I was servicing them one thing I'd do was to show people how to turn them on and how to use them."

William P. Graham was the first Syracuse University alumnus to hold the office of Chancellor. Probably he was not the first layman to be Chancellor, as sometimes is reported. The first Chancellor of the University, Alexander Winchell, served from 1872 to 1874 and was a noted geologist, lecturer, and author, but he was not a clergyman.

A story told of Winchell is that he would go to a church downtown and preach the gospel, then go back to the campus and teach evolution. The story is probably apocryphal; keepers of records of the Methodist Church have found no evidence that Winchell was ordained. He did enjoy lecturing to young people about science, as well as "the natural relations between science and religion," and spoke often in high school and college lecture halls and in Sunday school classrooms.

Chauncey D. Holmes, A.B. '25, A.M. '27, in a 1978 interview spoke of attending a geology lecture by a Professor X, who was to retire a few years later. "I was enjoying the course very much except that I couldn't understand some of the technical details. So I asked for clarification, and X turned back the pages and proceeded to read the same thing in the same way, and that was the extent of his knowledge."

The colleague who was interviewing Holmes at his home in Tully, New York, said: "There are lots of teachers like that. That's what happens when they have to cover such a large subject."

"I don't blame X," Holmes said. "It was what I heard later called a cookbook way."

Holmes, who once planned a career in the ministry, earned his Ph.D. at Yale University and for most of his career taught geology at the University of Missouri, specializing in glaciology. He was department chairman there from 1945 to 1951 and retired in 1964. Recalling his graduate student days at Syracuse, he said: "I intended to stay with the Methodist Church, but when I learned what was required I knew I could not compete. I also decided I wasn't cut out to be small church pastor."

Betty Dumars '30 recalled that when she was a freshman a woman doctor lectured to one of her classes about the opposite sex: "She said men are like an alarm clock. You wind them up, and they have to go off."

A volume in the University's rare book collection shows that Theodore Dreiser accepted a suggestion by a Syracuse alumnus when he was finishing his novel *Jennie Gerhardt*. The prized SU copy of that book has this inscription on the flyleaf: "My dear Rider: Here is Jennie, revised to your order. Will you shelter her beside Carrie? [signed] Theodore Dreiser, New York, Oct. 19, 1911."

Fremont Rider, a 1905 graduate of the University, was a good friend of the novelist. He made the presentation to his alma mater in 1938 in appreciation of the honorary degree it had bestowed on him in June of that year. Rider was then librarian at Wesleyan University, Middletown, Connecticut. SU Librarian Wharton Miller said the Dreiser revision was a change in the ending suggested by Rider and incorporated into the novel by the author. "Carrie" was Dreiser's earlier novel, *Sister Carrie*.

Chancellor Graham had a negative attitude toward expanding Social Security to include people who worked on campuses. He said in his final report to the board of trustees, on June 5, 1942, that there had been "considerable agitation in connection with the Social Security proposal." He cited a survey of the American Council on Education which indicated that more than four-fifths of the nation's college presidents favored coverage of their employees. Dr. Graham added: "Apparently our sister institutions do wish the Government to step in. That unemployment idea seems rather curious. Why should we insure college employees or why should the Government want to do that?"

Q. What was the campus like when you first came to the University as a student?

Newell W. Rossman '39: Well, that was in '35. It was a campus of about four or five thousand people, hardly any graduate students. There were some in law, education, and medicine. But we never saw the lawyers; they were all downtown. We never saw the medical students; they were all downtown until they built the medical building on Irving Avenue.

The buildings were very simple. We had one men's dormitory and two dormitories for women—Winchell and Haven—and the rest of the students all lived in rooming houses or fraternities and sororities.

For example, I lived on Livingston Avenue in an old two-family house. Three of us studied and slept in the same room; I think it was $5 a week. The heat wasn't very good in the winter, and no meals, and that's about the way most of the rooms were. I think there were twenty people in the house.

Nobody had any money. There was a depression, and every student, as far as I could tell, had some kind of job. Mrs. Allis' office administered the National Youth Administration program and would provide jobs for us for a maximum of $15 a week. ... Most of us had some financial aid. I had a Methodist scholarship fund, and later Dean Powers, the first dean of Hendricks Chapel, administered the Pfeiffer Fund. Mrs. Pfeiffer was a very generous woman and I got, I think, $100 my junior and senior years from that fund, which in those days was very helpful. I could borrow from the Methodist Church and borrow from the University, but the $15 a week was pretty good pay.

Jane Bishop entered Syracuse as a journalism student in 1925, beginning one of the longest continuous associations that anyone has had with the University.

In an interview in the summer of 1982 Jane Bishop Frost '29 said she chose journalism because "my idea was to write children's books, which my older sister, Dorothy Bishop McLaughlin '28, would illustrate." She added: "We had five first cousins at the University, two in Agriculture, two in Business Administration, and one in Applied Science. Dorothy was in the College of Fine Arts, majoring in illustration."

As a junior Jane Bishop worked for Ralph Strebel, head of the placement bureau of Teachers College, earning 25 cents an hour. She was employed at the college the following summer, and after graduation Dr. William T. Melchior, director of the education extension school, hired her full time, at $25 a week. "I worked six days a week—to 1 P.M. on Saturdays," she said. "There was no overtime pay or compensatory time, but we had privileges. A month's vacation and free tickets to all home games were two of them!" Free tuition came later for her daughter, Dorothy Frost VanMarter, bachelor of music 1960.

Jane Frost worked next for D. Walter Morton, who succeeded Melchior and combined the education extension and adult education schools into what later became University College.

In 1940 Mrs. Frost formed the Syracuse University Secretaries Association, whose original aim was to raise money for a Women's Building. It was also a social organization. "It was of great value to all secretaries. We got to know not only the personnel but the functions of their departments—and we were proud of the name 'secretary.' We met each month in a different building for a program put on by the secretaries there. The association continued for three years, but because of war work and outside activities, such as volunteer services, it became inactive.

Mrs. Frost remained with University College until its dean, Alexander N. Charters, was named a vice president. She worked on the Hill with him until she retired from the University in 1972. After retirement she formed Jane Frost Associates, a New York State corporation, "rather like Manpower," and continued to do work for the University in various capacities. As a skilled typist and editor she has worked closely with authors of dissertations and other manuscripts, preparing them for publication. Books she has worked on have been published by Macmillan, Princeton University Press, University of Chicago Press, Jossey-Bass, and Syracuse University Press, among others.

She was on each reunion committee of her class, including the fiftieth in 1979. Among her classmates are: J. Leonard Gorman, editor, the Syracuse *Post-Standard;* actor-producer Sheldon Leonard; underwater explorer Marion Clayton Link, Dean Bernice Meredith Wright of the College of Home Economics, Mary Gilmore Smith, counselor at University College, and Ted Webster, long-time swimming coach. Stuart Pomeroy, lawyer and president of the class of '29 for fifty years, was the recipient of the University Alumni Award as were Dean Wright and Mary Smith.

Jane Frost's ties to the University continue. In the 1982–83 academic year, she typed some of the chapters for this book.

Kalman Druck, editor-in-chief of the *Daily Orange* in 1936 and later a New York public relations executive, was one of the organizers of a campus group calling itself Veterans of Future Wars. Taking its cue from World War I veterans pressing for a federal bonus, the students demanded a bonus in advance, "before we're dead." The movement, begun at Princeton as a burlesque, grew into a national antiwar protest.

Toward the end of his administration Chancellor Graham abolished the honorary degree of doctor of divinity. He told the trustees on May 31, 1940: "I think this action is going to save us a vast amount of trouble, for the reason that each year we have had twenty more or less applicants, all equally deserving candidates, for the degree of doctor of divinity. We could select two or three. Those who were selected were, of course, grateful, and those who were rejected could not understand why they were not chosen for this honor. So I think we are going to gain good will."

Dr. Graham acted against this background: The Reeves report of 1930, based on a survey requested by Chancellor Flint, showed that in the ten-year period from 1920 to 1929 inclusive, 190 honorary degrees had been awarded. Of these, 105 had been given in the first three years of that period—at commencements and on other occasions under the administration of Chancellor Day. The compilation also showed that 56 of the 190 were doctor of divinity degrees. From 1930 to 1940 inclusive, twenty-three more D.D.'s were awarded—the last two in 1940.

W. Freeman Galpin, as University historian, has noted that Chancellor Day awarded 365 honorary degrees, 158 of them D.D.'s, during his administration. Dr. Day himself had at least six honorary degrees, including the D.D. Professor Galpin wrote: "Possibly Dr. Day, realizing that his life was coming to an end, sought to bestow distinction on some of his friends before his tenure expired."

About halfway through his administration Chancellor Charles W. Flint asked the Board of Education of the Methodist Episcopal Church to make a study of Syracuse University. The Educational Association of the church, consisting of school and college presidents, at its meeting of January 1927 had heard a paper suggesting a scientific study of educational institutions affiliated with the Methodists. In 1928 the presidents voted unanimously to survey all such institutions. They directed the board to establish a commission on survey to supervise the task. One purpose of the survey was "to furnish the bases to determine the nature and quality of the service rendered the cause of Christian Education by our Educational Institutions, to appraise their work and suggest improvements of it, to cooperate in formulating a constructive statesmanlike policy for them, to inform the church so that it may be inspired to increased confidence and more generous support."

The presidents named Methodist Bishop Thomas Nicholson chairman of the commission and appointed as its other members the heads of Drew University, Garrett Biblical Institute, the School of Education of the University of Chicago, the University of Louisville, Morningside College, Wilbraham Academy, and Albion College.

At Syracuse, Dr. Flint asked the Methodist group to put the University among the first to be looked at in the general survey program. A staff of eight directed by Floyd W. Reeves made the thirty-four-day study in April and May of 1930. Reeves, a professor of education at the University of Chicago, had the assistance of a local committee appointed by the Chancellor consisting of three members of the University's board of trustees, including the president, Hurlbut W. Smith, Vice Chancellor Graham, and the deans of Teachers College and the Colleges of Liberal Arts and Business Administration. The registrar helped compile statistical data.

Pertinent parts of the Reeves report have been quoted or summarized elsewhere, but some sections of the study deserve a more extended look. Here are some excerpts:

> An indication of the intellectual quality of the student body at Syracuse University may be obtained from comparative data reported by the American Council on Education. *The Educational Record* for April 1930 contains a report on the results of the 1929 edition of the *American Council on Education Psychological Examination.* Scores are reported for 131 colleges well distributed over the country at large. The report shows that the median score for this group is 140.67, while the score reported for Syracuse University is 162.77. Of the 131 institutions included in the report, only 23 have average scores higher than that of Syracuse.

> One of the most significant indexes of the quality of the program offered by an educational institution is the salaries that are paid faculty members.... At the date of the writing of the report on Syracuse University data were available from 10 Methodist colleges. Six of these institutions are on the approved list of the Association of American Universities. Syracuse University is also on this list ... and the six are taken for comparison with the College of Liberal Arts of Syracuse University,... chosen because the other institutions are primarily colleges of liberal arts ... only two of the six college (pay) as low an average salary to professors as is paid

in Syracuse University. ... The inadequacy of the salaries in Syracuse University becomes even more evident when consideration is given to the location of the six colleges with which Syracuse University is compared. They are for the most part in small places and in the middle west, both of which conditions are likely to operate in the direction of reduced living costs.

The six colleges mentioned by the Reeves report were Dickinson College, Allegheny College, Hamline University, University of Chattanooga, Cornell College (Iowa), and Simpson College.

Some abuses have resulted from the lack of proper coordination of the extension and resident instruction programs. It is reported that a number of professors have urged resident students not to take their courses offered on the campus but to go down town and there register and attend the same or an 'equivalent' class offered by these professors. This procedure has been resorted to by certain instructors in order to avoid a decrease in their earnings when extension registration fell to a point below which the class could be permitted to continue. In some cases professors have paid registration fees for students in order that extension classes would be of sufficient size to permit of their continuance. As a result the reputation of the institution and of the professors was jeopardized.

The Graduate School has an arrangement whereby students may earn the Master's Degree in four summer sessions of six weeks each. Considering the fact that the University is not a member of the Association of American Universities this is a questionable practice. The survey staff recognizes the fact that some of the strong competitors of Syracuse University have a similar plan. The University should not attempt to meet such competition by a lowering of standards; it would be a desirable forward step to place the requirements for the Master's Degree in the summer session on exactly the same basis as those of the regular year.... The presence of large numbers of graduate students who are interested only in the purchase of a Master's Degree at a minimum outlay of time and effort does not make for a strong program of graduate work. It is accordingly recommended that the requirements for the Master's Degree in the summer session be made the same as those in the regular year.

At one time the institution had the unenviable distinction of having the largest outstanding debt of any educational institution in America. In recent years the policy of the administration has been to reduce this debt and to work towards its eventual extinction. [A table showed that from 1922 to 1929 the total debt had been reduced from $1.3 million to $861,858.] The debt is still large but the University has shown a surprising degree of vitality in paying off the accumulated deficits of former years.

> The service of Syracuse University to its students cannot be complete until a Student Union building is provided, and the construction of such a building is recommended as part of the building program. The estimated cost would be from $750,000 to $1 million.

> In nearly all buildings, but particularly in Slocum Hall, janitors are used as bell boys to come at the call of any faculty member who wants something done. In some cases there is so much interference from this source that the janitors have difficulty in properly performing their janitorial duties. Errand jobs requested of the only janitor on duty at Slocum Hall during one morning... included the following: sorting and delivering mail to faculty members; carrying milk to the home economics department; delivering express to proper departments; delivering typewriting paper to the commercial department; delivering mimeographed material to another building; cracking 50 pounds of ice for the home economics department.

Maybe one had to have been there in the 1930s to appreciate the complexity of the Reeves group's task, but to a time traveler from the 1980s it seemed that some conditions at the University were more thoroughly scrutinized than others. For example, the Reeves report covered the work of the Graduate School in two and a half pages but devoted nearly nine pages to the care of blackboards and erasers. Here is a paragraph on the latter, reported by the Reeves investigators under the heading "Methods of Cleaning Erasers":

> The usual method employed by janitors is to beat the erasers together out of doors or out of windows. This method is effective in freeing erasers from chalk dust only if they are beaten together a great many times. This probably is not done by janitors. One janitor pounds erasers against a brick wall. One "cleans" erasers merely by scraping them on the chalk trays. Another janitor brushes them with a scrubbing brush. This method is ineffective for it will not remove dust from between felt strips, but only brightens the surfaces. The first time the eraser is used it will again become as dirty as before being brushed. One janitor uses the portable residence vacuum cleaner for cleaning erasers. This method is effective if sufficient vacuum is produced to remove the dust. In one building, in which the janitor stated that he never had cleaned erasers, there is much evidence that the students have tried to clean them by pounding them on the seats and walls.

Information the Alumni Office provided to the Reeves group showed the variety of jobs held by people who graduated from the University between 1900 and 1929:

Occupation	Number	Percentage
Educational Service	4035	25.5
Homemaking	2645	16.8
Business	2605	16.5
Medical Service	1225	7.8
Law and Government	1220	7.7
Unknown	1155	7.3
Engineering	881	5.6
Religious Service	413	2.6
Forestry	398	2.5
Art	321	2.0
Scientific Research	202	1.3
Journalism	201	1.3
Music	196	1.2
Social Service	158	1.0
Farming	145	0.9

In its "General Conclusions" the Reeves team wound up its 685-page report by saying:

> The location of Syracuse University is a fortunate one. The city itself is of sufficient size to offer an institution of higher learning large opportunities for service. Furthermore, Syracuse is the center of travel and trade for a large area that is thickly populated. That a distinctive service is being rendered to the immediate community is shown by the fact that 45 per cent of the student body lives within 50 miles of the University. But its service is not narrowly restricted territorially as is borne out by the thousands of students that are drawn from more remote areas. In the main the program of education the University is carrying forward is well conceived.
>
> The present Chancellor came to the position he now occupies at a critical time in the development of the University. He has clearly demonstrated his ability to administer a large university. Under his leadership the position of the University has been greatly strengthened both financially and academically.
>
> To carry forward the program of the University, as now conceived,

will require additional funds both for capital outlays and endowment. In view of the large service being rendered locally the University administration may properly look to the people of the city of Syracuse, and to friends throughout the constituent territory, for generous support in its efforts to obtain the necessary funds. Donors may make their gifts with assurance that they are giving to a well-conceived program of education that is being ably administered.

"Observations by the Vice Chancellor," on a list so headed, included two pages of blunt comment on the Reeves survey:

This is inconsistent with the previous recommendation.
Such a body would be unwieldy and almost useless.
This body we already have.
This would not do at all.
Sounds good, but freshmen are not passive receptacles.
What we have been doing.
A misunderstanding.
I am wholly opposed to this recommendation.
Is it not beneath the dignity of the University to detail its accrediting agencies?

The last official reference to the Reeves survey appears to have been Chancellor Flint's report to the board of trustees of December 13, 1930. Dr. Flint noted that the survey had been completed and added: "This study has subjected every college and school of the University to the closest scrutiny, and the recommendations that the final report contains will be intended to make Syracuse one of the soundest universities, educationally, in America."

Michael O. Sawyer, an undergraduate at Syracuse before World War II, and a graduate student, professor, and administrator after he served in the war, was asked in an interview whether he mourned some departed traditions and whether there were others he did not miss.

I don't mourn many that are gone. Maybe some of the things carried a certain measure of style—I believe in some sense that the right is the mannerly. You're more apt to get to the right or the truth through a mannered approach, and a mannerly approach. At the same time I'm very attracted to the openness of young people at this point, the informality.

One change that I don't bemoan at all is that when I was an undergraduate, in Chancellor Graham's time and earlier and somewhat afterward, the Greek system was very strong. I applaud the Greek system, I think it's a fine thing, the sense of brotherhood and sisterhood. But there were clearly very cruel things done to young people who were not accepted into the houses, and often certainly for reasons of class and caste. It was endemic in American higher education, and I think that has improved enormously for the better, and I don't bemoan the loss of any of those things.

There was more of an intimate interest in sports. ROTC was very large and had an honorable standing and place on campus.... There were all sorts of ceremonies—Moving Up day, step singing, the lantern ceremonies, sort of Mardi Gras parades at homecoming. I think they were very colorful and very nice. There was a certain insanity at Colgate game time. But I don't know that the way people engaged in tribal rites at one time was necessarily better than the contemporary list of activities.

Step singing at Hendricks Chapel in the early forties is fresh in the memory of Eleanor A. Ludwig '43, director of alumni programs. Each sorority—hers was Kappa Alpha Theta—prepared vocal renditions of well-known songs and sang before judges from the School of Music. People by the hundreds came from downtown to hear them. "There was absolutely no question that you were going to compete," Miss Ludwig said. "The only way to get out of it was to be a monotone, but even then you had to stand there and move your mouth." Step singing is no more. "I guess attitudes have changed," she said.

For years a twelve-foot bronze statue of a huntress, her bow stretched high and her dog below, brought luck to students about to take exams; or so enough of them thought to have rubbed the paint off the dog's extended forepaw, leaving it shiny. The statue is of the goddess Diana and was a gift of its creator, Anna Hyatt Huntington. She and her husband (his first name, appropriately: Archer) presented the bronze to the University in 1932. Diana's dog's paw took a lot of rubbing as it stood in the main hall of the Carnegie Library from the time it was placed there until the new Bird Library opened. Diana and her dog remained in Carnegie, but the main traffic of the University passed them by.

Another vanished tradition is the flour rush. Freshmen attacked Crouse College hill and sophomores did their best to repel them. The event was annual but its date variable, supposedly coinciding with the last day of fall registration.

The *Post-Standard* campus correspondent, Ernest J. Bowden, wrote of "the philosophy of a flour rush" in the late 1920s, asking "Why are the gates of wisdom garnished with such an uproarious spectacle?"—that of several hundred freshman, armed with bags of flour, storming a hill defended by several hundred sophomores armed with a fire hose. Bowden saw a safety valve in the fray. "For a few hours the campus is given over to the wildest horseplay—but in daylight, and under the friendly though unconscious supervision of juniors and seniors. "This is the lightning rod for higher temper or strained susceptibility. And it works. Freshmen and sophomores settle down to the business of the campus, and midnight forays and hazing are forgotten."

The flour rush was abolished toward the end of the Graham years, in November 1941, after a defending sophomore fell and suffered a leg injury. This tradition and others had begun to wane before that, a student government representative said. Howard Miller '42, who was doing research on the subject, said that at Syracuse throughout its history "traditions have been observed—at some times with great spirit and at others with less." He added: "We are now in one of those 'less' periods."

"One of the loveliest traditions" was Women's Day, celebrated each May, said Marguerite Woodworth '18 of the dean of women's office in her introduction to the 1926 book, *Songs of Syracuse.* From early morning to late evening it was a festive carnival, beginning with breakfast on the old stone bridge of Yates Castle. The first strawberries of the season were served to all comers with cream, crisp bacon, rolls, and hot, fragrant coffee.

In the morning at Hendricks Field there was a hockey game, tennis, track events, and a baseball game between women students and faculty; and in the afternoon a pageant, featuring a May Queen, elected from the senior class, with her court of attendants. Music, dance, and pantomime were on the program, which followed presentation by the dean of women of the Junior Medal, awarded by Eta Pi Upsilon to the most representative junior woman.

Editha A. Parsons of the School of Speech as pageant-master of Syracuse was in charge of the colorful pageant that was a major part of the Women's Day program each May. "Syracuse University has been in the vanguard in the development of Pageantry and during the past 14 years," she wrote in 1929. The theme of the pageant that year was the story of silk from its inception in the cocoon through the life of a butterfly to its appearance in the robes of a Japanese queen and her

The May Queen and her consort, Woman's Day, 1922.

court of beautiful maidens. Margaret Driscoll of the physical education department was dance coach for the spectacle, an original production by Betty Lansing '29 called "In a Garden" and presented on the lawn of the College of Forestry. A hundred young women were in the cast, and 200 more had worked behind the scenes.

The Sophomore Cup, other awards, and an interclass song contest were features of a banquet at the College of Home Economics. Then came the symbolic Lantern Ceremony on the slopes of Crouse College—seniors in caps and gowns, holding lighted lanterns, formed the numerals of their class. The seniors then sang the Women's Alma Mater as the white-gowned juniors took the lanterns and formed the numerals of their class. The day closed as all the women students sang the Women's Day Hymn—"Thank Thee for friendship, service, light and love."

29

An Old Era Ends

I assume that the committee on the selection of a Chancellor will continue its search for a younger man.
—William P. Graham

THE CHANCELLOR SEARCH COMMITTEE that was established in 1936 to find a successor to Charles W. Flint was a cumbersome apparatus. A main committee, headed by Hurlbut W. Smith, president of the board of trustees, had several offshoots. A lengthy University announcement, issued a month before the July 31 official resignation of Dr. Flint to become Methodist Bishop of Atlanta, said the main committee represented "three major University interests—faculty, alumni, and the Methodist Church." The members were Smith, chairman; Dr. Graham, representing the faculty; Lewis C. Ryan, president of the Alumni Association; B. E. Salisbury and Henry Phillips, "representing both business interests of the city and the Methodist Episcopal Church"; George H. Bond, a member of the state board of Regents; and Neal Brewster. The announcement noted: "All are members or officers of the University's board of trustees, including Mr. Bond, a former trustee and counsel for the board, and Vice Chancellor Graham, assistant secretary of the board, who gained a place on the committee by virtue of a faculty poll taken at Mr. Smith's request."

There were four consulting committees. At a background briefing that accompanied the Saturday release of the announcement it was stressed that the consulting committees would be just that, and not advisory groups. The selection committee under Smith would be the dominant one, it was explained.

A report at that time said there would be no Acting Chancellor during the interregnum; Dr. Graham would continue as Vice Chancellor, directing the affairs of the University just as he would if Dr. Flint were still Chancellor but out of town. The report was wrong; Dr. Graham soon was named Acting Chancellor.

Nineteen people, including several deans, three bishops, a top national columnist, and the vice president of a Hollywood film studio were on the consulting committees. The announcement said they would give "faculty, alumni, and the church further indirect representation in the selection."

It was a distinguished list. The faculty consulting committee consisted of Herman G. Weiskotten, dean of the College of Medicine; William L. Bray, dean of the Graduate School; Charles L. Raper, dean of the College of Business Administration; Ernest Reed, director of Summer Sessions, and Horace A. Eaton, chairman of the English department. These five had received the highest number of votes, after Dr. Graham, in the faculty poll.

The alumni consulting committee members were Samuel H. Cook '02 of Syracuse; Mrs. Huntington B. Crouse '99 of Syracuse; Dr. Gordon D. Hoople '15 of Syracuse, former president of the Alumni Association; Edward H. Kraus '96, dean of the College of Liberal Arts, University of Michigan; David F. Lee '07 of Binghamton, former justice of the state Supreme Court; Dorothy Thompson Lewis '14 of New York, reporter and columnist; J. Robert Rubin '04 of New York, vice president and general counsel of Metro-Goldwyn-Mayer; Mary Landenberger Scandrett '26 of Cornwall, New York; and Eugene Randolph Smith '96 of Chestnut Hill, Massachusetts.

On the church consulting committee were Bishops Francis J. McConnell of New York, Wallace E. Brown of Chattanooga, Tennessee, and Frederick T. Keeney of Syracuse and Miami, whom Dr. Flint was succeeding in Atlanta.

Representing the New York State College of Forestry in a consulting capacity were Samuel N. Spring, dean, and William H. Kelley, vice president of the board of trustees of the college.

There were unofficial predictions that the search by the committees might take a year or longer.

In listing the church as one of "three major University interests" the announcement said: "In addition to playing the chief role in the founding of the University in 1870, the Methodist Church still maintains a large place in its development as a nonsectarian institution."

Since Dr. Flint had made his decision to leave Syracuse, nearly 200 applications for his old job had been received, the Syracuse *Herald* reported. Quoting informed sources, the newspaper said it was "quite unlikely that a clergyman would be selected for the chancellorate next time." But the *Herald* also reported that no decision had yet been reached "as to the type of man to be sought."

Nevertheless the search committee soon had several lists of the qualities its various members hoped to see in an applicant. One such document that survives among the working papers of the 1936 committee is headed "Specifications for Chancellor of Syracuse University for Confidential Guidance of the Committee in Appraisal of Prospects." It lists an even dozen attributes. The typed list is heavily edited in pencil in the distinctive handwriting of Dr. Graham, who expanded it to thirteen and wrote at the top "Call H.W.," presumably Hurlbut W. Smith. As edited, it reads:

1. Age Between 40 and 50
2. Good Health
3. Pleasing and Friendly Personality
   Flexibility of mind
4. An active and a continuing interest in the religious and spiritual life of the University and the community
5. Reasonably well known and with good contacts, both financial and educational
6. Good speaker
7. Good Administrator
   1. Good educator
   2. Tact
   3. Good business judgment
   4. Prompt decision
   5. Sense of humor
   6. Experience
8. Scholarship
   Degrees, writings and experience as an educator
9. Past success
10. Sound economic views
    Believes in a practical view of the balance between property rights and human rights
11. A competent judge of character and ability in the choice of men
12. A wife who possesses discretion in helping with the demands and dignity of her husband's position

13. He should be active in support of athletics as he finds it at Syracuse without being willing to relax standards

An item that found its way into the records of the 1936 committee was a carbon copy of a letter from Dr. Graham dated September 14, 1922. In it the then Vice Chancellor set forth what he considered to be "the three most important questions in the educational world at this time." He had been asked for his opinion by the president of the Association of Colleges and Preparatory Schools in the Middle States and Maryland, William Mann Irvine, who was seeking themes for the organization's annual meeting. Dr. Graham's reply apparently was of interest to the search committee fourteen years later. It said:

> How can the schools counteract the tendency to place undue emphasis on the purely utilitarian side of education? How can we encourage young people to do thorough, productive work? How can we counteract the tendency to commercialize athletic ability? Another question that seems to me important is: Will the rapid increase in the number of students attending institutions of higher education result in a lowering of the actual (not the nominal) entrance requirements and of the standard for graduation?

The unofficial forecast that the committee's task would be a long one was borne out. Educators and others from across the United States were considered by the committee. One name put forth was that of former president Herbert Hoover.

Another was William P. Tolley '22, president of Allegheny College. He was mentioned in at least three letters of recommendation received during the summer of 1936. Dr. Tolley, then thirty-five years old, was the first choice of one of the writers and the second choice of two.

But that young man's time had not yet come. The committee continued to screen candidates into the fall of 1936 and the spring of 1937.

Meanwhile sentiment among alumni, faculty, and students mounted in support of Dr. Graham. In March 1937 at the annual engineers banquet, when toastmaster George Parker announced the opening of a Graham-for-Chancellor drive, the 350 students, faculty, and alumni rose to cheer.

The momentum that followed, combined with the search committee's inability to find a suitable outside candidate, brought this announcement from the committee on May 28, 1937:

Chancellor Charles Wesley Flint says good-bye to Vice Chancellor William Pratt Graham, who is to succeed him, 1936.

> It has ... become increasingly apparent ... that we have on our own campus a man well qualified to assume the duties of this office, and moreover, a man who in every respect deserves this high honor. The unanimity of this sentiment is not only a distinct compliment to him, but also a clear indication of the action which our committee should take.
>
> We, therefore, recommend to the board the election to the office of chancellor of Syracuse University the present acting chancellor, William Pratt Graham.

The board agreed unanimously. Somewhat reluctantly and in his self-effacing, almost bashful manner, Dr. Graham accepted, but added that his term should be for one year only or "until my successor shall be appointed."

Dr. Graham also said in his letter of acceptance: "I assume that the committee on the selection of a chancellor will continue its search for a younger man."

In a subsequent letter to the board Dr. Graham, then sixty-five, insisted that the special committee continue its search, and said he would help. He continued: "I am reaching the age when most men begin to think about retirement and I am not sure how long I should be able to give the energy to this position which it requires."

There were no formal installation ceremonies for Dr. Graham but throughout the fall of 1937 many campus and local organizations honored him with dinners and receptions.

Dr. Graham was the first alumnus and the second layman to become Chancellor. The first layman in that office was Alexander Winchell, the first Chancellor. Dr. Graham was also the first Chancellor with an earned doctorate. He received his Ph.D. from the University of Berlin in 1897 after studying under some of that institution's outstanding professors, notably Max Planck.

Unlike "The Phantom Chancellor," as the *Daily Orange* had dubbed Dr. Flint, Dr. Graham was highly visible on campus—except perhaps when he was in his plant-filled office. He almost always walked to the campus from his residence at 701 Walnut Avenue, nodding to students or speaking to them along the way. "He was a tall, gaunt man with a mustache," one of the students recalled years later. "He always wore a long coat and a homburg, and from the back you'd think you were looking at Abraham Lincoln. He was very slender. I don't think he ever got excited about anything."

Contemporary descriptions of Dr. Graham were "unobtrusive but quietly firm and efficient" and a man with "a gracious kindliness and a courtly simplicity." One interviewer said: "Like a magnet his quiet personality draws people to him. ... The uneasy are met with patience without condescension; the brilliant by a meaning wit; the troubled with sincerity; the angry with justice and the stupid with enlightenment."

The new Chancellor's wish to serve for only a year was not realized. In carrying on the work of his predecessor he faced many problems, particularly those growing out of the international tensions that exploded into World War II. During his administration the Schools of Citizenship and Education achieved graduate status, a radio workshop was established, the Alumni Office was reorganized, the Reserve Officers' Training Corps unit expanded, and a system of student deans for women and resident advisers for men was established in their living centers. The student dean program for women was hailed as the first of its kind on a U.S. campus and was later copied by other universities. When Chancellor Emeritus Graham died at the age of ninety he was eulogized by Charles C. Noble, dean of Hendricks Chapel, as a man whose genius had burst the bounds of any one discipline. "He came as close to being the indispensable man as Syracuse University has ever known," Dean Noble said.

In mid-April 1942 Chancellor Graham told the trustees "it is time a younger man assume my position." The trustees yielded to his request and appointed a committee to find the seventh chancellor of Syracuse University.

As in 1936, Hurlbut Smith was president of the board of trustees, and he named the first nine members of the new search committee—a group representing alumni, faculty, and trustees. They were George H. Bond, Neal Brewster, Harold J. Coon, president of the Alumni Association, Gordon D. Hoople, Judge Edmund H. Lewis, Henry Phillips, Lewis C. Ryan, Professor W. M. Smallwood, and Mrs. James D. Taylor. The executive committee of the board then named Smith himself as a member of the search committee and elected Dr. Hoople chairman after Smith declined the position, pleading the pressure of war work.

Again there were predictions that the committee might take a year to make a selection, but the new group worked fast. Appointed in April, it was able to agree on a candidate in August. Dr. Hoople told how the committee made its way through a list of 264 candidates. A four-member subcommittee considered the qualifications of all. After that, in discussions with the full committee, the list was cut to thirty, then to ten, and then six. The entire committee interviewed the six finalists. Criteria the committee kept in mind in screening the candidates were generally similar to those of 1936. The list was shorter:

1. Good health; not over 55 years of age.
2. Sympathetic leadership such as could inspire respect for his general policies and effectively meet opposition.
3. Reasonably well known and with good contacts both financial and educational.
4. Active interest in the religious and spiritual life of the University and the community.
5. Awareness of present trends in our national life—social, economic, political.
6. Competent judgment of character and ability in choosing subordinates.
7. Such an understanding of scholarship as to command respect for his educational leadership.
8. A wife who possesses characteristics in keeping with her husband's position.

Commissioning ROTC students as Army second lieutenants at 1942 commencement.

The announcement that a new chancellor had been chosen would not be made until August 8.

Before that, as Dr. Graham's administration moved through its final year, the guns of war boomed ever closer. Long before Pearl Harbor, as America's traditional allies were being pounded by the Axis war machine, universities and colleges were under pressure from Washington to train young men for the national defense. There were these headlines in the Syracuse newspapers: "University Plans Summer Courses to Train Airmen," "Applied Science Revises Courses to Aid Defense," "Syracuse To Train Radio Technicians."

Then it was defense no longer. On December 7 Japan attacked the United States at Hawaii, thirteen days after Dr. Graham turned seventy. Now the campus was geared to the war effort.

Chancellor Graham enumerated the ways Syracuse University was cooperating, but in one area he demurred: "I don't think that we can hurry education," he said. He reported to the board of trustees on June 5, 1942:

> There are a number of opportunities for students to enroll in the Army or the Navy. We placed them on the reserve list and they may continue their college program. The Naval Reserve—V-7—applied to students in the upper classes, already in college. That is being replaced by V-1. This is open to freshmen and sophomores and also to freshmen admitted but not already in college. . . .
>
> There is very close cooperation between the Physics Department and the Signal Corps. Twenty-five or 30 men are interested and will be deferred until graduation. The ROTC men in the advanced programs will be given commissions at graduation. The Coast Guard is open to college graduates. We have 60 men now in V-7, 30 in V-1, 50 in the Marine Corps Reserve; 100 men have been accepted for Air Force flight training and 15 men for the ground group. By fall we expect that about one-fourth of our undergraduate men will be in one of these three reserves. . . .
>
> There was great pressure from Washington to speed up the production of properly educated men—one of the most serious shortages, as I see it, that we have. As I told the Medical Alumni, I don't think that this shortage can be made good. . . . I don't think that we can hurry education, but we are showing our good faith and we are doing what we can in the matter of acceleration. We are taking in freshmen in July and offering an opportunity to get a full semester's work during the summer sessions. Thus a student could complete a college program in three years or somewhat less. . . . Personally, I can't get any enthusiasm or confidence in this idea of acceleration. It is possible to train men rapidly for certain specific jobs, but that is not our problem in education and I don't see how education can be hurried.

Chancellor Graham concluded his remarks on the University's role in the war by saying:

> An item came to my attention not long ago which pleased me—we were visited by a special Air Force board. We were one of the colleges in New York State visited in such a way—to recruit for the Air Force. The various institutions that furnished recruits were as follows:

Columbia	26
College of the City of New York	27
New York University	19
Rutgers	38
Cornell	53
Princeton	58
Syracuse	120

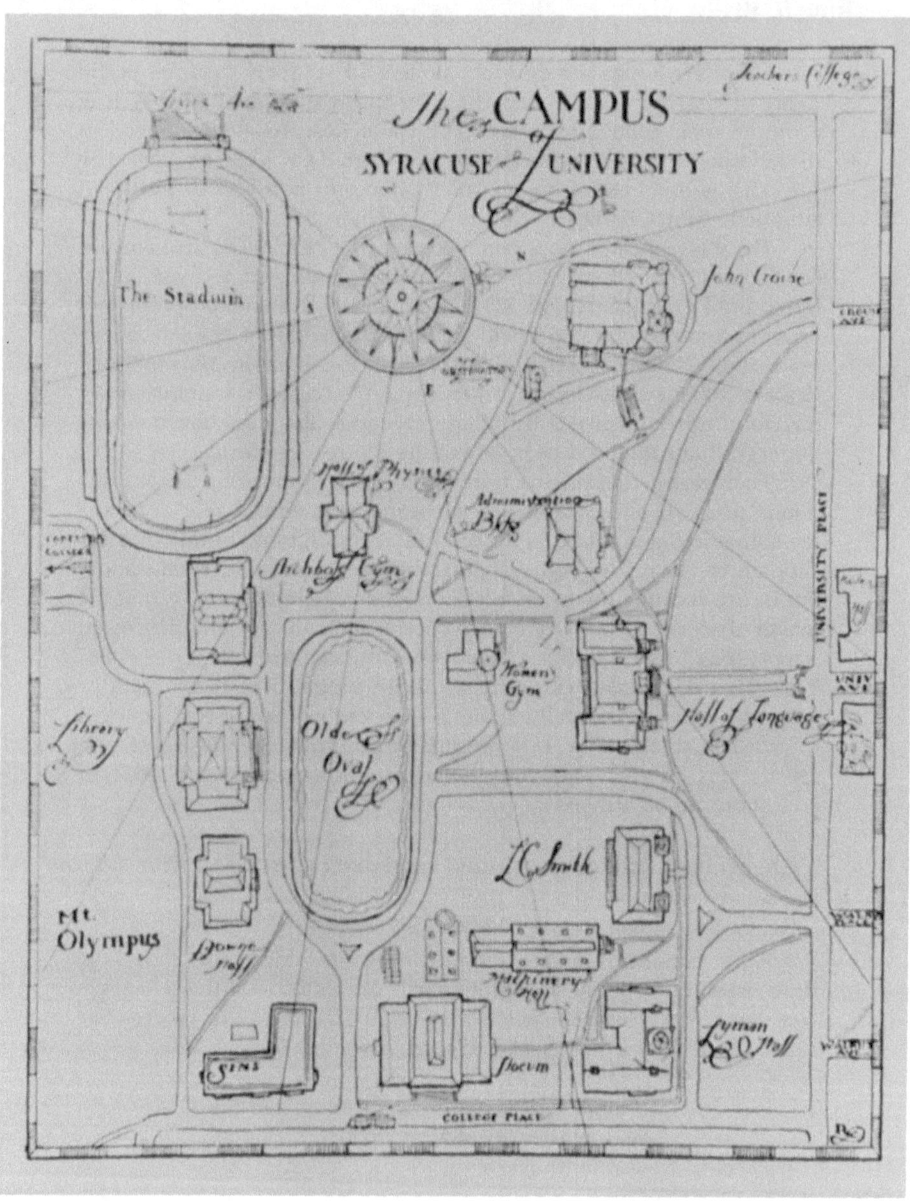

Campus map from the 1928 *Onondagan*.

> So there we are doing our part.

Then it was honors time.

At the annual alumni dinner Harold J. Coon, president of the Alumni Association, bestowed on Dr. Graham the George Arents Pioneer Medal. He said:

> As student, assistant professor, professor, dean, vice chancellor, and chancellor, your association with this institution covers a period of 53 years, nearly three-fourths of its corporate life. You have witnessed the erection or dedication of every building on this campus except the Hall of Languages and Holden Observatory. You have seen the student body grow from 600 to 6,000. ... Thousands of Syracuse alumni and undergraduates know you as a "human" administrator, placing the welfare of the individual above and beyond administrative machinery.

Capping his career, the University at its seventy-first commencement June 8 awarded Dr. Graham the honorary degree of doctor of laws.

Two months later to the day, on August 8, Hurlbut Smith announced the name of the man who was to lead the University for the next quarter century and more.

There was a kind of inevitability about it. He was the younger man Dr. Graham had hoped would be found to succeed him. He had graduated from the University at the end of the Day regime in 1922 and was returning in 1942, as the Flint-Graham administrations came to a close. An old era was ending.

That man, who would not be forty-two for a month and five days, was William Pearson Tolley.

Index

SYRACUSE UNIVERSITY
VOLUME THREE
The Critical Years

was composed in 10-point Merganthaler
Linotron 202 Baskerville and leaded two points
by Utica Typesetting Company, Inc.;
and published by

SYRACUSE UNIVERSITY PRESS
SYRACUSE, NEW YORK 13244-5290

www.ingramcontent.com/pod-product-compliance
Lightning Source LLC
LaVergne TN
LVHW091643100826
845152LV00006B/147/J

* 9 7 8 0 8 1 5 6 8 1 0 8 3 *